ANCIENT EUROPE AND THE MEDITERRANEAN

Studies presented in honour of Hugh Hencken

This Festschrift is written in honor of a distinguished scholar who has worked for five decades in the field of post-glacial European and Mediterranean archaeology and who has contributed immensely to the understanding of these studies in the North American universities and archaeological institutions. In fact most if not all professors who presently teach these disciplines in North America were his students. It is thus a great privilege and pleasure to present this volume to Dr. Hugh Hencken on his seventy fifth birthday. Following his line of interest, we have limited the topics to include only Europe and the Mediterranean area. The articles consist of contributions by his friends, former students and his colleagues.

Vladimir Markotic

1931   The excavation at Chysauster, Cornwall. Hugh Hencken, in the white shirt, is in the centre.

1936   Hugh Hencken (third from left) receiving his Hon. D. Litt. from the National University of Ireland.

ANCIENT EUROPE
AND
THE MEDITERRANEAN

Studies presented in honour of Hugh Hencken

edited by Vladimir Markotic

ARIS & PHILLIPS Ltd

Warminster : England

ISBN 0 85668 083 4

Jacket design by Ralph M. Rowlett

Printed in Great Britain by
BIDDLES LTD., Guildford, Surrey

Published by **ARIS & PHILLIPS LTD.**
Teddington House, Warminster, Wiltshire BA12 8PQ, England.

CONTENTS

ILLUSTRATIONS

NOTES ON CONTRIBUTORS

EMMANUEL ANATI is Director of the Centro Camuno di Studi Preistorici, Italy, and General Secretary of LASPER, the International Association for the Study of Prehistoric and Primitive Religions. Educated at the Sorbonne and at Harvard, he has led several archaeological expeditions and excavations in Europe and the Near East. His major interest is prehistoric and primitive art and religions; he is author of over twenty books and of numerous papers. Among his major works are: *Palestine before the Hebrews, Camonica Valley, Naquane, Hazorea, Rock-Art in Central Arabia, Evolution and Style.* He was born in Florence, Italy; he is married and has two children.

H. ARTHUR BANKOFF is Assistant Professor in the Department of Anthropology at Brooklyn College of the City University of New York (CUNY). Both his doctoral dissertation (Harvard, 1974) and his present research interests have been directed towards problems of the Bronze Age of southeastern Europe.

HUMPHREY CASE is Keeper of the Department of Antiquities in the Ashmolean Museum, and teaches prehistory at Oxford. He has contributed papers to British, Irish and other European journals or monographs on the Neolithic and Bronze Age of western Europe and on the philosophy of archaeology, and has directed research and rescue excavations in England, France and Ireland.

JOHN GRAHAME CLARK was born 1907 in Kent, England. He has been Master of Peterhouse, Cambridge since 1973; lecturer 1936 to 1952; Disney Professor of Archaeology from 1952 to 1974 in the Department of Archaeology and Anthropology at Cambridge, where he taught the Prince of Wales (as Prince Charles) and the Queen of Denmark (as Princess Margrethe), and a large proportion of the leading prehistoric archaeologists holding professional posts in the United Kingdom, as well as many overseas.

He was awarded the Hodgkins Medal of the Smithsonian Institution, the Viking Medal of the Wenner-Gren Foundation and the Lucy Wharton Drexel Medal of the University of Pennsylvania Museum. A Fellow of the British Academy since 1951, a Foreign Associate of the Academy of Sciences USA and an honorary fellow or member of many European academies. He is currently a trustee of the British Museum. His research interests focus on the ecological study of prehistoric man with special reference to his economy e.g. *Prehistoric Europe, the economic basis,* 1952; *Excavations at Star Carr,* 1954; *The Earlier Stone Age Settlement of Scandinavia,* 1975. Expository works include *Archaeology and Society,* 1939, 1947, 1957; *The Stone Age Hunters,* 1967; *Aspects of Prehistory,* 1970; and *World Prehistory, an outline,* 1961 and 1969, a much enlarged and illustrated edition of which is now in press.

JOHN M. COLES was born in Canada. M.A., Ph.D., F.S.A. He is a Reader in European Prehistory, University of Cambridge, England. A Fellow of Fitzwilliam College, Cambridge University. Honarary Editor, Proceedings of the Prehistoric Society. Publications include *The Archaeology of Early Man* (with E. S. Higgs); *Field Archaeology in Britain; Archaeology by Experiment* and numerous articles in professional journals.

ROBERT W. EHRICH, born April 23, 1908. Professor Emeritus, Research Associate, Archaeological Research Institute of Brooklyn College and Honorary Research Associate, Peabody Museum, Harvard University. He received his Ph.D. from Harvard University. He taught at Brooklyn College, City University of New York, 1947-1973.

He excavated with Vladimir J. Fewkes at Homolka, 1929-31, and with Fewkes and the late Hetty Goldman in 1932 and 1933 at Starčevo, Yugoslavia; made an anthropometric survey in Montenegro in 1932; excavated at Tarsus, Turkey with H. Goldman, 1934-1939; National Park Service archaeologist at the Saratoga Battlefield, 1940-1941. In 1960 and 1961 he completed the excavations at Homolka with Emilie Pleslová-Štiková of the Archaeological Institute in Prague and in 1969 and 1970 returned to Starčevo for control excavations.

He is area editor for COWA (Council of Old World Archaeology): East Central Europe and the Balkans, since 1956. His major publications include *Homolka, an Eneolithic Site in Bohemia,* with Emilie Pleslová-Štiková; Bulletin 24 of the American School of Prehistoric Research, Monumenta Archaeologica XVI. 1968. He has edited *Chronologies in Old World Archaeology.* Chicago, 1965.

GEORGE EOGAN is a graduate in archaeology of the National University of Ireland and Dublin University. He has been lecturing in archaeology in University College since 1965. He is a Member of the Royal Irish Academy and a Fellow of the Society of Antiquaries of London. He is much involved in the wider issues of archaeology and is a member of the National Monuments Advisory Council, Dublin and the Historic Monuments Council, Belfast.

His principal field of research is the Irish Late Bronze Age and the comparative archaeology of that period. He published an overall study of the period (Proceedings of the Prehistoric Society 30, 1964) and numerous papers on various aspects of the Late Bronze Age. Since 1962 Dr. Eogan has been directing excavations at Knowth and to date several papers on these investigations have appeared.

ANTONIO GILMAN, born in 1944, is Assistant Professor of Anthropology at California State University-Northridge. He received his Ph.D. in Anthropology from Harvard University in 1974, and undergraduate degrees from Cambridge University in archaeology in 1967, and Harvard College in Classics in 1965. His publications include: "Neolithic of Northwest Africa", Antiquity 48:273-282 (1974); *The Later Prehistory of Tangier, Morocco* Bulletin of the American School of Prehistoric Research 29 (1975); "Bronze Age Dynamics in Southeast Spain", Dialectical Anthropology[1] (1976): 307-319.

MITJA GUŠTIN, born 1947 at Maribor, received his degree at the University of Ljubljana in 1972. Since 1974 he is curator for archaeology and editor of the *Varia Archaeologica* in the Posavski Museum at Brežice.

His publications include "Mahaira Krumschwerter: Vorgeschichtliche Verbindungen Picenum-Slowenien-Basarabi". *Situla* 14/15 (1974): 77-94; "Die eisenzeitlichen Grabhügel aus der Umgebung von Boštanj." *Varia archaeologica* 1 (1974): 87-119; and with Raffaele De Marinis "Qualche considerazione sulla cronologia e diffusione delle fibule seminunate." *Praistoria alpina* 11 (1975): 237-253.

RICHARD JOHN HARRISON was born at York, England, and educated at Selwyn College, Cambridge, and at Harvard. He spent two years in the Department of Prehistoric and Romano-British Antiquities of the British Museum, and is now Lecturer in Prehistoric archaeology at the University of Bristol. His main work is on Eneolithic and Early Bronze Age Cultures of Spain, Portugal and France, with current projects on jade analysis and Late Bronze Age metal work. He published numerous articles on all these topics.

KATHLEEN KENYON was educated at St. Paul's Girls' School and Somerville College, Oxford. She received her training in archaeology under Dr. R. E. M. (Sir Mortimer) Wheeler at Verulamium. She was an assistant on excavation at Zimbabwe, Southern Rhodesia and at Samaria, Palestine. The first excavations she directed were on Romano-British and Iron Age sites in England. In 1951 she became Director of the British School of Archaeology in Jerusalem and on behalf of the School directed excavations at Jericho and Jerusalem between 1952 and 1967. From 1935 to 1962 she was on the staff of the University of London Institute of Archaeology, first as Secretary, and from 1948 as Lecturer in Palestinian Archaeology. From 1962 to 1973 she was Principal of St. Hugh's College, Oxford. She is a Fellow of the British Academy and a Trustee of the British Museum. D.Lit., London and D.Litt., Oxford.

VLADIMIR MARKOTIC received his Ph.D. from Harvard under Hugh Hencken with his thesis "Starčevo and Vinča". He is the area editor for "Russia" for Council of Old World Archaeology, associate editor of *Croatia,* and member of the editorial board of *Canadian Ethnic Studies.* He is also editor of the *Calgary Archaeologist.* He has written on the Neolithic, Croatia, the European part of the Soviet Union, and on ethnic problems in North America.

ELEANOR M. MEGAW (née Hardy) read Archaeology and Anthropology at Cambridge under H. M. Chadwick and J. M. de Navarro. She assisted Hugh Hencken at the excavation of Lagore Crannog, Ireland, in 1934. Later she worked at pollen-analysis, particularly in relation to archaeology in Sweden and Cambridge. She was Acting-Director of the Manx Museum during the war, and carried out rescue excavation of the late Neolithic site at Ronaldsway, Isle of Man. She is married to Basil Megaw F.S.A., F.R.S.E. She has published articles on palynological work and on archaeological topics.

CARL-AXEL MOBERG was born in 1915 in Lund, Sweden. He received his Ph.D. from the University of Lund in 1941. He was director of the Gothenburg Archaeological Museum between 1957 and 1968; since 1960 he has been professor of Archaeology, especially of the Northern Europe at the University of Gothenburg. He has published on Mesolithic and later periods of Northern Europe such as *Zonengliederungen der vorchristlichen Eisenzeit in Nordeuropa*, 1941. Ornavasso - Horn, Acta archaeologica 21-25, 1950-54. He is the co-author on socio-economic factors in prehistory, *Ekonomisk-historisk början,* 1973; he has also written on principles of archaeological research *Introduktion till arkeologi*, 1969; *Introduction à l'archéologie,* 1976 and on mathematical methods in archaeology. His present research interest is the social basis of the La Tène period.

J. M. de NAVARRO, former fellow of Trinity College and former lecturer in the Faculty of Archaeology and Anthropology, Cambridge; corresponding Fellow of the British Academy; Ordentliches Mitglied d. Deutschen Archäologischen Instituts; corresponding member of the Schweitzerische Geselschaft fur Urgeschichte; Fellow of the Society of Antiquaries. He is author of various papers in English, German and Swiss periodicals and Festschrifts and of the *Finds from the Site La Tène,* 1972.

JIŘÍ NEUSTUPNÝ, born 1905. He received his Ph.D. from the Charles University in Prague in 1928, and D.Sc. from the Czechoslovak Academy of Sciences in 1962. He was Assistant Curator at the Department of Prehistory of the National Museum in Prague since 1925; Chief Curator since 1935; Lecturer in Prehistory and Museology at the Charles University since 1950; Full Professor since 1969.

He received a State Order for outstanding work in prehistory and museology; he is a member of the State Council for Museums; member of the boards of many museums in Czechoslovakia; member of the Permanent Council of the Union of prehistoric sciences; full member of the German Archaeological Institute; member of the ICOM-Committee for archaeological museums, etc.

His main interests are archaeology of the Stone Age, theoretical, social and economic problems in prehistory. He wrote about 600 papers and 18 books. Among them are *Czechoslovakia before the Slavs,* with Evžen Neustupný, London, New York, Milano 1961-3; *Museum and Research,* Prague 1968, *The Prehistory of Mankind,* Prague 1947, Sarajevo 1960. He is also editor of *Fontes Archaeologici Pragenses.*

STUART PIGGOTT, born 1910, began his archaeology in museums and the field in Britain, early specializing in the Neolithic period. Military intelligence duties in India in the 1940's led him to the prehistory of India and Western Asia, and on his appointment as Abercromby Professor of Archaeology in the University of Edinburgh in 1946 he turned increasingly to that of Europe. His publications include *Prehistoric India,* 1950; *Neolithic Cultures of the British Isles,* 1954; *Ancient Europe: a survey,* 1965; *The Druids,* 1965 and papers in learned journals.

RALPH M. ROWLETT, Ph.D. Harvard University, was from 1959-1968 a student of Dr. Hencken, who directed his doctoral dissertation and who helped arrange his study at the Institute of Archaeology of London University and the Ecole des Hautes-Etudes Pratique of the University of Paris. Since 1965 he has been a member of the Anthropology Department of the University of Missouri-Columbia. He was an early experimenter with the thermo-luminescence dating of archaeological lithics. He has directed excavations primarily concerned with the Iron Age at Ebly, Belgium in 1969, Espekaer, Denmark in 1967 with Elsebet Sander-Jørgensen Rowlett, and the Titelberg, Luxembourg in 1972-76. His work at Chassemy, Aisne, France was done while a student of Dr. Hencken.

JAROSLAV ŠAŠEL is Senior Research Fellow at the Archaeological Institute, Slovenian Academy, Ljubljana. He received his Ph.D. in Roman archaeology and history from the University at Ljubljana. In the academic year 1969-70 he was visiting member at The Institute for Advanced Study at Princeton, New Jersey. Since 1960 he organized the systematic research of the *Claustra Alpium Iuliarum* and volume I was published with collaborators in 1971. He is also editor of the *Arheološki vestnik*, Journal of the Archaeological Institute from volume XXIII. He collaborated on the publication of "The Archaeological Sites of Slovenia" in 1975, and edited the *Tabula imperii Romani,* Sheet K 34 (Naissus-Serdica-Thessalonike, 1976). His main interest is Roman epigraphy. He published, with his wife, the *Inscriptiones Latinae quae in Iugoslavia inter annos MCMXL et MCMLX repertae et editae sunt* in 1963. He has also written on the ancient history of the Balkan area.

H.N. SAVORY, F.S.A. Born 1911; lived in Oxford 1915-38. He graduated at Oxford University, Literae Humaniores Class I, 1934. He received his D. Phil. in 1937 with his thesis on Early Iron Age migrations in northwest Europe. He was a MacIver student in Iberian Archaeology, at the Queen's College, Oxford, 1936-8; Assistant Keeper in Archaeology at the National Museum of Wales 1938-55; the Keeper 1955-76; Research Associate since 1976. Circumstances delayed the publication of Iberian studies until 1968 (*Spain and Portugal,* Thames & Hudson). Excavations in Wales included several megalithic communal tombs, notably Pen-y-wyrlod (Talgarth).

BIBA TERZAN finished her studies at the University of Ljubljana where she now teaches the Metal Ages in the Department of Archaeology. Included in her publications are: "Die hallstattzeitlichen Grabhügel aus Brusnice bei Novo Mesto", *Varia archaeologica,* 1974; "Contributo alla Cronologia del gruppo preistorico di Santa Lucia". *Arheološki vestnik* 1975, etc.

HOMER L. THOMAS received his M.A. degree at the University of Chicago in 1941 and his Ph.D. in Archaeology at the University of Edinburgh in 1949. He is currently Professor of Art History and Archaeology at the University of Missouri-Columbia. Dr. Thomas has served on numerous executive and advisory councils, including the Archaeological Institute of America, the Missouri State Park Board, and the Smithsonian Institution. He is a Fellow of the Society of Antiquaries of London (1972), and he has worked on many aspects of European pre- and protohistory. Among his publications are: *Near Eastern, Mediterranean and European Chronology,* 2 volumes. Studies in Mediterranean Archaeology XVII, Lund, 1967; with R. W. Ehrich, "Some Problems in Chronology" *World Archaeology* I, 1969; with R. M. and E. S. Rowlett "The Titelberg: A Hill Fort of Celtic and Roman Times" *Archaeology* XXVIII, 1975.

PETER S. WELLS received his B.A. in 1970, M.A. 1973, and Ph.D. 1976 (all at Harvard University). Year of study 1971-72 at the Institut für Vor- und Frühgeschichte of the University of Tübingen, West Germany. Doctorate in anthropology, with special field in later European prehistory. Special interests include contact between cultural groups and change related to such contact, and economic problems. European excavation experience in France, Germany, Ireland, and Italy. He has done much museum study on Iron Age collections in west-central Europe. Currently he is Research Fellow in European Archaeology at the Peabody Museum, and Lecturer on Anthropology at Harvard University.

ACKNOWLEDGEMENTS

The editor wishes to thank Peter L. Shinnie, Richard G. Forbis and J. Scott Raymond of the Department of Archaeology, The University of Calgary, for the use of departmental facilities. Thanks are also due to H. Anderson for her secretarial help, S. Dowling for compiling the Index and for her editorial assistance, and finally to the publishers, Aris and Phillips, for their unwavering support.

Vladimir Markotic

HUGH HENCKEN: HIS VITA

Hugh Hencken was born in New York City, on January 8, 1902, the son of Albert Charles and Mary Creighton (O'Neill). In 1935 he married Thalassa Cruso, who was born in London, England. She was later to achieve distinction of her own. In the 1930's she excavated and published on a British Iron Age hill fort on Bredon Hill. She regularly writes a column, "The Garden", in the *Country Journal.* She is also the author of the books: *Making Things Grow, Making Things Grow Outdoors, To Everything There is a Season,* and *Making Vegetables Grow.* They have three children: Ala, born in 1938, and the twins, Sofia and Thalassa, born in 1940.

Dr. Hencken received a B.A. from Princeton in 1924, a B.A. from Cambridge University in 1926, an M.A. in 1929, and a Ph.D. in 1930. Later, in 1936 he was to receive an Hon. D. Litt. from the National University of Ireland, and Sc. D. from Cambridge University in 1972.

Dr. Hencken excavated in England in 1928, 1930, and 1931. He was the Director of the Harvard Archaeological Expedition in Ireland from 1932 to 1936. He directed excavations of the American School of Pre-historic Research in Morocco in 1947, and in Algeria in 1949.

During 1930-31, Dr. Hencken was Associate in European Archaeology at the Peabody Museum, Harvard University. In 1931-32, he was appointed Assistant Curator of European Archaeology at the Peabody Museum, becoming Curator of European Archaeology in 1932, a position he held until his retirement in 1972. He was a Lecturer at the Lowell Institute in 1942, and Special University Lecturer at London and Oxford Universities in 1947. From 1945 to 1972 he was Director of the American School of Prehistoric Research, and its Chairman from 1959 to 1972. He held the Monro Lectureship at Edinburgh University during 1959. In 1970, he was elected Honorary Fellow, St. John's College, Cambridge University.

In addition to being a member of many other societies, Dr. Hencken is a member of the Honorary Committee, International Union of Prehistoric and Protohistoric Sciences, as well as honorary member in the International Institute of European Research and Education. He has been honored by a corresponding membership in the Jysk Archaeologisk Selskab of Denmark.

England has recognized Dr. Hencken's contribution to prehistoric research with the following memberships: British Academy (corresponding); Society of Antiquaries of London; Royal Archaeological Institute of Great Britain; Prehistoric Society (honorary); Penzance Natural History and Antiquarian Society (honorary).

The Societé des Antiquaries de l'Ouest of France has bestowed a corresponding membership on Dr. Hencken.

In Germany, he is a member of the Deutches Archäologisches Institut.

The Royal Irish Academy has recognized his work with a membership.

Italian memberships held by Dr. Hencken include Istituto di Studi Etruschi ed Italici (corresponding) and Istituto di Preistoria e Protoistoria.

An honorary membership in the Society of Antiquaries of Scotland is among his many honors.

The Instituto de Estudios Ibéricos of Spain has recognized Dr. Hencken with a corresponding honorary membership.

In the United States he holds the following memberships: American Academy of Arts and Sciences; Archaeological Institute of America (honorary president); and Phi Beta Kappa (honorary).

A bibliography of his scholarly works, not including reviews, is as follows:

1928   An Excavation at Chysauster. Journal of the British Archaeological Association: 145-164.
1931   A Fortress Four Thousand Years Old. Harvard Alumni Bulletin, Cambridge.
1932   The Archaeology of Cornwall and Scilly, London.
1933   The Excavation by H.M. Office of Works at Chysauster, Cornwall 1931, Archaeologia
              LXXXIII: 237-284.
1933   Notes on the Megalithic Monuments in the Isles of Scilly (with Hallam L. Morius). Antiquaries
              Journal XIII: 13-29.
1933   A Gaming Board of the Viking Age. Acta Archaeologica LV: 85-104. Kφbenhavn.

1934   The Cemetery-Cairn at Knockast. Proceedings of the Royal Irish Academy XLI, Section C:232-284.

1934   The Ancient Cornish Tin Trade. Proceedings of the International Congress for Prehistoric and
        Protohistoric Sciences: 283-284. London.

1934   Harvard and Irish Archaeology. The Irish Review I, No. 1, April.

1935   A Tumulus at Carrowlisdooaun, County Mayo. Journal of the Royal Society of Antiquaries of
        Ireland LXV, June, 73-83.

1935   A Cairn at Poulawck, County Clare. Journal of the Royal Society of Antiquaries of Ireland
        LXI: 191-222.

1935   Inscribed Stones at St. Kew and Lanteglos by Fowey, Cornwall. Archaeologia Cambrensis, XC: 156-159.

1936   Ballinderry Crannog, No. 1. Proceedings of the Royal Irish Academy XLIII, Section C, 5:103-239.

1936   The Ancient Irish from Stone Age to 1000 A.D. The Illustrated London News, June 6.

1938   Cahercommaum: A Stone Fort in County Clare, Royal Society of Antiquaries of Ireland, Dublin.

1939   The "Irish Monastery" at North Salem, New Hampshire. The New England Quarterly XII,
        3, September: 429-442.

1939   A Long Cairn at Creevykeel, County Sligo. Journal of the Royal Society of Antiquaries of Ireland
        LXIX, part II: 53-98.

1941   The Harvard Archaeological Expedition in Ireland. American Journal of Archaeology XLV:1-6.

1942   Ballinderry Crannog, No. 2. Proceedings of the Royal Irish Academy XLVII, Section C, 1:1-78.

1943   Archaeological Evidence of Invasion. American Journal of Archaeology XLVII:88-90.

1946   Future Aims and Methods in Research in Prehistoric Europe. American Journal of Archaeology L,
        Series 2:341-344.

1947   The London Conferences on Archaeology, 1943 and 1944. Archaeological Journal 102:1-11.

1948   The Prehistorical Archaeology of the Tangier Zone, Morocco. Proceedings of the American
        Philosophical Society 92, No. 4: 282-288.

1949   Tipasa, An Ancient City in North Africa. Archaeology 2:170-176.

1950   Lagore Crannog, An Irish Royal Residence. Royal Irish Academy Proceedings LIII:1-247.

1950   Herzsprung Shields and Greek Trade. American Journal of Archaeology 54:295-309.

1951   Palaeobotany and the Bronze Age. Journal of the Royal Society of Antiquaries of Ireland 81,
        part 1:1.

1952   A Two-looped Socked Axe of the 7th Century B.C. Proceedings of the Prehistoric Society
        XVIII:121-4.

1952   Beitzsch and Knossos. Proceedings of the Prehistoric Society, 36-46.

1955   Indo-European Languages and Archaeology. American Anthropological Association. Memoir No. 84.

1955   Some Early Irish Illuminated Manuscripts. Gazette des Beaux-Arts: 135.

1955   A Western Razor in Sicily. Proceedings of the Prehistoric Society XXI: 160-162.

1955-56 Fragmentos de Cascos de Huelva. Ampurias XVII-XVIII: 254.

1956   Quelques épées à langue de carpe en Espagne, France et Italie. Crónica del IV Congresso
        Internacional de Ciencias Prehistóricas, Madrid 1954. Zaragoza. Pp. 679-682.

1956   Carp's Tongue Swords in Spain, France and Italy. Zephyrus 7:125-178. Salamanca.

1956   The Fibulae of Huelva. Proceedings of the Prehistoric Society XXII: 213-215.

1957   Horse Tripods from Etruria. American Journal of Archaeology 61:1-4.

1958   Early Graves with Metal Objects from Syracuse. American Journal of Archaeology 62:259-272.

1959   Archaeological Evidence for the Origin of the Etruscans. Contributions to CIBA Foundation
        Symposium on the Origin of the Etruscans: 29-47. London.

1966   A View of Etruscan Origins. Antiquity 40:205-211.

1968   Tarquinia and Etruscan Origins. Thames and Hudson. London.

1968   Tarquinia, Villanovans and Early Etruscans. Bulletin, American School of Prehistoric Research,
        No 23, 2 volumes.

1971   The Earliest European Helmets, Bronze Age and Early Iron Age. American School of Prehistoric
        Research. Bulletin 28.

1974   Bracelets of Lead-Tin Alloy from Magdelenska gora. Situla 14/15:119-127.

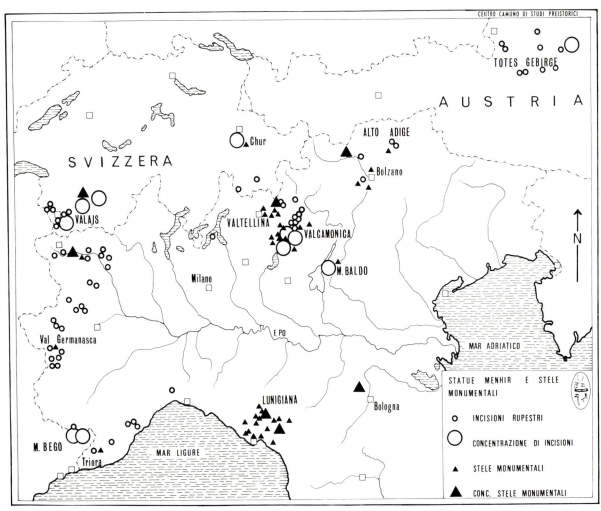

FIG 1   Distribution map of statues - stelae in Northern Italy.

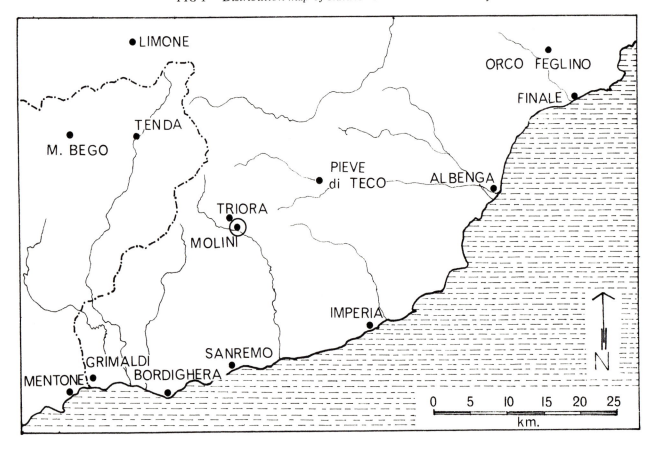

FIG 2   Location map of Triora near the Ligurian coast.

THE TRIORA SLAB (LIGURIA)
by Emmanuel Anati

Discovery and Site

The Triora slab was discovered on August 15, 1941, by the lawyer Nunzio Senigaglia, near Molini di Triora at the site of Perallo (Fig. 1). Realizing the interest of the discovery, he brought it to his home in Milan. We thank him for having loaned the stele to the Centro Camuno di Studi Preistorici for study. In small groups of abondoned huts in Perallo hundreds of such slate slabs had been used to cover the roofs (Fig. 2). In fact, the same day the stele was discovered, a search was made for other fragments and a piece of another decorated slab was also found, but subsequently lost.

The site where the stele was found is about 600 meters above sea level at the foot of the Maritime Alps, less than 20 km. as the crow flies, to the north of the Ligurian coast, 25 km. south-east of Mount Bego, the principal zone of prehistoric rock art in the Maritime Alps (Louis and Isetti 1964), and 15 km. to the west of Pieve di Teco, a minor centre of rock art. Although rock carvings have been reported in the vicinity of Triora, at Monte Pellegrino, their age is in question.

Previous Publications

The stele has already been studied by M.O. Acanfora who, after publishing a short note in 1955, presented a more detailed description to the IV Congress of Prehistory in Madrid (Acanfora 1956: 115-127). She noted the particular carving technique (Fig. 3), "a tremolo"[1], which is also used in Neolithic "cardial" ware, common also in the Ligurian area; she recognized that the engraving must have been done using a flint burin, not a metal instrument. She also made a series of comparisons with figures from stelae and rock art which permitted her to place the Triora in a general cultural framework, and to propose its probable dating to the late prehistoric period.

The stele had also been dealt with by the present author in the general framework of prehistoric statue-stele (Anati 1968: 117-136).

The Technique of carving

The Triora stele is a slate slab on which is engraved, "a tremolo", a schematic composition which generally resembles menhir statues.

Through a microexamination of the surface of the stone, it was determined that the carving was made with an instrument whose point was very thin, 0.3 – 0.4 cm. wide and less than 0.1 cm. thick. It was also possible to establish that, in the course of the engraving, several changes in rhythm occurred in the execution of the design, at least three of which may be distinguished very clearly. Every time one line was finished and another started, the instrument was lifted and reapplied to the surface. At least three times the engraving was stopped in the middle of a line, and each time it was started again the mark appears sharper and more precise, consequently it may be deduced that the point of the burin was broken or dulled and had to be repaired or changed. The microscopic analysis has determined that there are 90 starting points for the engraving. On the left side of the stele (left side facing the artist), an uninterrupted sequence lasts from the base until right after the upper curve, a length of 33 cm., when the instrument is lifted and the engraving becomes finer. Also, on the right side, one notes an uninterrupted sequence of over 30 cm. Such lengthy work without lifting the instrument, and thus without stopping the had, would be difficult to sustain for more than a few minutes. Therefore, the work must have proceeded rather quickly.

Several experiments on the same type of stone have shown that the materials most likely used to engrave "a tremolo" on slate, are shell and stone. Seashell, however, tends to splinter easily and it is improbable that, with cardium or any other shell, one could engrave a line, "a tremolo", for more than 30 cm. Of the several suitable types of stone, a good quartz could have been used, but more probably, as Dr Acanfora deduced, flint was used. In fact a microscopic examination of the engravings supports this deduction. From what is revealed by the traces, the instrument seems to have been a delicate burin on a small blade with a sharp point made by the removal of a single flake on one part and of two or three very small flakes on the other. In the engraved lines one can see the negative form of the concave point of the flakes, which is characteristic of flint.

FIG 3   Detail of the central register.

FIG 4   Photograph of the Triora slab.

0   5   10   MOLINI DI TRIORA

FIG 5   Tracing of the Triora slab. Arrows show the procress of engraving of the stele.

Since the engraving, "a tremolo", enables us to recognize the starting point, the direction of engraving, and the stopping point of each line, it was possible to reconstruct the direction followed by the engraver in each line and, consequently, the process of engraving. The direction of the line is:

from bottom to top :	57 lines
from left to right :	25 lines
from right to left :	3 lines
from top to bottom :	5 lines TOTAL 90 lines

The three lines executed from right to left are the most distorted and imprecise. To prove this fact, it is enough to compare the two middle horizontal lines: that on the top was engraved from right to left, that on the bottom from left to right. The latter is much more straight and precise than the former. From these considerations we may assume the following:

1)   The artist was left-handed and worked primarily with the left hand.
2)   More than 60 percent of the design was executed while the artist held the stele with the base on the ground and the rounded part upward.
3)   The design appears to have been conceived as a unified composition since the engraving has only secondary variations of rhythm and maintains the same fundamental characteristics throughout the work. A difference in the engraving that one finds on the left side at the top, right after the curve, would seem to indicate a partial repair of the burin's point through a further chipping. The principal differences are those found between the major part of the work done with the left hand and the little done with the right, which leads one to believe that the whole monument was done by the same person and probably at one sitting (Fig. 4).

Description of the slab

The slab has an irregular, oval form, with slight concave depressions on the side. It is 53 cm. long and 28 cm. wide, with a maximum thickness of 3.5 cm.. The base is rather thin and would have been easy to stick in the earth. The figure is 20.5 cm. high and incised on the centre of the slab. Besides the engraving "a tremolo", there are various other finely incised lines, some completed earlier, others later than the principal design. These are not dealt with in this article.

The main figure has a semi-elliptical shape, with a horizontal base and two curved side lines. Following the process of execution, one sees that the base is composed of two lines. The first starts from the left side and, toward the centre, turns down into the right curved line. The second was executed from the lower left line, is superimposed from about 3.6 cm. on the first line and ends on the far right side. Therefore, the two bottom curved lines are intentional parts of the base (Fig. 5).

The two sides are engraved in a slightly curving line from the base towards the top after having described a curve in their upper sector which, in its course, changes from an almost vertical to an almost horizontal direction. At the top the two lines are joined by a cruciform sign which necessitated the lifting of the burin. The new vertical line began, and was superimposed at the end, on the line of the left side; it passes, superimposed as well, on the line of the right side, reaching a length of 2.7 cm. The horizontal line of the cruciform, slightly inclined to the left, is superimposed on the vertical line and reaches a maximum length of 2.8 cm.

The internal space, defined by the base and by the curving lines closed at the top by the cruciform, is divided into three horizontal registers. The top register contains the figure of a sun with rays; the middle one is composed of two horizontal lines on which are based vertical carvings; the bottom space has a central stair-like design which divides the area into two unequal rectangular spaces, each of which contains a "phi" design.

The solar disk, which has a maximum length of 6.7 cm., is an irregular oval, for some of its parts are almost straight and others curved. The 21 rays vary in length from 1.5 cm to 4.2 cm.. By microscopic study, it was possible to reconstruct the execution of this figure: first, the figure was "sketched", or very lightly incised, traces of this thin line being still visible to the naked eye on both the right side and on the left, where the sketch was enlarged and leaving the thin lines inside the outline of the disk.

The engraving (Fig. 6) was begun at the right angle of the base and continued in an inclined line almost straight, for 4 cm. after which the line stops and continues with a different rhythm. No signs of the instrument's breaking are visible, but the progress is notably different, being more fluent and secure. The "tremoli" are more forceful, indicating that the artist must have changed hands, beginning the figure with the right hand and after 4 cm. changing to the left. He followed the curve from the bottom and then stopped, where a change in the position of the stone is obvious, accomplished either by changing his seat or the position of the stone. The engraving then

FIG 6   Detail of the solar disk.

FIG 7   The stele of Granja di Toninuelo, Badajoz, Spain

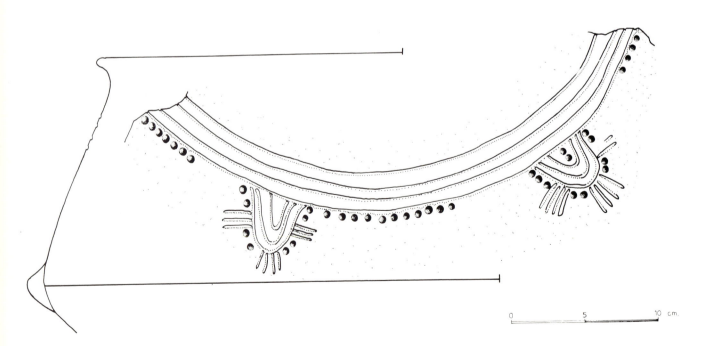

FIG 8   Decoration of a Bronze Age pot, from the Fiave pile-dwelling (Trentino). Courtesy R. Perini, Museo Tridentino di Scienze Naturali.

curves to the top at the left and follows, without interruption, to the top right angle. Here the burin is lifted and the artist begins the engraving from the bottom right angle, tracing an arc from bottom to top, joining the two lines together and closing the circle.

The rays were done in three groups from three different positions. One of the groups, done while the artist was sitting a little to the right of the slab, is composed of seven rays, from the almost horizontal line on the extreme left to the smallest in the line on the extreme left.

The rays are all executed from the disk outward while the last one is superimposed under the first of the second series. Here, apparently, the artist moved to the left side of the stone and engraved the second group of 9 rays, also from the disk outward. Finally, the artist returned to his original position in front of the stone and finished the last five rays which, instead, go inward; the distance between the first of these rays, at the centre in the bottom part of the disk, and the last one of the preceding group, is well-balanced, then it curves, leaving between the two a larger space than between the others. The last ray of the third group, turning toward the bottom on the extreme left, is superimposed on the first ray of the first group.

The sun, with its twenty-rays, dominates the upper register which is closed at the top by the semicircle of the upper part of the outer line and at the bottom by the central register.

The central register is formed by two horizontal lines on which there are two series of engravings. The centre of the upper line contains a semicircle surmounted by a cross and inside by a seven pointed star. This semicircle is the type designated as "hut figure" and since it is found in the centre of the composition it seems to be a focal point of the figure. On the left of the central semicircle there are four vertical lines and five on the right, making nine vertical lines on the upper line; added to the seventeen on the bottom, there is a total of twenty-six lines. Their lengths vary from 3.6 to 5.1 cm.; all are engraved from the bottom toward the top. These lines at the centre of the stele have certain analogies with the "belts" of some stele of the French Midi and of the Alpine zone. In other cases, a possible symbolic significance has been postulated (Anati 1964b: 25–26; 1968a: 101–107).

It was recognized in the study of the stele of Ossimo (Anati 1972: 81–120), that the number 26 is repeated in other monuments and seems to be connected with the lunar cycle. At Ossimo, in the upper zone there is a long "face" in the form of a "crescent moon", with a series of parallel lines on the sides, 26 on one side, 24 on the other. The "crescent moon" seems to separate two moon cycles and the crescent itself also seems to have been counted. If the lunar cycle is 27 days long and the lunar month is 28–29 days long, when the two sets of rays are added together (26+24=50), plus the crescent, this last must be the valence of four days if, as it seems, the "cycle" rather than the "month", was considered by the prehistoric artist. As already seen in studying the stele of Ossimo, an idol of Abakan in Siberia has two series of lines (26+24) on the sides of its face, functioning as hair and/or as rays: here we have again 26 and 24 plus the central face (Okladnikov and Timofeeva 1972: 225–235).

In the Triora stele, the central register is composed of two series of vertical lines, 26 altogether, and a semicircle with a symbolic star inside. If, together, this represents a lunar cycle of 27 days, the semicircle must have the value of a day or of a "station", perhaps a special or particularly important moment that the monument commemorates. One may ask if it is purely coincidence to find repeated on some stelae of the Iberian Peninsula the number 26. For example, on the Idol of the Granja di Toninuelo (Fig. 7), the large "belt" is decorated by 2 series of 13 points, which, added together, equal 26 (Anati 1968b: 72). The presence of 26 elements in series is not limited to statues-stelae; an analogy of this numerical composition can be found on a fragment of a clay vase discovered by Perini in the pile-dwelling of Fiave, in Trentino (Fig. 8). There is a series of dots connected with astral symbols on the neck of the vase. One of these series, apparently complete, contains 26 dots, from left to right: a row of 7,4 groups of 2 each between the rays of the sun and a row of 11, after the sun (total 26).

The third zone of the Triora stele is composed of a stair-like form with one "phi" figure on either side. All three figures were engraved from the bottom toward the top, beginning with the base line, while the eight steps of the "stair" were all done from left to right. The stair, as well as the sun, was first sketched by a fine incision and then redone by the "tremolo" technique.

The "phi" figure on the left side was started with a line at the angle of the base and the side. After 3.5 cm., without interrupting the engraving, the left arm was made, partly superimposed on the left side line of the composition. The central line of the figure, almost straight and vertical for 7.3 cm. was carved next. The right arm, executed last, is superimposed at the starting point on the two preceding lines and proceeds for 3.6 cm. before the burin is lifted to change direction. Although this figure is called "phi" for convenience, it is clearly and intentionally different from the other, for which the term is more appropriate (Fig. 9).

The second "phi" figure, enclosed in an almost square space, occupies more than half of the bottom register. It is made of an unusual series of 7 superimposed lines which enables one to follow almost exactly the process of its

FIG 9   Detail of the "phi" figure, to the right of the lower register.

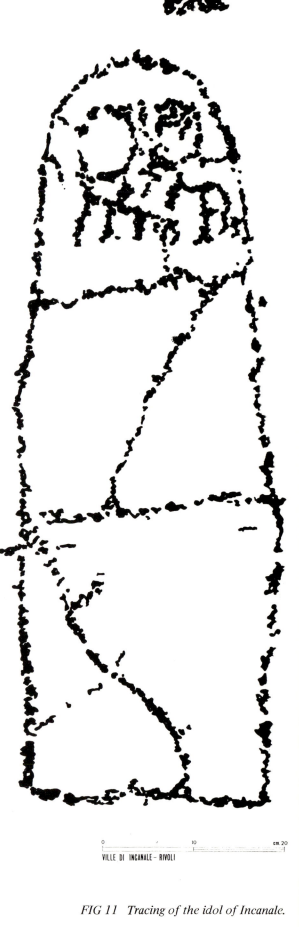

VILLE DI INCANALE - RIVOLI

FIG 11   Tracing of the idol of Incanale.

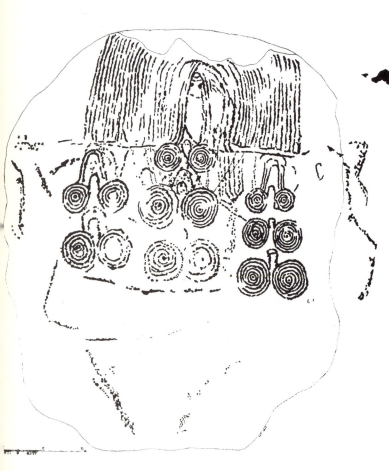

FIG 10   Tracing of the Ossimo stele.

execution. The engraving was started about 0.8 cm. below the base line and continued upwards for 7.5 cm.; the burin was then lifted and replaced in the same spot to make the central line which curved to the right at the top, then stopped about 14 cm. from the start. The beginning of the left "arm" is tentative, almost sketchy; in fact, at a height of 3 to 4 cm. from the base one notes 2 incision marks, from right to left. However, this attempt, probably made with the right hand, was quickly abandoned and the engraving started again, probably with the left hand, beginning at the extreme top left of the "arm". The engraving then proceeds without interruption, in a curved line, down to the point of the first tentative engraving. Starting from this same point, the engraving then goes toward the right, making the right arm by an oblique line which is about the same height as the left arm. At this point the right and left "phi" figures were similar, with a trunk and two "arms"; however, the second figure was continued and completed. Starting on the left, a lightly rounded line connects the top of the left "arm" with the central trunk. The line is superimposed at this point and then continues to the right for another 2 cm.. Then, the end of the right "arm" is connected to the first line by an oblique line directed toward the top. This line of 2.4 cm. is made from right to left and has characteristics of execution similar to those of the bottom right lines of the sun. In fact, the lines keep coming closer together, indicating both a lack of confidence in the execution and a weaker muscle in the arm, making one wonder if the artist, besides being left-handed, had some muscular defect in his right arm. The remaining two curved lines are almost parallel, executed from the bottom left to the top right, connecting the horizontal line of the arms with the top of the figure, seeming to make a face. The left line is super-imposed on the horizontal line.

Through microanalysis it was possible to reconstruct the process of engraving and thus to follow the artist, almost moment by moment as he produced an artistic composition characterized by determination and confidence derived from precise concepts which were well thought out beforehand. There are, in fact, neither second thoughts nor erasures: the artist has kept intact all that he engraved.

A trial by the same method on a similar slate slab, with the same kind of burin strokes and in the same "tremolo" rhythm, permits us to estimate the time required by the artist to complete the work at about two and a half to three hours.

We have tried to bring alive several hours in the life of a left-handed prehistoric artist who shifts from the left hand which holds the burin to the right hand where control is not as secure. Through this reconstruction we have tried to retrace the process of creativity, from the stone to the tool, from the tool to the hand and from the hand to the mind. We see a man at work, engrossed in his creation, but we do not know as yet his motivations or his state of mind.

One of the first questions to arise is the following: has the artist of Triora spent other half-days of his life in the same manner? If so, where are his other creations? On the other hand, it is very probable that such a self-assured and expert artist was not the only one of his group to make stone engravings. The Triora slab is part of a tradition, not an isolated case; eventually similar works will come to light.

Dating

As we can ascertain from the preceding pages, the composition must have had a clear and definite symbolic meaning. The artist knew exactly what he wanted to represent, which enables us to establish that in the era in which the stele was engraved, specific concepts existed which he expressed in his work.

In fact, the figure of the sun, the idea behind the three registers of the composition, and the symbolic character of the monument enables us to place some of the statue-stele and the monumental compositions of Valcamonica and Valtellina and perhaps also the older ones of Lunigiana ("Pontevecchio" type) in the same ideological world. For later periods, compositions of the type of Triora are as yet unknown. The later statue-stele often become more naturalistic and figurative. The Triora stele lacks elements of direct chronological value, such as figures of daggers, axes, and pend-ants which we find in other monuments of the period; however, its character and type of composition seem to indicate that it belongs to a rather archaic phase of the statues-stelae epoch.

Acanfora has already made a comparative study of single figures in the stele in question and has dated the monument generally to the prehistoric age. To these comparisons one can add the method of engraving justly compared to that of the impressed Neolithic pottery found also in Liguria (Acanfora 1956, Fig. 2; Bernabo-Brea 1947, Plate XIV).

The areas of Liguria and the French Midi have various manifestations of post-Paleolithic prehistoric art as already discussed (Anati 1960; 692–712; 1961: 580–585; 1968c: 57–68). In these regions, there are three principal types of monumental art: 1) the statues-stelae and menhir-statues which are concentrated mainly in Aveyron-Tarn and in Liguria; 2) symbolic-figurative rock art, which is found mostly in Mount Bego but also in minor groups of both engrav-ings and paintings throughout the subcoastal area from the Pyrenees to the Ligurian Apennines; 3) schematic

"Ligurian" rock art, whose area of diffusion covers the maritime provinces of France, Savoy, the French Maritime Alps, Liguria, and the Alpine valleys of Piedmont.

The statues-stelae in the areas under consideration are generally a Neolithic phenomenon whose production was prolonged into the Bronze Age and, in the most peripheral areas, persists sometimes in a decadent form until the Iron Age. In the Midi of France statues-stelae are often found reused in megalithic monuments of Middle and Late Neolithic Age.

Symbolic figurative rock art, begun in the Neolithic and reaching maximum development in the Bronze Age, has conceptual and stylistic points of contact with the statues-stelae in the Late Neolithic and in the Early Bronze Age. At Mount Bego the complex of rock art ceased rather abruptly with the beginning of the Iron Age after a fervid and uninterrupted flowering during the whole Bronze Age. At Mount Bego itself there are later examples of schematic rock art executed in various techniques, including "a tremolo" and incised filiform figures which are completely diverse conceptually.

In all the cases in which we find schematic rock art of the "Ligurian" type superimposed, it is always later than the statues-stelae and the symbolic-figurative rock art. This holds true throughout the entire area of distribution. Near La Spezia, a menhir of Monte della Madonna has later schematic engravings superimposed on the original design (the monument is in the museum of La Spezia). At the extreme opposite end of the area under consideration, the covering slab of the Dolmen del Barranc (Espolla) has a large figure of the statues-stelae type with numerous schematic engravings of a later period superimposed on it (Anati 1968b: 117). There are examples of superimposition at Mount Bego and in the French Midi that establish a relative chronology between symbolic-figurative rock art and schematic rock art; in all the cases in which a chronology is possible, schematic rock art is the latest of the three groups.

A similar succession of rock art styles is found in the western regions of the Iberian Peninsula where the style called "geometric symbolic" starts at the beginning of the Iron Age and lasts into the full historic period (Anati 1968b).

In looking for the initial date of the schematic rock art group termed "Ligurian", we can deduce that it must be located after the main development of schematic-figurative art of Mount Bego type and that, therefore, it should post-date the Bronze Age. The beginning of this art style probably coincides with the beginning of the Iron Age. On the other hand, "Ligurian" schematic rock art lasts into historical times up to the Middle Ages without any substantial typological, technical, and conseptual changes. It reflects, as it seems, a sort of ideology belonging to a population that entered the area during the Iron Age and persisted until the full Christianization of the region. Pastoralism was a major characteristic of these people which we may identify with those called "Ligurians" by the Romans. It would seem that these people took possession of their land at the beginning of the Iron Age and firmly dominated it, not allowing other ethnic groups of other ideologies to enter.

As was already mentioned, the stele of Triora conceptually and constituently re-enters the group of statues-stelae in an archaic phase. In view of the above considerations an Iron Age, Roman, or medieval date for the stele should be excluded. Nothing concerning the stele in question reflects the manner, concepts, or style of these periods in the area in which it was found. In effect, the monument can be placed either in the Neolithic Age, or it could be a recent work, carved in the last century by some shepherds. We know that some carvings executed "a tremolo" have been found at Mount Bego and elsewhere in Liguria. These were made by shepherds in the last three or four generations but were done with an iron point while on the stele of Triora the engravings are almost certainly done with a flint instrument, a material that shepherds have not been familiar with for at least several centuries.

It seems, therefore, that the Triora stele may be dated to a prehistoric epoch and can, in all probability, be attributed to the Neolithic Age; in other words, late fourth or third millennium B.C..

Significance and Conclusions

The composition of the front of the slab is made up of three registers contained within a semi-elliptical outline. The form of this outline is interesting in itself: under the base line there are two fangs and at the top, a cruciform figure. The three zones are composed of: the top, a solar disk with rays; the middle, two series of vertical lines resting on horizontal bases; the bottom, two figures vaguely anthropomorphic, divided by a stair-like shape. In spite of certain formative differences one sees conceptual analogies with the Ossimo stele (Anati 1972: 81–120) and perhaps the differences existing between the two monuments are as significant as their similarities. The interpretation of the significance which follows is presented as a working hypothesis and we wish to warn the reader as to its tentative character.

From the study of the Ossimo stele (Fig. 10) it was possible to show that the carving represents an abstract conception of the universe. It appears to be a very interesting cosmological vision in which the "entity", shown as the universe, was seen as subdivided into three parts which, from top to bottom, represent respectively the sky, the earth and the underworld. The upper register of the Ossimo stele has a lunar face in the centre with two series of lines on the sides, equalling two lunar cycles. On the Triora stele there is a sun in place of the moon, another celestial symbol which permits the hypothesis of an analogy between upper register of the two stelae.

The central register of the Ossimo stele has been interpreted as an image of the terrestrial world with eight spectacle-spiral-pendants which, as documented in the study of the stele, are symbols of birth and death (or of rebirth in another world?). One should not attribute, a priori, the same concept to the series of lines numerically identified with the days of the lunar cycle in the Triora stele. But this possibility should be examined. The lunar month was, and still is, identified by many people with the life cycle, the fertility of the earth, and of woman. Many people even today in Liguria and in other parts of Italy, decide the proper time of the month for grafting, for harvest, and for woodcutting by the phases (waxing and waning) of the moon. The lunar cycle determines the weaning of infants and sometimes also the time of a social occasion, of a contract, or of a marriage. Often, the best moment for sexual union and for the fertility of a woman are calculated by the moon's phases. Actually, the lunar cycle has a certain correspondence with the physiological cycle of women and of certain animals, and is also connected with certain recurrent phenomena in nature. Prehistoric man was an acute observer of these phenomena, constantly trying to find associations and correlations. If the lunar cycle had such great significance in many aspects of daily life for numerous prehistoric and historical people, it may be considered to have had an analogous significance for the prehistoric people who made the statues-stelae.

It can therefore be considered a possibility that the middle register of the Triora stele symbolizes the lunar cycle or a lunar cycle, divided in two parts under two lines, the one executed from right to left, the other from left to right. Altogether, the first part is formed of ten days, divided into five days + a particular day + four other days; the second part has seventeen days. If as it seems, there is an analogy between the stele of Triora and that of Ossimo, the lunar cycle could symbolize, for the artist, earthly life. If such an interpretation is held valid, it suggests even more the fact that the day or the particular moment, which perhaps was a fundamental one for the maker of the stele, is shown under the "hut" form which has the star figure inside and the cruciform figure above. Both these symbols are amply diffused in various historical epochs and also well-represented in the symbolism and beliefs of today.

In the stele of Ossimo, the third register, which was originally buried below surface, probably represents the underworld perhaps the world of the dead. In the stele of Triora, the third register is represented by two "phi" figures, by the sides of a stair-like form. There are several examples in Europe of statues-stelae in which a main entity, located on the upper part, is opposed by two entities of lesser importance or of negative value on the sides or at the bottom of the stele; such examples are found throughout Europe, from the stele of Kazanki in Crimea (Gimbutas 1965: 496) to a stele of Castello Branco in Portugal (Anati 1968b: 70). Their ideological significance has already been discussed in another study (Anati 1968a: 117–136).

We will not examine, in the present study, the very large number of mythological references suggested by the lower register of Triora. Here are found two "spirits" or watchmen, who guard the entrance of hell, by the side of the stairs, symbol of separation from the upper world and of the ascent or descent from one world to the other. It is enough to say at this stage of research that the third register of Triora, like the other two, appears to have conceptual analogies with that of the stele of Ossimo and that, as in the latter, seems to be part of cosmological vision of a universe divided into three parts, symbolizing respectively heaven, earth, and hell.

As in Ossimo, the trinity, composed by the three "logos" in this conception of the universe, is unified in one indivisible body intentionally closed and sealed, at Triora, by the external line surmounted by a cruciform symbol. It seems that the "entity" represented is an expression of a cosmological unity of this trinity in one transcendental synthesis.

This preliminary work simply presents a general view of this monument with the intention of stimulating some thought and does not intend to solve all the problems raised by this interesting monument. Two figures, that of the "hut" and that of the cruciform, remain among the most problematical. For the first, a precise and complex shape is established. Inside the hut is a seven-point star and above it there is a cruciform. It is inserted in the upper series of parallel lines in the central register. If, as it seems, the signs have a calendric significance, the hut would take the place of the sixth "day" of the series described. As we know, in primitive art, the hut can sometimes have the meaning of "woman" of of the "vagina". In other places, it can represent the presence of a divinity of of spirits, which, where invisible, are represented by their own receptacle. In still other instances, the hut is the symbol of matrimonial union and of the creation of new family. There are many examples in comparative ethnology of possible interpretations for this figure but a precise interpretation does not seem possible at this stage.

Very often the cruciform sign is " the symbol of man" but there are other alternatives. The cruciform, also in the rock art of Valcamonica, has sometimes been interpreted as the author's or tribe's mark or signature and, in these cases, it simply indicates the paternity of the figure with which it is associated. In other cases in rock art, it sometimes represents a schematic bird or the spirit of the departed person. In yet other examples this same symbol lacks a convincing interpretation. Therefore, even in this context, the meaning must remain open to debate.

In conclusion, the entire composition in a well-defined, semi-elliptical space seems to indicate the unity of three "logos" in one universe, the indivisibility of three "houses" in one entity. This form, with an elliptical sky, a rectangular body, and a flat base, must reflect a particular vision of the universe. It is interesting to note that this is exactly the form of many statues-stelae and of engraved idols. The Neolithic idol engraved on a rock at Incanale (Verona) (Fig. 19) is perhaps one of the simplest most compendious figures of this sort.(Nissi 1974: 177–179).

References Cited

Acanfora, M.O.
    1956   Singolare figurazione su pietra scoperta a Triora (Liguria). Studi in onore di Aristide Calderini e
            Roberto Paribeni. Milano, Vol. III, Studi di Archeologia e Storia dell'Artentica, 115–127.
Anati, E.
    1960   Quelques reflections sur l'art rupestre d'Europe, BSPF LVII, No. 11–12: 692–712. Parigi.
    1961   Prehistoric Art in the French and Italian Alps. Year Book of the American Philosophical Society,
            Philadelphia 1960: 580–585.
    1964a   Civilta Preistorica della Valcamonica, Milano (Il Saggiatore). pp. 1–299.
    1964b   La Stele di Bagnolo presso Malegno, Breno. pp. 1–42.
    1968a   Arte preistorica in Valtellina, Archivi, Capo di Ponte (Edizioni del Centro) No. 1: 1–74.
    1968b   Arte rupestre nelle regioni occidentali della Penisola Iberica. Archivi, Capo di Ponte (Edizioni del
            Centro), No. 2: 1–136.
    1968c   Arte immobiliare della tarda preistoria nel Sud della Francia e nell'Italia del Nord. Bollettino del
            centro camuno di studi preistorici II: 57–68.
    1972   La Stele di Ossimo, Bollettino del centro camuno di studi preistorici VIII: 81–120.
Bernabo' Brea, J.
    1947   Le Caverne del Finale. Bordighera.
Gimbutas, M.
    1965   Bronze Age Cultures in Central and Eastern Europe. The Hague: Mouton & Co.
Glory, A., Martinez, K., Neukirch, H., and P. Georgeot
    1948   Les peintures del'age du metal en France meridionale.   Prehistoire X, Paris.
Isetti, G.
    1957   Scoperta di incisioni repestri a Triora. Rivista Inguana e Intemelia, XII, No. 1–3: 78–79.
Louis, M. & Isetti, G.
    1964   Les Gravures prehistoriques du Mont-Bego (Itineraires Ligures, 9) Bordighera (Institut
            international d'Etudes Ligures), pp. 1–99, maps I–II.
Nisi, D.
    1974   Arte preistorica presso incanale di Rivoli (Verona). Bolletino del centro camuno di studi preistorici
            XI: 177–179.
Okladnikov, A.P. and Timofeeva, N.K.
    1972   Le Enigmatiche Statue-stele dello Ienisei e un Nuovo Idolo della Cultura di Okuniev. Bolletino di
            centro camuno di studi preistorici VIII: 225–235.

METAL ORES AND TRADE ON THE MIDDLE DANUBE[1]
by H. A. Bankoff

Although the copper sources of both Serbia and Transylvania have long been known in the literature (cf. Childe 1929; Gaul 1942), most research has tended to stress either the earliest appearance of metallurgy in this area (for example, Jovanović 1971; Renfrew 1969a), or its period of greatest development (Rusu 1963). Relatively little interest has been shown in that rather amorphous period which is termed "Middle Bronze Age". This is especially true for the southern part of the Middle Danube region, embracing the Banat, Oltenia, and eastern Serbia. Studies concentrating on chronology, and metal typology, such as Popescu (1944) and Hänsel (1968) include this area as a matter of course, treating it as a cul-de-sac or a region peripheral to the major metallurgical centers of the interior of the Carpathian Basin or the east Alpine region. While this view is to some extent justified, it takes into account neither the probable mechanics of copper production nor the vital role played by the cultures of this region with respect to their northern neighbors.

Temporally, the Middle Bronze Age in the southern part of the Middle Danube area may be roughly correlated with Reinecke Bronze B–D in the Central European chronological system (Müller-Karpe 1959; Garašanin 1959, Foltiny 1955), or Tószeg B2–D (Childe 1929), Tószeg D (Nestor 1932) or Bronze III–IV (Mozsolics 1957) in several interpretations of the Hungarian system (cf. Hänsel 1968 for an exhaustive overview of the relative chronology). In absolute terms, this span still basically depends on chronological connections with Egypt through Aegean intermediaries (Hachmann 1957). Depending on the choice of a high or low chronology, the Middle Bronze Age may begin as early as 1650 or as late as 1525 BC (Thomas 1970). The central part of this period, corresponding to Reinecke Bronze C, may be taken as contemporaneous with Late Helladic IIIA in Greece, but problems again arise in connection with the dating of Reinecke Bronze D–Hallstatt A, the end of the Middle Bronze Age. Müller-Karpe (1959), dates this in the thirteenth to twelfth centuries, depending on the date given for the LH IIIB–HC transition in the Aegean, which may be as early as 1230 or as late as 1180 (Thomas 1970). What radiocarbon dating can do to these limits remains to be seen, but for the moment we will not be far wrong in setting the sixteenth and thirteenth centuries B.C. as our *termini.*

Culturally, the Danube alluvium from the mouth of the Morava to the Isker drainage in Bulgaria is most closely associated with the "Žuto Brdo" or "Girla Mare" culture in the Middle to Late Bronze Age (Vasić 1907, 1910, 1911; Garašanin 1959, 1973; Dumitrescu 1961; Mikov 1970). Known largely from "urnfield" cremation cemetery assemblages, the hallmark of this culture is a highly ornate style of pottery decoration, predominantly incised and stamped volutes, spirals and arcs on the slipped and polished exterior surfaces of biconical and two-stage urns, roughly conical bowls, and cups with spherical bodies and cylindrical necks (see Dumitrescu 1961 or Garašanin 1959 for a complete description and illustrations). This ceramic group may be distinguished from the assemblages further upstream along the Danube alluvium in the Banat and Srem, including the lower Tisza, Timiş, Mureş, and Karaš drainages, which define the Vatina "culture" (Milleker 1905; Childe 1929: Vulić and Grbić 1938; Garašanin 1959, 1973). Although certain shapes, especially in the cup series, occur in both Žuto Brdo and Vatin assemblages, the latter is distinguished by the presence of false cord-marking, simpler urn bowl shape and decoration, and relatively lesser complexity of design motifs. "Vatina", like "Žuto Brdo", is known primarily from cremation cemetery assemblages. It must be stressed, however, that Vatina is not "provincial" or imitation Žuto Brdo ware, but partakes of a different esthetic tradition. On this ground, as on others which fall outside of the scope of the present study, these two groups may be considered to represent two different "cultures" or "peoples" (see Bankoff 1974 for a fuller discussion).

Having thus briefly sketched the chronology and cultural subdivisions of the area, let us turn to the problem of the relationship of these groups to each other and to their more northerly neighbours with respect to mining, manufacture and trade of mineral resources.

The entire region of older folded metamorphic rocks that make up the Timok Basin of eastern Serbia is of crucial importance for a study of the metal resources of the southern part of the Middle Danube. The zone of copper-bearing strata stretches from the Danube to Dimitrovgrad on the Yugoslav-Bulgarian border. To the east are the large copper deposits at the north end of the Isker gorge at Eliseina, which do not extend farther east than Etrepole (Gaul 1942). Within this entire area, copper occurs both in oxidized forms and in some places as native copper (Jovanović 1971). Eneolithic copper mines have been identified at Rudna Glava near the modern mines at Majdanpek (Jovanović

1.   I would like to thank Dr. H. Hencken, who first suggested that I turn my attention to the problems of the Middle Bronze Age in southeastern Europe. His work has long been a source of inspiration and guidance. I also gratefully acknowledge the help of the Wenner-Gren Foundation for Anthropological Research, which in addition to a grant from the United States Government, under the Fulbright-Hays Program, enabled me to spend 1970–1971 doing research in Yugoslavia.

1969, 1971), and Late Bronze/Early Iron Age workings at Zlotska Pećina near Bor (Tasić 1969). Erosion in the ancient crystalline schists of which this mountainous region is composed, has exposed ore-bearing strata, not only in the Danube gorges (Yugoslavia 1944–45), but also along the Pek and Timok, as well as their smaller tributaries (Riznić 1888). Copper ore is also found in some quantity in Macedonia and in western and central Serbia (Jovanović 1971). There is no sign at this time of "scrap metal" being shipped or hoarded for re-use.

Data are less certain for Romanian copper sources. Nonferrous ores are found particularly in Maramureş, in the southwestern edge of the Bihor Massif. Here the so-called Munţii Metalici are rich in primarily polymetallic ores, containing copper, lead and zinc, and sometimes silver and antimony (Matley 1970; Osborne 1967). These mountains are transected by many rivers, flowing eastward into the Mureş or Someş, which in turn flow westward out of Transylvania (Pounds 1969). The valleys are steep, narrow, and heavily forested, thus providing but limited access to the interior of the massif. There is no evidence that these ores were utilized in the Middle Bronze Age.

Tin sources, of course, are also a major problem. Analyses of finds from the latter part of this period (Reinecke Bronze D–Hallstatt A) show a percentage of tin of up to ten percent in pieces from both the southern part of the Middle Danube and Transylvania (Junghans, Sangmeister and Schröder 1960; Popescu and Rusu 1966; Veselinović 1952; Nadj 1955; Vinski 1958). Since tin is unknown in this area, Milleker (1940) and Childe (1929), would bring the tin used in Transylvania from mines in the Saxo-Bohemian Erzegebirge or Bavaria. However, as Muhly (1973a) has recently noted, the Erzegebirge tin deposits are hydrothermal deposits in veins of granite rock, and would have been completely inaccessible to the metal-workers of the Bronze Age. In that case, we must either posit now-depleted tin sources in the Banat (Milleker 1940) or include the (tin-) bronze producing centres of Transylvania in a Cornish tin network (cf. Muhly 1973b). The possibility that either or both of these alternatives may be "imaginative fantasy" (Muhly 1973a: 170) should be kept firmly in mind.

Since the ore-producing parts of the area are thus sharply defined, we must examine the ways by which material could be traded or shipped from one part of the region to another. Although easy movement both by land and by water was possible along the Middle Danube and along the Tisza, Trogmayer (1963) states that the area between the two rivers formed a boundary that was only semi-permeable. This area is a low sandy plateau with loess tracts that become more pronounced to the south. Ehrich (1965) sees this interfluvial area as a major north-south dividing strip during the Neolithic, somewhat differentiating Transdanubia from the west, and itself sometimes differentiated from the Hungarian Plain. It forms the division between Paulik's (1968) eastern and western Carpathian areas. Thus, while the interfluvial area divides the southern part of the Middle Danube drainage from the larger Hungarian Plain to the north, it also forms a natural dividing line between east and west, possibly reflecting a vegetational difference on either side of the 760 mm isohyet. In terms of trade routes or exploitation of copper sources, it is thus possible that central and western Serbia was a source of metal for an area to the northwest, while the copper deposits of the eastern Serbian and Bulgarian region supplied a predominantly Transylvanian market.

Routes into or out of the eastern edge of the Banat along the Danube are difficult to reconstruct. At low water narrow sand banks line the sides of the Djerdap defiles, but the only possible overland path which would not stray far inland from the Danube would involve zig-zagging along the slopes on either side. While not impossible, this is certainly not the easiest route of contact between the ore sources and the interior of the Carpathian Basin (Pounds 1969). The Romanian side of the Djerdap is linked to the interior of the Banat by way of the Porta Orientalis formed by the confluence of the Cerna and the Danube (Yugoslavia 1944–45). From the Danube at Orşova it is possible to ascend the Cerna to the small divide that separates it from the headwaters of the Timis (at Teregova) and then follow the Timiş down-stream past Caransebeş, to where the valley broadens and turns westward into the Banat.

Other routes may have linked the ore-producing regions of central and western Serbia to the north. Sites on the Jadar and its tributaries (Belotić, Bela Crkva) point to a route along the Jadar valley from the ore sources in the vicinity of Valjevo to the confluence of the Jadar with the Drina, thence down the Drina to the Sava. The fine flat land skirting the northern edge of the Cer Mountains would have made it unnecessary to follow the Drina all the way to its mouth. This route would then proceed into Srem, possibly crossing the Sava near Hrtkovci (Gomolava), and continue into the Banat via a route which followed the right Danube bank to Slankamen, where it would branch off up the Tisza. An alternative route could ascend the Kolubara from the ore sources around Valjevo and proceed up the Sava. Assuming western Transylvania, or eastern Hungary to have been the destination, the former journey could have been made directly in somewhat less than two weeks, while the Kolubara route would have taken about half that time, assuming a maximum daily distance of less than thirty kilometers on the plains and fifteen kilometers in the mountains. It is even possible that the regions around Kragujevac in central Serbia were connected with the north via a route running down the Morava and utilizing the valleys of its eastward-flowing tributaries, such as the Lepenica, to gain access to the ores of this area. It must be kept in mind that despite the relatively short distances to be traversed, this trade might equally have been indirect rather than direct.

The distribution of sites along the southern Middle Danube strongly suggests that the cultures of the Middle Bronze Age in this area represent a group of interlinked local trade networks. Trade in limited metal resources, would, among other effects, promote contact between communities and the interchange of ideas through personal contact (Renfrew 1969b). While this hypothesis must be dealt with in greater detail elsewhere, it seems reasonable to propose that the primary suppliers of copper in the region were the people living along the Danube, those of the "Žuto Brdo", "Cirna" or "Girla Mare" culture, whose site distribution closely follows the distribution of the oxide ores of the Timok eruptive basin (cf. Gaul 1942; Garašanin 1959; Berciu 1967). The Vatina culture of the Banat alluvium represents secondary suppliers, purveying southern resources to the more northeasterly Transylvanian markets. Even a cursory glance at the distribution of finished metal objects of Middle Bronze Age date from the Middle Danube area (cf. Hänsel 1968:II, Verbreitungskarte 1–30) shows that the large majority of types and artifacts occur far to the north of the metal source areas. The primary exception is the "winged pin" (Majnarić-Pandžić 1971), which may represent status goods in a "kula-like" trading partner exchange or elite distributional system (Sherratt 1972). Even these pins, however, are limited to the Vatina area, reflecting the northern part of the trade network. While one is tempted to postulate a trade in perishables or agricultural products directed southwards from the richer Banat alluvium towards eastern Serbia, this remains in the realm of speculation. The Karaš-Nera interfluvial region, thickly settled with Vatin and Žuto Brdo sites, seems to have been an intensive point of contact between the two groups, perhaps meriting consideration as a "port of trade" (Polanyi, et al. 1957).

The central and western Serbian sites, both of the "West Serbian Vatin culture" (Garašanin and Garašanin 1956; Garašanin 1959), and the "Belotic-Bela Crvka" group (Garašanin 1958, 1962, 1967) are part of a related trade network. Their relative wealth of metallic grave goods, tumulus burial practices, and amber, all differentiate these sites from those of the Vatina and Žuto Brdo areas, and suggest more direct northwesterly contacts than were available to regions farther to the east. It is distinctly possible, although untestable, on the basis of present data, that the contacts of this central and western area were directed west of Fruška Gora up the Danube through Bačka to the Hungarian Plain. The complexity of interrelationships within the area may very well be underestimated, and the unity of western and central Serbia may be questioned. One can sense a close connection between the eastern part of thie group and the area around Beograd (via the Kolubara) and farther east (via the Lepenica), which could be differentiated from the more western Serbian material. Further investigations along the Jadar and Drina are sorely needed; the lack of settlement material in particular is extremely crucial. Needless to say, each of these problems requires study before a more complete picture of cultural interaction in this highly complex area can emerge.

This paper has tried to illustrate several facets of the problem of metal resources and trade in the Middle Bronze Age in a very limited area. I have tried to propose hypotheses which can be tested by metallurgical analyses or further archaeological data. None of the postulated routes may have been used, nor may any of the groups have interacted in the way which has been proposed. Nonetheless, a necessary step for the further development of any sort of coherent picture of life in the area in the Middle Bronze Age requires that we stop treating cultures as assemblages of pots and begin treating them as groups of interacting individuals whose activities and motives are the focus of our inquiry.

References Cited

Bankoff, H. A.
    1974   The end of the Middle Bronze Age in the Banat. Doctoral dissertation, Harvard University.
Berciu, D.
    1967   Romania. Ancient peoples and places. London.
Childe, V. G.
    1929   The Danube in prehistory. Oxford.
Dumitrescu, V.
    1961   Necropola de incinerație din epoca bronzului de la Cirna. Biblioteca de arheologie, 4. Bucurest.
Ehrich, R. W.
    1965   Geographical and chronological patterns in Central Europe. In R.W. Ehrich (ed.), Chronologies in Old World archaeology. Chicago.
Foltiny, S.
    1955   Zur Chronologie der Bronzezeit des Karpatenbeckens. Bonn.
Garašanin, M.
    1959   Neolithikum und Bronzezeit in Serbien und Makedonien. Bericht der Römisch-Germanischen Kommission 39:1–130.
    1973   Prehistorija Srbije. Beograd.
Garašanin, M. and D. Garašanin
    1956   Neue Hugelgräberforschung in Westserbien. Archaeologia Yugoslavica 2:11–18.
    1958   Iskopavanja tumula u Belotiću i Beloj Crkvi. Zbornik radova Narodnog Muzeja 1:17–50.
    1962   Iskopavanja tumula u kompleksu Belotić-Bela Crkva 1959. i 1960. godine. Zbornik radova Narodnog Muzeja 3:47–68.
    1967   Iskopavanja u kompleksu Belotić-Bela Crkva 1961. godine. Zbornik radova Narodnog Muzeja 5:5–30.

Gaul, J. H.
    1942   Possibilities of prehistoric metallurgy in the East Balkan Peninsula. American Journal of Archaeology
            46 (3): 400–409.
Hachmann, R.
    1957   Die frühe Bronzezeit im westlichen Ostseegebiet und ihre mittel- und südosteuropäischen Beziehungen.
            Hamburg.
Hänsel, B.
    1968   Beiträge zur Chronologie der mittleren Bronzezeit in Karpatenbecken. Bonn.
Jovanović, B.
    1969   Rudna Glava, Majdanpek. Arheološki pregled 11:29–31.
    1971   Metalurgija eneolitskog perioda Jugoslavije. Beograd.
Yugoslavia
    1944-45 Geographical Handbook series, BR 493. 3 volumes. London. Naval Intelligence Division.
Junghans, S., E. Sangmeister and M. Schroder.
    1960   Metallanalysen kupferzeitlicher und frühbronzezeitlicher Bodenfunde aus Europa. Studien den Anfängen
            der Metallurgie, 1, Berlin.
Majnarić-Pandžić, N.
    1971   Prilog tipologiji i rasprostranjenosti krilastih igala. Rad Vojvodjanskih Muzeja 20:13–23.
Matley, I. M.
    1970   Romania. a profile. New York.
Mikov, V.
    1970   Materiali ot posledni'ia period na Bronzovata epoha ot severozapadna Bulgari'ia. Arheologi'ia 12(3):
            48–63.
Milleker, F.
    1905   A vattinai östelep. Temesvar.
    1940·   Vorgeschichte des Banats: Bronzezeit. Starinar, 3 ser. 15:3–42.
Mozsolics, A.
    1957   Archäologische Beiträge zur Geschichte der Grossen Wanderung. Acta Archaeologica Academiae
            Scientiarum Hungaricae 8: 119–156.
Muhly, J. D.
    1973a   Copper and tin: the distribution of metal resources and the nature of the metals trade in the
            Bronze Age. Transactions of the Connecticut Academy of Arts and Sciences 43: 155–535.
    1973b   Tin trade routes of the Bronze Age. American Scientist 61(4):404–413.
Müller-Karpe, H.
    1959   Beiträge zur Chronoligie der Urnenfelderzeit südlich und nördlich der Alpen. Bonn.
Nadj, S.
    1955   Bronzana ostava iz Novog Bečeja. Rad Vojvodjanskih Muzeja 4:43–61.
Nestor, J.
    1932   Der Stand der Vorgeschichtsforschung in Rümanien. Bericht der Römisch-Germanischen
            Kommission 22:11–181.
Osborne, R.
    1967   East Central Europe. New York.
Paulik, J.
    1968   K problematike východneho Slovenska v Mladsej Dobe Bronzovej. (Zur Problematik der Ostslovakei
            in der jüngeren Bronzezeit). Sbornik Slovenskeho Narodneho Muzea 62, Historia 8:3–43.
Polanyi, K., C. Arensberg, and W. Pearson
    1957   Trade and market in early empires. New York.
Popescu, D.
    1944   Die frühe und mittlere Bronzezeit in Siebenbürgen. Bucurest.
Popescu, D. and M. Rusu
    1966   Roumanie; Dépots de l'Age du Bronze Moyen. Inventaria Archaeologica. Bucurest.
Pounds, N.
    1969   Eastern Europe, Chicago.
Renfrew, C.
    1969a   The autonomy of the south-east European Copper Age. Proceedings of the Prehistoric Society
            35:12–47.
    1969b   Trade and culture process in European prehistory. Current Anthropology 10 (2–3): 151–169.
Riznić, M.
    1888   Starinski ostaci u srezu Zviškom (okr. Požarevački). Starinar, 1 ser. 5(1): 31–39.
Rusu, M.
    1963   Die Verbreitung der Bronzehorte in Transylvanien vom Ende der Bronzezeit bis in der mittlere
            Hallastattzeit. Dacia 7: 177–210.

Sherratt, A. G.
    1972   Socio-economic and demographic models for the Neolithic and Bronze Ages of Europe. In D. Clarke (ed.), Models in archaeology. London.
Tasić, N.
    1969   Zlotska Pećina. Arheološki pregled 11:36–39.
Thomas, H.
    1970   Europe and Near Eastern historical chronology. Actes du VIIe Congrès International des Sciences Préhistoriques et Protohistoriques, Prague, 21–27 août 1966, I:603–605.
Trogmayer, O.
    1963   Beiträge zur Spätbronzezeit des südlichen Teils der ungarischen Tiefebene. Acta Archaeologica Academia Scientiarum Hungaricae 15:85–122.
Vasić, M.
    1907   Žuto brdo. Starinar, 2 ser. 2(1):1–47.
    1910   Žuto brdo. Starinar, 2 ser. 5:1–207.
    1911   Žuto brdo. Starinar, 2 ser. 6:1–94.
Veselinović, R.
    1952   Bronzana ostava iz Gaja. Rad Vojvodjanskih Muzeja 1:38–47.
Vinski, Z.
    1958   Brončanodobne ostave Lovas i Vukovar. Vjesnik Arheološkog Muzeja u Zagrebu, 3 ser. 1:1–34.
Vulić, N. and M. Grbić
    1938   Yougoslavie: Belgrade-Musée de Prince Paul. Corpus Vasorum Antiquorum. Paris.

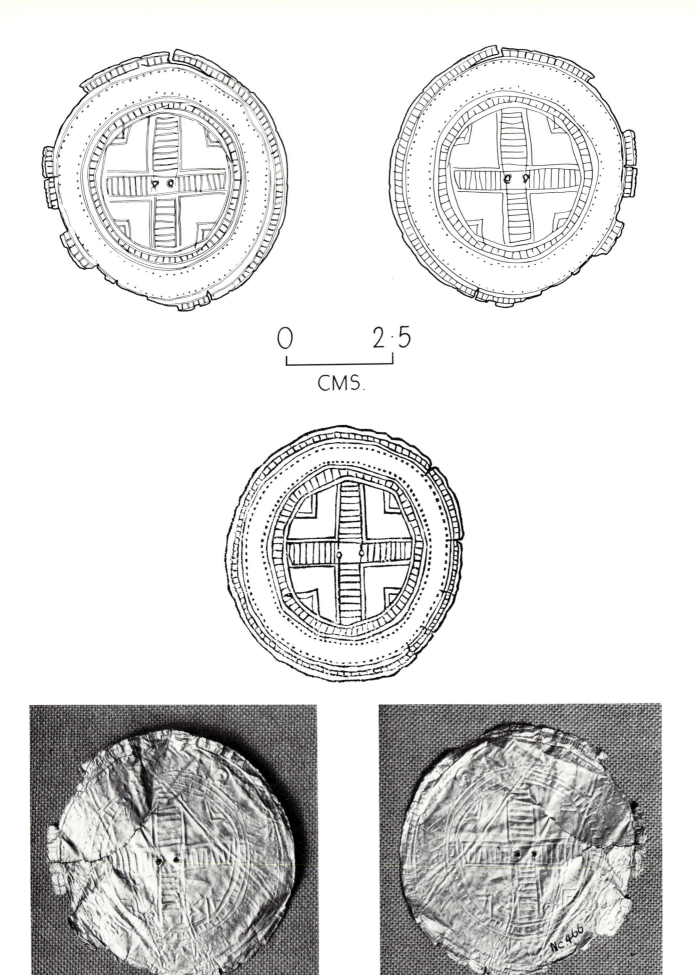

FIG 1 *Gold disc from Ballyshannon, Donegal, Ireland.* Top and bottom left: *face of the disc.* Top and bottom right: *its reverse.* Centre: *illustration of the disc in Gibson's edition of* Camden's Britannia *(1695). The scale applies to all the drawings; the photographs are at a slightly larger scale.*

AN EARLY ACCESSION TO THE ASHMOLEAN MUSEUM
by Humphrey Case.

The gold disc from Ballyshannon, Donegal, Ireland illustrated on FIG. 1 is a fine specimen of an ornament of the British and Irish Beaker Culture dating to the early second millennium b.c. in conventional radiocarbon chronology. It must be not only one of the oldest surviving accessions to a public museum, having been in the Ashmolean for nearly three centuries, but also one of the earliest surviving recorded finds from an excavation, and one of the first excavated finds to be illustrated by a scale drawing (FIG. I, centre). It is interesting too for its possible connections with bardic prophecy, or folk memory. Its associations are thus a microcosm of that blend of experimental science and the semi-occult which contributed to Natural Philosophy, for the pursuit of which the Ashmolean was founded; and its rather tattered condition may show how Elias Ashmole's intentions for his foundation failed to be realised, even from its opening in 1683.

I offer these notes to my learned fellow curator, Hugh Hencken, in appreciation of his many scholarly papers on the prehistory of Atlantic Europe and in gratitude for his long and benevolent association with the Ashmolean Museum.

The disc and its archaeological context

The disc is an approximately circular piece of hammered gold, diameter where surviving about 56 mm; it is 0.122 mm thick at the centre, and 0.085 at the rim. It tends to have a slightly convex profile, but this may have no significance as it has suffered repeated deformation. Three prominent linear marks, where it was folded and bent double on more than one occasion can be seen on FIG. 1: parts of the rim are missing or torn and two of the surviving segments were bent under until 1975; numerous minor scratches and bruises are also apparent. It is decorated with linear and dotted repoussé ornament made with strokes and pressure of a sharp implement without a cutting edge (a pointed copper or bronze awl suggests itself) against a firm but yielding surface, for example a leather strip on a wooden bench or a stone; the work may have been held with battens located by the craftsman's free hand or possibly with the help of an assistant. The decoration is entirely free-hand, and no special attempt was made to form the patterns accurately or neatly. Two holes were punched through from the face — assuming the face to be the side with raised ornament (FIG. 1, left: top and bottom).

Discs of this kind variously termed "sun-discs" or "button-covers" have been studied by Jacob-Friesen (1931), MacWhite (1951, 50–6), Butler (1963, 167–75) and Clarke (1970, 94–5). Twenty-four such gold discs from Ireland and Britain are listed in Tables 1 and 2 with published references and are illustrated diagrammatically on FIGS. 2 and 3. Twenty-one of these discs have or appear to have had similar twin central perforations, and free-hand linear and repoussé ornament of concentric and cruciform patterns; but those from Ballydehob, Cork and Farleigh Wick, Wiltshire (nos. 15 and 11) are unperforated and the unusually small one from Site D, Knockadoon, Lough Gur, Limerick (no. 14) is undecorated. By its higher polish, or neater or more definite decoration, the side with raised patterns may be assumed in most cases to have been the face worn or displayed outwards, as with the Ballyshannon disc, but most of the decoration on the face of the Farleigh Wick disc was depressed.

At least half the discs were found in pairs: those from Ballina, Mayo (nos. 6 and 7), Tedavnet, Monaghan (nos. 22 and 23), Cloyne, Cork (nos. 17 and 18), a pair from Co. Wexford (nos. 20 and 21) and possibly another from Co. Roscommon (nos. 4 and 5). The Ballyshannon disc was also originally one of a pair (nos. 1 and 2) as was that from Mere G. 6a, Wiltshire (nos. 12 and 13). The Farleigh Wick and Mere discs were from graves; but none of the Irish ones was so recorded and most, or all of them, may have been in caches. The Farleigh Wick and Mere G. 6a graves contained at least two burials and the former grave yielded one disc and the latter two. Perhaps therefore the discs were intended to be worn singly; with more reason therefore those recorded in pairs may have been placed in caches. The Lough Gur and Ballydehob finds (nos. 14 and 15) were certainly caches. The Lough Gur disc was recorded as "found amoung the stones which supported the uprights of the lower terrace wall" of Site D, and "bent double along a line across the perforations". The Ballyshannon discs which may also have been in a cache (see below, page 30) had been apparently similarly "bent double", as had been one of the discs from Co. Wexford (no. 21) and

Table 1:   *TYPE A DISCS AND AN UNDECORATED DISC (FIG. 2)*

Locality	Circumstances of finding: Associations	Museum	Catalogued in Armstrong 1933	Other references besides Armstrong and Hartmann	Analysed in Hartmann 1970
					Table: Serial No.
I, (2). Ballyshannon, Donegal.	Two discs found together.	Ashmolean NC. 466	—	Gibson 1695: 1021-2, note b.	—
3. ? Corran, Armagh.	? found in a box bound with a gold band, with 2 stone wrist-guards of Atkinson's type B1, (an)other gold disc(s), and jet beads.	NMD Disc: W. 270 Wristguards: W.69 and 70.	No. 337 Pl. XIX, 438	Wilde 1857: 89 Wilde 1862: 94	3 : 555
4. Co. Roscommon 5. " "	? found together.	NMD 835a: P. 949 W. 268	No. 332. Pl. XIX, 439 No. 333. Pl. XIX, 435	—	3 : 549 3 : 550
6. Ballina, Mayo 7. " "	Found together.	NMD W. 267 W. 271	No. 326. Pl. XIX, 430 No. 327. Pl. XIX, 429	—	3 : 546 3 : 547
8. Kilmuckridge, Wexford.	—	BM 493-1.31	—	Clarke 1970, Fig. 141 c	—
9. Castle Treasure, Douglas, Cork.	—	BM 54.12 - 27.2	—	Croker 1850: 150-2,22 ? Clarke 1970: Fig. 141a	—
10. Ireland	—	NMD 92:1881	No. 338 Pl. XIX, 434.	—	3 : 558
11. Farleigh Wick, Wiltshire.	**Jug's Grave. In a stone** cist with at least two disarticulated inhumation burials, with a beaker and sherds of another, a bone belt ring, four barbed and tanged arrowheads and struck flints. Although the disc shows four incipient borings it was not in fact perforated (electrotype only examined).	Disc in **private collection.** Other finds: **Bristol.** Electrotype: **Devizes**	—	Underwood 1947: 447-51; 1948:270-1. Clarke 1970: 440; Fig. 259	—
12, (13). Mere, Wiltshire	Barrow G.6a. Two discs (one since lost) in a grave with the inhumation burial of an adult man and "a young person", a beaker, tanged copper knife, wristguard of Atkinson's type B1, and bone spatula.	**Devizes** Annable and Simpson 1964, nos. 93-96	—	Colt Hoare 1812: 44; Pl. II	—
14. Lough Gur, Limerick.	**Undecorated disc** found among the stones which supported the lower terrace wall, Site D, Knockadoon.	NMD	—	Ó Ríordáin 1954:410	—

NMD = National Museum, Dublin.   NME = National Museum, Edinburgh.   BM = British Museum.

another recorded simply as from Ireland (no. 24), and the same may have been true of some of the other Irish examples (Coffey 1913, Pl. III). The surviving disc from the Mere grave has not been folded but the disc from Farleigh Wick had; but the latter was unperforated and may never have been worn.

The discs are classified here into *type a* and *b*. *Type a* discs (Table 1, nos. 1–13; FIG. 2) have ladder-patterned cruciform motifs, such as on the Ballyshannon example, and show a northern Irish tendency although the two English finds are of this type. *Type b* (Table 2, nos. 15–24; FIG. 3) comprises the remainder, including those with cruciform mofits without ladder-patterns, and those with zig-zag bands; it includes the biggest examples and has a southern Irish tendency. The undecorated disc from Lough Gur (Table 1, no. 14: FIG. 2) is considered with *type a*.

Dating *type a* is not difficult. The Mere and Farleigh Wick graves belong to the Middle phase of the Beaker culture in Great Britain and Ireland. This Middle phase was within the insular Late Neolithic and dates from the latest 3rd millennium b.c. in conventional radiocarbon chronology or mid 3rd in calibrated chronology (Case 1976b). It saw the major innovations of Beaker Culture settlement in these islands and culminated in the culture's high peak, exemplified notably in rebuilding at Stonehenge, Wiltshire (Atkinson 1956, Stage II; Case 1976a & b). *Type a* discs and allied gold finery discussed below (pages 26-7) were essentially Irish contributions to a major exchange network of pottery, metal and other objects which defines the Middle phase, and which may be conveniently summarised as Clarke's ranges of association 2 and 3 (Clarke 1970: 447-8).

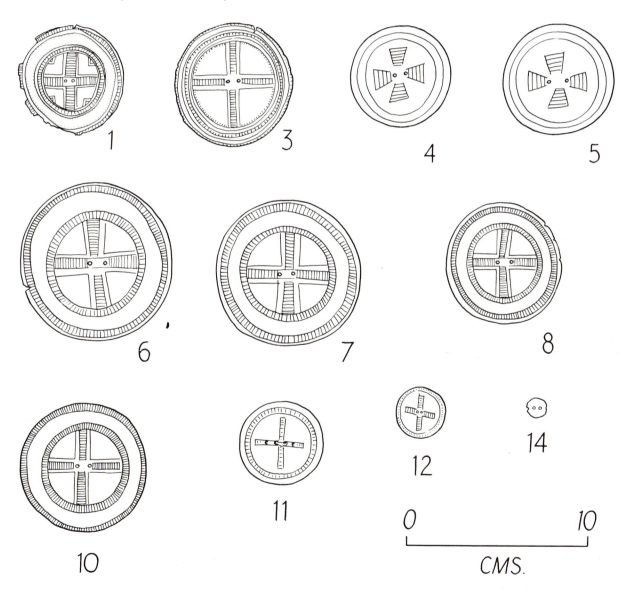

FIG 2   *Gold discs of* type a: *1, Ballyshannon, Donegal; 3, possibly Corran, Armagh; 4, 5, Co. Roscommon; 6, 7, Ballina, Mayo; 8, Kilmuckridge, Wexford; 10, Ireland; 11, Farleigh Wick, Wiltshire; 12, Mere, Wiltshire; 14, Lough Gur, Limerick. (3-7 and 10 after Armstrong 1933 ; 8, after* A Guide . . . . . Bronze Age *(British Museum 1920), fig. 120; 14, after Ó Ríordáin 1954).*

The undecorated disc from settlement site D, Lough Gur, Limerick was also in Middle Beaker association, and the same may have been true of the *type a* disc possibly from Corran, Armagh (Table 1, no. 3). This is the only disc recorded as formerly in the Dawson collection (Wilde 1862: 94) and may possibly therefore have been found in a cache with two stone wristguards now in the National Museum, Dublin (Accession nos: W.69 and 70), also formerly in this collection, which were "found in a bog at Corren three miles from Armagh, in the year 1833, in a box bound

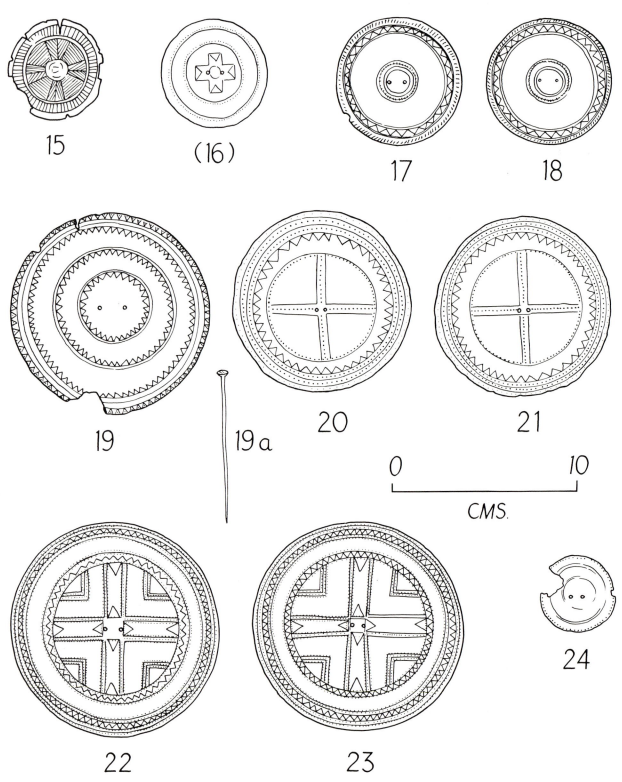

FIG 3   Gold discs of type b *(15 - 19, 20 - 24) and a gold pin (19a): 15, Ballydehob, Cork; 16, Baltimore, Cork; 17, 18, Cloyne, Cork; 19, 19a, Ballyvourney, Cork; 20, 21, Co. Wexford; 22, 23, Tedavnet, Monaghan; 24, Ireland. (15, 17 - 24 after Armstrong 1933; 16 after a drawing by Stukeley published in Herity 1969. The dimensions of 16 are uncertain).*

Table 2:   TYPE B DISCS AND A PIN (FIG. 3)

Locality	Circumstances of finding: Associations.	Museum	Catalogued in Armstrong 1933	Other references besides Armstrong and Hartmann.	Analysed in Hartmann 1970 Table: Serial No.
15. Ballydehob, Cork	Unperforated disc, the only recorded surviving piece from a cache which included "two or three similar pieces", found "in a cleft in the rock carefully covered with earth and a rude pavement of stones. Along with it were two or three similar pieces . . . . were destroyed . . . . In the same place were found some specimens of bronze . . . 'ring money', which were broken by the finders . . . ." One of the bronzes was described as "a massive circular bronze armlet, 4¼ inches in diameter"	NMD S.A. 130; 1913	No. 340. Pl. XIX, 427	MacAdam 1856:164 Day 1899: 414 **Bronze bracelet:** Sotheby *et al.* 1913: lot 350	3 : 559
(16) Baltimore, Cork.	An early 18th-century find since lost. (?) found with another.			Herity 1969: 3; Pl. Ia	—
17. Cloyne, Cork. 18. " "	Found together	NMD S.A. 129:1913 S.A. 129:1913	No. 334.Pl.XIX,436 No. 335.Pl.XIX,437	—	3 : 553 3 : 554
19. Ballyvourney, Macroom, Cork. 19a. " "	Found with 19a: a gold nail-head pin.	NMD Disc: S.A.128: 1913 Pin: S.A.127: 1913	No. 339. Pl. XIX, 431 No. 449. Pl. XIV, 252	—	3 : 545 6d : 544
20. Co. Wexford 21. " "	Found together	NMD W. 266 W. 272	No. 328. Pl. XIX, 432 No. 329. Pl. XIX, 433	—	3 : 552 3 : 551
22. Tedavnet, Monaghan. 23. " "	Found together between the roots of an old oak tree.	NMD 34 : 1872 35 : 1872	No. 330.Pl.XIX,425 No. 331.Pl.XIX,426	—	3 : 557 3 : 556
24. Ireland	—	NMD W. 269	No. 336.Pl.XIX,428	—	—

NMD = National Museum Dublin

with a gold band, together with some gold circular plates, and several jet beads of various shapes" (Wilde 1857: 89). These wristguards of Atkinson's type Bl (typology quoted in Clarke 1970) would be consistent with a Middle Beaker date. No jet was recorded from the Dawson collection (Wilde 1857: 240–2), but jet beads could conceivably also belong to the same Middle Beaker phase; a jet ring from Cassington, Oxfordshire (Clarke 1970: Fig. 240) comparable with a fragmentary bone one from the Farleigh Wick grave (*loc. cit.,* Fig. 259) can be so dated.

Type *a* discs therefore can be assigned to the Middle Beaker phase. The date of the *type b* discs is rather less clear, although it seems likely that they were current later. First one must consider the continuity within the Beaker Culture following the Middle phase and then the variety of gold objects both of that culture and of contemporary and ensuing developments. The transition to the Late phase of the Beaker Culture, during the early 2nd millennium in conventional radiocarbon chronology – or from the late 3rd in calibrated – was a matter largely of internal development (Case 1976a & b). The phase corresponded to an early part of the insular Early Bronze Age. Its exchange network may be conveniently summarised as Clarke's ranges of association 4 and 5 (Clarke 1970: 447–8). Food Vessels, the origins of which can be traced to Middle Beaker pottery, and various forms of Urn were also current during it.

The gold and other decorated metal objects which were part of the exchange networks of the insular Late Neolithic and Early Bronze Age are quite various. The rather rough freehand repoussé decoration on discs of *type a* and *b* and on the allied ear-rings and plaques discussed below is very different from the fine, elegant and confident freehand tracing on the Irish lunulae, which are also of thicker metal than are the discs; yet some of the decorative motifs of the lunulae are matched by those of Middle Beaker pottery (Taylor 1970), and it seems likely that their origins go back to the Middle Beaker phase. The decoration on the discs is different again from the freehand traced decoration of the bronze or copper bracelet from a Late Beaker grave at Knipton, Leicestershire and of other comparable objects (Britton 1963: 279–81; Clarke 1970: Figs. 946, 955), and the decoration of all the objects mentioned so far differs strongly from the precisely executed and compass-and-template drawn tracing of the best Wessex Culture gold work of the later part of the Early Bronze Age. The repoussé decoration of the armlets from Melfort, Argyllshire is different again (Piggott and Stewart 1958a; Britton 1963: 278). The Melfort armlets may be Middle Bronze Age, but the lost gold armlet from Lisnakill, Waterford seems to have been comparable and this may have been found in a Vase Food Vessel (Herity 1969: 10–11) and thus may have been Early Bronze Age; the repoussé decoration on the armlets is at any rate in a Beaker Culture

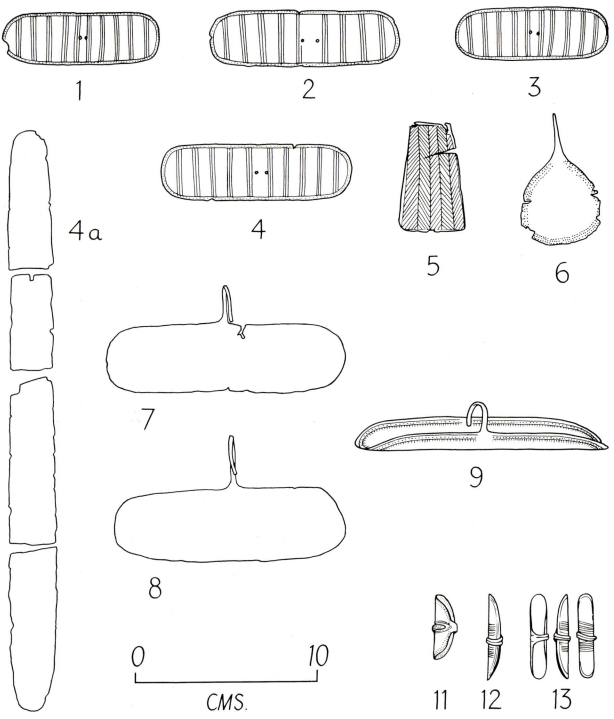

FIG 4   Gold objects allied to discs of types a and b: 1-3, plaques from Belleville, Cavan; 4, 4a, plaque and band from Cavan; 5, plaque from Castlemartyr, Cork; 6-9, 11-13, ear-rings from Deehommed, Down (6), Ireland (7), Ireland (8), Orbliston Junction, Morayshire (9), Alston, Northumberland (11), Radley, Berkshire (12, 13). (1-8, after Armstrong 1933; 9, after Paton 1871; 11, after Maryon 1936).

tradition, and this appears to have been rather dramatically confirmed by a gold bell-beaker recently reported from Switzerland (Bürgi and Kinnes 1975).

The only association of an Irish *type b* disc reported by Armstrong is of that from Ballyvourney, near Macroom, Cork, with a gold nail-headed pin (Table 2, nos. 19 and 19a). He did not comment on the possible associations of the similar type disc from Ballydehob (Table 2, no. 15), and it is unfortunately impossible to be certain from Day's description (1899: 414) or MacAdam's (1856: 164) whether or not it was indeed found with bronzes including " a massive circular bronze armlet, 4¼ inches in diameter " (sold in 1913, Sotheby *et al*, lot 350). The description of the bronzes as " ring money " suggests that they may have been of Eogan's Late Bronze Age Dowris phase rather than the earlier Bishopsland phase, which is connected with the so-called Ornament Horizon of the English Middle Bronze Age (Eogan 1964: 272–88).

Table 3:   GOLD OBJECTS ALLIED TO DISCS OF TYPES A AND B (FIG. 4)

Locality	Circumstances of finding: Associations.	Museum	Catalogued in Armstrong 1933	Other references besides Armstrong and Hartmann.	Analysed in Hartmann 1970 Table:Serial No.
PLAQUES AND A BAND					
1. Belleville, Cavan 2. " " 3. " "	Found together in 1852 in drainage operations in the bed of a stream.	NMD W. 71 W. 72 W. 75	No.391.Pl.X,55 No.392.Pl.X,53 No. 393.Pl.X,56	Wilde 1862: 39-40	3 : 603 3 : 604 3 : 605
4. Co. Cavan 4a. " "	No. 4 (a plaque) found in the "same locality" as 4a (a fragmentary band).	NMD Plaque: W. 76 Band: W.78-81	No.394.Pl.X,54 No.395.Pl.X,49	Wilde 1862:44	3 : 606 3 : 607-10
5. Castlemartyr, Cork.	Found when quarrying in 1805, in a cave with an inhumation burial said to have been covered with "exceedingly thin plates of stamped and embossed gold, connected by bits of wire . . . . also several "amber beads" described as "mitre shaped". The plaque is the only surviving object from this grave; " . . . . . . rather more than the contents of half a coal box of gold" was said to have been sold and melted. Other alleged (indeterminate) gold finds in Croker 1854: 145-8.	NMD S.A.131:1913	No.398.Pl.X,57.	Croker 1854:143-5 Day 1899:414	6d : 1077
6. Deehommed, Down	—	NMD 18:1876	No. 350. Pl. XVIII,413	—	8 : 1062
7. Ireland	—	NMD W.73	No. 348. Pl. XVIII,423	—	3 : 991
8. Ireland	—	NMD W. 74	No. 349. Pl.XVIII,424	—	3 : 992
9,(10). Orbliston Junction, Morayshire.	Two ear-rings (one lost) found in a stone cist possibly with an inhumation burial.	NME	—	Paton 1871: 30, Fig. Walker 1964/6: 93-4, 118-9	-
11. Kirkhaugh, Alston, Northumberland.	**Barrow I.** Possibly associated with a beaker and (?) with other finds.	Newcastle	—	Maryon 1936:207-17 (cp. Clarke 1970:438) Clarke 1970 : Fig. 3	—
12,(13), Radley, Berkshire.	**Barrow 4a.** Two ear-rings with the contracted inhumation burial of an adult man, a beaker and three barbed and tanged arrowheads.	Ashmolean	- —	Williams 1948: 1-9, 15-17 Clarke 1970: Fig.63	—

NMD = National Museum Dublin. NME = National Museum, Edinburgh.

The dating of nail-headed pins as recorded from Ballyvourney needs clarifying. Eogan assigned such Irish gold or bronze pins to the Late Bronze Age Dowris phase (1964: 282–3), but they seem to have originated earlier. A bronze one was recorded in House I at Site D, Lough Gur, Limerick in Middle Bronze Age association, with a stone mould for looped palstaves, clay moulds for socketed spearheads and Class II pottery (Ó Ríordáin 1954: 411); the presence of another at nearby Site C in the so-called gravel layer in which the latest classifiable finds were sherds of Food Vessels and Class II ware (Ó Ríordáin 1954: 360–1), is inconclusive (Case 1961: 207), but not inconsistent with an Early or Middle Bronze Age dating. Eogan himself drew attention to one in a late context of the north European Early Bronze Age (1964: 282–3); and an oval-headed bone pin comparable to a metal nail-headed one was found in Early Bronze Age association at Caltragh, Galway (Rynne 1961) in a cist grave with a cremation burial, a Food Vessel Urn with affinities to the Drumnakilly series (ApSimon 1969), sherds of another Urn recalling Beaker Culture settlement pottery, and a flint plano-convex knife. (I am grateful to Mr ApSimon for commenting on this grave group.) The pin seems better compared to a metal nail-headed pin than to the so-called crutch-headed pins of the English and central European Early Bronze Age (as for example, Annable and Simpson 1964: 98, no. 166, Wilsford G.23, Wiltshire).

The Irish evidence therefore suggests that *type b* discs may have overlapped with the Late Beaker phase but are likely to have survived in use later. Elsewhere in these islands, a disc from Kirk Andrews, Isle of Man, is somewhat similar to *type b* ones, as are four fragmentary ones found together in Barrow 1 of the Knowes of Trotty, a barrow cemetery on Mainland, Orkney. The Kirk Andrews disc has three concentric rings of dots at the rim, and perforations there instead of at the centre as in the discs considered so far. Butler suggested that it could thus be related to fourth- or early third-millennium northern and central European discs of gold and copper (1963: 169). These resemblances are plausible and if justified would mean that it could not be taken in context with the early second-millennium discs considered here. Similar dotted decoration however occurs around the rim of the basket-shaped ear-rings from Deehommed, Down and Kirkhaugh, Alston, Northumberland (FIG. 4, nos. 6 and 11) discussed below; and Dr. Jean L'Helgouach has drawn my attention to a gold disc perforated around its rim in the Musée de L'abbaye Sainte-Croix at Les Sables d'Olonne, western France. This disc is some 22 mm. in diameter, and was found with perforated gold strips, amber, V-shaped buttons, a copper or bronze awl and bell-beaker sherds in the Dolmen de Pierre-Folie at Thiré (Vendée).

If the date of the Kirk Andrews disc is thus debatable, the four from the Knowes of Trotty give quite clear indications. Although they had each originally a single large perforation, their raised repoussé decoration of concentric bands, including zig-zags, is quite in the style of *type b* Irish discs. They were associated with a cremation-burial with amber beads, pendants and spacer-plates, dated by Piggott (1958) to "within or immediately after, the floruit of the Wessex Culture" of southern England, thus in the later part of the Early Bronze Age. In addition to the later continental Early Bronze Age comparisons quoted by Piggott, one may add the bronze discs from Ostro, Kamenz (von Brunn 1959: 65; Taf. 75, nos. 5 and 6) and compare also their off-centre perforations with those of the Kirk Andrews disc; the concentric dotted repoussé ornament of that disc and that of *type b* discs generally may also be compared with the decoration on other similarly dated central European ones from Kiebitz, Döbeln (von Brunn 1959: 61; Taf. 52, no. 16).

The conclusion must be that the *type b* discs were current in a mature phase of the Early Bronze Age; in view of their stylistic continuity with the *type a* discs, their origins are likely to have been in the Late Beaker phase. It would not be surprising if they had survived in use into the Middle Bronze Age.

The comprehensive series of composition-analyses of Irish gold objects published by Hartmann (1970) throws further light on the dating of *type b* discs (see below page 27), but first one must consider other Irish or English sheet gold ornaments with repoussé decoration, which can be brought into the same orbit as the discs of both types. These are basket-shaped *ear-rings* and various *plaques* or bands (Table 3; FIG. 4).

Three so-called *ear-rings* have been reported from Ireland: one was recorded from Deehommed, Down (FIG. 4, no. 6) and two simply as from Ireland (FIG. 4, nos. 7 and 8); a pair came from a Beaker culture grave in barrow 4a, Radley, Berkshire (FIG. 4, nos. 12 and 13); another may have been associated with another Beaker Culture grave at Kirkhaugh, Alston, Northumberland (FIG. 4, no. 11), and a pair of which one only survives was found in a stone cist at Orbliston Junction, Morayshire, possibly with an inhumation burial (FIG. 4, no. 9). There seems every reason to regard Radley 4a as belonging to the Middle Beaker phase, like the Wiltshire graves of Mere G.6a and Farleigh Wick, and the Beaker Culture settlement at Site D, Lough Gur. The same should be true of the putative assemblage from Kirkhaugh; the all-over-corded beaker with which the ear-ring may have been associated should by no means be regarded as a type exclusively of the Early Beaker phase (Case 1976a & b). Finally a fragment of possibly another ear-ring, but of copper or bronze, was with a secondary burial similarly of the Middle Beaker phase in the Sale's Lot long barrow, Withington, Gloucestershire (O'Neill 1966: 24; Case 1966: Fig. 10, nos. 17 and 18). Some of the basket-shaped ear-rings should therefore have been contemporary with the *type a* discs, in the Middle Beaker phase; but the fashion for them in copper or bronze continued into the Late phase, as shown by the grave-groups from Stakor Hill, Buxton, Derbyshire (Clarke 1970: Fig. 910) and Tallington, Lincolnshire (information kindly given by Mr Gavin Simpson); and contemporaneity with a stone battle-axe of Roe's Stage III at Barrow 58, Cowlam, Yorkshire

(Roe 1966: Table IV, 220—1, 223) and their occurrence in the Migdale hoard, Sutherland, Scotland (Piggott and Stewart 1958b; Britton 1963: 273—5) confirm that they persisted into the Early Bronze Age.

Four Irish *sub-rectangular plaques* (Table 3, nos. 1—4; FIG. 4) have twin central perforations like the discs, and dotted and linear borders and intermittent grouped transverse hatching — forming a kind of ladder-pattern. Armstrong's catalogue entries (1933: nos. 391—4) are less complete than those of Wilde (1862: 39—40; 44) according to whom nos. 1—3 of Table 3 (FIG. 4) were found together at Belleville, Kilmore, Cavan. No. 4 of Table 3 (FIG. 4) was also found in Cavan, according to Wilde in the "same locality" as an undecorated band (no. 41), surviving as four fragments and originally at least 300 mm long. This band, possibly originally a diadem or hair-band, may have been of the same kind as the one used to bind the Corran box (see above, page 22). These plaques are plainly allied to the discs and this sub-rectangular kind stands decoratively and regionally closer to those of *type a*.

The plaque from Castlemartyr, near Cloyne, Cork (Table 3, no. 5, FIG. 4) however is more clearly allied to the *type b* discs. It is the only surviving example of "exceeding thin plates of stamped and embossed gold, connected by bits of wire" from an inhumation burial (Croker 1854; Day 1899), which was associated also with amber beads said to have been of "mitre shape", thus possibly similar to the gold-covered shale buttons from the Wessex culture graves of Wilsford G.8 and Upton Lovell G.2e, Wiltshire (Annable and Simpson 1964: nos. 181, 233). The amount of gold from the Castlemartyr grave which was sold and melted was said to have been "rather more than the contents of half a coal box". The close-hatched decoration of the plaque closely resembles that of the *type b* unperforated disc from Ballydehob (Table 2, no. 15; FIG. 3).

We thus have a tradition of craftsmanship producing discs, ear-rings, plaques and bands with generally roughly drawn freehand dotted and linear repoussé patterns, which originated in the Middle Beaker phase and whose traditions continued into the Late phase and beyond. Further light is thrown on the existence of this tradition and on its duration by the very comprehensive series of composition-analyses of Irish gold objects, published by Hartmann (1970). All the analyses of the discs, plaques, ear-rings and associated objects listed here in Tables 1, 2 and 3 can be seen, with four exceptions, to have been of gold with high or very high silver, medium copper, low tin or a trace, and with nickel present only as a trace or undetected; some examples of analyses are shown in Table 4. Interestingly 40 out of the 41 analysed Irish lunulae show a similar pattern of composition, suggesting that gold of a similar kind was widely used both in the Late Neolithic and Early Bronze Age and by two quite distinct but chronologically overlapping Irish schools of craftsmanship. The metal is termed L-group by Hartmann (1970: 84—5, Table 3), who no doubt correctly considers it to be of Irish origin. His specific suggestion that it was from Wicklow may to some degree also be correct, although the analytical evidence for that is very slender (Hartmann 1970: 24—5) and scepticism seems justified as to whether trace-element analysis is capable of giving clear indications of provenance in the case of gold (Tylecote 1970). Other Irish sources besides Wicklow should also not be ruled out (Briggs *et al.* 1973).

The four objects among those considered so far which are exceptional in not being of L-group metal are listed, in Table 5 with their analyses. They are: the Ballydehob disc (FIG. 3 no. 15), the Ballyvourney pin (FIG. 3, no. 19a), the Castlemartyr plaque (FIG. 3, no. 5) and the Deehomed ear-ring (FIG. 3, no. 6); a likewise exceptional lunula is from Mullingar, Westmeath (Armstrong 1933: no. 28). These are of great interest in being of gold alloyed with copper. Whatever may be the failings of trace-element analysis in defining provenance, its value for indicating technological change is well-founded, and the occurrences of quantities of copper as in Table 5 seem clear indications of alloying (Tylecote 1970). Hartmann (1970: 28) noted that this practise of alloying with copper, presumably done with the intention of deepening the colour of the metal, became general in the Late Bronze Age Dowris phase (*loc.cit.*, 28) but that it was practised to some extent in the preceding Bishopsland phase (*loc.cit.* cp. Tables 4 and 5). It occurred too in the later part of the English Middle Bronze age, with which the Bishopsland phase must have more or less completely overlapped (Hawkes 1962). The fact that experiments in such a simple technique were taking place towards the end of the Early Bronze Age in Ireland should not therefore be surprising.

The metals of the Deehomed ear-ring and the Mullingar lunula are unfortunately indeterminate. However, the metal of the Castlemartyr plaque could have been simply obtained by alloying an L-group metal, such as that of the lunula from Rossmore Park, Monaghan (Hartmann 1970: Table 3, Au 543), with copper. Conceivably the metal of the Ballydehob disc was also produced in a similar way, although it is closer to metals of the kind which became prevalent in the Bishopsland and Dowris phases (Hartmann 1970: cp. Groups OC and MC/NC, Tables 5 and 6). The metal of the Ballyvourney pin seems closer again to the gold characteristic of the later Bronze Age. Although a glance at Table 5 will show that the gold of the pin is statistically inseparable from those of the Castlemartyr plaque and the Ballydehob disc, it differs from that of the associated disc (Table 4, serial nos. 544, 555) by more than an order of magnitude not only in copper but also in tin. These differences are unmatched in any of the other associated finds of discs or allied objects as shown in Table 4, and suggest that the disc may have been an archaic survival in a Middle Bronze Age context; on the other hand Early Bronze Age craftsmen should not necessarily be assumed to have invariably used gold from identical sources in Ireland or from elsewhere, especially since they were plainly experimentally inclined.

FIG. 5 summarises the ralationship of the discs and allied ornaments to cultural and technological stages of the British and Irish Late Neolithic and Early Bronze Age.

Table 4:   *ANALYSES OF ASSOCIATED FINDS: DISCS AND ALLIED GOLD OBJECTS*
          (after Hartmann 1970)

Object	Locality	Listed in this paper	Hartmann 1970: Serial No.	Ag	Cu	Sn	Ni
Disc Disc	Co. Roscommon	Table 1:4 5	549 550	∿ 11.0 ∿ 11.0	0.50 0.52	0.029 0.027	Tr. Tr.
Disc Disc	Ballina, Mayo	Table 1:6 7	546 547	∿ 9.0 ∿ 16.0	0.62 0.54	0.009 0.006	Tr. Nd.
Plaque Plaque Plaque	Belleville, Cavan	Table 3:1 2 3	603 604 605	13.0 ∿ 8.0 ∿ 16.0	0.25 0.29 0.18	0.022 0.02 0.011	∿0.01 Tr. ∿ 0.01
Plaque Band, fragments	Cavan	Table 3:4 4a	606 607 608 609 610	∿ 13.0 ∿ 13.0 12.0 12.5 12.5	0.22 0.29 0.36 0.31 0.32	0.007 0.004 0.005 0.004 0.005	Tr. Nd. Nd. Nd. Nd.
Disc Disc	Cloyne	Table 2:17 18	553 554	∿ 21.0 ∿ 18.0	0.21 0.23	0.008 0.008	Nd. Nd.
Disc Pin	Ballyvourney, Macroom, Cork	Table 2:19 19a	545 544	∿ 17.0 17.0	0.36 9.4	0.022 0.39	Nd. Nd.
Disc	Co. Wexford	Table 2.20 21	552 551	∿ 17.0 ∿ 18.0	0.21 0.24	0.015 0.024	Nd. Nd.
Disc Disc	Tedavnet, Monaghan	Table 2:22 23	557 556	9.0 11.0	0.82 0.82	0.070 0.081	0.031 0.03

Table 5:   *ANALYSES OF GOLD-COPPER ALLOYS (after Hartmann 1970)*

Object	Locality	Listed in this paper or in Armstrong 1933	Hartmann 1970: Serial No.	Ag	Cu	Sn	Ni
Disc	Ballydehob, Cork	Table 2:15	559	∿ 10.0	6.2	0.036	Tr.
Pin	Ballyvourney, Macroom, Cork	Table 2:19a	544	17.0	9.4	0.39	Nd.
Plaque	Castlemartyr, Cork	Table 3:5	1077	∿ 14.0	7.0	0.20	Nd.
Ear-ring	Deehommed, Down	Table 3:6	1062	∿ 11.0	11.0	Nd.	Nd.
Lunula	Mullingar, Westmeath.	Armstrong 1933, No. 28	526	∿ 8.0	3.0	Nd.	Nd.

The quantities are percentages.   ∿ = About.   Nd. = Not detected.   Tr. = Trace

I have suggested that the discs may have been worn singly. The manner in which they were worn must however remain speculative. They seem unlikely to have been decorative covers for the insides of buttons, such as the one which occurred in the rich Early Bronze Age Wessex Culture grave, Upton Lovell G.2a, Wiltshire (Annable and Simpson 1969: 48, no. 233); apart from any other considerations the thread-holes in the discs seem too small for serviceable buttons up to 100 mm or more in diameter.

Clarke (1970) suggested that they served as decorative covers for the outsides of buttons, wired separately to the button itself which could then have been sewn to a garment, presumably through V-perforations. The plaques of Belleville type could have similarly served as toggle-covers. These seem rather complicated and vulnerable arrangements. A more likely suggestion perhaps is that discs or plaques were sewn onto clothing or favouite possessions simply as embellishments, perhaps glued to leather stiffeners. However a fourth- or early third-millennium copper disc, with twin central perforations, was recorded as attached by wire to the wrist of an inhumation-burial in a dolmen at Rude, east Jutland (Randsborg 1970). Wire was reported with the Castlemartyr find (see above, page 25).

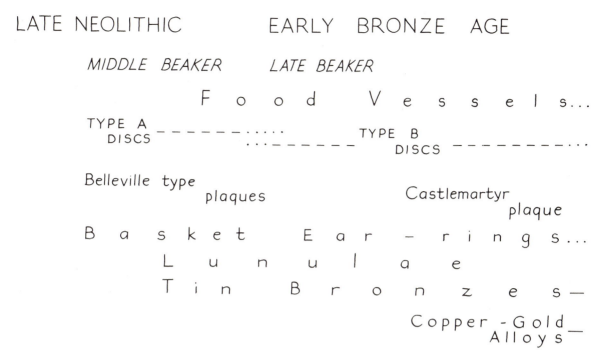

FIG 5   The relationship of gold discs and allied ornaments to cultural and technological stages of the British and Irish Late Neolithic and Early Bronze Age.

According to Clarke's suggestion (1970: 95), if worn on clothing the discs would have resembled disc-headed pins of the contemporary central European Early Bronze Age, some of which bear cruciform ladder-patterns (for example one from Unterrissdorf, Eisleben: von Brunn 1959: 68, Taf. 94, no. 5); but disc-headed pins by no means invariably show the concentric or cruciform motifs characteristic of the discs themselves and they are generally not repoussé but finely traced rather in the style of lunulae. At any rate, Irish discs and central European pins both show a contemporary taste for somewhat similar bright metallic ornament; and Clarke's comparison with central European pins seems more directly relevant than those with the bases of Iberian beakers (Hartmann 1970: 22) or with Danish Middle Neolithic pottery lids — however striking these resemblances may be (Butler 1963: 171–3). Direct resemblances were also noted by MacWhite who illustrated a disc from northern Portugal classifiable as *type b* (1951, lam. **VIII**), and listed others. Gold bands or diadems have also occurred in Beaker Culture or contemporary contexts in Iberia (Case 1966: 172, note 29; Harrison 1974). All these may show contacts between Atlantic regions which had been linked for millennia, as suggested by Clark elsewhere in this volume (reiterating Case 1969: 20); and midway between Ireland and Iberia we may note the gold disc from the Vendée, western France, mentioned above (page 26).

The gift of the Ballyshannon disc to the Ashmolean

The disc was given to the Ashmolean during the curatorship of the second Custos, Edward Lhwyd (1666–1709), and it was entered under the year 1696 in the calligraphically written and illuminated *Book of Benefactors* which was maintained between the years 1683 and 1766:—

> " A.D. MDCXCVI
> Dnus CAROLVS HOPKINS dedit orbiculatam quandam LAMINAM AVREAM prope Bali-Shani apud Hibernos nuper effossam; ad monitum vetustæ cujusdam citharaëdi Hibernici, cantilenæ; in quâ virum aliquem fortem prædicabat locum sepulturæ designans, de duabus laminis totidemqȝ annulis, aureis, cum ipso terræ mandatis, verba faciens. Narrationem fusius exaratam, vide apud Camdenum edit. Gibs. p. j022. cat. VC. 954. "

It thus came to the Museum during Lhwyd's sixth year in office and shortly before his great tour of Wales, Ireland, Scotland, Cornwall and Britanny made partly to gather material for his never-to-be-completed *Archaeologia Britannica* (Gunther 1945, for Lhwyd's career and selected correspondence; also Herity 1975:8).

The accession number (VC. 954) is that entered in one of the manuscript catalogues (*Liber Dñi Vice-Cancellarii*) begun in about 1687. All previous entries are in the handwriting of Robert Plot, Lhwyd's predecessor; it was therefore the first entry made during Lhwyd's curatorship, although in fact written by an assistant:—

> " Lamina aurea prope Bali-shani apud Hibernos effossa &c narrationem vide apud camdenum edit.
> Gib. p.j022. Ex dono D. Caroli Hopkins. "

It was subsequently recatalogued in 1836 as no. 372, and in the *New Catalogue* (1868) as no. 466, which is the number it carries today (NC 466).

The donor, Charles Hopkins (?1664 – ?1700), presumably had it from his father, Ezekiel Hopkins (1634 – 1690), who must have been given it by the excavators, between 1681 when he was consecrated Bishop of Derry and 1688 when he advised his flock not to resist the Earl of Tirconnel and departed for England (Stephen and Lee 1921–2: 1228). Charles Hopkins was brought up in Ireland and returned there apparently to campaign with Tirconnel, to his father's mortification. Having "exerted his early Valour in the Cause of his Country, Religion and Liberty . . . he came again for England and fell into acquaintance with Gentlemen of the best Wit", devoting himself to writing poetry and plays (Jacob 1723, II: 140–1). Among his works on ancient historical themes was *Boadicea Queen of Britain: A Tragedy* which "was acted with very great Applause" in 1697. It was dedicated to Congreve, acknowledging his influence and inspiration, and includes a blood-curdling Song of Druids. Hopkins was generous and convivial, "very much esteemed" by Dryden, "always more ready to serve others than mindful of his own Affairs; and by the Excesses of hard Drinking and a too Passionate fondness for the fair Sex, he died a Martyr to the Cause" (*op.cit*. I: 75) with "No money left, but Lines exceeding Number" (Prologue to *Friendship Improved or The Female Warrior: A Tragedy*) and in sombre repentance (Nicholas 1780: 321).

The circumstances in which the disc was found

The entries in the late 17th-century catalogues refer to a footnote in Gibson's edition of *Camden's Britannia* (Gibson 1695: 1021–2, note b). Lhwyd had been assisting Gibson with the *Britannia* between 1693–5; although only concerned with the Welsh entries, it is possible that he had heard the story of this Irish find and passed it on. Since the account has sometimes been misquoted or misinterpreted it is worth giving in full:–

> "South from *Donegall* is *Belishannon*, near which, not too many years ago, were dug up two pieces of Gold, discovered by a method very remarkable. The late Lord Bishop of *Derry*, Dr. *Hopkins*, hapning to be at dinner with Mr. *Edward Whiteway*, (a Gentleman whom he preferr'd in his former Diocese of *Raphoe*,) there came in an Irish Harper, and sung an old song to his Harp. Neither his Lordship nor Mr. *Whiteway* understanding any thing of Irish, they were at a loss to know what the song meant. But the Herdsman being called in, they found by him the substance of it to be this. That in such a place (naming the very spot) a man of a gygantick stature lay buried, and that over his breast and back there were plates of pure gold, and on his fingers rings of gold, so large that an ordinary man might creep through them. The place was so exactly described, that Mr. *Foliot*, brother in law to Mr. *Whiteway*, and one Mr. *Nevill*, his Lordship's Steward, were tempted to go in quest of the golden prize, the Irish man's song had pointed out to them. After they had dug for some time, they found two thin pieces of gold exactly of the form and bigness of this Cut. This discovery encouraged them next morning to seek for the remainder; but they could meet with nothing more. The passage is the more remarkable, because it comes pretty near the manner of discovering King Arthur's body, by the directions of a British Bard. See *Camden* in *Somersetshire*, p. 64, 65. The two holes in the middle seem to have been for the more convenient tying of it to the arm or some part of the body. "

The first noteworthy point in this account (in which the phrase "this Cut" must refer to a wood-cut scale drawing reproduced here as FIG. 1 centre) is that although the harper described a burial, the account of the excavation makes no mention of it. Possibly bones had been destroyed in acid soil. But possibly also and rather more likely, the discs were not in a burial deposit but a cache, like others of the Irish finds (see above, page 20). A second point to note is that since " the very spot . . . was so exactly described " it is likely to have been quite an easily recognisable part of the land-scape. A megalithic monument suggests itself. Borlase noted Irish folklore to the effect that megaliths were the graves of giants (1869: 773, 794, 812), Grinsell similarly for English long barrows and occasionally round ones (1953: 78). In Ireland, as in Scotland (Henshall 1972: *passim*), Giant's Grave is a commonly recorded name for monuments with elong-ated mounds or chambers, such as portal-dolmens and especially court-cairns and wedge-shaped gallery-graves (de Valéra 1960: 87–134; de Valéra and O'Nualláin 1961: 56–98). It was not usually applied to those with round mounds such as passage-graves, although they might too be associated with gold (Borlase 1877: 370; Grinsell 1953 82–3; 1959: 55–6). A likely possibility therefore is that the discs were in a secondary cache in a prominent field-monument, perhaps a court-cairn or more plausibly a wedge-shaped gallery-grave, since Beaker Culture material has been found repeatedly associated with such gallery-graves (Case 1969: 22; ApSimon 1969: 56).

The search cannot effectively be taken any further but it is interesting to note that court-cairns, passage-graves and wedge-shaped gallery graves have all been recorded in the Ballyshannon district. Interestingly too, Lhwyd included the district in the four-year field trip on which he embarked in the year after the disc had been registered in the Museum's catalogues. He recorded collecting fossils there in the spring of 1700 (Gunther 1945: 432), having previously sent his assistant William Jones on reconnaissance. Perhaps significantly and with the find of the disc in mind, Jones not only reported on Connaught geology (Bodleian: MS Ashmole 1815. f. 295), but planned megaliths there including some apparently in the neighbourhood of Ballyshannon, and, in one instance recorded finds (British Library: MS Stowe 1024). One such megalith has been identified by Herity as a passage-grave at Magheracar, near Bundoran (1974: 215) – although Wood-Martin's plan of this site (1888: Fig. 130) shows several differences from Jones's (Herity 1974: Fig. 11). Another field-monument nearby was planned by Jones with two galleries or large cists (British Library: MS Stowe 102A, f. 176); he noted, "N.B. That there was five Urns found here, as We were informed by Mr. . . . . Ellis, Who saw them". Possibly this was the site of which one gallery was recorded by Wood-Martin in the late 19th century but with larger dimensions (1888: Fig. 131).

The identification of the disc and its preservation

Two discs were found near Ballyshannon but only one can be traced. Perhaps Charles Hopkins, like Beaker man before him, kept one and gave the other to a female. There seems every likelihood at any rate that the one drawn for the *Britannia* – the wood-cut is reproduced here as FIG. 1, centre - is that which now survives, although comparison of the 17th-century and present day illustrations (FIG. 1) shows differences both in dimensions and preservation. The 17th-century draughtsman apparently drew the reverse of the disc; but he described an oval, perhaps mistakenly taking as the right-hand edge one which remained folded under until 1975. He may then have fitted a fairly idealised reconstruction into this oval shape. However, the possibility remains that the disc was indeed more complete when it was in Hopkins's hands than it is today; it would regrettably not be surprising for an object to remain unscathed in the hands of a wild and adventurous owner such as Hopkins, and disintegrate in academic custody in 18th-century Oxford. The reasons are painfully relevant to academic institutions today.

In giving his collections to the University, Elias Ashmole's intention had been to promote a centre for Natural Philosophy, an institute to serve the needs of general teaching and pure and applied research, with emphasis on experiment and to be staffed, among others, by an Ashmolean Professor (Gunther 1923: 43–51; 1925: 280–318; Josten 1966). Among his donations to its library, he no doubt hoped that his astrological books and papers would figure prominently in teaching and research – and similarly the specimens, many of which were concerned with the natural sciences but which included highly important ethnographic objects and some of archaeological or artistic interest. He intended that access to the specimens by strangers should be strictly controlled, only one party being shown them at a time (Gunther 1925: 314).

In the event, however, he failed to make provision for staff. The University's funds were exhausted by the building, and salaries and running costs had therefore to come from admission charges. The curators thus had a strong incentive to disregard the founder's intentions and open the collections fully to the public. This was disastrous, since the specimens were not locked up or arranged in a way suitable for public display. Some were in "cabinets" (Josten 1966: 252) but others were " all hung around " (*Op.cit.*: 255), and may have stood on open shelves, or trays, or in open drawers, as in the 17th-century Wormian Museum at Leiden (illustrated in Gunther 1925: 287–8).

The state of affairs in the Museum in 1710, a year after Lhwyd's death in office, was described by a visitor from Frankfurt, Zacharias von Uffenbach, a traveller and collector of manuscripts (Quarrell 1928): " . . . it was market day and all sorts of country folk, men and women, were up there . . . it is surprising that things can be preserved as well as they are, since the people impetuously handle everything in the usual English fashion and, as I have mentioned before, even the women are allowed up there for six pence; they run here and there, grabbing at everything and taking no rebuke from the *Sub-Custos*". Under such conditions, and with curators absent from their posts for long periods (four years in Lhwyd's case during his great tour), or idle, as in the case of his successor Parry who was in office at the time of von Uffenbach's visit (" the Custos . . . cannot show strangers over the museum for guzzling and toping . . . he is always lounging about in the inns so that one scarcely ever meets him " there), under such conditions it is not surprising that eventually the dodo fell to pieces, all the Lhwyd collection of annotated fossils was lost and as for William Borlase's similar collection given after 1758, he " might as well have sent his treasures to Twickenham to add to the decorations of his friend Pope's grotto " (Gunther 1925: 233). In 1710 the disc may have been reasonably safe, with "fibulae" and other "antiquities" including excavated finds, in a cupboard " in the vestibule not shown to everyone " which Parry eventually opened to von Uffenbach; but is would be surprising if such an attractive object had been permanently placed in reserve, and with repeated handling, its edges might soon have been torn.

Folk-memory, prophecy or second sight?

There remains the question of its finding "by a method very remarkable". To the average literate late 17th-century Englishman, apart from a sceptical minority, its discovery may indeed have seemed a remarkable vindication of bardic prophecy or second sight, employed too in the very proper pursuit of buried treasure (Thomas 1973). Furthermore, although possibly transmitted by a poet, the account seems too well authenticated for the legend to have emerged after the discovery, in the manner of similar stories concerning English barrows (as suggested in Grinsell 1959: 55–6). Moreover, folk-memory is very likely to have been strong in periods and places with a static population and oral traditions – although its authenticity is inherently impossible to check, and its duration for some three-and-a-half millennia seems incredible.

We do well to recognise, therefore, that the harper may only have been recounting a common stereotype, based on beliefs which evolved long after the Beaker period: that in such a megalith (as in other megaliths of the kind) a giant was buried, and that gold objects were buried too (as in other megaliths, and, as befitting a giant, exceptionally large objects). Croker (1854) and MacAdam (1856) quote traditional songs describing heroes buried with gold plates and rings. What seems remarkable in this instance is that in one minor detail the stereotypes matched the facts; and this exceptional coincidence may have been enough to have secured their charming record for posterity.

Acknowledgments

I am grateful to my fellow curators for invaluable assistance over details : Mr. Kenneth Annable, Dr. Joanna Close-Brooks, Dr. Ian Kinnes and Mr. Martin Welch. And similarly to Dr. Joan Taylor. I owe FIGS. 2–5 to my colleague Mrs. P. Clarke and FIG. 1 to her and to my colleague Miss O. Godwin.

References cited

Annable, F.K. and D.D.A. Simpson,
    1964   Guide Catalogue of the Neolithic and Bronze Age collections in Devizes Museum.
ApSimon, A.M.
    1969   The Earlier Bronze Age in the North of Ireland, Ulster Journal of Archaeology 32:28–72.
Armstrong, E.C.R.
    1933   Catalogue of Irish Gold Ornaments . . . 2nd ed.
Bodleian Library
            Manuscript letters.
Borlase, W.C.
    1869   The Dolmens of Ireland, III
Briggs, S., J. Brennan and G. Freeborn,
    1973   Irish Prehistoric Gold-Working; some Geological and Metallurgical Considerations. Bulletin of the
            Historical Metallurgy Group 7, no.2:18–26.
British Library
            Manuscript plans.
Britton, D.
    1963   Traditions of Metal-Working in the Later Neolithic and Early Bronze Age of Britain: Part 1.
            Proceedings of the Prehistoric Society 29: 258–325.
Bürgi, J. and I. Kinnes,
    1975   A gold beaker from Switzerland. Antiquity 49: 132–3.
Butler, J.J.
    1963   Bronze Age connections across the North Sea. Palaeohistoria IX.
Case, H.J.
    1961   Irish Neolithic Pottery: Distribution and Sequence. Proceedings of the Prehistoric Society
            27: 174–233.
    1966   Were Beaker-People the first metallurgists in Ireland? Palaeohistoria 12: 141–77.
    1969   Settlement-patterns in the North Irish Neolithic. Ulster Journal of Archaeology 32: 3–27.
    1976a   Contextual archaeology and the Beaker Culture. Glockenbecher Symposion: Oberried 1974.
            (ed. J.N. Lanting and J.D. Van der Waals), 198–204.
    1976b   The Beaker Culture in Britain and Ireland. Contribution to Colloque XXIV, IXe Congrès de l'Union
            Internationale des Sciences Préhistoriques et Protohistoriques. Nice.
Clarke, D.L.
    1970   Beaker Pottery of Great Britain and Ireland 1 and 2.
Coffey, G.
    1913   The Bronze Age in Ireland.
Colt Hoare, R.
    1812   The Ancient History of South Wiltshire.
Croker, T. Crofton
    1854   Notes on various discoveries of Gold Plates chiefly in the south of Ireland. In C. Roach Smith,
            Collectanea Antiqua 3: 131–52, 221–50.
Day, R.
    1899   Gold Plates and Discs found near Cloyne, County Cork. Journal of the Royal Society of Antiquities
            of Ireland 29: 413–6.
de Valéra, R.
    1960   The Court Cairns of Ireland, Proceedings of the Royal Irish Academy 60 C: 9–140
de Valéra, R. and S. O'Nualláin,
    1961   Survey of the Megalithic Tombs of Ireland:I,   Co. Clare.

Eogan, G.
    1964   The Later Bronze Age in Ireland . . . . Proceedings of the Prehistoric Society 30: 268–51.
Gibson, E.
    1695   Camden's Britannia, Newly Translated into English: with Large Additions and Improvements.
Grinsell, L.V.
    1953   The Ancient Burial Mounds of England.
    1959   Dorset Barrows.
Gunther, R.T.
    1923   Early Science in Oxford, I: Chemistry, Mathematics, Physics and Surveying.
    1925   Early Science in Oxford, III: Part I, The Biological Sciences. Part II, The Biological Collections.
    1945   Early Science in Oxford, XIV: Life and letters of Edward Lhwyd.
Harrison, R.G.
    1974   A closed find from Cañada Rosal, Prov. Sevilla and two Bell Beakers. Madrider Mitteilungen 15: 77–94.
Hartmann, A.
    1970   Prähistorische Goldfunde aus Europa.
Hawkes, C.F.C.
    1962   Archaeological significance of the Moulsford Torc analysis. Archaeometry 5: 33–7.
Henshall, A.S.
    1972   The Chambered Tombs of Scotland, II.
Herity, M.
    1969   Early finds of Irish antiquities from the Minute-Books of the Society of Antiquaries of London.
                    Antiquaries Journal 49: 1–21.
    1974   Irish Passage Graves
Jacob, G.
    1723   The Poetical Register: or, the Lives and Characters of the English Dramatic Poets. With an account of
                    their Writings, I and II.
Jacob-Friesen, K.H.
    1931   Die Goldsheibe von Moordorf bei Aurich mit ihren britischen und nordischen Parallelen. IPEK
                    (Jahrbuch für prähistorische und ethnographische Kunst) Jahrgang 1931: 25–44.
Josten, C.H.
    1966   Elias Ashmole (1617–1692) : I, Biographical Introduction.
MacAdam, R.
    1856   Gold Disks found in Ireland. Ulster Journal of Archaeology 4: 164–8
MacWhite, E.
    1951   Estudios sobre las relaciones atlánticas de la Península Hispánica en la Edad del Bronce.
Maryon, H.
    1936   Excavation of two Bronze Age barrows at Kirkhaugh, Northumberland. Archaeologia Aeliana 4th Series,
                    13: 207–17.
Nicols, J.
    1780   A Selected Collection of Poems with Notes Biographical and Historical, II.
O'Neil, H.
    1966   Sale's Lot Long Barrow, Withington, Gloucestershire, 1962–1965. Transactions of Bristol and
                    Gloucestershire Archaeological Society 85: 5–35.
Ó Ríordáin, S.P.
    1954   Lough Gur Excavations: Neolithic and Bronze Age Houses on Knockadoon. Proceedings of the Royal
                    Irish Academy 56 C:297–459
Paton, N.
    1871   Notice of two gold ornaments found at Orton on the Spey. . .Proceedings of the Society of Antiquaries
                    of Scotland 8: 28–32.
Piggott, S.
    1958   Knowes of Trotty, Barrow No.1. . . . . Inventaria Archaeologica:Great Britain 5th set, G B. 33.
Piggott, S. and M. Stewart,
    1958a   The Melfort Grave, Argyllshire, Scotland. Inventaria Archaeologica:Great Britain 5th set, G B. 25.
    1958b   The Migdale Hoard, Sutherland (Scotland). Inventaria Archaeologica:Great Britain 5th set, G B. 26.
Quarrell, W.H. and W.J.C. Quarrell,
    1928   Oxford in 1710: from the Travels of Zacharias von Uffenbach. (Translation of section describing Oxford
                    in Z.C. von Uffenbach, Merkwürdige Reisen durch Niedersachsen, Holland und Engelland, III, 1754).
Randsborg, K.
    1970   Eine kupferne Schmuckscheibe aus einem Dolmen in Jütland. Acta Archaeologica 41: 181-90.
Roe, F.E.S.
    1966   The Battle-Axe Series in Britain. Proceedings of the Prehistoric Society 32: 199–245.
Rynne, E.
    1961   Cist-burial at Caltragh, Co. Galway. Journal of the Royal Society of Antiquaires of Ireland 91: 45–51.

Sotheby, Wilkinson and Hodge,
    1913   Catalogue of the. . .collection of Irish. . . .implements, personal ornaments etc. . . . . . formed by
           Robert Day. . . .
Stephen, L.and E. Lee,
    1921/2 Dictionary of National Biography, IX.
Taylor, J.J.
    1970   Lunulae Reconsidered. Proceedings of the Prehistoric Society 36: 38–81.
Thomas, K.
    1973   Religion and the Decline of Magic
Tylecote, R.F.
    1970   The composition of Metal Artefacts: A Guide to Provenances. Antiquity 44: 19–25.
Underwood, G.
    1947   Early British Settlement at Farleigh Wick and Conkwell, Wiltshire. Wiltshire Archaeological Magazine
           51: 440–52.
    1948   Farleigh Wick. Wiltshire Archaeological Magazine 52: 270–1.
von Brunn, W.A.
    1959   Die Hortfunde der frühen Bronzezeit aus Sachsen–Anhalt, Sachsen und Thuringen.
Walker, I.W.
    1964/6 The counties of Nairnshire, Moray and Banffshire in the Bronze Age – Part I. Proceedings of the
           Society of Antiquaries of Scotland 98: 76–125.
Wilde, W.R.
    1857   A descriptive catalogue of the Antiquities . . . . in the Museum of the Royal Irish Academy.
    1862   A descriptive catalogue of the Antiquities of Gold in the Museum of the Royal Irish Academy.
Williams, A.
    1948   Excavations in Barrow Hills Field, Radley, Berkshire, 1944. Oxoniensia 13: 1–17.
Wood-Martin, W.G.
    1888   The Rude Stone Monuments of Ireland (Co. Sligo and the island of Achill).

THE ECONOMIC CONTEXT OF DOLMENS AND PASSAGE-GRAVES IN SWEDEN
by Grahame Clark.

In a volume offered to High Hencken to mark his unobtrusive but long sustained and formidable contributions to archaeology it may be appropriate to touch upon one of the most numerous and prominent categories of field monument surviving from the prehistory of Mediterranean and Temperate Europe, namely megalithic tombs. In doing so it is not my primary object to seek to reconstruct the history of their diffusion, still less to speculate about the character or motives to be attributed to those engaged in this process. (I) My first concern is rather to consider these monuments as social products. The time is indeed long overdue to consider megalithic and associated tomb structures as sources of information about the societies which in obedience to ideas of whatever kind or origin in fact erected them. Paradoxically it is by considering such monuments in functional and ultimately social terms that there lies the best chance of returning with greater hope of success to the historical problems which they undoubtedly pose.

In an admittedly speculative essay published in honour of another eminent prehistorian, Professor R.J.C. Atkinson (2) helped to point the way by considering some of the demographic and social implications of the earthen and megalithic long barrows of neolithic England. In the present essay I propose to examine the earlier forms of megalithic tombs, namely dolmens (dysse) and passage-graves, in economic terms and to do so in relation to an ongoing project of research into the early settlement of Scandinavia. (3) Although by far the larger number of these tombs is concentrated in Denmark (FIG. l), I intend for present purposes to concentrate on south Sweden, a territory on the very margin of megalithic distribution and one which for this very reason might be expected to throw light on the particular problem I have in mind. It has only been possible for me to do so because of the careful scholarship and helpfulness of Swedish colleagues. Much of their work is acknowledged in the usual manner by reference to their publications, but I would like especially to thank Dr. Lili Kaelas, Director of the archaeological museum at Göteborg to whom I am especially indebted for the up-to-date and precise information about the tombs in Bohuslän, incorporated in fig. 5.

A basic premise, of this paper, is that megalithic tombs were costly to erect in terms of man-power, more especially in terms of the demographic circumstances which we may suppose to have obtained in Neolithic times, in south Scandinavia. By way of illustration, reference may be made to certain calculations in relation to English long barrows. Taking due account of such factors as the amount of lifting and fetching the necessary chalk and soil, Paul Ashbee calculated (4) that the construction of the Fussell's Lodge long barrow, Wiltshire, would have consumed something near 5,000 man days of labour, for the mound itself. Even when it is conceded that this barrow is rather larger than the average of its kind, this is a striking figure. The implications, for our own problem, become even more formidable if we accept Professor Atkinson's further estimate (5) that the construction of a megalithic chambered long barrow, of the type found on the Cotswolds, would have required, at least, three times as much labour as an earthen and chalk one, of comparable size. Even if we discount this, in respect of the Swedish tombs, on the ground that their covering mounds were relatively small and were made from materials available on the surface, the assembly and erection of the megalithic slabs, used in the erection of their chambers, and the obtaining and erection of the barrow materials, imply, between them, a formidable input of human labour. This implies the existence of a fund of labour, capable of being diverted, in emergency, to purposes other than mere subsistence. In other words, the erection of the tombs seems to indicate the attainment of a certain level of prosperity, on the part of the people who built them. A question to be answered is what was the basis of subsistence which allowed so great an expenditure of economically unproductive labour?

Direct information, about the settlements of the megalith builders, being as scarce as it is, it remains to be asked what can be learned from the distribution and location of tombs. To answer this, we need to decide to what extent the pattern of settlement can safely be inferred from the distribution of tombs. Plainly a question of this kind is not one to be answered dogmatically. There is hardly any length to which men are not prepared to go in the face of ordinary economic forces under the impulse of ideology, as we are so well reminded in a megalithic context by the implications in terms of human labour of the assembly of bluestones and sarsens at Stonehenge. (6) What can nevertheless be said is that the same forces, which ensure that under a subsistence economy most food is obtained within an hour or so's radius of the focus of settlement, apply equally to the disposal of the dead and all the more so when this involved the periodical erection of tombs requiring a substantial volume of human labour. If the great events of history are proof in themselves that the forces of inertia do not invariably prevail in human affairs, they by no means alter the fact that human beings in most circumstances and for most of the time tend to conserve their energies. The hypothesis that burials are likely to reflect

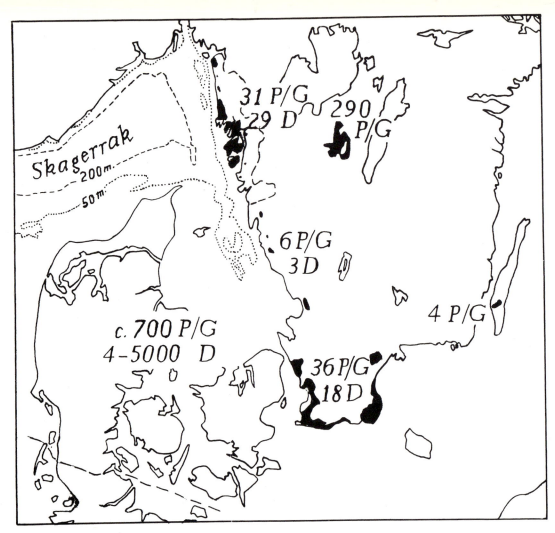

FIG 1. Map showing the distribution of dolmens and
passage-graves in Sweden. 1:5,000,000

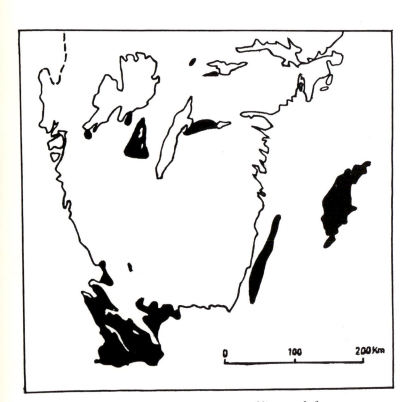

FIG 2. Map showing the extent of lime rock formations in south Sweden.

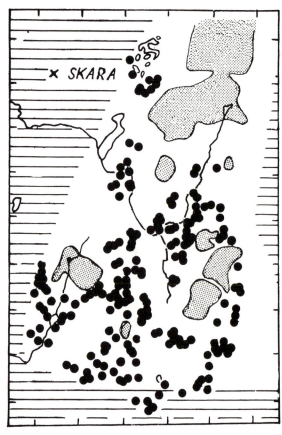

FIG 3. The distribution of passage-graves in
Skaraborgs lan, Vastergotland. The reserved
area coincides with the lime-rich Cambro-
Silurian formation and the stippled zones
with outcrops of dolerite. Scale I: 250,000.

the propinquity of settlement is one which at least merits first consideration. Weight has been added to this argument that megalithic tombs were not erected once and for all. As recent investigations in Jutland and Scania have shown they were foci of ritual and cult observance carried on over lengthy periods of time. This fact alone suggested to Strömberg (7) that the people who maintained these observances whether funerary or otherwise lived close at hand.

Where actual settlements as well as burials can easily be discerned the hypothesis is not difficult to test. This commonly applies in the Mediterranean. The most famous example in the Aegean world is probably Mycenae where nine princely and many more numerous private tombs are concentrated within some 600 m. of the citadel and even closer to the outer town. (8) The same situation is found in Iberia. The hundred or so tholoi at the third millennium settlement of Los Millares for example are crowded within 500 m. of the outer defences of the township (9) and a similar situation exists at Almizaraque. So much was this the case that Childe (10) felt no compunction in inferring the existence of similar townships from the existence of cemeteries at such sites as Belmonte, Puchena and Tabernas, even though these had not been precisely identified on the ground. Nearer home from northwestern Europe the evidence is more difficult to come by. Megalithic tombs are plentiful enough along parts of the Atlantic seaboard of western Europe, but settlements attributable to their builders are much more rare. Two suggestive conjunctions of tombs and settlements are known from hill-top sites surrounded by rich farm land in Co. Sligo, namely Carrowkeel (11A) and Knocknashee, (11B) but in neither case has contemporaneity been proved between the megalithic tombs and the circular walls of drystone construction which probably sheltered tents or light huts. In the case of Carrowkeel the site has largely been eroded down to the limestone rock. The situation at Knocknashee is much more promising due to peat formation having blanketed much of the site. The obvious way of settling the matter is by excavation. Even if it should turn out that analogies from Greece and Iberia fail to hold good in Ireland, this would have little application to south Sweden, an area of relatively mild relief in which there were no prominent hills to influence in a decisive way the choice of locations for either settlements or tombs. A converse of this is that the most relevant evidence from western Europe is that derived from lowland sites. Three suggestive occurrences may be noted from Ireland. Thus, Sean O'Riordain found three megalithic tombs, one wedge-shaped and two ruined, within a radius of half a mile of the Knockadoon settlement near Lough Gur, Co. Limerick and recovered Beaker pottery alike from the intact tomb and from the settlement (12), clear indication of archaeological contemporaneity. In the other two cases megalithic tombs have been found overlying traces of settlement; thus tomb 8, adjacent to the great mound at Knowth, Co. Meath, overlay pits and trenches containing "western neolithic" pottery (13); and at Ballyglass, close to Bunatrahir Bay, Co. Mayo, Sean O'Nuallain found the well-preserved plan of a rectangular neolithic house underlying at an oblique angle the mound of a centre-court cairn. (14A) A further indication of the close juxtaposition of tombs and settlement comes from the long barrow of South Lodge near Avebury, Wiltshire, which was found to overlie directly traces of ard cultivation. (14B)

Striking confirmation that megalithic tombs were closely linked to settlement comes from south Sweden itself and specifically from Scania, where as Mats Malmer has shown thin-butted flint axes relate to soil types in a similar way to megalithic tombs (15). Even more to the point Dr. Märta Strömberg is beginning to show that settlement traces adhere closely to actual tombs. Hearths and culture-layers have been found within a kilometer's radius of the Trollasten dysse (16) and systematic testing of the neighbourhood of four megalithic tombs clustered in the neighbourhood of Hagestad (17) revealed traces of no less than nine settlements in the immediate area of three of them.

The type of land taken up for settlement and its biological resources provide between them by far the best clue to the economic basis of the people responsible for the tombs. In the case of Sweden, with one important exception to which I shall return for detailed analysis, there is a marked degree of correlation between the distribution of the early types of megalithic tomb considered in this paper and the most productive farming land. This in turn coincides in south Sweden to a remarkable degree with the distribution (FIG. 2) of lime-rich and by consequence strongly alkaline soils. This has indeed been so since farming first began in Sweden. Whether one examines the distribution of cultivated land at the present day or the density of rural population during the mid-18th century the same general pattern emerges. It has always been lime-rich soils that have supported the wealthiest and densest farming populations. Lime is not merely in itself a plant food. Even more important it helps to make soils more tractable as well as serving to liberate other plant foods. So long as equipment was rudimentary ease of working was an essential requirement. By no means all lime-rich soils meet this specification. For instance many of the soils enriched with lime by glacial action, as happened when advancing ice passed over lime formations and incorporated this material in moraines, were too stiff and intractable for primitive ards. It was not until iron had become sufficiently inexpensive to arm ploughs and other implements of tillage that the heavier, potentially rich lime-bearing soils could be taken into systematic cultivation. The soils of eastern Sweden for instance, enriched though they were by lime derived by glacial action from rock formations at present under the Baltic off the east coast of Gästrikland, were not seriously tackled until the early Middle Ages during which they sustained the Viking power centered on the Mälar-Uppland region.

A striking example of the attraction of lime-rich and tractable soils is provided by the Cambro-Silurian region of southern Skaraborgs län, Västergötland, still to this day notable for the prosperity of its farming population. This narrow territory carries no less than 290 passage-graves (18) or about four-fifths of those known from the whole of Sweden. The concentration (FIG. 3) is all the more striking that part of the territory is occupied by prominent outcrops of dolerite and that other areas were occupied by lakes, many of them now peat-bogs. Since these monuments belong to a comparatively

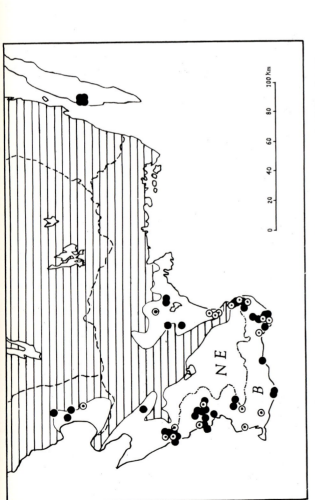

FIG 4. Map of dolmens (⊙) and passage-graves (●) in Scania, south Halland and Öland in relation to lime-rich soils (reserved). Within the latter the boundary between the soils of the Baltic end-moraine (B) and of the north-east moraine (NE) is marked by alternate dots and dashes.

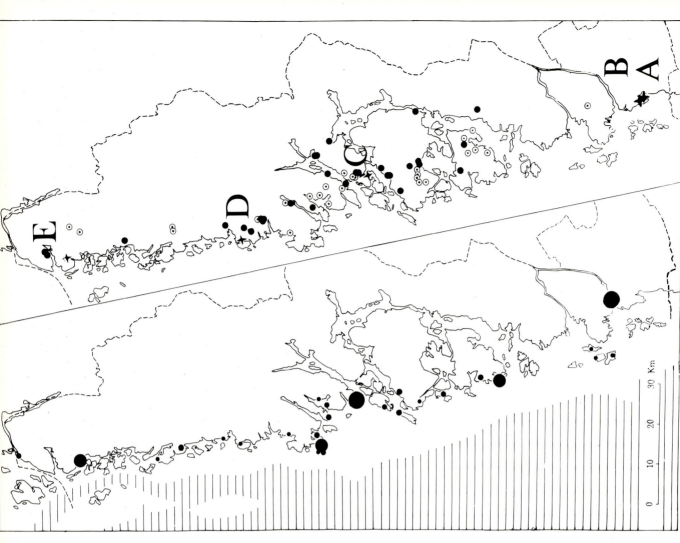

FIG 5. (right) Positions of midden sites A-E marked by ★ shown with the

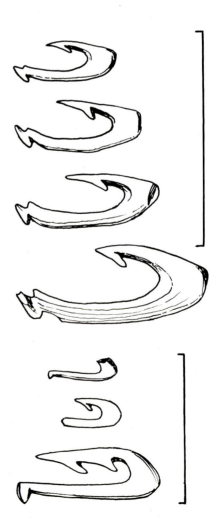

FIG 6. Bone fish-hooks from middens at Rottjärnslid (nos. 1-3) and Rörvik (nos. 4-7), Bohuslän, Sweden. Linear scales of 5 cm.

brief period of time their density, around one per square kilometer, is impressive. It is a reasonable hypothesis that in this case the surplus output of food symbolised by and utilised in such an outstanding constructive effort was derived substantially at least from farming. At the same time it is worth noting that Magnus Fries' pollen-analytical investigation (19) of lake deposits near Varnhem in this area suggest that cereal cultivation was still only of minor importance during Middle Neolithic times and that even when this was increased somewhat during the Stone-Bronze age it was still insignificant by comparison with the position during the Iron Age. Presumably stock-raising and ancillary sources of food were relatively important, though until adequate material from settlements is available no certain conclusions can be drawn.

Turning next to the dolmens and passage-graves of southernmost Sweden in south Halland, Scania and Öland the monuments are almost invariably situated on rock-formations rich in lime (FIG. 4) On the other hand when the situation in Scania is examined more closely the significance of surface soils assumes a greater weight. Of very great importance for agriculture is the distinction drawn by Ekström (20) between the relatively stone-free Baltic moraine with a clay component but relatively easy to work and the north-east moraine with its sandy soils practically free of clay and all too plentifully endowed with stones and boulders. No less significant is the fact that, whereas the soils of the Baltic moraine are alkaline or neutral, those of the north-east are mostly acid, except for part of the north-east corner of the province where the moraine is impregnated with lime from the underlying rock. The fact that dolmens and passage-graves and for that matter thin-butted flint axes are concentrated, as Malmer pointed out so clearly in 1962 (21), on this latter zone and on the Baltic moraine, that is on the agriculturally most favourable areas, argues that the economy of the builders was based primarily on farming. Confirmation in respect of crop-growing is indeed forthcoming from grain impressions on pottery from the megalithic tombs of Trollasten and Ramshog in Scania. According to Hjelmqvist (22) wheat predominated strongly over barley as shown in the following table:

	Trollasten	*Ramshog*
Einkorn (*Triticum monocccum*)	20	6 or 7
Emmer (*T.dicoccum*)	6	3
Einkorn or emmer	14	1
Wheat (Club ?) (*T.compactum* ?)	2	3
Spelt (*T.spelta*)	—	1
Total wheat	42	14/5
Naked barley (*Hordeum* sp.)	5	2
Percentage of wheat	89	82/88

TABLE 1.   Table showing predomination of wheat over barley from grain impressions on pottery from megalithic tombs in Scania

On the other hand there is some suggestion from the location of many sites (23) that coastal resources played some part in the subsistence of the megalith builders of this part of Sweden (24) As the following table shows slightly over 3/5th of dolmens were erected within 3 km. of the sea, that is within the potential daily catchment area. The fact that only a third of the passage-graves and transitional dolmens are within the coastal zone may perhaps suggest that

	3 km.	3–9 km.	10 km.	Totals
Passage-graves	12	15	9	36
Transitional dolmens	2	2	1	5
Dolmens	8	3	2	13
Totals	22	20	12	54

TABLE 2.   Table showing distances from coast of dolmens and passage graves in Scania

coastal resources came to play a less important role during the full Middle Neolithic in this part of Sweden. The main attraction of this south coast during the stone age was probably the seal. To judge from the finds at Siretorp (25) seals were already being taken from the final stage of the local mesolithic and in substantial quantities during successive stages of the neolithic. The fact that seal bones accounted for 84% of the total sample of 1469 bones suggest that the site was essentially a sealing station. Of the three species represented, Greenland and grey seals were strongly represented and spotted seals rather less so. The first species was also present at the neighbouring site of Mollehausen (26), though at this site seal-hunting was evidently only a subsidiary occupation. Although it looks very much as though the megalith builders in the coastal zone of Scania profited from seal-hunting, the importance of this in relation to farming ought not to be over-emphasised. It should be recalled that the Baltic moraine which carried the great majority of the Scanian megaliths formed only a comparatively narrow coastal girdle and on the other hand that over a sixth of dolmens and nearly a quarter of passage-graves were situated ten or more kilometers from the shore.

Analysis of the distribution of the third main group of early megalithic tombs in Sweden, those of Bohuslän, reveals a radically different pattern. So far from coinciding with areas of agricultural wealth the dolmens and passage-graves of Bohuslän diverge from this in a quite spectacular manner. From an agricultural point of view the province as a whole is poor: there is an absence of lime-rich soils, the distribution of cultivated ground is thin and the rural population as this is first known in the mid-eighteenth century is equally sparse. (27) Further, as our map (FIG. 5) shows, (28) the early megalithic tombs with which we are here concerned are confined to a narrow coastal strip which from an agricultural point of view is the poorest zone of a poor province. The dolmens and passage-graves are confined to the coastal strip in which more than half the land is officially classified as unproductive from a farming point of view against figures of 40% for the middle zone and 30% for the inner or eastern zone. (29) What, then, was the economic basis of this important group of megalithic tombs? A closer look at their pattern of distribution and location provides a clue. In discussing the Scanian tombs attention was drawn to the numbers sited within daily range of the coast and the suggestion was made that seal-meat may have supplemented to an important extent the income derived from farming. The coastal orientation of the Bohuslän tombs of these early groups of tomb is much more marked and contrasts with the inland distribution of the much younger gallery graves of the same province as pointed out by Moberg (30). The proportion of the early monuments erected within daily reach of the coast was greater and the degree of propinquity closer and each by a substantial margin. In our table propinquity is measured in relation to existing sea-level. Despite a certain fluctuation in the height of sea-level this was not sufficiently pronounced during the later half of the Stone Age to affect topography to any major extent.

	1	1–2	2–3	3–4	4–5	5–6	6–7 km.	
Passage-graves	14	6	6	3	–	1	1	31
Dolmens	16	8	5	–	–	–	–	29
Totals	30	14	11	3	–	1	1	60

Table 3.   Table showing distances from the existing coast of early megalithic tombs in Bohuslän.

A number of facts stand out from this. To begin with it will be noted that 100% of the dolmens and 84% of the passage-graves in Bohuslän are within 3 km. of the coast by comparison with 60.5% and only 33.3% respectively in the case of the Scanian tombs. Even more striking is the fact that no less than half the Bohuslän monuments are within 1 km. of the shore. A third thing to note is that as in Scania there was a tendency for passage-graves to be less closely associated with the shore than dolmens, though in the case of Bohuslän the indications of this are rather weaker.

Apart from Göteborg and its immediate neighbourhood and then only during the historic period, the coastal tract of Bohuslän has always depended on fishing as a main source of subsistence and wealth. The explanation for this is not hard to seek. The Bohuslän coast lies at the eastern extremity of the Skagerrak the deep waters of which front almost precisely the zone of early megalithic tombs (FIG. 5). Even to-day it is significant that the fish canning and conservation factories of Sweden are concentrated almost solely on this single stretch of coast. The degree to which this is so may readily be seen by tabulating the centres on the three main coastal zones of Sweden. (31) In doing so symbols of grade size have been used to designate the relative importance of the various factories.

Swedish coastal zones	●	●	●	•	·	*Totals*
West (Bohuslän)	2	3	5	5	8	23
South	–	–	–	–	2	2
East	–	–	–	–	2	2
Totals for Sweden	2	3	5	5	12	27

Table 4.   Table showing relative sizes of modern fish canning and conservation factories in Sweden.
Note.   The factories are listed according to size, the largest in the left-hand and the smallest in the right-hand column.

Close comparison of the maps shown on FIG. 5 will show that the modern factories occupy the sites most accessible from the outer sea, whereas the megalithic tombs and presumably the settlements associated with these are found in more sheltered situations. Yet the agreement over all is extremely striking. It suggests at least the hypothesis that the megalith builders gained much of their wealth from the sea and above all from fish.

The most obvious way of testing this hypothesis is to examine the faunal remains from Stone Age sites on the Bohuslän coast. In doing so regard must be had to the fact that this particular coast was subject, by reason of its position along the margin of the zone of isostatic displacement, to a complex series of changes in relative land and sea levels.

Although since mid-Atlantic times these were not of great magnitude in absolute terms, they were still sufficient to impair the archaeological record of coastal settlement in this part of Sweden. According to Mörner's paper of 1969 (32) the oldest coastal sites one could expect to find above sea-level would be those dating from his second PTM (Postglacial transgression maximum) that is from the centuries immediately either side of c.5000 B.C. Thereafter one must expect to find gaps in the surviving evidence corresponding with each of his main phases of regression, excepting only for lucky chances, as for example the coincidence of a deep dock or other excavation on the foreshore striking an actual settlement. We have for this reason to reconcile ourselves to an incomplete record. It is particularly unfortunate that the period of the earliest megalithic tombs in Bohuslän coincided with Mörner's sixth Postglacial regression (PR 6) and that by onset of PTM 6 (2300–2000 B.C.) passage-graves had neared or even passed the point at which they continued to be built. Yet even if the coastal settlements of the earliest megalithic phase are no longer available for study the picture of resource utilization for the preceding and immediately succeeding phases of settlement agree so closely that it seems reasonable to assume that they obtained during the intermediate and most directly relevant period.

The sites which by reason of their faunal remains are able to throw light on the utilization of coastal resources are lettered A–E from south to north of FIG. 5 right. They may here be briefly listed in chronological sequence:

A. *Bua Västergård, Göteborg* (33)

Occupied when sea-level was not more than 25 m above that of today. Radiocarbon analyses by two laboratories (St. 3566–70 and U 851–2; 2444–6: 2520; 4016) suggest a date (uncorrected) in the first half of the sixth millennium B.C. The occupation could well relate to Mörner's PTM (Postglacial Transgression Maximum) 2.

C. *Rottjärnslid, Dragsmark.* (34)

Flint core axes and stone stump-butted and Lihult axes suggest a late Mesolithic context in archaeological terms. The site stands between 34–36 m. above present sea-level and was occupied when the sea stood around 32–34 m. higher than it does at present. Its (uncorrected) radiocarbon age (St. 2421: 3650 ± 140 B.C.; St. 3878: 3620 ± 300 B.C.; St. 3879: 3505 ± 300 B.C.) suggests that this site relates to Mörner's PTM 4.

B. *Hasslingehult, V. Frölunda, Göteborg.* (35)

Archaeologically this site features tanged flake arrowheads of Becker's class A with only odd specimens of later forms. In conventional terms this would relate the site to a middle stage of MN III, that is to a time when passage-graves were no longer being constructed. The main occupation belonged to a time when sea-level was between 13–16 m. above its present level and presumably related to Mörner's PTM 6.

D. *Rörvik, Hamburgsund* (36)

Archaeologically the finds from this site indicate that it belongs to the same period as Hasslingehult. It is situated on a shellbank c. 15 m. above present sea-level and presumably also relates to Mörner's PTM 6.

E. *Anneröd, Skee* (37)

Archaeologically this points to a phase slightly younger than B and D. It is situated on a sandy strand deposit at 18.5 m. above present sea-level and in view of the number of discarded mollusc shells this suggests that sea-level stood only slightly below this level at the time of the occupation.

Analysis of the animal remains from these sites shows that land mammals made a certain contribution to diet. Red and roe deer are represented on the first three sites and pig at all but the third (B:Hasslingehult), the sample from which is in any case too small for absences to be at all significant. In addition elk occurred possibly at the first and certainly at the last site. The striking thing about the faunal remains on the other hand is unquestionably the emphasis on coastal and marine resources. As our table shows, these invariably included shell-fish, except at Anneröd, where 13 species occurred alongside numerous edible mussels and abundant oysters, these played only a subsidiary role and may well in some cases have served for bait rather than food. Sea-birds were present on all sites other than Hasslingehult, but in no case was there a marked concentration on any particular species, nor were birds as a class strongly represented in the fauna. Seals of one species or another, including Greenland, grey and spotted seals, were present among each assemblage and presumably contributed significantly to diet. Toothed whales on the other hand were much more sparingly represented. A leading role, at least in respect of numbers, was played by fish and notably by three species of bottom feeder, namely cod, haddock and ling, the first and third of which run to a very considerable size.

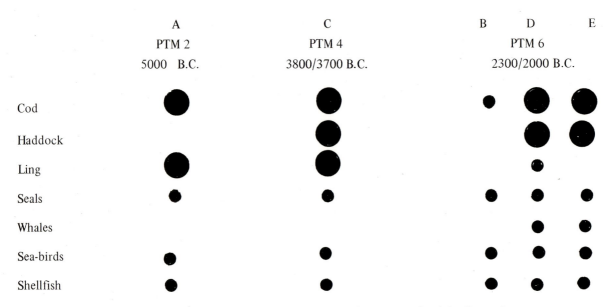

	A	C	B	D	E
	PTM 2	PTM 4		PTM 6	
	5000 B.C.	3800/3700 B.C.		2300/2000 B.C.	
Cod	●	●	●	●	●
Haddock		●		●	●
Ling	●	●		●	
Seals	●	●	●	●	●
Whales				●	●
Sea-birds	●	●	●	●	●
Shellfish	●	●	●	●	●

Table 5.   Table showing the contribution of sea-food at different periods of the Stone Age in Bohuslän as shown by the faunal content of five coastal sites.

Closer analysis of the fish represented in the refuse from the five sites reveals a remarkable consistency over a period spanning around three thousand years. The first fact to be noted is the complete absence of herring, which at the present day predominates over cod in the annual catch on the Bohuslän coast (50% against 30%) (38). Evidently fishing, which for seven thousand years at least has been a major source of wealth in the coastal tract of Bohuslän, depended during the Stone age primarily at least on fishing with line and hook for cod and other bottom-feeders. It is significant that bone fish-hooks (FIG. 6) were present on the three of our five sites where bone artifacts survived in any quantity. Those from Rottjärnslid (C) have straight shanks with head expanded rearwards and points having one or in the case of the larger ones two barbs. The hooks from Rörvik had single barbs and the shanks had thickened heads grooved to secure the line. A second point to note is, although the odd eel, flat-fish, mud-fish, pollack, whiting and wrasse were landed, the only species to be caught in sufficient quantity to indicate an organized fishery were cod, haddock and ling. At Bua Västergård (A) cod and ling accounted for no less than 140 out of 142/3 of individual fish identified, at Rottjärnslid (C) the three species accounted for 47 out of 49 individual fish and at Rörvik (D) to 146 out of 151. Thirdly, as if to confirm this, individual fish of these species were sometimes of exceptional size. Already in mesolithic times cod over 1 m. long were being caught both at Bua Västergård and at Rottjärnslid where the largest attained 1.5 m.; haddock up to 0.8 m. were caught at the latter; and ling up to 1.45 m. at the former and 1.7 m. at the latter. Large fish were also identified at the later sites, cod of 0.97 m. occurring at Rörvik and 1.0 m. at Anneröd, though at both these sites it is fair to add that smaller fish were also present. The significance of large bottom-feeding fish is that for most of the year these keep to deep waters such as those of the Skagerrak or the Atlantic itself. On the other hand as Ekman pointed out (39) in respect of Hasslingehult and Henrici (40) in respect of Rottjärnslid cod come into water as shallow as from 3 to 8 fathoms at spawning time. Yet even at this season ling rarely come into water much shallower than 20–25 fathoms and haddock seldom come above 12 fathoms. Either therefore the fishermen ventured out into the Skagerrak or they operated only during the spawning season, that is predominantly during the winter. In mesolithic times they may well have had to exercise both options, but during neolithic times it is likely enough that fishing was a seasonal activity that fitted into the farming year as it still did in Norway down to modern times.

Analysis of the location of early megalithic tombs in Bohuslän, taken in conjunction with the evidence of the potentialities of the province in early times, thus suggests that the exploitation of coastal resources contributed in a significant fashion to the wealth that made possible their erection. This has gained some support from an analysis of faunal remains relating to periods of relatively high sea-level before and immediately after the phase of marine regression (Mörner's PR 6) contemporary with the erection of the monuments. Although for this reason no information is or can be available from coastal middens of the actual builders the consistency of the pattern prevailing beforehand and immediately after is such as to make it a fair presumption that coastal resources were similarly exploited at the relevant time, as they certainly were being in Denmark. (41) Prominent among these resources, other than the seals which were also being exploited round the Scanian coast, were bottom feeding fish like cod, ling and haddock, the first two of which ran to a very large size. In order to catch these bottom feeders boats would have been needed. What kind they were can only be guessed at. The earliest direct evidence for the boats used on the Bohuslän coast is the Bronze Age rock-engraving from Kville (42) which shows two men line-fishing from a boat with upturned prow and projecting keel, almost certainly a craft with planks or strakes. Such a vessel can hardly have been made by the people who originated the fishery several thousand years earlier. The most likely boat employed in this fishery would have been made of skin stretched over a light frame, the kind of craft known down to recent times over a vast extent of the circumpolar zone, depicted on the late Stone Age rock art of the north-west Norwegian coast (43) and which significantly still remains active in the form of the curragh on the Atlantic sea-board of Ireland. The indications are, however shadowy, (44) that skin boats of this kind were active on the sea-ways between Ireland, Scotland and Brittany during the early Christian period and such could well have been descendants of those which linked these lands three or four thousand years earlier. Boats like the Eskimo *umiaq* were capable of carrying upwards of twenty people (45) across the open sea.

A main outcome of this enquiry into the economic basis of megalithic tombs in Sweden has been to emphasise the importance of the exploitation of coastal resources during the initial phase and in respect of Bohuslän to underscore the role of a line fishery for bottom feeding Atlantic fish, notably cod, haddock and ling, a fishery already established for a hundred generations or so in the Skagerrak before ever a passage-grave was built in Scandinavia. The relevance of this to the concept embedded in the literature of a dichotomy between "megalithic farmers" and "pit-ware hunter-fishers" during the latter half of the third millennium will only be mentioned in passing. (46) I would like to end this brief tribute by returning to a topic hinted at in the opening paragraph and consider the bearing of this study on the process of megalithic diffusion.

The coastwise distribution of megalithic tombs has long been accepted in conventional terms as evidence for the passage along the Atlantic sea-ways of "megalith-builders", variously inspired according to the predeliction of the writer by a thirst for metals, by missionary zeal or by sheer zest for adventure. The suggestion is worth considering whether fishermen may not have explored and opened up remoter territories as well as helping to feed the builders and even themselves assisted in the new cult. This applies not merely to south Scandinavia where the existence of the fisheries of the Skagerrak and the Kattegat and the seal and porpoise resources of the Swedish and Danish coasts make it easy to understand the close analogies in ceramic ornament and tomb form between N. Jutland and Bohuslän and between Zealand and Scania, (47) but also to the Atlantic sea-board of western Europe where the pursuit of fishing serves to knit together coasts and islands which to a landsman may seem far apart.

When Hugh Hencken first turned his attention many years ago to the archaeology of the extreme south-west of England he was immediately struck by the disproportionate number of megalithic tombs on the Scilly Islands, three times as many as in the whole of Cornwall even though the present land area of the islands only amounts to 3,500 acres. (48) Even if we allow for the possibility that the land in this region still stood sufficiently higher in relation to the sea than at present for the Scilly Islands to be joined together, 45 megalithic tombs is still a very large number; and the disparity is even greater when it is appreciated that all the Scilly monuments belonged to the category of V-shaped or Entrance Graves as opposed to only 4 or 5 of the Cornish monuments. Hencken was much in advance of his time when he found it "hard to understand how such an island, which could scarcely have supported much of a population, came to have on it such a profusion of burials". (49) He realised that in economic terms there was a problem: the land area was too restricted to support the investment. But the "Western Seaways" syndrome was still too strong and it was felt sufficient to recall that Scilly was "an obvious place for a sea-borne culture to strike deep root". A generation and a half further on we may prefer to respond to his initial insight and find an economic explanation that really answers the question how sufficient resources were in fact available for the monuments to be constructed, never mind whence the inspiration came. In the light of our analysis of the situation in Bohuslän the most likely source is the sea. And this accords entirely with what we can observe within a radius of 300 km. or so of the Scilly Islands.

The distribution of entrance graves, of the type described by Hencken, extends from the Land's End district of Cornwall (50) to the area of Tramore Bay, on the coast of Waterford, in the south of Ireland (51), east to the Channel Islands (Herm, Alderney and Guernsey, but not Jersey) (52), and south to Finistère and Morbihan, Brittany. (53) The one unifying factor, in such a distribution is the sea and the most likely underlying cause of this activity is surely fishing. In his popular account of *Britai̇n and the Western Seaways* (54), Prof. Emrys Bowen considered the maritime distribution of megalithic tombs in the west, in the light of mediaeval traffic, notably that inferred from the distribution of Ogham inscribed stones, church dedications, traditional journeys of Celtic saints, and known pilgrim routes, like those converging on Santiago de Compostela. He assumed that these journeys were accomplished by means of skin-boats, resembling the still-existing curragh of western Ireland, a gold model of which exists in the Broighter hoard, dating, in all probability, from the dawn of the Christian era (55). Prof. Bowen ended on a suggestive note:

"While we have concentrated on travelling in pursuit of some great objective, or for health or religious reasons, we must not forget that the cause of travelling in every age and in every land is primarily, but not exclusively economic. . . There is in this context one reason for travelling by sea which is not often mentioned, but which must have had an influence on movement over the western seas from the earliest times, and that is the pursuit of fish".

Whatever the factors that have led men to traverse the sea-ways of Atlantic Europe it seems safe to assume that the routes were first opened up by men intent on catching fish. Crustacea may locally have been a useful source of food during the Stone Age, as the crab claws from Obanian sites in south-west Scotland and from the midden at Skara Brae, Orkney, bear

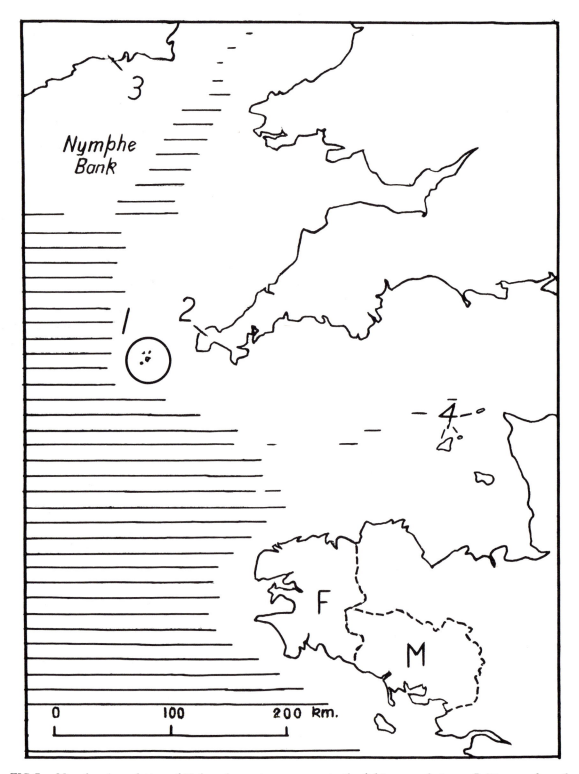

FIG 7.   Map showing relation of V-shaped or entrance graves to the fishing zone between Brittany and southern
Ireland. Shaded area marks sea over 100 m. deep. 1, Scilly; 2, St. Just-Zennor, Cornwall; 3, Tramore,
Co. Waterford; 4, Guernsey, Herm, Alderney F Finistère M Morbihan.

witness (56 B). On the other hand it is migratory fish and the seasonal movements of fishermen that these imply which provide the most likely clue to the coastwise distribution of megalithic tombs in Portugal, Brittany, the Celtic Sea, north-west Ireland and south-west Scotland. In the context of south-western and western Europe four main species have been the object of commercial fisheries during historic times, namely pilchards, tunny, mackerel and hake. Of these the first two are mainly taken by drift nets of a size beyond the capability of early man, nor is it conveivable that primitive line tackle could have stood up to catching tunney in the manner of modern sportsmen. The most likely prospects remain hake and mackerel.

The distribution of hake (gen. *Merluccius*) as given by C.F. Hickling (57) and B.W. Jones (58) is highly suggestive in the light of that of megalithic and related tombs. It extends from the west Mediterranean, round the Atlantic coasts of Iberia, western France up to Brittany, south-west England, south and west Ireland, south-west and west Scotland and the Isle of Man. In the course of modern commercial trawling these fish are taken from deep water, but in earlier times they were caught on hook and line when they came into shoal water for spawning. According to Hickling the time of the year when this happens may vary within a range of three months, but the important point to note is that it occurred earlier in the Celtic Sea for instance than further north off the west coast of Ireland or south-west Scotland. Thus fisher-men were able to extend the catching season by moving north during the course of the summer. The spawning cycle of the fish provided a mechanism for the northward movement of fishermen.

The importance of the Irish hake fishery between 1504–1824 has been well brought out by Arthur Went. (59) In connection with the pattern of distribution of entrance-graves it is interesting to note that in the area of the Celtic Sea there were two fishing grounds of key importance, namely the Melville Knoll off Scilly and the Nymphe Bank south of Co. Waterford. According to a mid-18th c. record quoted by Went a six-man boat might expect to take 1000 hake on hook and line in the course of a single night. It is small wonder that during centuries covered by Went's survey the Celtic Sea should have attracted fishermen from France and even from Biscayan Spain, as well as England and Ireland, or that the fish whether wet or dried and salted should have found its way to the markets of Iberia and France as well as England. Again, it is significant, when viewed in the context of Ruadhri de Valera's idea that the impulses which led to the construction of court and allied cairns in Ireland entered by way of the west coast, (60) that Oliver St. John should have noted in his *Description of Connaught* (1614) that a great trade in hake, cod, ling and conger from this coast was carried on by merchants from Brittany and Portugal as well as England. (61)

The other fish most likely to have played a significant part in prehistoric times in western as distinct from northern Europe is the mackerel (*Scomber scombrus*) (62). On this side of the Atlantic this is found mainly like the mackerel in the west Mediterranean and the warmer seas of western Europe. Since this fish moves near the surface in shoals, which off the coasts of N. America may be as much as 20 miles long and a ¼ mile wide, it is commonly taken in drift nets, but even in commercial fisheries it is still caught in large numbers on hook and line and is locally taken in small seine nets, both methods within reach of prehistoric man. (63) As with hake it is worth stressing seasonal movements linked with spawning: in winter the fish remain in deep water only to rise in the spring and make for their spawning grounds. Detailed information about the seasonal movements of mackerel is beginning to accumulate as a result of systematic recovery of tagged specimens. Thus according to experiments conducted by G.C. Bolster (64) fish tagged off the Atlantic shelf south-west of Cornwall and west-south-west of Co. Cork expanded over the whole extent of the Celtic sea in a matter of months and still more interesting individuals tagged off the south-west coast of Co. Cork found their way up the west coast of Ireland (65) and as far as south-west Scotland.

It is the more regrettable in view of these suggestive facts that the drowning of neolithic shore-lines in south-west Britain and Brittany makes it impossible to confirm the existence of hake and mackerel fisheries at this time in the way it was possible to demonstrate the existence from early times of the West Swedish line-fishery. The presence of accumu-lations of limpet shells offers one of the few clues, but this is unfortunately ambiguous: whereas Martin wrote of the inhabitants of St. Hilda at the close of the 17th century that "their common bait is the lympets or patellae", it is no less the case that these shell-fish were eaten directly in parts of Britain. (67) Dr. Hencken himself recorded "enormous quantities of limpet shells": from the midden at Halangy Porth on St. Mary's, Scilly, a midden which also yielded sherds resembling ones from entrance-graves and thick layers of limpets were noted in the chambers of the large-passage-graves of La Varde and Le Dehus, Guernsey (69) and of the gallery-grave of Ville-es-Nouaux, Jersey. (70)

Although stopping far short of proof it is at least a tenable hypothesis that the opening up of routes along the Atlantic sea-board of Europe was accomplished by fishermen. Moreover the superior cosmopolitanism of fishermen remarked by T.C. Lethbridge, (71) coupled with the god-fearing qualities of men accustomed to entrusting themselves to the unknown, further suggests that they may even have played some part in determining the maritime and coastal distribution of megalithic tombs in western Europe. Yet it has equally to be recognized that megalith builders were also farmers and that in many cases fishing was ancillary to stock-raising and cultivation, just as previously it had been carried on in a context of hunting and foraging. A final point to observe is that to judge from Dr. John Coles' work at Morton line fishing for cod was already well established on the coast of Fife, as on the west coast of Sweden, well before megalithic tombs began to be built in north-west Europe. (72)

Notes

1.   Dr. Glyn Daniel sensibly concluded a review of rival views on this matter by writing in *The Megalith Builders of Western Europe,* 1962:125 that "we may go on arguing for ever about the historical role of the megalithic builders."

2.   See his 'Old Mortality: some aspects of burial and population in neolithic England'. In *Studies in Ancient Europe: Essays presented to Stuart Piggott.* J.M. Coles and D.D.A. Simpson Eds. 1968.

3.   *The Earlier Stone Age Settlement of Scandinavia.* Cambridge University Press 1974 to be followed by a volume on *The Later Stone Age.* . .

4.   P. Ashbee in *Archaeologia* C(1966) : 35.

5.   *Ibid.* 91 Cf. Glyn Daniel, *Ibid.:* 22.

6.   R.J.C. Atkinson, *Stonehenge*: 98–107. London 1956.

7.   M. Strömberg, *Der Dolmen Trollasten in St. Köpinge, Schonen*: 227 Lund 1968.

8.   A.J.B. Wace and F.H. Stubbings, Eds., *A Companion to Homer,* Fig. 26. London: Macmillan 1962.

9.   M. Almagro and A. Arribas, *El Poblado y la Necropolis Magaliticos de los Millares,* folding plan. Madrid 1963.

10.   V.G. Childe. *The Dawn of European Civilization,* 6th ed.: 170. London 1957.

11A. R.A.S. Mcalister et al, *Proceedings of the Royal Irish Academy.* XXIX, sect. C (1910–12) 311–

11B. E.R. Norman and J.K.S. St. Joseph, *The Early Development of Irish Society*: 20–23. Cambridge 1969.

12.   S.P. O'Riordain, *Proceedings of the Royal Irish Academy.* LVI, sect. C (1954) : 443–56.

13.   G. Eogan, *Proceedings of the Royal Irish Academy,* LXVI, sect. C (1968) : 299–400; *Antiquity* 41 (1967) : 203–04.

14A. Sean Ó Nualláin, *Journal of the Royal Society of Antiquaries of Ireland* 102 (1972) : 49–57.

14B. P.J. Fowler and J.G. Evans, *Antiquity* (1967) : 290, Fig. 1.

15.   M. Malmer, *Jungneolithische Studien,* cf. abb. 117 and 120. Lund 1962.

16.   M. Strömberg, *op. cit.* (1968) : 231–32.

17.   M. Strömberg, *Die Megalithgräber von Hagestad*: 370–71, abb. 156.

18.   Our map (Fig. 3) is based on that by G.A. Hellman in 'Västergötlands gånggrifter', *Falbygden* 18 (1963) : 3–12. The geological basis is taken from *Sveriges Geologiska Undersökning* Sveriges Berggrund. Ser. B, nr. 16 (S. Sheet), controlled by outlines of the dolerite areas on Hellman's map.

19.   M. Fries, Vegetationsutveckling och odlingshistorie: Varnhemstrakten, *Acta Phytogeographica Suecia* 1958.

20.   G. Ekström, Skånes moränområden, *Svensk Geografist Arsbok* 12 (1936): 70–77; Skanes akerjordsomraden, *Socker* 6 (1950) : 53–61.

21.   *Op. cit.* 1962: 692–

22.   In Strömberg, *op. cit.* (1968) : 243–49; *Ibid.:* (1971) : 138.

23.   Strömberg, *op.cit.* (1971) : 195 noted the coastal situation of many Scanian passage-graves, but drew no conclusions from this about the economic basis of their builders.

24.   From the small scale maps in Dr. Strömberg's books (1968; 1971) it is hardly possible to measure distance as accurately as those I have been able to obtain from Bohuslän. It is nevertheless possible to see that certain tombs (notably Strömberg 1971, nos. 4, 11–13 and 32–34) are sited within l km. of the coast, although it is equally plain that the proportion is very substantially lower than in the case of Bohuslän.

25.   A. Bagge and K. Kjellmark, *Stenåldersboplatserna vid Siretop i Blekinge.* Stockholm 1939. See E. Dahr: 242–45.

26.   J.E. Forssander, 'Den sydsvenska boplatskuturen', *Medd. Lunds hist. mus.* 1940–41, 276–98.

27.   See *Atlas över Sverige,* maps 10, 66 and 49–50 (Fig. 3). Stockholm 1953.

28.   I am much indebted to Dr. Lili Kaelas for kindly supplying me with a detailed plot of Bohuslän passage-graves and *dysse* on the scale of 1: 200,000.

29.   *Op. cit.* map 67 (1).

30.   C.A. Moberg, Bohusläns forntid, map p. 33. From *Bohusläns Historia.* E. Lönnroth, Ed.

31.   Based on map 110 of *Atlas över Sverige.*

32.   N.A. Mörner, *"The Late Quaternary History of the Kattegat Sea and the Swedish West Coast,"* Sveriges Geologiska Undersökning, ser. C, nr. 640. Stockholm 1969.

33.   J. Wigforas, Arkeologisk Rapport and J. Lepiksaar, Zoologisk Rapport in *Stenåldersboplatsen Bua Västergård Göteborg.* 1972.

34.   J. Alin, 'En bohuslänsk kokkenmödding på Rotekärrslid, Dragsmark', *Göteborgs och Bohusläns Fornminnesforenings Tidskrift* 1935: 1–38; P. Henrici, 'Benfynd fran boplatsen på Rotekärrslid,' *Ibid.:* 38–42; S. Welinder, 'The Chronology of the Mesolithic Stone Age on the west Swedish coast. *Studier i nordisk arkeologi* 9. Göteborg 1973.

35.   C. Culberg, 'Hasslinghult, Göteborg,' Fynd 1972: 373–448. Also Jan Ekman on the bone material, *Ibid.:* 571–77.

36.   S. Janson, 'En boplats fran yngre stenåldern vid Rörvik i Kville sn. Bohuslän,' *Göteborgs och Bohusläns Fornminnesforenings Tidskrift,* 1936: 57–   ; P. Henrici, *Ibid.*

37.   O. Frödin, 'En svensk kjokkenmödding. Ett bidrag till de postglaciala nivåförändringarnas.' *Ymer* 1906: 17–35.

38.   Axel Sφmme, *A Geography of Norden.* London: Heinemann 1968, p. 314.

39.   In C. Culberg, *op. cit.* 1972: 576.

40. In J. Alin, *op. cit.* 1935 : 41—2.

41. This was recognized as early as 1900 in the report of the third commission on the Danish kitchen-middens by A.P. Madsen et al., *Affaldsynger fra Stenalderen i Danmark,* 176. Three of the six middens investigated were assigned to the period before megalithic tombs, but three (Aalborg, Ørum Aa & Leire Aa) were recognized to span the dolmen/passage-grave transition as this was then conceived.

42. J.G.D. Clark, *Prehistoric Europe : the economic basis,* Fig. 41. London: Methuen 1952 and 1974.

43. G. Gjessing, *Nordenfjelske Ristninger og Malinger av den arktiske Gruppe,* 197. Oslo 1936; J.G.D. Clark, *Prehistoric Europe: the economic basis.* London 1952: 283.

44. James Hornell, *Water Transport. Origins and Early Development.* Cambridge 1946: 136—142.

45. K. Birket—Smith, *The Chugach Eskimo.* Copenhagen 1953: 49.

46. This very broad topic will be dealt with in *The Later Stone Age Settlement of Scandinavia* now in preparation.

47. L. Kaelas, *Den äldre megalitkeramiken under mellan-neolitikum i Sverige.* passim. Stockholm 1953; M. Strömberg, *op. cit.* 1971: 199.

48. H.O'N. Hencken. *The Archaeology of Cornwall and Scilly.* London 1932: 17.

49. *Ibid.* : 33.

50. E.g. Giant's House, Pennance, Zennor; Treen near Gurnard's Head; Carn Gluze, St. Just; and Tregaseal, near Carn Gluze.

51. T.G.E. Powell, A new passage grave group in South Eastern Ireland. *Proceedings of the Prehistoric Society* 1941: 142, 143.

52. T.D. Kendrick, *The Archaeology of the Channel Islands.* I. London 1928. Figs. 86 and 113.

53. Glyn Daniel, *The Prehistoric Chamber tombs of France.* London 1960: 85—87, Fig. 35, Nos. 3 and 4.

54. E.G. Bowen, *British and the Western Seaways.* London 1973.

55. Against A. Mahr's claim (Proceedings of the Prehistoric Society III: 410) that "the greater part of the objects is Indian", Rainbird Clarke argued (*Proceedings of the Prehistoric Society* XX: 42) that the Broighter hoard was in fact Irish and dated from around the time of Christ.

56A. *Op. cit.,* 113.

56B. J.G.D. Clark, The Development of Fishing in Prehistoric Europe. *The Antiquaries Journal* XXVIII (1948) : 45—85.

57. C.F. Hickling, *The Natural History of the Hake.* Fishery Investigations. Ser. II, Vol. X, No. 2. H.M.S.O. London 1927.

58. B.W. Jones, World resources of hakes of the genus *Merluccius. Sea Fisheries Research.* F.R. Harden Jones, Ed. London 1974: 139—166.

59. Arthur E.J. Went, the Irish Hake Fishery, 1504—1842. *J. Cork Historical and Antiquarian Society* LI (1946) : 41—51.

60. *Proceedings of the Prehistoric Society.* XXVIII (1961) : 243 and 250, map.

61. Quoted by Went, *op. cit.* 43.

62. E.S. Russell, Fishery Investigations, ser II, Vol. III, No. I.

63. B. & E. Megaw, *Proceedings of the Isle of Man Natural History & Antiquarian Society* V, No. III (1952) : 250—260. The seine nets used from yawls in the 19th c. were only c. 20 yards long and had a ¾ inch mesh.

64. G.C. Bolster, The Mackerel in British Waters. *Sea Fisheries Research* F.R. Harden Jones, Ed. London 1974 : 101—16.

65. Arthur Went noted a flourishing mackerel and pilchard fishery in Cleggan Bay, Co. Galway. See *Proceedings of the Royal Irish Academy* LI (1946), Sect. B, No. 5: 81—120.

66. M. Martin, *A Description of the Western Isles of Scotland* c. 1695: 417. Reprinted Stirling 1934.

67. M.S. Lovell, *The edible mollusca of Great Britain & Ireland,* London 1884 : 178—179.

68. *Op. cit.* 29.

69. T.D. Kendrick, *The Archaeology of the Channel Islands* I. London 1928 : 79—80.

70. Jacquetta Hawkes, *The Archaeology of the Channel Islands* II : 262.

71. *Boats and boatmen.* London 1952: 84.

72. John M. Coles, The Early Settlement of Scotland; excavations at Morton, Fife. *Proceedings of the Prehistoric Society* XXXVIII (1971): 284—366. See esp. pp. 351—52.

References cited.

Almagro, M. and Arribas, A.
    1963   El Poblado y la Necrópolis Megalíticos de los Millares. Bibliotheca Praehistorica Hispana, III. Madrid.
Ashbee, P.
    1966   The Fussell's Lodge long Barrow Excavations 1957. Archaeologia C:1–80.
Atkinson, R.J.C.
    1956   Stonehenge. London: Hamish Hamilton.
    1968   Old Mortality: some aspects of burial and population in neolithic England. Studies in Ancient Europe. Essays presented to Stuart Piggott, J.M. Coles and D.D.A. Simpson, eds. Leicester University Press.
Birket-Smith, K.
    1953   The Chugach Eskimo. Nationalmuseets Skrifter Etnografisk Raekke 6. Copenhagen.
Bolister, G.C.
    1974   The mackerel in British Waters. Sea Fisheries Research. F.R. Harden Jones, ed. Pp. 101–16 London.
Bowen, E.G.
    1972   Britain and the Western Seaways. London: Thames and Hudson.
Childe, V.G.
    1931   Skara Brae. London: Kegan Paul.
    1957   The Dawn of European Civilization. 6th ed. London: Kegan Paul.
Clark, J.G.D.
    1948   The development of fishing in Prehistoric Europe. Antiquaries Journal XXVIII: 45–85. London.
    1952   Prehistoric Europe: the economic basis. London: Methuen.
    1974   The Earlier Stone Age Settlement of Scandinavia. Cambridge University Press.
Coles, J.M.
    1971   The Early Settlement of Scotland: excavations at Morton, Fife. Proceedings Prehistoric Society XXXVIII: 284–366.
Daniel, G.
    1960   The Prehistoric Chamber Tombs of France. London: Thames and Hudson.
    1963   The Megalith Builders of Western Europe. London: Hutchinson.
De Valera, R.
    1961   The 'Carlingford Culture', the Long barrow and the Neolithic of Great Britain and Ireland. Proceedings Prehistoric Society XXVII: 234–252.
Ekström, G.
    1936   Skånes moranområden, Svensk Geografisk Årsbok 12: 70–77.
    1950   Skånes akerjordsområden. Socker 6: 53-61.
Eogan, G.
    1968   Excavations at Knowth, Co. Meath, 1962–65. Proceedings Royal Irish Academy 66 C, no. 4: 299–400.
    1969   Excavations at Knowth, Co. Meath, 1968. Antiquity XLIII: 8–14.
Fowler, P.J. and Evans, J.G.
    1967   Plough-marks, Lynchets and Early Fields. Antiquity XLI: 289–301.
Fries, M.
    1958   Vegetationsutveckling och odlingshistorie: Varnhemstrakten. Acta Phytogeographica Suecia.
Gjessing, G.
    1936   Nordenfjelske Ristninger og Malinger av den arktiske gruppe. Inst. f. Sammenlignende Kulturforskning, Oslo. Ser. B, no. XXI.
Hawkes, J.
    1939   The Archaeology of the Channel Islands, II. London: Methuen.
Hellman, G.A.
    1963   Västergötlands gånggrifter. Falbygden 18: 3–12.
Hencken, H.O'N.
    1932   The Archaeology of Cornwall and Scilly. London: Methuen.
Hickling, C.F.
    1927   The Natural History of the Hake. Fishery Investigations, Ser. II, X, no. 2. London H. M. Stationery Office.
Hornell, J.
    1946   Water Transport. Origins and Early Development. Cambridge University Press.
Jones, B.W.
    1974   World Resources of hakes of the genus *Merluccius,* Sea Fisheries Research F.R. Harden Jones, ed., London.
Kaelas, L.
    1953   Den äldre megalitkeramiken under mellan-neolitikum i Sverige. Kungl. Vitterhets Historie och Antikvitets Academiens Handlingar. De 83. Antikvariska Studier V: 9–77.
Kendrick, T.D.
    1928   The Archaeology of the Channel Islands l. London: Methuen.

Lethbridge, T.C.
    1952   Boats and Boatmen. London: Thames and Hudson.
Lovell, M.S.
    1884   The edible mollusca of Great Britain and Ireland. 2nd ed. London: L. Reeve.
Macalister, R.A.S. et al.
    1912   Report on the Exploration of Bronze-Age Carns on Carrowkeel Mountain, Co. Sligo. Proceedings
                Royal Irish Academy XXIX C: 311—47.
Mahr, A
    1937   New Aspects and Problems in Irish Prehistory. Proceedings Prehistoric Society III: 261—436.
Malmer. M.
    1962   Jungneolithische Studien. Acta Archaeologica Lundensia. Octavo Ser. No. 2.
Martin, M.
    1934   A Description of the Western Isles of Scotland (c. 1695). Reprinted. Stirling.
Megaw, B. and E.
    1952   The Development of Manx Fishing Craft. Proceedings Isle of Man Natural History and Antiquarian
                Society   V, no. III: 250—60.
Norman, E.R. and St.Joseph, J.K.S.
    1969   The Early Development of Irish Society. Cambridge University Press.
Ó. Nualláin, S.
    1972   A Neolithic House at Ballyglass near Ballycastle, Co. Mayo. Journal Royal Society Antiquaries
                Ireland 102: 49—57.
Ó Riordain, S.P.
    1955   Lough Gur Excavations: the Megalithic Tomb. Journal Royal Society Antiquaries Ireland LXXXV: 34—50.
Petrie, G.
    1867   Notice of ruins of ancient dwellings at Skara, Bay of Skaill, in the parish of Sandwick, Orkney, recently
                excavated. Proceedings Society Antiquaries Scotland VII: 201—219.
Powell, T.G.E.
    1941   A new passage grave group in South Eastern Ireland. Proceedings Prehistoric Society VII: 142—43.
Russell, E.S.
    1914   Report on Market measurements in relation to the English Haddock Fishery during the years 1909—1911.
                Fishery Investigations, Ser. II, Vol. III (1). London: Board of Agriculture and Fisheries, H.M.S.O.
Strömberg, M.
    1968   Der Dolmen Trollasten in St. Köpinge, Schonen. Acta Archaeologica Lundensia. Octavo Ser. 7.
    1971   Die Megalithgräber von Hagestad. Acta Archaeologica Lundensia. Octavo Ser. 9.
Wace, A.J.B. and Stubbings, F.H.
    1962   A Companion to Homer. London: Macmillan.
Went, A.E.J.
    1946A   The Irish Hake Fishery, 1504—1824. Journal Cork Historical and Antiquarian Society LI: 41—51.
    1946B   The Irish Pilchard Fishery. Proceedings Royal Irish Academy 51 B, no. 5: 81—120.

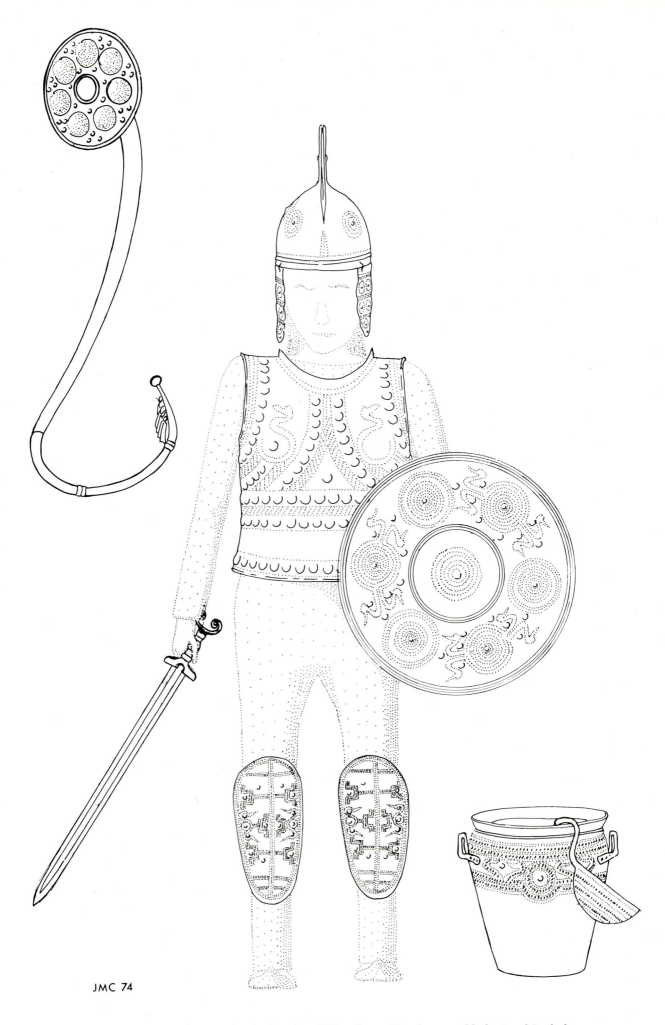

JMC 74

FIG 1.   *A pan-European dandy. Based on Müller-Karpe, Hencken, von Merhart and Broholm.*

PARADE AND DISPLAY: EXPERIMENTS IN BRONZE AGE EUROPE
by John Coles.

The field of archaeology as it applies to the Bronze Age and earliest Iron Age of Europe is liberally sprinkled with typological and stylistic studies. In part this is due to the quality of the surviving material, consisting of fine pottery, often highly burnished and decorated, and impressive metalwork of bronze and gold, striking either because of its sheer massiveness or because of its intricate decoration and composition. However, the other reason why archaeologists have been consistently attracted to such studies is the uneven and illogical nature of the total surviving evidence. A large proportion of our material, from which we aim to reconstruct the ancient societies of the early first millennium B.C., consists of isolated metalwork either alone or in hoards, or pottery the context of which is often funerary, and we tend to lack many of the attributes of an existing dynamic society, namely settlements and the elements of food production and subsistence. In some areas, of course, we possess ample information about settlements, and in others we have data on settlement types and economy as well, most notably the Swiss lakeside villages, but overall our view of European society in the early first millennium B.C. can be nothing but unbalanced.

This is the point at which archaeologists should search through their repertoire to find other methods of approach to the surviving material, in the hope that a "new look" may support or cast doubt upon interpretations based on the traditional studies. For Europe in the first millennium B.C. there have been several such approaches that supplement our knowledge. On the one hand, geographical studies using such concepts as site catchment analysis have contributed much to a theoretical understanding of subsistence practices by Bronze Age societies in southern Europe, yet there has been no attempt made so far to relate the results to the mass of material evidence noted above. This is indeed the reason for considering high quality metalwork, and some pottery too, as "supra-cultural", as representing particular features of the general society of the time but not identifiable with any ordinarily-understood economic function of a community.

The second approach that has been tried relates to the actual quality merchandise itself and does not pretend to do more than determine how such equipment was made and used, and therefore how it might have fitted into the society of the time. This approach, functional or experimental, is almost entirely non-theoretical, as it relies upon scientifically observable phenomena, and is undoubtedly less controversial than concept- or model- building. Only in the interpretation of such experimental results may the archaeologist be accused of subjective reasoning, and herein lie both the success and failure of the approach. In this paper an attempt will be made to show how experiments support and amplify our understanding of Bronze Age society, and suggest that we are dealing with a highly stratified organisation.

Experimental archaeology, as it has come to be called, is a method of investigating elements of material culture at greater depths than can be achieved through visual stylistic and typological studies alone. The method involves the reconstruction of ancient equipment and artifacts, or the simulation of such pieces, and the testing of these in various ways. The tests may be directed solely towards the manufacturing processes in an attempt to gain an insight into particular production problems, such as *cire perdue* casting, or firing of graphited pottery. The tests may also focus upon the possible functions of such products, the effectiveness of shields, or the penetration of arrows. The range of possible experiments of this kind is enormous, and little consistent work has so far been done. Yet to ignore such work, and its potential, is to eliminate a source of information that may well deny or support the results conjectured both from traditional and new interpretative studies. The words "deny" and "support" are deliberate, because while experimental results may effectively dismiss interpretations on the basic grounds of complete non-function i.e., the process or object does not carry out the inferred function, there can be few experiments where a positive conclusion can be acclaimed as the only possible one: support yes, confirm no.

Much of Hugh Hencken's work in the later prehistory of Europe has been concerned with what we might call the prestigious panoply of a favoured element in Urnfield and Early Iron Age society. His studies of shields and helmets are two aspects in the European armoury of the first millennium B.C. and through an examination of these in experimental terms we may hope to understand more fully their function in the society of the time. The shields and helmets are, however, only part of the ostentatious equipment that was produced, and in our study we might add other elements that seem to reflect a liking for showmanship, public display, even conspicuous consumption. Our treatment of these is in no way a summary of the very detailed stylistic studies that have been published on several occasions, but rather an attempt to see them in functional terms. The material is varied and extensive, and the experimental work is restricted in scope but perhaps is important even in its limited results to date; much remains to be done.

Among the impressive metal equipment of the European later Bronze Age is a series of beaten bronze shields. All of these are decorated with ribs surrounding the central boss, and many have multiple small bosses forming circles or arcs or other designs. They have been studied typologically on many occasions, but only once from the experimental-functional point of view. In addition to the many bronze shields, there exists one solitary example of a Bronze Age leather shield surviving through the accident of preservation in a peatbog, and there are several shields of wood similarly preserved. The range of evidence is completed by a couple of wooden shield-formers which must have been designed for leather or hide shields. All of the organic material is from Ireland, but the metal shields are found over a wide area, from Ireland and Britain to northern, central and southern Europe.

From studies of modern and recent primitive societies, archaeologists can be certain as may be of the widespread use of wood and other organic materials in prehistoric times. There can be little doubt that the startling preservation of even one leather shield, and several in wood, indicate a much more extensive use of these materials over a wide area. It is a fact that wherever in prehistoric European sites the conditions exist for the conservation of organic materials, through mud or peat or other waterlogged conditions, quantities of wood, leathers,textiles and bones have been revealed. Such materials were not unique in the past, but are likely to have formed the basis for the bulk of equipment in first millennium B.C. Europe. Here we are concerned only with the shields.

Experimental testing of these shields can serve in some ways as a model of all experimental work dealing with surviving archaeological material. In the first place, a series of observations are made on the original materials, to determine composition, precise shape,size, and strength; then copies are made to conform exactly to the originals so far as is humanly possible today. The copies are then assessed for their reliability as true replicas, before they are put to the test of functional capabilities. The tests themselves are devised on archaeological grounds as being likely to represent actual events in the past, and therefore employ techniques and equipment that were within the scope of the original owners or users of the material copied. In these ways the experimental archaeologist tries to replicate as closely as possible the modes of the past, without introducing any concepts that might have been revolutionary enough to distort the results. In other words, don't make copies with modern machines, and don't subject them to modern stresses, both alien to prehistoric technologies.

For the Bronze Age shields all these theoretical steps were carried out in practical terms, and divergencies from the prehistoric materials and technologies were avoided where possible, and assessed where necessary. Metal shields would have begun with a cast plate-ingot of bronze, subsequently beaten out with a convex-faced hammer in opposite directions to stretch the metal evenly; ingots of this type are known. By annealling, the metal could have achieved a thinness of about .3mm, to match the shield sheets. In the experiment, these stages were omitted due to an inability to obtain sheet bronze; instead, copper sheet was beaten out to the required thinness, and then was planished with a flat-faced hammer to remove dents. The hardness of the ancient bronze sheet and the modern copper sheet, after hammering, was almost exactly similar, so that distortion by the use of inappropriate materials was reduced and in overall effect eliminated.

The hammering of the central boss, the strengthening ribs and other decoration, was the next stage, and involved the manufacture of a yielding bed of soft clay, although warm pitch might have been more suitable. It is likely that the ribs and small bosses would have been formed first in antiquity, with the use of small appropriately-shaped wooden punches hammered onto the back of the sheet as it lay firmly attached to the pitch or clay; the need for a resisting yet flexible bed, to prevent accidental puncturing of the thin metal, is obvious. It would not be necessary to anneal the bronze during this operation. Next would be the careful hammering out of the central boss which would very seriously thin the sheet to .2mm. In the experiment the central boss was formed first because provision for it was made in the bed onto which the shield was placed for the ribs and small boss decoration. A lead bed was also tried and found to be successful. Thereafter all the decoration was outlined by the use of flat-ended punches beaten onto the face of the shield while it lay on a wooden board, and in this way the slight bends and unevenness in the sheet could be reduced and balanced; however, any accidental thinning of the sheet could not be eliminated, and some buckling did occur on one of the experimental shields, as on some of the ancient shields.

These operations completed the shield body and all that was needed to finish the object were a handle, riveted onto the back of the central boss, and the turning of the rim of the shield to give it added strength and eliminate the sharp edge. It is likely that the rim was turned over a metal or wooden rod, and hammered in sequence until the rod was withdrawn as the last of the edge was bent over. Several of the Bronze Age shields still possess the rod. One of the copies retained the bronze rod to give it maximum strength. Many of the ancient shields also have small tabs of metal riveted onto the back, to hold a leather carrying strap. These seem to rule out the possibility of the shields ever possessing a wooden or leather backing, and this is a crucial point in the functional testing. Most shields have been found in muds or peats where wood and leather should have survived, and indeed the carrying strap on one of the Swedish shields confirms this, but there are no clear traces of any backing on any shield today.

In the manufacture of the replicas, no estimates of time could be usefully made as the need to anneal sheet bronze, and to beat it from a cast plate-ingot, were not reproduced. However, it was clear that both care and skill were needed to produce a highly-decorated shield, some of which have up to 30 ribs and 6000 bosses, clearly not a task undertaken lightly. This was perhaps the main conclusion of the exercise, other than the obvious one, often in fact overlooked, that a sheet bronze shield when fresh must have been an outstanding sight, reflecting light in many directions. The evidence then suggested a prestige product requiring much time and skill.

There is only one surviving leather shield of the Bronze Age, but the wooden moulds that also survive show that at least in Ireland the leather shield must have been a popular alternative to the metal shield. The experimental work on this leather shield began with its identification as ox-hide and as vegetable-tanned. The preparation of the hide itself, by soaking, kneading, sweating and scraping, is well-known and would have presented little difficulty. Softening the hide by puering with dung might have preceded the tanning operation which would have involved soaking in oak-bark solutions of increasing strengths for perhaps a year. The result would be a leather stable in water and resistant to putrefaction, yet retaining flexibility and strength. All of these operations were accepted in the experiment as representing reasonably closely the ancient techniques, although there is no doubt that the ox-shoulders obtained for testing were tanned in a more concentrated fashion than would have been the case in the past. They were also "oiled-off", that is, spread with oil to prevent discolouration; this effect was ignored in the testing.

The difficulty with the working of leather into a shield is that of flexibility. The importance of leather as a substance is in its flexible nature, yet in a shield this is an undesirable feature. Bronze Age craftsmen had to overcome this, and the experiments set out to discover the methods they might have used.

A wooden mould was made based upon surviving Bronze Age moulds; it consisted simply of a heavy plate of wood in which grooves and a central depression had been cut. Part of an ox-shoulder 4—6mm. thick was soaked in cold water for 2 hours and was then laid flat and scrubbed with a piece of wood to push out any excess tannin that otherwise would firm the hide surface and cause it to crack when it was bent into the mould. The leather was then placed over the mould and a wooden punch with convex face was hammered to stretch and drive the leather into the central depression. A lead weight was then put into the hollow to hold the leather while the innermost rib was formed by beating the leather with punches into the mould groove. Subsequent ribs were formed in the same manner, with weights to hold the various stretched ribs in place. The whole operation, including the trimming of the leather into a circular shape, took ten minutes only. Weights were then put over the entire shield and it was allowed to dry for three days; during this time the leather tended to shrink and pull out of the grooves, and hammering back took place every four hours throughout this period, clearly a job for an apprentice. After three days the shield was touch-dry, and could be removed from the mould. After a further week it was completely dry, firm to the touch yet slightly flexible, only 3 per cent shrinkage having occurred. A handle of laced leather was fixed to the shield by thongs and it was ready for use.

However, reliance on a shield of this character in Ireland would have been a risky business, because in a moderate rain of one hour or more, the shield would collapse, the leather regaining its flexibility, and the warrior would no doubt gaze down in horror as his shield gently folded itself over his arm. The experiments continued, to discover how such a shield could have been made water-resistant in order to hold its shape. The problem here was that the unique character of the leather, its suppleness, had to be destroyed, and the most obvious method was the application of heat. Five experiments were carried out on separate shields, four of which had been formed in the manner described above. By this variety of approach it was hoped that some approximation to Bronze Age methods could be obtained.

The first procedure was a hot bath at 80°C., for 30 seconds, a process that softened the leather but not sufficiently to cause it to lose its shape. The result was a shield that could withstand a lengthy soaking by rain or flood. The second method used dry heat in an oven at about 75°C. for 2 minutes, and the result was satisfactory other than some distortion. A third procedure was to pour near-boiling water over the shield, on both sides, for a total of two minutes; the finished product withstood light rain and damp but not a prolonged soaking. The fourth method employed molten wax in place of water; paraffin wax rather than beeswax was used, both having been tested for comparison on small pieces of leather. The shield was placed in a vat at 71°C. for 3—4 minutes, sufficient for full penetration, and it became very soft yet easily regained its shape with careful handling. The result was a high gloss shield, rigid and completely impervious to water. Finally, tests were run on the possibility of pre-heating the leather, immediately before it was beaten into the mould; a sheet was dipped in a bath at 80°C. for 1¼ minutes, and by rapid manipulation it could be shaped before shrinkage distortion took place. This method, however, was difficult to control.

Of all the procedures employed, it seems likely that the hot water dip was the most satisfactory and easiest to perform, although the wax method was extremely successful in its result. Of course, there may have been other ancient manufacturing processes that were not tested in the experiments, but analysis of a fragment of the leather from the Bronze Age shield did not detect any sustances other than traces of vegetable tanning agencies and the leather itself. One rule adopted by necessity by experimental archaeologists is that the simplest and most economical method is generally preferred over any others in the absence of conflicting evidence, yet from ethnographic data there may well have been elaborate procedures or rules of conduct that determined the technologies employed; if these were not reflected in a material sense, in the incorporation of physical elements into the product and if we have not in any case been able to detect them,then experimentally we cannot suggest more elaborate methods than the surviving evidence indicates. Yet we should be well aware of the likelihood in the past of traditional standards of procedure considered unnecessary by us today. This need not reflect adversely upon our results, and experimental archaeology is no worse, and no better, than many other archaeological approaches in this regard.

Before looking further in this series of experiments other Bronze Age materials will be noted.

Among the hundreds of Bronze Age weapons recovered from central and western Europe, a relatively small number stand out as particularly impressive either in size or in decoration, sometimes both. Very few experiments have been devised for these, and much of the conjecture about their function is based entirely on their appearance and archaeological context. Studies of Urnfield swords, for example, have indicated that a significant proportion of lengthy weapons, some with inlay decoration of iron and gold, have been recovered from rivers and streams, or from the sites of former lakes. Similarly, Urnfield spearheads of impressive size and quality have often been extracted from watery surroundings. In western Europe, spearheads with gold decoration on their sockets have been shown to be disproportionately long and probably unusable as projectile heads. The sockets of these spearheads are very slender, the weight of spearhead great, and tests suggest that a normal wooden shaft would tend to bend and probably break if the weapon was held horizontally like a spear. The only reasonably likely position appears to have been vertically upright, when the decoration would be evident and the balance reasonable.

These swords and spears are not the only impressive armament in existence in the later Bronze Age. In addition to the sheet metal shields there are helmets, corselets and greaves, all of which were made of thin beaten bronze, elaborately decorated with slight ribs and multiple bosses (Fig. 1). In the definitive work on helmets, Hugh Hencken has described them as almost uniformly too large for Bronze Age heads, and we assume that an inner cap of leather or cloth was worn to afford a better fit, and to cushion any blow that might have penetrated the thin metal of the helmet itself. We might also comment from experimental work that the reverberations from a glancing blow or accidental knock on an unpadded metal helmet would not be an experience deliberately repeated. It is unfortunate that no full-scale tests have been carried out on padded helmets, or on the body armour of the Bronze Age, because this equipment is highly relevant to the question of the function of craftsmen's products at this time. Bronze shields appear to have been used without backing, and nothing has survived from helmets, corselets or greaves, that could be said to demonstrate certain padded backing. The question then arises, how effective were these pieces of armour in actual physical combat? Here experimental archaeology can again contribute to the interpretation of the evidence.

Without doubt the manufacture of helmets and other armour can be said to represent the same elements at work as for the shields, that is, craftsmanship of a high order, organisation of a workshop, and considerable time. Would such armour be put at risk of total destruction by a single blow? Perhaps only for a conspicuous consumption type of activity. The corselets and greaves survive only in fragments, so traces of use are not discernible, but of the many helmets, it could be said that hardly any have any certain signs of sword slashes or spear thrusts. That they would bear such traces from direct physical conflict cannot be doubted, although only the shields have been experimentally tested.

In these tests, a water-hardened leather shield and a sheet metal shield, with strengthening rod around the rim, were subjected to thrusts and blows with Bronze Age spear and sword. The spearhead punctured the metal shield readily, and the first slash of the sword cut the shield entirely in two, only the rod holding the pieces together (Fig. 2). The leather shield, however, resisted the spear thrusts and absorbed a large number of violent sword slashes with only superficial damage to the surface of the leather. The wax-hardened shield was not tested, but would probably have been less effective because it was entirely rigid, and any side-blow would have strained the handle thongs to the point of breaking. The flexible leather shield bent sufficiently to take the major impact without such stress. The result of these tests, subsequently repeated in part, was that leather shields could have served as effective defensive equipment in the Bronze Age. That they actually did so is not certain. The metal shields, however, and by inference the helmets, corselets and greaves, were not at all effective against physical attack, and unless produced for deliberate owner-inflicted destruction, are much more likely to have been primarily showpieces, for ostentatious display on a number of occasions. Here the archaeological evidence, their findspots, their representations in art, and their very nature, suggest a parade aspect perhaps involving ceremonial deposition sometimes in graves but more often than not in watery places. The experimental results support the archaeological considerations.

Among the weaponry of the Bronze Age, the bow and arrow is a neglected item. Produced not in metal, except for rare arrowheads, but by using perishable wood for bows and shafts, and the commonplace flint for arrowheads, the bow and arrow tends to be an underestimated weapon, yet its range, accuracy and penetrating ability far exceeded any

FIG 2.   Experimental testing of Bronze Age shields. Metal shield on left, leather shield on right. Note slashed and distorted metal shield. Photo by Ralph Crane, Life Magazine, Copyright Time Inc. 1964.

other contemporary weapon. For these reasons there is little doubt that the bow was a popular implement, and the arrowheads found in great abundance in many parts of Europe attest to this. Rarely have actual bows survived, although their ancestry extends back some ten millennia, in Europe. How effective were these, and against what were they employed? Experiments again have provided some answers for the first question and suggestions for the second.

A series of tests on ancient bows and arrows has shown the formidable qualities of such diverse weapons as the English long-bow, Tartar and Turkish composites, and American Indian wooden bows. The experiments involved reconstructing and testing bows and arrows, bowstrings and arrowheads. The major element is of course the bow itself, and here weapons were tested for cast and weight. Among the results, yew-wood bows, with an ancestry in the Neolithic of western Europe, were shown to be highly effective, throwing arrows over 200 metres at drawn weights of about 30kg. The best performance came from a composite bow, made of cow-horn, hickory, catgut and rawhide; this weapon had a range over 250 metres. Arrowshafts of hickory, birch, ash, pine and willow were tested for strength, flight, ease of manufacture and, surprisingly, the pine shafts, representing the earliest known arrowshafts in the world, were ranked below the first three woods listed. These arrows travelled up to 80 m.p.h., and penetration tests showed conclusively that medium-sized game and simulated human bodies could be totally perforated at ranges of 15—25 metres. Important for prehistoric Europe was also the realisation that finely flaked flint arrowheads had a greater cutting potential than any other material including ground steel. The minute serrations along the edges of a flint or obsidian arrowhead act as a saw and cut through flesh and slender bone very readily. In comparison, metal arrowheads, which are known in limited quantities from Bronze Age and Iron Age Europe, were less effective. Here then is the clear and obvious explanation of the widespread popularity of flint arrowheads throughout European prehistory, from late Glacial times down to the Roman Empire, and the reason why bronze and iron arrowheads are relatively sparse in quantity and in distribution. Against such weapons as the long bow of yew, or the composite short bows, Urnfield and Iron Age metal armour would stand no chance, and it would be an interesting test of the defensive capabilities of shields and body armour of leather to subject these to the cast of a reconstructed Urnfield or Iron Age short bow, remains of which are well-known. An experiment, designed to test an historical document, suggests that such a test would demonstrate the need for protection alternative to sheet metal armour alone. The document records the successful penetration of two suits of chain mail by a flint-tipped arrow fired by a Florida Indian. In experiment, a steel arrowhead shot from 75 metres perforated a chainmail suit on a simulated human body. The historical document records that chain mail armour was abandoned by the Spanish explorers after the demonstration, and that felt cloth padding was worn instead. The latter may well have been a popular type of protection in first millennium B.C. Europe; fragments survive but as yet not from any unequivocal armoured context.

It is perhaps an interesting commentary on the development of human society and its values at this time if we compare the appearance and performance of, on the one hand, sheet metal armour and enormous unbalanced metal spears and swords, all of impressive visual display, with, on the other hand, thick cloth padding or leather jerkins and the wooden bow with flint-tipped arrowhead, all of menial aspect. Experimental archaeology confirms beyond much question that the performance qualities of these two sets were in inverse ratio to their appearance. Yet as prehistoric archaeologists we should not forget the medieval equivalents, of a striking force of knights with metal weapons of great weight and impressive appearance, and their supporting forces of foot-soldiers clad in leather and cloth and carrying wooden staves, spears and bows. The experimental results should perhaps then be expressed in terms not of comparison and contrast but of complements. The archaeological evidence for this is not likely to be difficult to find.

In considering both Bronze Age shields and helmets, prehistorians have often referred to the contemporary sheet metal buckets and cauldrons, found widely distributed over Europe, and demonstrating not only craftsmanship of high quality but also broad stylistic and technical similarities to the metal armour. These metal vessels, of enormous capacity, holding anything up to 25 litres (44 pints) of liquid, and weighing fully 28 kg (62 pounds) when water filled, are clearly not for everyday use. Elaborately decorated, fitted together with difficulty, and fragile, they can be hardly anything but prestige vessels, although the special occasions are unknown to us; they may have played a part in the presumed wine-making and wine-tasting activities in southern Europe during the earlier first millennium B.C.

One other item in late Bronze Age and Iron Age material culture cannot be disregarded in any consideration of parade and display, and of experiment, because here too the traditional and experimental results are in broad agreement. The objects in question are the elaborate metal trumpets and horns of northern and western Europe. Matched in size and range only by the array of instruments of the Roman Empire, the prehistoric horns of Scandinavia and Ireland represent an important element for the first millennium B.C. in their technological, social and musicological implications. They have been studied on numerous occasions and with varying results and emphasis.

The evidence consists of one hundred bronze horns from Ireland, and about half that number from Denmark, southern Sweden and northern Germany. All may be dated by rare associations and by stylistic and technical features to the later Bronze Age in these areas. They form an element in the material culture of the regions not as unusual as they might seem at first glance. Large and impressive as some of the instruments are, they can be shown to fit perfectly into our admittedly conjectural ideas about the society of the time; they are a particularly useful manifestation of the parade and ceremonial aspect that is hinted at by some of the material described above. Experimental work, far from merely supporting these ideas, has been mainly responsible for them.

From Ireland, the horns are single unassociated finds. Only one horn is attested as part of an otherwise normal Bronze Age hoard. The horns are of two distinct types by decorative style, and of two musicological types. All are relatively short instruments, about one metre long, and are of cast bronze. Some are end-blown horns, others are side-blown horns, both by shape clearly having origins in an organic animal horn of *Bos longifrons* type. Neither of these types, however, is complete, for in almost all cases the horns have provision for separate detachable mouth pieces; the end-blown horns have an inserting flange, the side-blown horns have a wide unprepared mouth-hole, and by experiment both clearly require some form of lip-support. Yet in no case has such a mouthpiece been recovered other than a few horns with cast-on mouthpiece. This fact alone suggests an unusual deposition sequence, with the instruments deliberately dismantled before consignment to the marsh.

Stylistically the horns are of two types, one restricted to the south-west of Ireland, the other to the north-east. Both side- and end-blown horns occur in both regions. Only in one place at Dowris, in central Ireland, are all found together. Here, some form of *Opferplatz* may well have existed to collect all manner and quantity of objects over a long period of time.

The lack of normal associations, the find-spots uniformly marshy and boggy, the absence of the one item essential to allow the horns to be played, and the Dowris find, all indicate a use and a design not entirely directed towards ordinary economic or social pursuits. Such ordinary pursuits might include the delivery of musical compositions, signalling for the hunt or for war, and sounding on funereal occasions.

Experimental work on these horns has been entirely confined to the musicological aspects. Technical examination of the castings has indicated that particular attention was paid to the exterior of the horn, and its internal surfaces left unsmoothed. This suggests that the visual impression may have been considered more important than the aural. Musically, the experiments support this. The end-blown horns have a limited range, restricted to two notes for many horns, four or five for a few and most importantly no evidence seems to suggest any tonal system. The notes seem random, and without overall pattern. Even the Dowris horns, possibly specially made for their purpose at that site, are a heterogeneous lot in musical terms. It must be said, however, that the absence of any mouthpiece makes these conclusions less certain than they would otherwise be, because a carefully prepared mouthpiece, of wood or metal, would allow some tonal matching and range increase. Yet the mouthpieces cast on the few Irish horns are poor in quality and design, and do little to help the player.

In similar manner the side-blown horns exhibit attention to appearances, and disregard to musical qualities. Their mouth-openings are enormous, far greater than those of almost all ethnographic side-blown horns of ivory or animal horn. The internal chambers are left rough as from the casting, and part of the clay core still resides in the solid tip of many. When blown, with great difficulty, each horn yields one note only, and together the notes seem entirely random, both with each other and with those of the end-blown horns. These side-blown horns have provided the only known fatality to the subject of experimental archaeology, through an excess of indiscrete enthusiasm for the production of a euphonomous musical note.

When taken together, the experimental results on these Irish horns seem to support the archaeological results yet again, that these instruments have about them an aura of parade and display, and ceremony, fully befitting their contemporary position with the great range of massive gold and bronze objects, gorgets and torcs, buckets, cauldrons, shields and swords, that litter the Irish landscape in the early first millennium B.C. In passing, we might point to the evidence from the later Irish prehistoric contexts, wherein massive bronze horns again align with a wealth of Celtic gold and bronze objects of very high artistic quality, the whole providing a shadowy background to the society and events recorded in the early Irish chronicles. May we see in our Bronze Age material the beginnings of such a phenomenon? The archaeological and experimental evidence supports it.

For the other great area of Bronze Age lip-reed instruments, southern Scandinavia, the archaeological evidence is very broadly similar to that of Ireland. The instruments themselves are of cast bronze, of very high technical quality, and are far larger than the Irish horns. The experience and expertise required to manufacture these horns was of the highest order, and they probably represent the apex of European Bronze Age cast metalwork. Yet all went into appearances, the exterior highly smoothed and polished, the decorative jointing and embellishments finely cast and emphasized, whereas the internal chamber was left rough and unsmoothed. Cast-on repair patches were merged with the original body outside, but left as protrusions inside. Mouthpieces were cast as part of the horn, yet on occasion were broken off and hidden in a different place from the horns themselves which were uniformly deposited in marsh and moorland. The mouthpieces are crude and unsophisticated elements, showing little resemblance to the evolved cups of today's horns, trombones and trumpets. Such an evolution might well have been achieved with Bronze Age skills, inventiveness, and desire. Of the first two qualities there is no doubt. The lack of the third is apparent.

Experimental work has again been restricted to the musicological aspects of these horns, and results are comparable to those of Irish workmanship. The earliest testing of the horns, however, purported to demonstrate their impressive musical quality, and the invention of harmonics by Nordic peoples, because unlike the Irish horns, the Nordic horns generally occur as matched pairs made in each other's mirror image like a pair of animal horns of *Bos primigenius* type. It was considered by the early experimental musicologists that even if the playing of these pairs of horns was meant to be in unison, someone was bound to make a mistake and thus the invention of harmonics. Such an explanation was on the face of it reasonable because as the horns were clearly cast as pairs, identical in size and shape, the pairs should be identically tuned, yielding the same range of notes. However, more vigorous experimental work has demonstrated that the lack of attention paid to internal consistencies within each pair of horns created a situation where externally the horns were indeed absolutely similar yet internally they were different enough to yield different notes within the same range. Hence, to our ears at least, unison playing would have on occasion sounded positively non-harmonic; who, however, can say what Bronze Age musical tastes were?

The point here, however, is that experimental work has shown the great range of notes available from these instruments, unconnected notes it is true, but perhaps eight or nine available to normal blowing techniques. The minor inconsistencies within matched pairs could only be recorded by experimental work, and the sonorous character of the horns, noted. Problems in handling the long curved horns gave reason for dismissing theories about the use of the horns in battle at least insofar as rapid retreat was concerned. What then does the experimental work tell us? The musicological studies support the archaeological evidence that these horns were probably of special significance to Bronze Age society, created primarily for display when their sounds were no doubt heard and appreciated with perhaps the particular notes or sequences of minor concern. This interpretation may be going too far, as it is quite possible that particular notes and series were required on certain occasions. The major result of the studies, however, must be that appearances counted for much, and that a high development of musical notational system is not attested by these horns. As such, the horns fit into the general picture of a society where parade and display of certain objects, on certain occasions, figured highly. The deliberate breakage of mouth pieces, and burial in marshlands, also suggest a general picture of ceremonial activity for these magnificent horns. Our sources of data are not yet exhausted, however, for support emerges from a brief glance at the contemporary rock art of the period.

The carvings so abundantly represented on the living rock of Scandinavia are capable of many interpretations, and here we will look only at certain aspects, those that seem to support some of the suggestions made above. One of the problems of any open rock art is of course its dating, another is its association with other art nearby, and a third is its interpretation. Although there are several art panels in Sweden depicting humans with curved horn-like objects held above the head, only one group shares all of the problems above. This is the series of stone slabs in the grave at Kivik in Scania, clearly of the Bronze Age, and clearly depicting some activity not at all related to normal Bronze Age economic pursuits such as are shown on many other art panels. The precise meaning of the scenes is unknown, of course, but cloaked figures in procession stand apart and in apparent rank above uncloaked humans, animals depicted in disarray, and unusual objects. Several humans are shown with horns held in the act of blowing. The whole scene is reminiscent of the find spots of some of the metal horns, in moorland strewn with animal and human bones, the horns broken deliberately before deposition. What the ceremonies were, and why they ended, we do not know, but the ceremonial aspects of the horns themselves, fortified by their experimental testing, suggest some actions involving display and ritual. Again the experiments have provided strong support, not confirmation, for the archaeological interpretations.

In this paper the archaeological evidence for the production and display of prestige equipment in Bronze Age Europe has been briefly assessed in relation to experimental work. Other aspects of such conspicuous material culture exist, particularly in the form of personal ornaments, and in the neglected field of burial monuments often prominently positioned and elaborately constructed. The very considerable care taken in the erection of some Bronze Age funerary monuments, and the prestigious grave goods accompanying the dead for whatever purpose, speak of a stratification of society at least in death and one would assume in life. In all the cases cited here, shields and armour spears and swords, horns and art, the experimental work has sometimes supported the archaeological interpretation, sometimes suggested new avenues to explore. In none of these cases has experimental work refuted absolutely the archaeological concepts, although the field of experiment is littered with such rejections for other aspects of past human activities. In the subjects discussed here, we may perhaps see the strengthening hand of experimental archaeology in supporting our ideas about the materials and some of the mechanisms of parade and display in Bronze Age Europe.

References cited

Broholm, H.C., W.P. Larsen and G. Skjerne
    1949   The Lures of the Bronze Age. Copenhagen.
Coles, J.
    1962   European Bronze Age shields. Proceedings of the Prehistoric Society 28: 156–190
    1963   Irish Bronze Age horns. Proceedings of the Prehistoric Society 29: 326–356.
    1971   Bronze Age spearheads with gold decoration. Antiquaries Journal 51: 94–95.
    1973   Archaeology by Experiment. Hutchinsons, London.
Hencken H.
    1971   The Earliest European Helmets. Peabody Museum, Cambridge.
Müller-Karpe, H.
    1962   Zur spätbronzezeitlichen Bewaffnung in Mitteleuropa und Griechenland. Germania 40: 255–286.
Piggott, S.
    1959   A Late Bronze Age wine trade? Antiquity, 33: 122–123.
Pope, S.T.
    1918   A study of bows and arrows. University of California Publication in American Archaeology and Ethnology 13(9): 329–414.
Torbrügge, W.
    1971   Vor- und frühgeschichtliche Flussfunde. 51–52 Bericht der Römisch-Germanischen Kommission.
von Merhart, G.
    1952   Studien über einige Gattungen von Bronzegefässen. Festschrift des Römisch-Germanisch Zentralmuseums in Mainz 2: 1–71.

STARČEVO REVISITED
by Robert W. Ehrich

Since the American School of Prehistoric Research was one of the sponsors, and since some of its students participated in the major excavation of Starčevo, in 1932; since the present administration of the School has expressed a lively interest in its final publication, and since Dr. Hencken himself has always had a deep concern for the completion of the project, a paper concerning Starčevo would seem to provide an appropriate topic for this volume.

It is understood that what follows, either in its present or somewhat altered guise, will form part of the introductory material of the final publication. However, since this will almost certainly appear first, it seems worth while to begin to clarify some long-standing misconceptions. In deference to my collaborator, Dr. Draga Garašanin, who is not yet convinced that our control excavations of 1969 and 1970 completely support my point of view, I will not attempt to cite much detailed evidence from them until we have completed our joint manuscript. We have agreed that if our disagreements persist, we will state our divergent views separately.

What follows, then, is a history of the investigations and an account of the gradual incorporation of numerous errors and misinformation that have crept into the record to form the basis of what I consider to be some completely false interpretations of both the site and of the Starčevo culture. Normally, perhaps these matters would be of limited significance but, since Starčevo is not only the eponymous site for the Yugoslav part of the Starčevo-Körös-Cris complex, but also the first site of this culture to have been the scene of extended excavation, it has served as a key against which other material has been evaluated. Furthermore, since some of the misconceptions stem from errors in our preliminary report (Fewkes, Goldman and Ehrich; 1933), it seems more than high time to set the record straight.

The Site

The site lies at the northwestern edge of the village of Starčevo, along an old bank of the Danube some 8 km. downstream from Pančevo and approximately 20 km. ENE of Beograd, on the Banat or left side of the Danube. Pančevo is situated at the mouth of the Tamiš (Temes, Timiş) River. Houses along the westernmost street of the modern village lie roughly parallel to the bank and some 100 m. from it, with narrow garden strips running behind them both on the Banat plain and on the bank itself, which slopes irregularly for a distance of some 90 m. to the lower flood plain lying approximately 3 m. below it. The Danube now flows approximately 3.5 km. to the west. Until the relatively recent construction of dikes at about the turn of the century, this lower flat was subject to periodic inundation, particularly during the spring floods, and the area seems to have been marshy like other unprotected segments. It is not surprising, therefore, to find the traces of prehistoric settlement apparently concentrated on the slope itself and at the edge of the upper plain. One cannot, of course, be certain as to how much may have been swept away by the river, but even today the lower plain is uninhabited.

The brown deposits containing traces of human occupation and agriculture lie on yellow loess, which in turn rests on fine sand.

History of the Investigations

Although the flatland above the slope generally formed a part of the properties which lined the street to the east, in the area of the excavations the slope itself was public land. This was allocated for the use of itinerant brickmakers who had begun to work there in 1912 and appeared annually during the summer months. Starting on the lower plain, they worked eastward, stripping away the topsoil and cultural deposits and cutting or "mining" away the loess, which they utilized. Needing water, they dug wells on the lower plain and used well sweeps to draw it to the surface. They also dug large rectangular pits back into the higher ground to serve as kilns. One cannot say definitely that their numbers increased markedly over the years, but their depredations at the site certainly did. After 1919 they had made heavy inroads, which continued year after year. Although it is presently against the local ordinances, the villagers still remove the disturbed and fertile upper earth to spread on their gardens, and they also dig the loess to make mud brick and mud plaster to daub both their inner and their outer walls. Since they do not always use the customary vegetable tempering, they mine the underlying sand for this and other purposes.

Once the museum at Pancevo had obtained a small collection of material, the site came to the attention of the National Museum in Beograd. In 1928, Miodrag Grbic, then at the National Museum, excavated seven pits and also made a fairly extensive collection of the material turned up by the brickmakers. I have been unable to find any notes of Grbic's excavations, and in the catalogue of the National Museum's collections there is no distinction made between what he actually dug and what he collected. All the material is simply pooled as having been acquired in 1928.

At that time clearly related wares of the Körös culture were appearing in Hungary, but initially were assigned to the later Tisza culture (Fewkes 1936: 73, note 491; Kutzián:1947 1—2), and in his brief paper of 1930 Grbić equated his material from Starčevo with Lengyel and Tordos and considered it to belong to the end of the Neolithic. Across the Danube at Vinča, Vasić was finding Starčevo material in his deepest and earliest deposits (See Letica 1968, for a review).

In 1931 Grbić offered the site of Starčevo to V.J. Fewkes for possible future work, and the two spent ten days making a brief sounding there, to test whether a substantial excavation would be justified. By this time the brickmakers had completely obliterated all traces of the earlier explorations. During the course of their work Grbić and Fewkes opened an irregular rectangle, 18.75 x 6.75 m., along the chewed-up face of the site, and investigated the remains of two pits which had been mostly cut away but were still visible in the profile of the bank. They also uncovered two burials. The pits were designated Pits 1 and 2, and their contents, together with what was saved from the other deposits, are in the collections of the Peabody Museum of Harvard University.

The year of 1932 saw the major excavation at Starčevo. Financial support came from the Peabody and Fogg Museums at Harvard University and from the American School of Prehistoric Research. Fewkes was the Field Director, while Hetty Goldman, representing the Fogg Museum, and I, together with Grbić (on behalf of the National Museum in Beograd) comprised the senior staff. Other members included Oleh Kandyba, a specialist on the painted pottery of central and eastern Europe, and Adolf Fiker, surveying engineer, both of Prague, and Mrs. Gwyneth Harrington of Boston, who served as staff artist.

Fewkes was also Field Director of the American School of Prehistoric Research, and his students participated as assistants. These were the Misses Josephine Graton (Bryn Mawr College), Gertrude Howe (Mount Holyoke College), Ruth Sears (Radcliffe College), and Messrs. Curtice M.C. Aldridge (Cornell University), Frederick A.L. Richardson (Harvard University), and Dwight W. Morrow, Jr. (Amherst College).

The excavation lasted from July 15 to September 20, opening an irregularly triangular section, the long side of which ran approximately north-south along the west face of the bank for 45 m., returning westward for 26.5 m., at its northern end, and approximately 3 m. at its southern end. In addition, two sounding trenches (1932 A and B), measuring 13.75 x 7.60 m. and 10 x 2.5 m. respectively, were dug some 275 m. north and somewhat west of the major section. Further, a cut just south of the 1931 soundings investigated a sharply outlined disturbance showing in the profile, which we had correctly taken to be the return of a relatively recent eastward-running ditch already examined in the main trench.

During the winter of 1932—33 Fewkes worked on the preliminary report of Starčevo while I continued with our previous commitment to the Bohemian site of Homolka, helping Fewkes occasionally with the initial draft of his report. In the summer of 1933, supported by the Fogg Art Museum only, we continued our reconnaissance in Yugoslavia and, upon our return, I continued as before with the description of the Homolka material and worked on my own anthropometric data from Montenegro. Miss Goldman was in New York during this period. After the 1933 field session, my official position at the Peabody Museum was terminated, and in the early spring of 1934 I joined Miss Goldman's Expedition to Cilicia.

I cite these details to explain how, although I did participate in the initial drafting of the preliminary report, and was co-signer at Fewkes' generous insistence, I saw neither the final manuscript nor the proofs of the article, which appeared before my return from Turkey in the fall of 1934. There are a number of errors in that report, some of which I recognized at that time. Fewkes and I discussed them and agreed that we would correct them in the final publication, never dreaming that this would not take place for over forty years. Other errors and questionable interpretations appeared later, and I also discuss them below.

Although Fewkes continued intermittently to lead the American School in 1933, 1934 and 1938, he left the Peabody Museum and moved to Philadelphia, taking with him all our notes from Yugoslavia, and all the material and data from Czechoslovakia. The material from the 1931 excavations at Starčevo remained at the Peabody where Miss Sears, under Fewkes' direction, had studied the contents of Pits 1 and 2 as part of her graduate work.

After Fewkes died in 1941, all that he had taken to Philadelphia was packed together in cartons and crates and returned to the Peabody Museum in an incredibly jumbled condition. The undertaking of sorting out the disarray of various notes and records was a lengthy affair that took some years of the little time that I could spare for it.

Although Fewkes did return to Starčevo when leading the School in 1938 (Fewkes 1939: 11), I can find no record that he ever did any further excavation there. This is important, for he changed his views on the question of stratification and, without any real evidence, had already come to the conclusion that at Starčevo unpainted pottery preceded painted pottery, which he stated unequivocally as fact (Fewkes 1936: 27 note 109, 73, note 491; 1937: 391). I have been unable to discover any actual basis whatsoever for this statement.

In 1951, while writing a review of J.H. Gaul's "The Neolithic Period in Bulgaria" (1948) for the *American Anthropologist,* I came upon a statement by Milojčić (1949: 70) that at Starčevo unpainted pottery preceded painted pottery. He attributed this to Fewkes (1936 and 1937 as above). I checked the original references and went into the matter further while preparing a paper for the 1952 meetings of the Anthropological Association (Ehrich 1954). At that time I wrote, "The sampling is insufficient, but there may be some cleavage between sites which show the presence of the painted wares and those which do not. Chronological interpretations are at least partly hinged on flat and unsubstantiated statements by Fewkes (1936: 27, note 109, 33, 73 note 491; 77; 1937: 391) that at Starčevo unpainted l wares occur earlier than do the painted. Fewkes made those statements subsequent to the publication of our preliminary report, in which we indicated clearly that the characteristic painted ware appeared in all the earliest deposits, including the pits dug into the virgin soil (Fewkes, Goldman and Ehrich 1933: 38ff). I have rechecked our notes and our field catalogue of material and have consulted with other members of our expedition. I can find no basis whatsoever for any stratigraphic indication that the first appearance of painted wares at Starčevo is any later than the period of original settlement." (Ehrich 1954: 112)

In a draft of an article which I wrote at that time but which remains unpublished, I find the following comment: "As to the grounds upon which Fewkes based his later statements that at Starčevo the unpainted wares preceded the painted, the present writer is uncertain. All collaboration terminated at the close of the 1933 season, and after that he [Ehrich] was no longer active in the European field. A half-remembered conversation with Fewkes some years later brings to mind a statement that Fewkes returned to Starčevo for a hasty additional check, that, because of the absence of painted ware in the inadequate sampling of the Danubian sites, he was looking for a stratigraphic sequence in which the painted wares appeared later at Starčevo, and that he found it." I have found no record of any further excavation and, if it did take place, no one either here or in Beograd knows about it. I can only assume that, at most, he reexamined the face of the bank.

Milojčić, in the passage referred to above (1949: 70), also cites personal information from Grbić that in some of the pits, there were only geometric painted ware designs, while others contained spiral ornament. It was partly on these statements and partly on some reports from other sites that Milojčić elaborated his four Starčevo phases. (1950: 109–111) All of this took place before the advent of Carbon 14 dating. On the basis of stylistic similarities we were then equating the black-on-red spiral wares with Dimini, and attributing the white-on-red geometric patterns and some of the coarser ware forms to Sesklo origins or survivals. Parenthetically, it is also worth noting that, conditioned by these factors (and by a somewhat evolutionistic outlook), Fewkes and Grbić thought they recognized what they had expected to find. This, in my view, illustrates one of the methodological pitfalls in the current pressure for hypotheses to be stated before investigation.

In 1954 Draga Arandjelović-Garašanin published her *Starčevačka Kultura,* a general study of the Starčevo culture but based primarily on a detailed analysis of the pits at Starčevo. The publication rights were released to her by Grbić who was apparently unaware that I had the field notes in my charge and that I was planning to work on them. At that time she had available to her only the tags on the bags of material, the list of bags, the field catalogue of special objects, and a copy of our imprecise and error-laden preliminary report. Although our labels were clear enough, in several instances they were misleading, for they designated unfolding situations during the course of excavation. Thus "Pit 6" initially referred to a large disturbed area that eventually resolved into three separate pits which, for convenience and continuity, we still called Pit 6, followed by additional verbal description. No one unfamiliar with this situation and without the accompanying field notes could possibly have avoided pooling all three units. Nor could one have deduced that Pit 5B was a later intrusion cut into Pit 5A, nor that "Pit 4" was, actually, a recent ditch or trench.

There were also intricacies in the labeling of the painted wares, all of which had been packaged separately.

For some reason the copies of the site plans and drawings, as well as other information we had left with Grbić, had disappeared, — either through the exigencies of the war years or in the relocation of the Museum. In any event, Dr. Garašanin was handicapped by the lack of data that she properly should have had.

Obviously influenced by Milojčić, she distinguished the following phases: Starčevo I, II a and b, and III, the last of which, not occurring at Starčevo, characterizes the Körös culture. There is no point in embarking on a detailed analysis here, for subsequent finds and information have somewhat invalidated this interpretation.

What we are concerned with at the moment is the history of the research into the site of Starčevo, and why a control excavation was necessary. A detailed analysis of the documentation will, of course, form an important part of the final publication.

In 1955 I returned to Yugoslavia for the first time since 1933, apart from a brief transit from Turkey in 1939, and suggested to Grbić that we jointly complete the Starčevo publication as originally planned. Since he felt out of touch with the project and was involved in other matters, he introduced me to Dr. D. Garašanin and suggested that we collaborate. Because both of us had prior commitments, it was not until 1969 that we were able to complete the necessary arrangements and begin a control excavation at the site.

Thanks to a grant from the Foreign Currency Program of the Smithsonian Institution, Mrs. Ehrich and I, with Dr. D. Garašanin as Field Director, excavated with a small labor force for 35 days in 1969 and again for 10 days in the fall of 1970. At that time the entire slope in the settlement area had been eaten back to the edge of the upper plain, with only a few irregularities remaining. All traces of our previous operations were eradicated, and our work was thus confined to public land under cultivation on the upper flatland, somewhat to the north and west of our old excavations, and to some soundings on the privately owned garden strips to the south.

Subsequently, during the winter of 1970–71, Mrs. Ehrich and I carefully went through the material from the 1932 excavations and, during the winters of 1973–74 and 1974–75, after the archaeological aspects of the Smithsonian Foreign Currency Program had been discontinued at the request of the Yugoslav government, a grant from the National Science Foundation enabled us to study the results of the 1969 and 1970 excavations and also the material collected by Grbić in 1928.

Since Dr. Garašanin and I still disagree on numerous points and, since our vast accumulation of descriptive data has not yet been properly synthesized, my own opinions — though strongly held at present — are still subject to change or modification. So far I have not published my current views, although they are no secret. I gave a talk on them at the VIII International Congress of Prehistoric and Protohistoric Sciences in Beograd, 1971, with Dr. Garašanin present, and later in that year I spoke at the Columbia University Seminar on the Archaeology of the Eastern Mediterranean, Eastern Europe and the Near East. Subsequently, particularly in 1974 and 1975, I have discussed certain questions with colleagues in Yugoslavia, Hungary, Bulgaria and Rumania, many of whom seem in varying degrees of accord with some of my conclusions. Some are not.

Some criticisms, corrections and comments on the preliminary report of Fewkes, Goldman and Ehrich, 1933.

(1)   "The most significant painted ware, some 30% of the total, was recorded in watercolor" (p. 37) is misleading. This statement was intended to convey that 30% of the total painted wares had been recorded in watercolor. Actually, the proportion of painted wares to the total pottery recovered is extremely low, averaging perhaps 1.5% or even less in different units or areas. This is an estimate only, for exact distribution calculations have not yet been made.

(2)   The passage concerning the deposits (pp. 37–43) is both confused and confusing, and needs clarification. Here we list four strata, consisting of: 1) an active humus; 2) a relatively thick "subhumus", described as a transition level; 3) an underlying "culture level" characterized as "predominantly Neolithic with intrusions caused by later burials"; and 4) "the occupational niveau (called pit level)", from which the pits opened and descended into the loess below.

In a sketchy journal kept by Fewkes it is clear that in the soundings of 1931 he and Grbić did not recognize any distinction between the culture level and pit level, and that they used the term "culture level" to characterize all of the deposit below the subhumus, which was clearly distinguishable.

In those days in Europe it was not generally the practice to draw profiles directly from baulks or from trench walls, but rather to dig horizontally in artificial levels or with careful and thorough nivellation of visibly changing deposits, and to reconstruct cross sections schematically, leaving small pillars to serve as stratigraphic controls. We did, however, have a vertical exposure in the bank cut by the brickmakers, and Fiker drew a cross-section of Pits 5A and 5B, in part directly from the exposure as shown in Plate VIb of our 1933 report, and in part from the excavation data.

For purposes of clarity, Draga Garašanin and I have agreed to revise these strata designations, eliminating the active humus and numbering the rest as Stratum I = "subhumus", Stratum II = our old "culture level", and Stratum III = "pit level". Although the cleavage line between Levels II and III, was not sharply distinguishable, there were some observable differences in color and texture, with Level III being browner and containing a higher proportion of loess lumps.

In our excavations of 1969 and 1970, particularly in the upper plain area to the north and east of the 1932 operation, these strata were again present. Level III, however, seemed to be of somewhat patchy and irregular occurrence. The same levels appeared again in some of the soundings in the field strips to the south of our old workings, although here they were sometimes in attenuated form and less clear, due to the scraping away of the deposits on the brow and upper part of the slope.

There is, I think, no real question as to the identifications of Levels I and III with our earlier subhumus and pit levels. Although there is no question in my mind that Level II equates with our former culture level, there is still a question as to its proper interpretation, and about this we still have some disagreement. In my view, our initial assessment of Level II as a Neolithic deposit, disturbed by intrusions but essentially an occupation layer laid down after the destruction or abandonment of the original Starčevo dwellings as represented by the pits, is completely wrong. My reasons for thinking so are as follows:

(a)   "In one case, a sharply defined "pit", starting below the humus and penetrating the deeper deposits, was noted; this subsequently proved to be a modern intrusion." (p.38) If this statement refers to the 1932 excavations, it can only apply to "Pit 4", which was a relatively modern ditch or trench, clearly visible in the bank profile. A careful reading of the levels, however, shows its top edge to lie 2.03 m. below the surface, and since the general summary, on pp. 39–40, gives the following deposit thicknesses : Humus, .60 m. ; Subhumus, .80 m. ; Culture level, .65 m. ; Pit level, .35 m. ; the top edge of even this modern ditch would appear to fall at the boundary between our Culture level and Pit level, or Levels II and III.

We could recognize no other pits or clear-cut disturbances above Pit level. It was from Level III that all the pits opened, including 4 circular pits containing hearths, two of which were demonstrably late and the other two apparently so. I now believe that everything above this division between Levels II and III represents disturbance.

(b)   Also on page 38 we wrote, "The culture dirt was made up of musty earth with admixture of ashes, refuse, and cultural material, as well as a graded portion of the original loess which lessened steadily toward the base of the humus, where it disappeared entirely. This suggests that the land has been under cultivation from the end of the actual house occupation."

On page 39, "Culture level: representing that accumulation of debris which took place after the abandonment of the area as a dwelling site. The irregularly distributed burnt layer within it identified fire destruction of the superstructure, which was further evidenced by ashes. It may have been partly built up by cultivation subsequent to the period of occupation." Here and there there were small patches of burnt earth, usually quite fragmentary, and there were also occasional small smears or pockets of ash. There was not enough, however, to justify these as an irregularly distributed burnt layer representing fire destruction of a superstructure. The phenomenon may well have been the remains of fires that served other purposes during later times.

(c)   The photograph of the bank exposure of Pit 5, Plate VIb, (opposite page 40) clearly shows the cross-section of Pit 5B which was cut into Pit 5A from above, and which obviously must be later. What is significant here is that the top of 5B was planed off by the lower edge of a disturbance that apparently cut away at least a part of the top of 5A at the same time. The depth of Pit 5B is given as .65 – .68 m., in our measured field drawing. If we take this as our scale and measure to the bottom of Pit 5A as shown in the photograph, we get a total figure of 1.95 m. as against 1.99 m. which is the sum of the thicknesses of the lower deposits as given on page 40. Since the total depth from the surface to the bottom of 5A adds up to 4.04 m., and since the sum of the depths to the top of the pit level (III), is 2.05 m., the planing off of the tops of Pits 5A and 5B obviously falls at the boundary between our so-called Culture and Pit levels (II and III), whatever may have been the process that disturbed and mixed the deposits of what is now Level II. This is also in conformity with one of my own field notes.

Pit 5B yielded very few sherds, among them some small mediaeval or perhaps Bronze Age coarse wares. They are too small to be closely identifiable, but they are certainly not Neolithic. In the drawing of the cross-section made in 1932 a thin layer, visible in the photograph, which overlay Pit 5B is labeled as Pit Level, but this is obviously a mistake, for Pit 5B is patently post-Neolithic and "Pit Level" is generally agreed upon as representing the Neolithic occupation. If not Neolithic, this overlying layer must have been later than the pit level, and was certainly the "culture level" which planed off the top of 5B. Furthermore, the sharply cut sloping walls of 5B, which widens at its base, are markedly similar to the remains of a pit in the bank as it existed in 1969. Excavation of this pit yielded unmistakable Hallstatt pottery in considerable quantity. This Hallstatt pit in turn was clearly covered by the highly recognizable Level II of our 1969 and 1970 excavations. Level II also covered a pit in 1969 Trench II in which a couple of Hallstatt sherds appeared.

(d)   Level II of 1969 and 1970 was marked by small flecks of a white substance identified as calcium carbonate, and equally small flecks of burnt earth and occasional bits of charcoal. This lay over the area to the north and west of the 1932 excavation and appeared somewhat more erratically in the sounding trenches to the south. No disturbances or pits earlier than Roman times penetrated it, nor were there any identifiable remains of habitation within it.

The identification of Level II with the Culture Level of 1932 seems definite, by virtue of their relative positions. In our initial description of an "ashy" culture level, we apparently interpreted the calcium carbonate bits as ash. Furthermore, the statement (p. 41) that in undisturbed parts it was purely Neolithic seems also in error. One must remember that, although the material from the site as a whole is predominantly Neolithic, in no way could we isolate or describe such "pure" areas. There was of course an uneven distribution of material which obviously represented concentrations that had been disturbed by cultivation but had apparently not been carried too far from where they had initially been deposited.

(e)   As in the area 275 m. north of the excavations, where modern brick was recovered in Level 10 of Trench B (1932) at a depth of 1.60 m., in the main excavation relatively late material occurred sporadically to the top of Level III, or Pit Level, appearing even in the deposit directly over Pit 5.

(f)   In the upper levels there were few if any sherds that could be joined unless they were found together or immediately adjacent either horizontally or above or below each other. For the most part these seem to be merely large sherds broken up by secondary disturbance. In no case, however, did such matchings yield a relatively complete vessel, as should have been the case in a reasonably closed context. Sherds representing whole profiles did occur, but really reconstructible, as opposed to restorable fragments were found primarily on the burnt deposit in Pit 5A. The painted pedestalled bowl from Pit 6 (Plate XIII), for example, was made up of several fragments from one side only and was clearly only a large fragment that was subsequently further broken.

It is for these reasons that I interpret Level II as a horizon of cultivation that planed off the upper part of the Neolithic settlement accumulation and mixed it with later earth and deposits. Because of its position above Pit 5B and over two pits containing Hallstatt material recognized in 1969, and because it seems to have been penetrated by at least three pits containing Roman material, it seems logical to date this disturbance as post-Hallstatt, possibly between Hallstatt and Roman times, possibly even later, whereas Level I, or subhumus, seems relatively modern.

Since the houses of the village lie well back of the presumed Neolithic settlement area, which is now cultivated or is unused except as a source of loess and sand, it seems highly likely that a somewhat similar pattern existed during post-Neolithic periods, and that these Hallstatt, Roman, mediaeval and other disturbances lay well outside of their various contemporary settlements.

The main location of the Neolithic settlement seems probably to have been on the lower slope because this was the area of heaviest concentration of Neolithic material, because the line of pits which were uncovered here in 1932 lay in a band along mid-slope with no further early disturbance of the loess behind them, because of the relatively high occurrence of animal bones and the presence of fish bones, and because of the possibly analogous positions of the Starčevo settlements at Padina and Lepenski Vir. This statement, however, applies only to this central area, for Pit 3 in 1932 Trench B, 275 m. to the northeast, was on the upper flatland, and some pits in the private land to the south (1969–70) were on the upper slope and on the edge of the upper plain. It is, of course, impossible to tell whether the Neolithic settlement at Starčevo extended further out on the lower plain but, in view of the periodic flooding and its presumed marshy character, this seems unlikely.

Furthermore, if one observes today's daily drives of cattle and pigs from the courtyards of the village along the main streets and down the cross streets to the lower plain, and sees how they churn up the Banat gumbo mud after even the lightest rain, the lack of any recognizable stratification in Level III, the presumed Neolithic occupation level, becomes predictable and explicable.

From what has been said it thus seems clear that above Level III we are dealing with a stratification of disturbance, and that even within Level III, the constant mixing of the soil during wet periods pretty well obviates the possibility of recognizing any stratification within it.

(3)   The question of house remains, as described on p. 41, has over the years become increasingly dubious.

(a)   First, I am now convinced that our statement that traces of postholes were distinctly recognizable is completely in error and is my own fault. During Fewkes' absence with the School I was completely in charge of the excavation. While cleaning the surface of the yellow loess approximately 1000 small dark circular spots were revealed. As we emptied each one, many curved away or joined underground tunnels and were promptly recognized as animal holes. However, some seemed to go straight down and tended to run in consecutive strings or circles, often at the peripheries of the pits, the insides of which were riddled with burrows.

With hindsight I realize that these should have been sectioned, which I did not do. Although Fewkes and Fiker had severe reservations (Miss Goldman had been called home), for the preliminary report at least these were retained as postholes as a courtesy to me. In 1961, in the excavation at Homolka (Ehrich and Pleslova-Štikova 1968) we came across a small area with similar circular chains of holes which proved to be burrows in an area of what might have been a heap of grain or a spot used for threshing. At Starčevo a few such holes appeared at the edge of the pit in Trench A 1969, and others perforated a Roman period hearth, where they looked like flue holes. In both cases, however, sectioning showed clearly that they were animal holes. This, together with the uniform size of all the holes, both recognizable animal burrows and presumed postholes that we found in 1932, pretty well eliminates them from consideration.

b)   The function of the pits as house foundations, although a usual interpretation, now seems to me to be very doubtful. They are of no consistent shape. Some of them are roughly circular (*e.g.* Pits 6 A,B, and C) while others (7,8,9) are long, shallow, wandering and irregular. Since no postholes can be attributed to them and, since in none of them was a true hearth found (the burnt level in the upper part of 5A seems more probably the result of a special function such as pottery firing), I am now inclined to view them as probably borrow pits for earth or loess, to construct or daub houses elsewhere, or to supply material for pottery making. The pits from Bylany in Czechoslovakia (Soudský 1960: 11; Tringham 1971: 119, Fig. 20a), were clearly associated with the long post houses typical of the Linear Bandkeramik culture. Furthermore, the shapes of the pits, particularly 5A, are quite different from the quadrilateral and trapezoidal house forms found at some other Starčevo and Körös sites. It seems more than likely that any possible traces of actual houses, either as postholes or as mud or brick construction, had completely disappeared. Although some of the smaller, rounder pits could have been inside of houses, there is no convincing evidence that they were.

(4)   On page 43, the discussion of the graves raises some questions also. Of the three Neolithic graves, two are correctly placed in the Pit Level. These were in Trench B 1932, a sounding north of the main excavation. The third, described as occurring in the culture level, was found in 1931 when no distinction between culture level and pit level was made. If Fewkes was correct in thinking it to be Neolithic, then it almost certainly must have been in the lower part of this culture-bearing stratum or pit level. If of a very late post-Neolithic period, it might have been in Level II. The burial we thought Dubovac is actually Roman in date and is so catalogued and exhibited in the National Museum. The LaTène skeletal burial might possibly have been in Level II, and that labeled Vatin might also have belonged there if the building up of Level II began in Hallstatt times. It seems more probable, however, that the Vatin grave penetrated some irregularity in the top of Level III. At this time I am more inclined to think that Level II represents a stratum of cultivation in which the LaTène grave and the large burial urn found in 1931 might possibly have been laid, and that the Vatin cinerary burial actually intruded into Level III as the others may have. Since surface erosion or disturbance may well have caused the interface between Levels II and III to be quite irregular, one simply cannot be too definite on this point.

Other considerations

My present interpretation of the site of Starčevo is that only Level III represents the niveau of Neolithic occupation. Within it, because of the consistency, churning, and periodic flooding by the Danube, no internal stratigraphy could be discerned. In Level II the rather uniform distribution of the highly recognizable calcium carbonate white flecks, tiny bits of red burned earth or plaster, and the absence of any units within it (except for intrusions from above) all indicate a post-Neolithic period of cultivation. The relative sparsity of later material would indicate that the area lay well away from the contemporary settlements, while the high proportion of Neolithic material would simply represent the disturbance of the underlying deposit of Level III. In our 1933 report (p.43) we made the comment that much of the area at one time or another was probably under vineyard cultivation, as was a tract close by. It is highly suggestive in this regard that, writing on Dalj, Hoffiller in *Corpus Vasorum Antiquorum Yugoslavia* 2, (Zagreb 2, III, VIc, page 2) mentions the deep working of the vineyard areas to renew them after the devastation wrought by Phylloxera which, according to the *Encyclopedia Britannica,* had spread throughout Europe by 1885. He also refers to similar deep working at Sarvaš, in 1890–95 (*Ibid.* II, VIc, p. 1). This could account for the depth and condition of Level I (our subhumus).

When we come to the question of the purported periodization of the material from Starčevo, I can see no clearcut demonstration in the results of our 1932 excavations. If, as I believe, the pits do not represent house foundations and their contents are not living accumulations but simply backfill deposited during the Neolithic occupation, any attempt to develop a horizontal stratigraphy for the culture on the basis of a relatively small area is risky in the extreme, while the contents of the two layers of the fill of Pit 5A do not show any marked differences or cultural change that would indicate a long period of occupation. While there may have been some slight internal chronology originally visible during the neolithic occupation of the site, the depredations of the brickmakers, the churning of the soil mentioned above, and other disturbances which would have brought sherds from the deeper into the upper levels, effectively obliterated any such evidence for phasal differences, if indeed it did exist.

Since M. Garašanin (1971: 76) equates D. Garašanin's IIa with Milojčić Phase II, and her IIb with Milojčić III, and her III with Milojčić IV, in both instances we are dealing with a fourfold division. Citing D. Garašanin (*Ibid.* 79), he stresses his statement that no sherds with spiral decoration occurred in any of the closed units at Starčevo, and then argues that the final or fourth phase, characterized by spiral ornament, is later than the pits and partially overlaps the appearance of Vinča A.

I consider his interpretation to be erroneous. Although sherds with complete spiral patterns are lacking in the pit assemblages, there are several which bear parts of curvilinear designs that apparently are from spiral or spiraloid patterns. These range from those that strike me as convincing through varying degrees of probability. Twelve of these sherds are from Pit 5A, four from Pit 6, and two possible ones from Pit 7. Since three of these are labeled as from the Upper Level of Pit 5A, and two from the top of Pit 6, any statement that these five sherds are from closed units would be questionable. The closed find status of the others, however, seems clear. Those not inventoried in the collection of the National Museum carry our field inventory numbers.

Thus, in reconsidering the 1932 excavations at Starčevo, we find painted wares occurring in every pit, and no evidence of an earlier pre-painted pottery phase. Likewise, there seems to be sufficient reason to discard the notion that no spiral or spiraloid decorated sherds occurred in the pits, and that spirals and spiraloids thus necessarily serve as a diagnostic of a final later phase which overlaps with Vinča A. This leaves us with only two of the Milojčić-Garašanin phases. In spite of the disturbances in the ground, I can see no evidence for more than one of these phases at Starčevo, at least in the area under discussion.

Limitations of time and space unfortunately preclude a detailed treatment of other pertinent sites of the Starčevo-Körös–Cris complex in this essay. Furthermore, it is far better to refrain from analyzing the impact of what I have said here on the interpretation of this wider sphere, at least until I can include the results of the 1969–70 campaigns, which I have not yet thoroughly digested.

My current view is that to date there is no satisfactory evidence from other sites in Yugoslavia, Hungary, Rumania and Bulgaria that warrants a division of the culture complex as a whole into more than two major periods. At any site, of course, minor changes may occur during a major period, but I see these as purely of idiosyncratic or local significance, perhaps of some use in a step-by-step construction of a relative chronology, but of no general cultural import. If this be correct, as I firmly believe it is, we can divide the whole Starčevo-Körös-Cris complex into Early and Later periods, with the area excavated at Starčevo itself, in 1928, 1931 and 1932, belonging to the Later Period.

The following highly consistent radiocarbon determinations on animal bones from different assemblages and on human bones from the two close-lying Neolithic graves in Trench A, 1932, are suggestive. These dates were furnished by Dr. W.G. Mook of the Laboratorium voor Algemene Naturkunde of the Rijksuniversiteit at Groningen, and are reported according to the standard 5570 ± 30 half life, with 1950 as the reference year. Further adjustments to correct for a half life of 5730 ± 40, plus calibration for the variation in C14 formation as indicated by the bristlecone pine data, would make them approximately 800 years older. The only inconsistent determination is derived from potsherds with a carbon content that was almost certainly too low for accuracy. Comparatively, apart from this exception, they accord well with results of Late Starčevo date.

GrN	6626	Starčevo	1	(bones)	6610 ± 65	BP
GrN	6627	Starčevo	2	(bones)	6545 ± 105	BP
GrN	6628	Starčevo	3	(sherds)	7615 ± 50	BP
GrN	6629	Starčevo	4	(bones)	6615 ± 65	BP
GrN	7154	Starčevo	5	(Human bones)	6610 ± 100	BP
GrN	7155	Starčevo	6	(bones)	6835 ± 70	BP

Concluding remarks

In view of some of the misconceptions regarding the site of Starčevo, many of which stem from errors in the earlier reporting of the site, and in view of the importance attached to it, I have tried to set the record straight. The initial excavations of 1928, 1931 and 1932 were of both an exploratory and a salvage character. From the original nature of the site and from the subsequent disturbance, any incontrovertible evidence for multiple phases, even if they had originally existed, would seem impossible to document. I regard the site as having represented a relatively modest settlement that was probably of fairly brief duration in the Late Starčevo period.

I have given a short history of the research at Starčevo itself and of some of the misinterpretations that were subsequently based on them; I have pointed out some of our own errors and mistakes, as embodied in our preliminary report. With further digestion of the Starčevo data and with new published results of other excavations, I may very well modify some of the things I have said here. However, this seems to me to be an appropriate occasion on which to put my current views on the record, and to explain why I hold them.

Acknowledgements

I am indebted to Ann M.H. Ehrich and H. Arthur Bankoff for critical readings and suggestions.

References cited

Arandjelović-Garašanin, D.
    1954   See Garašanin, D.
Ehrich, Robert W.
    1954   The Relative Chronology of Southeastern and Central Europe in the Neolithic Period. In Relative
            Chronologies in Old World Archeology. R.W. Ehrich. Ed. Pp. 108–129. University of Chicago
            Press.
Ehrich, Robert W., and Emilie Pleslová-Štiková
    1968   Homolka. An Eneolithic site in Bohemia. American School of Prehistoric Research, Peabody
            Museum, Harvard University. Bulletin No. XXIV. Monumenta Archeologica XVI, Prague.
Fewkes, J.V.
    1936   Neolithic Sites in the Morava-Danubian Area (Yugoslavia). American School of Prehistoric Research
            Bulletin 12: 5–82.
    1937   Neolithic Sites in the Yugoslavian Portion of the Lower Danubian Valley. Proceedings of the American
            Philosophical Society LXXVIII : 329–402.
    1939   Report on the 1938 Summer Term of the School. American School of Prehistoric Research Bulletin
            15: 6–12.
Fewkes, Vladimir J. ; Goldman, Hetty; and Ehrich, Robert W.
    1933   Excavations at Starčevo, Yugoslavia. American School of Prehistoric Research, Bulletin 9: 33-54.
Garašanin, D.
    1954   Starčevačka Kultura. Univerza v Ljubljana, Arheološki Seminar. Ljubljana.
Garašanin, Milutin
    1971   Genetische und Chronologische Probleme des frühkeramischen Neolithikums auf dem mittleren Balkan.
            Actes du VIIIe Congrès des Sciences préhistoriques et protohistoriques. Tome première. Beograd.
Gaul, J.H.
    1948   The Neolithic Period in Bulgaria. American School of Prehistoric Research, Bulletin 16.
Grbić, Miodrag
    1930   Bemalte Keramik aus Starčevo im Banater Donaugeländer – Jugoslavien. Odbitka z Ksiega Pamiatkowa
            ku czci Prof. Dr. Włodzimierza Demetrykiewicza. (Bibljoteka prehistoryczna, Poznan).
Hoffiller, Victor
    1938   Corpus Vasorum Antiquorum. Yougoslavie 2. Zagreb – Musée National – Fasc. 2.
Kutzián, Ida
    1944,   The Körös Culture. Dissertationes Pannonicae. Ser. II, no. 33. Budapest. Plates, 1944; Text, 1947.
    1947
Letica, Zagorka
    1968   Starčevo and Körös Culture at Vinča. Archaeologia Iugoslavica IX: 11–18.
Milojčić, Vladimir
    1949   Chronologie der jüngeren Steinzeit Mittel – und Sudosteuropas. Berlin: Gebr. Mann.
    1950   Körös – Starčevo – Vinča. Reinecke Festschrift. Gustav Behrens and Joachim Werner, Eds. Mainz.
            Pp. 108–117.
Soudský, Bohumil
    1960   Station néolithique de Bylany: résultats historiques préliminaires des six premières campagnes des
            fouilles. Historica II. Pp. 5–36. Praha.
Tringham, Ruth
    1971   Hunters, Fishers and Farmers of Eastern Europe: 6000–3000 B.C. Hutchinson University Library:
            London.

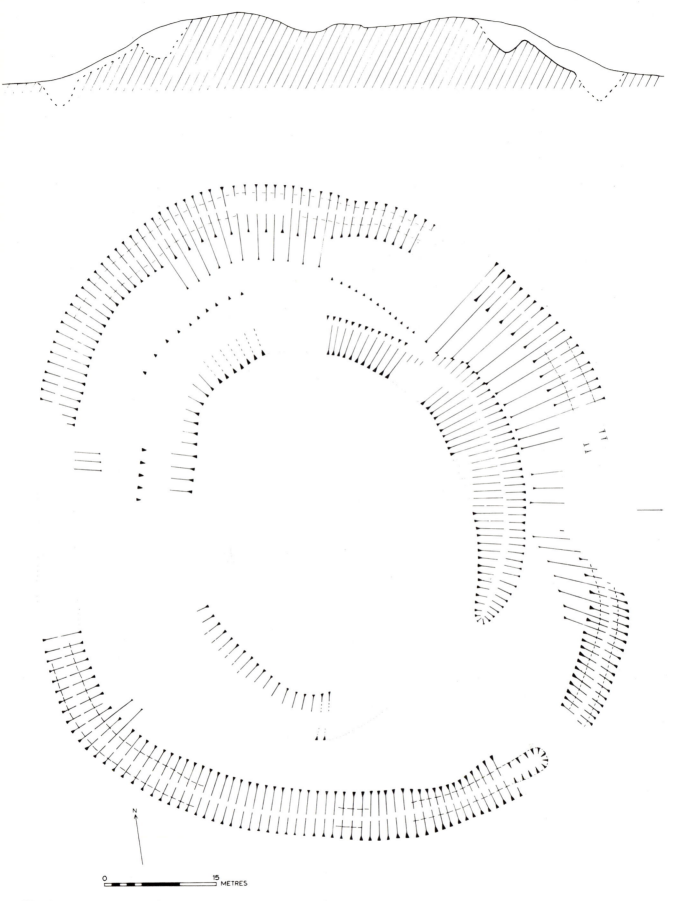

FIG 1.   *Ground plan of First phase of Settlement*

THE IRON AGE - EARLY CHRISTIAN SETTLEMENT AT KNOWTH, CO. MEATH, IRELAND
by George Eogan

For Irish archaeology an event of outstanding importance took place in the Summer of 1932. At that time the Harvard Archaeological Expedition in Ireland commenced their investigations with the excavation of a crannog (No. 1) in the townland of Ballinderry, county Westmeath. The Director of the Expedition was Hugh O'Neill Hencken and excavation was carried out at sites in all of the four provinces. The work of the Expedition made a tremendous contribution to Irish archaeological studies. Modern excavating techniques were applied and large and complex sites were investigated. Furthermore, the work in the field was followed up with the prompt publication of comprehensive reports. Indeed, the Harvard Expedition marked the beginning of modern archaeological research in Ireland.

The Expedition excavated for five consecutive seasons, 1932-1936. During that time excavations were carried out at fifteen sites that ranged in date from the Stone Age to Early Christian times. Amongst these were notable and spectacular sites such as Creevykeel but probably the most notable of all was the great crannog (lake dwelling) at Lagore close to the village of Dunshaughlin in county Meath. This was truly a remarkable site, it was the first crannog to be noted in Ireland back in 1839 when a number of artifacts were discovered. Hugh Hencken's excavation took place in 1934-36 and his work produced a wealth of information about virtually every aspect of Early Christian Ireland. But, in addition, the site was well-documented in the early Irish literature, in fact it was the capital of the Kingdom of Deiscert Brega (Hencken 1950 with a section on the history of the site by Liam Price).

For some years past excavations have been in progress at another site in Co. Meath about twelve miles to the north as the crow flies from Lagore. This is Knowth (Eogan 1968 with a section on the history of the site by F. J. Byrne; 1973; 1974). The hill of Knowth was used by man on many occasions. During the neolithic period a cemetery of passage graves was constructed there. Amongst these is a huge mound that covers up to an acre and a half. It is about 10 m in height and it covers two massive passage graves (Site 1). Subsequently occupation took place on the site by Beaker, Celtic and Norman peoples. During Early Christian times there were parallels between Knowth and Lagore. Although differing in environment - Knowth was a dry-land site; Lagore a wet-land site - both became prominent occupation sites during the latter half of the 1st millennium A.D. They were also important political centres, Knowth was apparently the 'capital' of the Kingdom of northern Brega; Lagore was the 'capital' of the Kingdom of southern Brega. Although the dynastic families were of the Síl nAedo Sláine and therefore cousins they were, nevertheless, rivals. There are similarities between the material culture from both sites. Indeed, the study and interpretation of the Late Celtic settlement at Knowth is benefiting considerably from the Lagore results. It is, therefore, a pleasure to offer this preliminary account of 1st millennium A.D. Knowth as a tribute to Hugh Hencken's achievements at Lagore and in gratitude of his wider work in Irish archaeology.

As the excavations are still in progress the following account is based on partial evidence and views put forward are only tentative and subject to modification as the excavations proceed. The excavations have been in progress since 1962. They are financed by State Grants administered through the National Parks and Monuments Branch, Office of Public Works, Dublin on the recommendation of the National Committee for Archaeology of the Royal Irish Academy. Financial assistance has also been given by University College, Dublin. The writer wishes to record his gratitude to these bodies and also numerous individuals who have assisted in many ways. In the preparation of this paper and also for assistance in the field over a number of years he is particularly grateful to Mr Barra Boydell. Thanks are also due to Miss Catherine Daly for assistance and especially for preparing the plans which form Figs. 1 and 2.

The Settlement

This took place on and close to the large mound (Site 1) which was built by the passage grave people during the 3rd millennium B.C. Two main structural phases have been determined. The first is characterised by fosses; the second by souterrains and evidence of occupation.

The first phase (FIG. 1). The summit was enclosed by two penannular ditches placed concentric to each other. The outer fosse was at the base of the mound and its outer edge was only a short distance in from the kerbstones. It was dug through the edge of the mound and it penetrated the subsoil to an average depth of 1.7 m. On the inside the side of the mound was cut back and this created a formidable scarp 6 m in maximum height. The mean average depth of the fosse was 2.8 m and in width it was 5.8 m. The inner fosse surrounded the top of the mound. This reached its maximum dimensions on the eastern side where it was 3 m in depth and 6 m in width at the mouth. An undug causeway on the south-eastern side provided an entrance. As yet no evidence for a gateway, or other features around the entrance, have come to light. Neither is there any evidence for banks. There is no evidence as to how, or where, the material from the inner fosse was disposed of. At the base, on the outside of the fosse, a layer of material that must have been derived from the outer fosse overlies primary slip. It is possible that a bank stood there and that it was levelled out as a result of subsequent activity.

The reason for digging the fosses, and the time that they were dug, has not yet been established. On structural grounds the site could be compared to a large ring-fort, or even a small hill-fort, although hillforts in the eastern half of Ireland only have a single fosse (Raftery 1972: 40-44). However, on analogous evidence for both hill-forts and ring-forts it appears that the ditches were dug so as to create a fortified or well-protected prestigious habitation site. One could assume that a house, or houses, stood in the centre but as this area was removed, possibly early in the last century, no such evidence survived. Due to the nature of the mound construction considerable slip should have taken place soon after the digging of the fosses and unless the ditches were kept cleared out they would soon have become fairly ineffective.

Dating is difficult. Stratigraphically the fosses are earlier than the second phase. In addition two objects that provide slight help with dating have been found low down in the fill of the inner fosse. One of these is a rim sherd of Class E ware (Thomas 1959); the other is a single-edged bone comb with curved back and dot and circle ornament. Combs of this form may have forerunners in the Iron Age. An example was found at Lagore, an old find (Hencken 1950: 189, Fig. 102A) and combs of similar shape have been found in Britain in Anglo-Saxon contexts (Laing 1975: 301). The site has produced other finds which can be assigned to a pre-8th century date but this is based on type, not on their stratigraphical position. Three bronze items are in the Roman tradition. These are what may be an ear scoop and two varieties of "spoons" (*ligulae*?) (cf. Brailsford 1964: 11). Two sherds of Roman pottery have also been found. Both are sherds of Terra Sigillata bowls of Dragendorff form 37 (Eogan 1968: 375). There are in addition three bronze penannular brooches with zoomorphic terminals. One, with its simple terminals, is an early variety (e.g. Kilbride-Jones 1937, Fig. 29). The other two are later. One has an enamel setting. A melon bead was also found and while this might also be pre-8th century this is difficult to establish (Eogan 1968: 375; Hencken 1950: 136).

In addition to the foregoing there are nine inhumation burials with grave goods (Eogan 1968: 365-73; 1974, 68-87, with one subsequent addition). These graves were outside the mound but not far from its base. The remains were in simple pit graves and they were flexed. The persons buried varied in age and in sex and the orientation was inconsistent. The grave-goods also varied. They include conical stone objects (Raftery 1969: 79-82), bone dice (Clarke 1970), bone "gaming pieces", blue glass beads, bone beads, and bronze rings. These objects could have been in use during the pagan Iron Age.

It is difficult to get an overall picture of this first phase but it can be suggested that during the early centuries A.D. a group of people, or probably a prominent family, took over the main mound at Knowth and transformed it into a well-protected settlement site. The people who were buried with grave goods might have been some of the inhabitants. If they were then it can be taken that they played board games, that they wore personal ornaments such as necklaces of glass beads, armlets of glass beads and bone beads; the bronze rings could have been finger rings. Adding to this the isolated finds of penannular brooches, bone comb and *ligulae* (?) it appears that personal adornment was a feature of the inhabitants. The presence of ditches indicates that whoever organised their digging had considerable command of labour and from the size of the ditches it appears that the site was intended as a place of prominent settlement. The earliest literary references are to Gormgal, son of Eladach, who was King of Knowth and died in 788. Gormgal was not of the Uí Néill but of an old population group, the Gailenga. Before about 800 it appears that Knowth was in the hands of the Gailenga (Byrne *In* Eogan 1968: 397).

The Second phase (FIG. 2). In contrast to the first the second phase was an unprotected settlement. The evidence for settlement during the second phase is also much more extensive. To-date the remains of at least nine houses have been discovered. All appear to have been rectangular. Evidence for stone walls survived in four examples. It has not been established how high these stood originally, perhaps they were just foundations. There is not enough stone lying around at the other house sites to form walls neither were the remains of other material, such as sods or mud, found. It would, therefore, appear that the walls were made from wood or at least a framework of posts with say straw or hay in between. Apart from House B no definite post-holes were found but this can be due to the fact that the houses were constructed over the fill of the ditches and it would be impossible to recover post holes in the soft fill. A reasonable amount of daub was found a short distance downhill from House H. This must have come from a wattle and daub structure, possibly even from the walls of House H. Houses C, E, H, I had paved floors over which there was a layer of occupation debris and the shape of the houses can be determined from the paving. Remains of paving were found at Houses D, F and G. House I lacked a paved floor, in fact there was no evidence for a floor of any sort, but there was a definite layer of occupation debris. In House C there were two main layers of occupation. These layers were separated from each other by a layer of sterile silt-like material implying that the house was abandoned for a time. At the other house occupation appears to have been continuous.

House A. At the time of publication it was not certain if this was a house site (Eogan 1968: 359-61). Further investigations in this area indicate that the features constitute a house site and they have also caused a modification

FIG 2.   Ground plan of Second phase of Settlement.   ho. = House S. = Souterrain

in the published interpretation. The evidence for a house was provided by the layer of dark occupation material that consisted of a mixture of ashes and charcoal. Small scraps of bone were mixed through the material. This layer covered a roughly rectangular area approximately 5.6 m in length and 4 m in width. On the northern side the edge of the layer was irregular. There was a fire-place near the north-eastern end. This was defined by a mixed deposit of ash and charcoal. Initially the fire-place was unprotected but subsequently a stone setting for the purpose of delimiting the fire was laid down. The stones were set on three sides of a rectangle, the south-eastern side was left open. Internally the setting measured 60 cm by 30 cm. Outside the setting on the south-western side there were a few loose stones. Artifacts from the occupation layer consisted of a gilt bronze buckle, a bronze and an iron stick pin with biconical heads, a bone pin with unexpanded head, four bone objects of uncertain use, two one-edged iron knives and two flint scrapers.

In the published report references were made to layers of ash in the ditch fill (Eogan 1968: 359, Fig. 6, Sections 11-12).Subsequent excavation has established that these are earlier than the House A. In fact they represent three earlier stages of activity at the same place. These are fire places but there was no evidence for associated occupation, indeed the purpose of the fires has not been determined. In each instance after the fire had gone out of use earth had accumulated over it.

On the eastern side of the large mound (Site 1) overlying both the inner and outer fosses there is evidence for intensive occupation. This consists of areas of paving, isolated fire pits and a minimum of six houses (B-G). The evidence for House B, which overlies the inner ditch, is not comprehensive but it appears to have consisted of a wooden structure that was burnt down. Overlying paving shows that the area was subsequently used. Most of the evidence for houses comes from the base of the mound. The incomplete remains of House C consists of a unifaced wall on the northern and western sides. This is 60 cm in maximum height and the corner is rounded. The paved floor at present measures 6 m by 5 m. The finds, which date from the first phase of use, included portion of a Viking type weighing scales. This house predates Souterrain 5 as part of the chamber protrudes into it on the western side and it was probably the souterrain builders who destroyed portion of the house.

The remains of House D consist of two short walls 2m and 1.40 m in length respectively. These stumps run north-south and east-west. There is an inturn on the north-south wall and this may be part of an entrance feature. There was also an area of paving. Overlying this and the floor of the house generally, there was a spread of charcoal. There was also a hearth. Animal bones over the floor included cow and lamb or kid. Carbonised grass and straw with carbonised grains (wheat?) mixed through it also turned up. This and the charcoal spread suggests that the house could have been burnt down, the straw being either part of the roof or floor matting. However, the large amount of grain suggests that grain may have been roasted in the house. The construction of souterrain 5 damaged the house.

At the southern end of this area of settlement there were at least three houses and these occurred in stratigraphical order.

House E was the earliest so far uncovered in this particular area. Parts of two side walls survived. The southern one was 3.80 m long; the western 3.75 m. Most of the interior that survived had a floor of small cobbles. There was an area of burning and some flags beside it, possibly a hearth. There was a charcoal spread over the floor and the charred remains of beams could also be traced. The remains of straw were also present. It would appear that this house was burnt down, the straw coming either from the roof or a matting.

This house was no longer functioning when Houses F and G were constructed.

Only portion of one side wall, a well defined hearth and some paving was all that survived of House F. This was overlain by House G.

The walls of House G survived on the south and north ends, 2.20 m and 2 m long respectively. The hearth had side stones and paving in the base. It was centrally placed in relation to the side walls. This gave the house an external width of 3.25 m. If the hearth was centrally placed in relation to the house as a whole it would have been about 4 m long externally.

House H. Excavation is still in progress but the remains appear to be those of a rectangular structure approximately 4.20 m long by 3 m wide. There was a fire place.

House I was 15.50 m long and slightly under 5 m in width. Near the centre on the south-eastern side there was a hearth. The base of this was formed by a prominent flagstone. A souterrain (No. 10) was associated with this house and the inhabitants also had access to the western passage grave. Finds from the layer of occupation debris included bronze ringed and stick pins of different types; iron knives, needles, part of a horse bridle bit and a buckle; bone combs, pins and needle; fragments of jet bracelets; disc-shaped quern stones and grindstones (Eogan 1974, 87-110).

Other evidence of occupation

In the fill of the ditches, particularly the inner ditch, there is considerable evidence for occupation. This is provided by occupation debris, isolated fire places and areas of paving. Further excavation may yield additional house plans.

Souterrains

Souterrains 1 and 2 are similar in plan and in structure. Both are drystone built and they consist of a straight passage that averages a little over 3 m in length and 60 m in width. The passage was roofed with lintels. The beehive-shaped chambers average 2 m in diameter and 1 m in height.

Souterrain No. 3 had suffered fairly intensive damage, nearly all the capstones of the passage had been removed and portion of the chamber had been destroyed. The meandering passage is 21 m in overall length. There is also a lateral passage 4m long. The chamber measured about 2.50 m in length by 2.10 m in width. A fragment of a jet bracelet was the only find.

There was a complex of five souterrains on the eastern side (Nos. 4-8) and in addition the Eastern passage grave was incorporated into the complex. As was the case with the western passage grave a dry-stone built passage was built more or less on the line of the original tomb passage. There must have been a sequence of souterrain building but apart from establishing that Souterrain 7 is later than Souterrain 4 a sequence of construction has not otherwise been established. The short drystone passage already mentioned gave access to the tomb but also to Souterrains 4 and 5.

Souterrains 4 and 6 are beehive structures with straight passage. No. 6 was previously investigated (Roe *In* Macalister 1943: 141-49). The roof of the chamber had collapsed. The chamber was 3.50 m in diameter and the passage 4 m in length and averaged 1 m in width. Souterrain 4 is intact. Its passage is 5.30 m in length. The chamber is about 2.70 m in diameter and 1.80 m in height. Souterrain 5 is the largest of the complexes being 28 m in overall length. It is L-shaped and it was built on the side of the mound. There is a small chamber at the base of the mound. The lower part of the passage extends along the base of the mound and links up with Souterrain 4 and the tomb passage. Souterrain 7 consists of a curved passage, part of which is missing, and a circular chamber. On the eastern side, about 4 m in from the entrance there is a small recess. Only the basal portion of the chamber survives, it was probably a beehive structure. Souterrains 4 and 5 produced a range of finds, including two 10th century Anglo-Saxon pennies from Souterrain 5 (Dolley, 1969).

The remains of the entrance portion of a souterrain passage (No. 8) was dug into House E and is therefore later. This may have linked up with the entrance to the main complex.

Souterrain 9 has a curved passage 10 m in length. It extends down the slope to a bee-hive shaped chamber 2.50 m in diameter. The roof of the chamber and parts of the passage had collapsed. The finds consisted of a few nondescript iron and bone pieces.

Souterrain 10 associated with House I, is a poorly built structure. The walls are of dry-stone with a lintelled roof. This souterrain consists of a main passage, 12.5 m in length and averaging 60 cm in width, and a small lateral passage. The digging of the outer ditch destroyed part of the passage of the western passage grave but the Early Christian occupants remodelled it. This largely consisted of the building of a dry stone, lintelled-roofed passage approximately on the line of the megalithic passage for a distance of about 2.50 m.

Farming

Grazing was widely practised as is shown by the quantities of animal bones that have been found. Amongst the animals represented were cattle, horse, pig and sheep. Corn must have been grown by the inhabitants. Grains (wheat?) and straw have come to light. Quern stones attest corn grinding. Horse bridle bits, made of iron, show that horses were harnessed.

Technology and industrial activity

Craftsmen worked in different media on the site.

Metal working.

Iron was smelted. This took place at the base of Site I on its northern side and overlying the outer ditch. The area was defined by an extensive spread of charcoal and iron slag, the main concentration of which was rectangular and measured 2m by 4m. The furnace did not survive but it appears to have been near the western end of the spread. In this area the concentration of charcoal was more pronounced and pieces of iron slag were mixed through it. In this part a large lump of slag and also some of the smaller pieces bore on one side the rounded impression of a furnace base. In addition there were pieces of rough clay which had been subjected to a high degree of heat. These could be fragments from a clay-lined furnace. Underneath this concentration there were two circular pits that averaged 1 m in diameter and 25 cm in depth. There was a narrow trench between these pits. This was 40 cm long and it might have served as an air flue. The fill of the pits consisted of charcoal and slag but near the bottom there were pieces of molten iron and burnt animal bones. Adjacent to the "furnace area", on its eastern side and extending over an area 2 m by 1.20 m there was a concentration of iron slag.

Fine metal-working and enamelling was carried out on the southern side of Site I and on the west of the slope. The principal area is defined by a spread of charcoal roughly circular and averaging 1.70 m. in diameter. The main concentration of charcoal was against, and spreading out from one face of a rectangular stone. This was set on edge and it measured 30 cm in length by 12 cm in height. It appears that the fire was kept burning in the area beside the stone. The finds consisted of two complete heating pans and a fragment of a third. These were made from clay and the largest, which is circular, is 5.5 cm in diameter. Parts of clay crucibles also turned up. These varied from one piece which consisted of more than half a crucible (30 mm in height, 33 mm in external mouth diameter) to small rim and body fragments. All appear to have been of the bag- or cup-shaped variety (Hencken 1950: 235-40).

Manufacture and decorating of metal objects. A wide range of iron and bronze artifacts were found on the site and it is very likely that some of these were made at Knowth. The heating pans indicate that bronze was worked. In addition the large heating-pan from the fine metal-working area contained considerable evidence for the use of enamelling. Traces of gold-working were also present. In addition grinding stones and stone hones have been discovered. These were probably used in finishing off the metal artifacts.

Some very fine metal objects were found but, of course, it cannot be proved that these were manufactured at Knowth. Amongst these is a bronze mount in the shape of a stylised bird. On the head there is a square plaque of light blue and yellow millefiori set into red enamel. The body is decorated with an elongated S curve in yellow enamel set in red enamel in champlevé manner. There are four square plaques of blue and yellow millefiori set in spaces round the S design. The tail is decorated in red enamel. The background for the red enamel is scored and this may also be the case for the yellow enamel. The mount was cast and the cells were afterwards worked by hand. The object was attached to a backing by projecting tongues and it was secured by transverse pegs through a hole in each tongue. Another fine piece is a buckle, probably gilt bronze. On one side there was a hinge which held a tongue and on the opposite side the tongue rested on a flattened expanded part of the surface. The decoration is on one face, it is worn but it included four stylised bird heads. The heads were set opposite to each other; two on the hinge side and two on the tongue rest side. On each side, between the birds there is a sunken panel decorated with an interlaced design (Eogan 1968, 359-61).

Stone working. Stone was worked on the site as unfinished quern stones, grinding stones and spindle whorls show.

Bone working. Pieces of bone that have been slightly utilized have been found. No partly complete artifact has, however, turned up.

Wood working. Positive evidence is lacking but it may be inferred from the presence of a hand gouge and the houses.

Costume, textiles and leather

Spindle whorls indicate that thread was spun. Apart from one example, the plano-convex variety cut from a femur, the others are made from stone. Nearly all of these are flat disc-shaped but the plano-convex or bowl-shaped variety is also present. Needles and awls, made from both iron and bone, have also been found. There is one elaborate bronze buckle (above) but iron buckles are also known. It is being assumed that these were from belts.

Tools and implements

As has been already shown the inhabitants had the use of specialist tools - awls, gouge, etc. - but other implements were also available. Foremost amongst these are tanged one edged iron knives with straight cutting edge.

Toilet articles

Combs are the commonest type. These are made from bone. The plates with the teeth and end plates, which are individual segments, are mounted between two strips which are held in position by rivets. Apart from one double-sided example all the combs are one-sided. Decoration usually occurs. This is confined to the binding strips. The principal motifs are long horizontal lines, short vertical and oblique lines and dot and circle motifs.

Miss Mairead Dunlevy has divided the Irish toilet combs into eight classes, A to H (unpublished but quoted in Eogan 1974: 99). Most of the Knowth combs fit into her Class F (late 9th to 12th century) and G (late 9th - early 10th to 13th century).

Personal adornment

A variety of objects of personal adornment were found. These items were made from bronze, iron, bone/antler, jet and glass.

Pins were the most common type and the ringed and stick varieties are present. The vast majority are of bronze but some are made from bone or antler.

The leading forms of ringed pin are those with baluster-shaped head and plain circular ring, polyhedral-shaped head on stem and kidney-shaped ring, crutch-shaped head on stem and stirrup-shaped ring, rolled over head and circular ring, and ring brooches (cf. Fanning 1969).

The most common form of stick pin has a swollen or somewhat biconical-shaped head with notches on the top. Ball-headed pins with sockets for settings are also fairly frequently found. Other types of bronze pins represented are bramble-headed pins, pin with expanded, sometimes mushroom-shaped head with radial grooves, frustum-headed, crutch-headed, faceted diamond-headed pin and kidney ring and skeumorph. Amongst the bone stick pins are examples with unexpanded head, with triangular head that is often perforated and cushion-headed pins (cf. Laing 1975: 324-31).

Jet bracelets with body of D-shaped cross-section were commonly worn. On occasion blue glass bracelets of D-shaped cross-section were worn. Some of these had a white inlay, either as dots or in the form of a "rope" pattern rather like examples from Lagore (Hencken 1950: 145-50, Fig. 70).

Glass beads suggest necklaces. Some of these are small and plain but the occasional elaborate example occurs such as a cable bead that consists of blue glass with flanges at each end. There are yellow knobs on the body and the 'cable' is a white inlay (cf. Hencken 1950: 137, Fig. 66: 125).

Remarks

Occupation during the second phase was much more intense than during the first. In addition the nature of the settlement was different, it was unprotected with souterrains. The structural remains (houses and souterrains) and the finds indicate that the settlement was an important one. It may also be postulated that a house, or houses, stood in the centre of the summit in the part that has been removed. Mixed farming and to a lesser extent industry formed the economic basis of the settlement which appears to have been largely self-contained. Inscriptions scratched on some orthostats of the western tomb of Site I shows that the inhabitants were literate and from at least the 10th century they made use of coins. Professor Byrne's researches have shown that the Kings of Brega lived at Knowth, indeed the title King of Brega and King of Knowth (Cnogba) was interchangeable. It has not been conclusively established that the Kings of Brega (northern) lived on the site that is currently under investigation but the range and nature of the material culture that is coming to light indicates that it was the site of their residence. According to documentary sources the Kings of Brega were living at Knowth from the 9th to the 11th century. It is interesting to note that this is also the date that, in the main, one would also apply to the second phase of the settlement on archaeological grounds. Some of the items, for instance Class G combs and kidney ring skeumorph pins, could have been in use later. Indeed, Celtic settlement may have continued down to near the end of the 12th century. At that time the site was taken over by the Normans.

References Cited

Brailsford, J. W.
    1964   Antiquities of Roman Britain, British Museum.
Clarke, D. V.
    1970   Bone Dice and the Scottish Iron Age. Proceedings of the Prehistoric Society 36: 214-32.
Dolley, Michael.
    1969   The Anglo-Saxon Pennies from the "Upper Souterrain" at Knowth. The British Numismatic Journal 38: 16-21.
Eogan, George.
    1968   Excavations at Knowth, Co. Meath, 1962-65, with historical note by F. J. Byrne. Proceedings of the Royal Irish Academy 66C: 299-400.
    1973   A Decade of Excavations at Knowth, Co. Meath. Irish University Review 3: 66-79.
    1974   Report on the Excavations of some Passage Graves, Unprotected Inhumation Burials and a Settlement Site at Knowth, Co. Meath. Proceedings of the Royal Irish Academy 74C: 11-112.

Fanning, Thomas.
    1969   The Bronze Ringed Pins in the Limerick City Museum. North Munster Antiquarian Journal 12:
            6-11.
Hencken, Hugh.
    1950   Lagore Crannog: An Irish Royal Residence of the 7th to 10th Centuries A.D. Proceedings of the
            Royal Irish Academy 53C: 1-247.
Kilbride-Jones, H. E.
    1937   The Evolution of Penannular Brooches with Zoomorphic Terminals in Great Britain and Ireland.
            Proceedings of the Royal Irish Academy 43C: 379-455.
Laing, Lloyd.
    1975   The Archaeology of Late Celtic Britain and Ireland c. 400-1200 A.D.   London.
Macalister, R. A. S.
    1943   Preliminary Report on the Excavations of Knowth, Co. Meath. Proceedings of the Royal Irish
            Academy 49C: 131-166.
Raftery, Barry.
    1969   Freestone Hill, Co. Kilkenny. Proceedings of the Royal Irish Academy 68C: 1-108.
    1972   Irish Hill-forts. In The Iron Age in the Irish Sea Province, Charles Thomas, Ed. Council for British
            Archaeology Research Report 9.
Thomas, Charles.
    1959   Imported Pottery in Dark Age Western Britian. Mediaeval Archaeology 3: 89-111.

BEITRÄGE ZU DEN VORGESCHICHTLICHEN BEZIEHUNGEN ZWISCHEN DEM SÜDOSTALPENGEBIET, DEM NORDWESTLICHEN BALKAN UND DEM SÜDLICHEN PANNONIEN IM 5. JAHRHUNDERT

by Mitja Guštin and Biba Teržan

Der Zeitraum des späten 6., des 5. und 4. Jahrhunderts ist im jugoslawischen Raum durch die zeitlich weit ausgedehnte späthallstättische Stufe -- Ha D 2/3 (nach mitteleuropäischer Terminologie) gekennzeichnet, die wenig erforscht ist, sowie kärgliches Fundmaterial aufweist und deshalb keine präzise Differenzierung der Zeithorizonte und der entsprechenden materiellen Kultur zuläßt.[1] Eine Ausnahme bildet die späthallstättische Gruppe in Slowenien,[2] in der das reichliche Gräbermaterial aus dieser Zeit die Einteilung in drei Zeithorizonte ermöglicht hat: den Horizont der Schlangenfibeln der zweiten Hälfte des 6. Jahrhunderts,[3] den Horizont der Certosafibeln der ersten Hälfte des 5. Jahrhunderts und den Horizont der Negauer Helme des späten 5. und des 4. Jahrhunderts.

Durch die Auswahl charakteristischer Gegenstände kann man in diesem Zeitraum bestimmte Strömungen zwischen Pannonien, Slowenien und dem nordwestlichen Balkan verfolgen, die einerseits durch die Erscheinung der skythischen Materialkultur in Ungarn bezeugt sind,[4] andererseits aber Ausdruck der schon angebahnten Beziehungen zwischen diesen Regionen sind.

Die östlichen (skythischen) Einflüsse machen sich im jugoslawischen Raum im Ritual der Pferdebestattung bemerkbar, in der materiellen Kultur dagegen vor allem im Typ des Pferdegeschirrs und im Gebrauch gewisser Waffengattungen.

In Slowenien kommt die Pferdebestattung im Gefüge der Sippen -- Familien -- Grabhügel vor (Magdalenska gora, Stična, Novo mesto, Brezje, Boštanj).[5] Die Pferde wurden in der Regel ohne Geschirr bestattet und liegen in der Nähe oder dicht bei den männlichen Skelettbestattungen, denen dagegen das Geschirr beigelegt ist. Gestützt auf diese Beigaben können wir die Pferdeskelette verläßlich in den Horizont der skythischen Einflüsse einordnen. Im Unterschied zum slowenischen Raum tritt jedoch in Doroslovo bei Sombor die Brandbestattung eines Kriegers mit einem Pferdeskelett vergesellschaftet auf.[6] Die Bestattungsweise, sowie die geographische Lage des Fundortes, lassen die Annahme zu, daß das Gräberfeld in Doroslovo in den Kreis der Alföldgruppe gehört.

Das Pferdegeschirr war in Slowenien bereits in der Ha C und in der Ha D 1 Stufe bekannt, und zwar der sogenannte thrako-kimmerische Typ.[7] In die Zäsur zwischen dem thrako-kimmerischen Horizont und dem Auftritt der skythischen Einflüsse gehören die Trensen mit Psalien aus Libna,[8] Boštanj[9] und aus Grab 1, Grabhügel Malenšek in Novo mesto (T. 1: 1-3).[10] Das Begleitmaterial und Vergleiche mit verwandten Beispielen ordnen das Pferdegeschirr aus Libna sowie die Trense aus Boštanj in die Mitte des 6. Jhs. ein.[11] Dagegen wird die Datierung des Pferdegeschirrs aus Grab 1, Grabhügel Malenšek in Novo mesto dadurch erschwert, daß wir keine entsprechende Analogie kennen; auch befindet sich im Grab keinerlei charakteristisches Begleitmaterial, wodurch das Pferdegeschirr datiert werden könnte. Dieses Geschirr wurde im zentralen (ältesten) ummauerten Grab gefunden. Die übrigen zwei Gräber, Grab 2 und 3 in diesem Grabhügel, sind ins späte 6. (T. 3) bzw. ins 5. Jh. (T. 4) zu setzen, deswegen glauben wir uns berechtigt, Grab 1 in die zweite Hälfte des 6. Jhs. einzuordnen. Diese Einordnung wird auch durch den Vergleich mit halbrunder Form der Psalien sowie Kopfschmuck aus Libna bestätigt.[12]

Im folgenden Horizont erscheint in Slowenien in Verbindung mit östlichen Einflüssen ein neuer Typ--das skythische Pferdegeschirr. Die charakteristischen skythischen Trensen mit Psalien hat M. Parducz klassifiziert.[13] Er hat sie in fünf charakteristische Varianten aufgegliedert. Wir haben seine Einteilung noch um die Variante 6 bereichert, die anscheinend Lokalcharakter hat; sie ist nämlich nur im Bereich Sloweniens zu finden (Karte 1).[14] Die Varianten 1 und 5 seiner Einteilung sind in unserem Raum nicht bekannt und beschränken sich nur auf den Bereich der Alföldgruppe. Interessant ist, daß ins Gebiet des nordwestlichen Balkans, nach Slowenien und ins Randgebiet der Ostalpen nur Variante 4 der Skythentrensen gelangten (Karte 1). Die gleiche Form der Skythen-trensen in Stična, Donja Dolina, Garibovac und Atenica weist auf die Gleichzeitigkeit der Skythischen Einwirkungen auf das gesamte besprochene Gebiet hin, die Gräber aus Atenica und Grab 99 aus Stična gehören ja ungefähr derselben Zeit an. In Stična sind die Trensen der Variante 4 mit frühen Certosafibeln vergesellschaftet (Karte 2), wodurch das Grab in den Beginn des 5. Jhs. datiert wird.[15] Grab II/13 von Magdalenska gora,[16] das ebenso eine Trense dieser Variante enthält, gehört einer etwas jüngeren Zeit an, wofür das mit Sphingen ornamentierte Gürtelblech[17] und der charakteristische Gürtelbeschlag sprechen, wogegen der Doppelkammhelm[18] und die Trense selbst dieses Grab mit Grab 99 aus Stična parallel setzen.

In Slowenien kommen jedoch außer Variante 4 auch noch Trensen der Varianten 2 und 3 vor (Karte 1). Die Erscheinung der Variante 2 bindet sich an die Zeit, in die das Grab mit ornamentiertem Gürtelblech aus Zagorje gehört.[19] In diesem Grab wurden unter anderem zwei Fibeln in Form eines Hündchens gefunden, die eine unmittelbare Parallele im Grab 2, Grabhügel Malenšek aus Novo mesto haben (T. 3: 1). Grab 2 aus dem

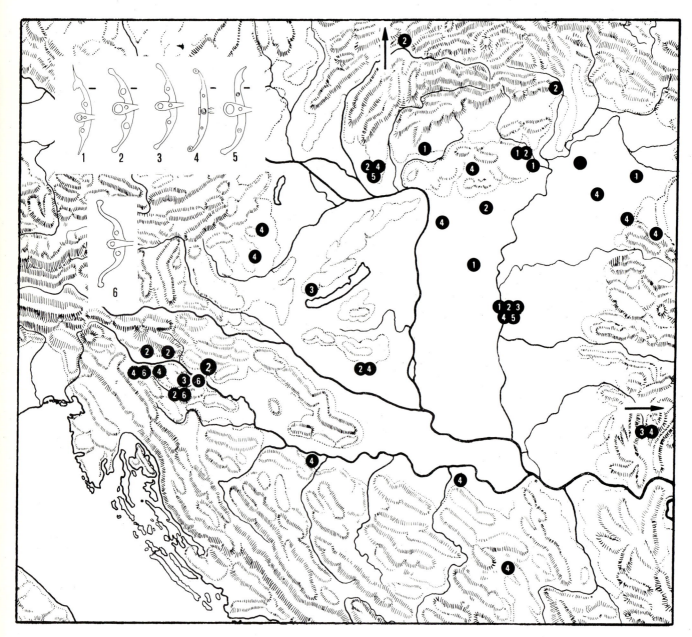

KARTE 1. Verbreitung der skythischen Trensen (ergänzt nach M. Parducz).

Grabhügel Malenšek bindet sich mit seinen zweiflügeligen Pfeilspitzen (T. 3: 2) und Verteilungsknöpfen (T. 3: 3) an den älteren Formenschatz, zugleich sind aber darin noch keine skythischen Elemente anwesend. Die zwei Grabeinheiten beweisen, daß das Erscheinen der skythischen Trense der Variante 2 an ungefähr dieselbe Zeit gebunden ist, wie die Variante 4; durch die Tierfibeln werden nämlich diese zwei Einheiten ins späte 6., bzw ins frühe 5. Jh. datiert,[20] gleichzeitig aber deuten sie die Sukzessivität der Einführung des Skythengeschirrs in Slowenien in diesem Zeitabschnitt an. In das Zeitintervall zwischen der Trense aus Zagorje und jener aus Novo mesto--Grabhügel Malenšek, Grab 3 (T. 4: 2), das auf Grund seiner Certosa-Armbrustfibel (T. 4: 6) schon in die Mitte des 5. Jhs. gehört,[21] können noch die Gräber VI/1 aus Brezje und 43 aus Vače eingereiht werden, welche Trensen der Variante 2 bzw. 3 enthalten.[22]

Die jüngste Trensengruppe stellt die Variante 6 dar, bekannt aus den Gräbern von Magdalenska gora II/19a, V/29[23] und aus Novo mesto IV/3,[24] die wir auf Grund der Frülatèneschwerter, der Negauer Helme, der ostalpinen Tierkopffibeln und der Situlen der jüngsten Variante ans Ende des 5., und vor allem ins 4. Jh. datieren können.[25]

Zugleich mit dem Aufkommen der Pferdebestattung, des skythischen Pferdegeschirrs, der charakteristischen Schmuckgegenstände in Form der Swastika[26] sowie der skythischen Eisenstreitäxte[27] erscheinen in den Gräbern aus dieser Zeit neben den bereits bekannten zweiflügeligen (T. 3: 2) auch dreiflügelige Pfeilspitzen, die mit den Einflüssen aus skythischem Gebiet auf den südöstlichen alpin-nordwestlichen Balkanraum in Zusammenhang stehen,[28]

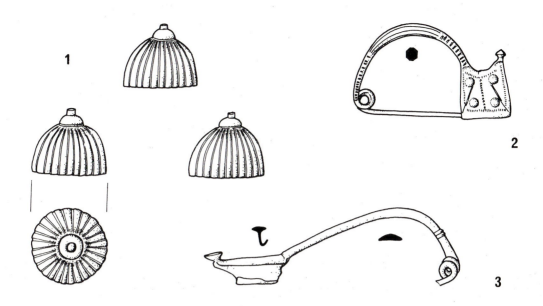

Abb. 1   Grab aus dem Tumulus CIII in Crvena Lokva auf Glasinac. 1, 3 Bronze, 2 Silber; [alles 1:1]

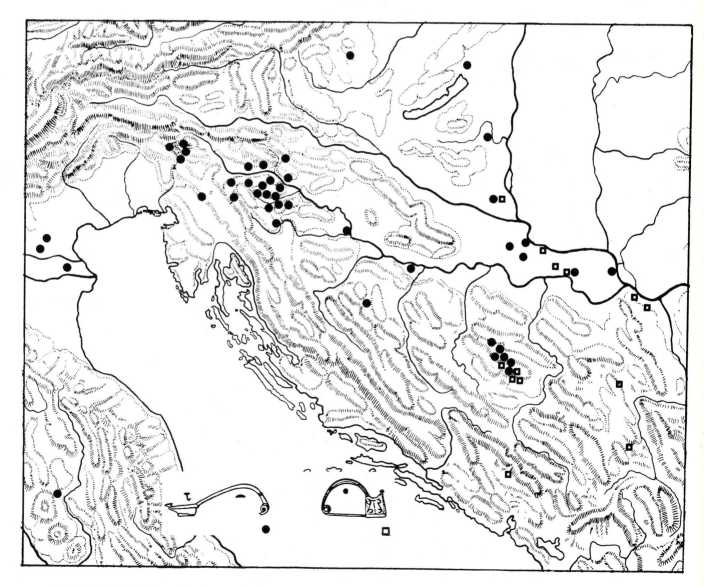

KARTE 2.   Verbreitung der Certosafibeln und Fibeln mit viereckigem Nadelhalter.

wobei wir ihren Ursprung und ihr Erscheinen im breiteren europäischen Raum beiseite lassen. [29]

Ende des 6. und im 5. Jh. kann man eine Zunahme von Gegenständen der südostalpinen Materialkultur im Gebiet des Balkans und Pannoniens feststellen, wie z.B. Certosafibeln, Bronzeszepter, Zisten und Ornaments-motive. Jene Certosafibeln, die in den pannonisch-balkanischen Raum gelangten (Karte 2), [30] gehören zu den ältesten Varianten, nicht nur in diesem Bereich, sondern auch in Slowenien. In Slowenien erscheinen sie in der Zeit um das Jahr 500, die Gleichzeitigkeit im pannonisch-balkanischen Raum aber wird durch Grab 2 aus Beremend [31] und das Grab aus Crvena Lokva auf Glasinac (Abb. 1) bezeugt, wo sich im selben Grab auch eine einschleifige Bogenfibel mit viereckiger Fußplatte befindet (Abb. 1: 2). Gestützt auf die Fibel mit viereckiger Fußplatte, die in Atenica und Novi Pazar in dieselbe Zeit datiert, [32] ist die Gleichzeitigkeit der Certosafibeln auf dem Balkan mit jenen in Slowenien erwiesen. Diesem Horizont gehört auch die Certosafibel mit bandförmigem Bügel aus Tapioszele an, [33] deren Ursprunggebiet ebenso im slowenischen Raum zu suchen ist. Zugleich mit den Fibeln tauchten in Pannonien auch die für den Este-Kulturkreis und den slowenischen Hallstattraum charakteristischen Bronzeszepter auf. [34]

Dieselbe Welt führte in den pannonisch-balkanischen Raum auch noch als Ornament das "Kreis-Tangenten-band" ein. In Slowenien tritt dieses Ornament recht häufig auf. Es findet sich in Grabeinheiten, die in die Zeit um das Jahr 500 datieren: Stična, Grab 104 mit Negauer Helm der italischen Variante, Magdalenska gora II/38 mit Doppelkammhelm und skythischen Elementen, sowie in Sveta Lucija (Most na Soči) auf der Gürtelplatte aus Grab 1008, worin auch die sogenannte jonische Schale gefunden wurde. [35] Das Motiv dieses Ornaments auf dem Pferdegeschirr aus Grab 1--Grabhügel Malenšek in Novo mesto (T. 2) deutet jedoch darauf hin, daß dieses Ornament im slowenischen Gebiet schon vor dem Jahr 500 anwesend war, was als Bindeglied zu den älteren, aus Klein-Glein und Hallstatt bekannten Beispielen aufgefaßt werden kann. [36] Das Vorkommen des "Kreis-Tangentenbandes" in Grab 2 in Beremend und Atenica [37] sowie in etwas abgeänderter Ausführung in Kaptol bei Slavonska Požega und in Novi Pazar [38] legt abermals Zeugnis für die Gleichzeitigkeit der oben erörterten Grabeinheiten ab, und damit auch für jenen bestimmten Zeithorizont der Funde, den wir im weiten Gebiet von der Soča bis zur Morava beobachten können.

Die neuveröffentlichten Nekropolen in der Baranja [39] weisen zusammen mit dem Fundmaterial in Ostslawonien und in Srem [40] auf eine geschlossene Gruppe hin, die im späten 6. bzw. im frühen 5. Jh. in Erscheinung tritt und durch einheitliches Grabmaterial gekennzeichnet ist. Ein charakteristisches Merkmal dieser Gruppe sind flache Gräberfelder mit Skelettbestattungen, die mit Pferdebestattungen vergesellschaftet sind. Im Unterschied zu Slowenien sind in diesem Raum die Pferde samt ihrem Geschirr bestattet. [41] Doch weist die materielle Kultur dieser Gruppe auch pannonisch-skythische Elemente auf (Trensen, dreiflügelige Pfeilspitzen), ferner südöstlich-alpine (Certosafibeln, Szepter) und balkanische (Fibeln mit viereckiger Fußplatte) Elemente. Eine der starken Datierungsstützen des Erscheinens dieses Horizonts im oben erwähnten Raum bietet die Fibel mit viereckiger Fußplatte der jüngeren Variante (Abb. 1: 2). Derartige Fibeln (Karte 2) sind auf Grund der Gräber aus Atenica und Novi Pazar bereits für die Zeit um das Jahr 500 bezeugt, ihr Weiterleben durch das ganze 5. Jh. wird aber durch die Gräber in Kačanj bewiesen. [42] Prototypen solcher Fibeln treten im Gebiet zwischen Gogosu, Donja Dolina und Grivac jedoch schon um das Jahr 600 auf. [43] Die erwähnte materielle Kultur gruppiert sich nur am rechten Ufer der Donau, was dafür spricht, daß die Donau in jenen Zeitläufen eine starke, die skythische Alföldgruppe von den späthallstättischen Kulturen des nordwestlichen Balkans abgrenzende, Trennungslinie darstellte (Karte 3).

Der vorgestellte reiche Horizont des späten 6. und des 5. Jhs. in Slowenien, im nordwestlichen Balkan und im südlichen Pannonien vereint in sich auch zahlreiche griechisch-italische Importe. Man kann sie von der Mänade aus Tetovo, der Tänzerin aus Prizren, dem Figuralgriff aus Janjevo, dem Hydrienfragment aus Atenica, der schwarzfiguralen Keramik und dem Bronzegerät aus Novi Pazar, den korinthischen Helmen aus Čavarine auf Glasinac und aus Kaptol bei Slavonska Požega sowie von dem Negauer Helm der italischen Variante aus Stična bis hin zur jonischen Schale aus Sveta Lucija (Most na Soči) verfolgen. [44] Auf Grund des Imports, namentlich jenes aus Atenica und aus Novi Pazar, wird die Datierung nicht nur der Grabeinheiten mit griechisch-italischem Import ermöglicht, sondern auch des gesamten besprochenen Horizonts der vorgestellten Region.

Nördlich von diesem Raum ist der Fund des reichen Grabes mit Hydria aus Artand wichtig. [45] Obwohl die Hydria aus Artand typologisch älter ist als der hier erörterte Zeithorizont, [46] befinden sich außerdem in diesem Grab mehrere charakteristische Gegenstände, die sich mit entsprechenden Beispielen aus den Gräbern in Atenica vergleichen lassen. In beiden Fundstätten sind skythische Trensen der Variante 4 und völlig gleiche Schildbuckel vertreten. [47] Außerdem wird die Gleichzeitigkeit noch durch kleine Goldrosetten und filigranmäßig ausgeführte Perlen bestätigt, [48] die abermals zusammen mit Novi Pazar, Sremska Mitrovica (Abb. 2) und Grab 1 aus Beremend im erörterten Horizont eingeordnet sind. [49] Das Grab aus Artand ist auf Grund der angeführten Vergleiche gleich-zeitig mit dem Horizont der reichen Gräber mit griechisch-italischem Import des späten 6. und des 5. Jhs. im nordwestlichen Balkan und in Slowenien.

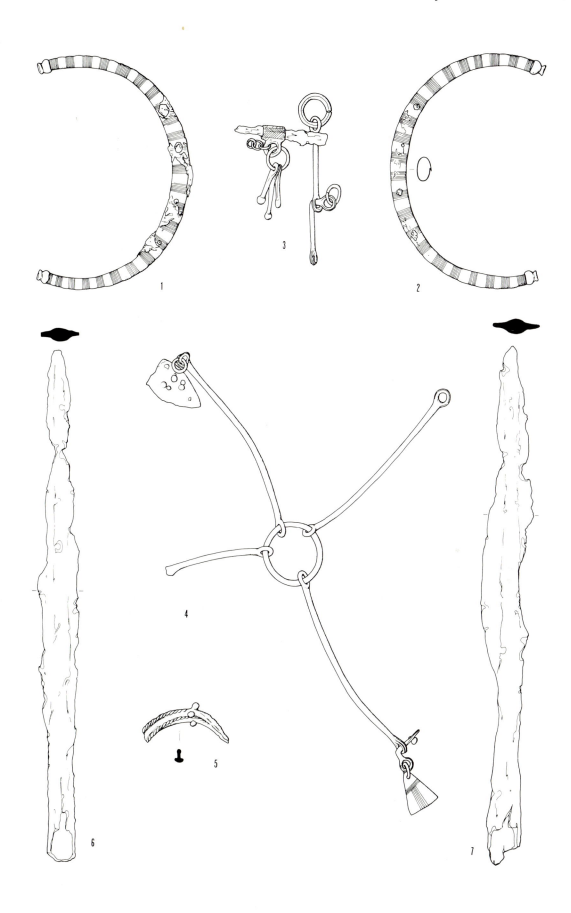

TAFEL 1. Novo mesto - Grabhügel Malenšek, Grab 1. 1-2, 4-5 Bronze, 6-7 Eisen, 3 Eisen und Bronze.

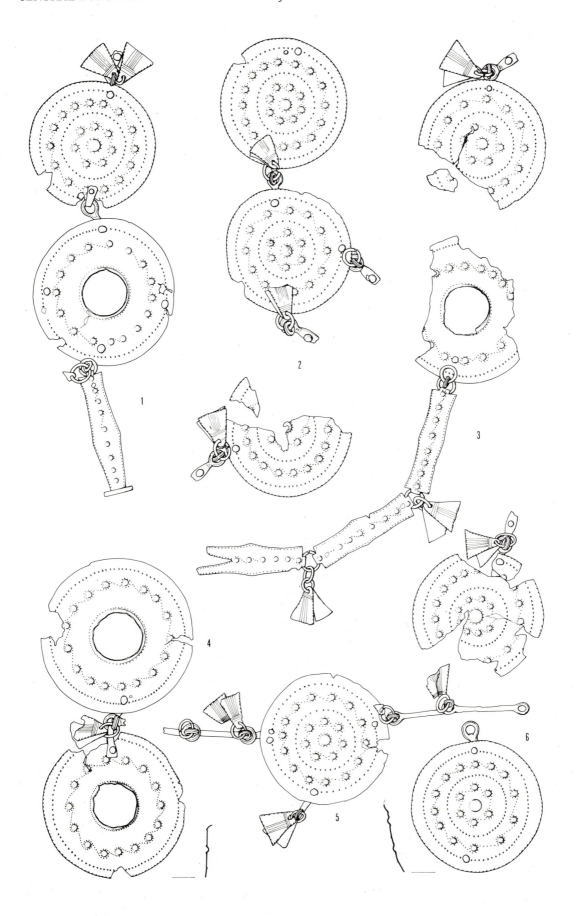

TAFEL 2.   Novo mesto - Grabhügel Malenšek, Grab 1. Bronze.

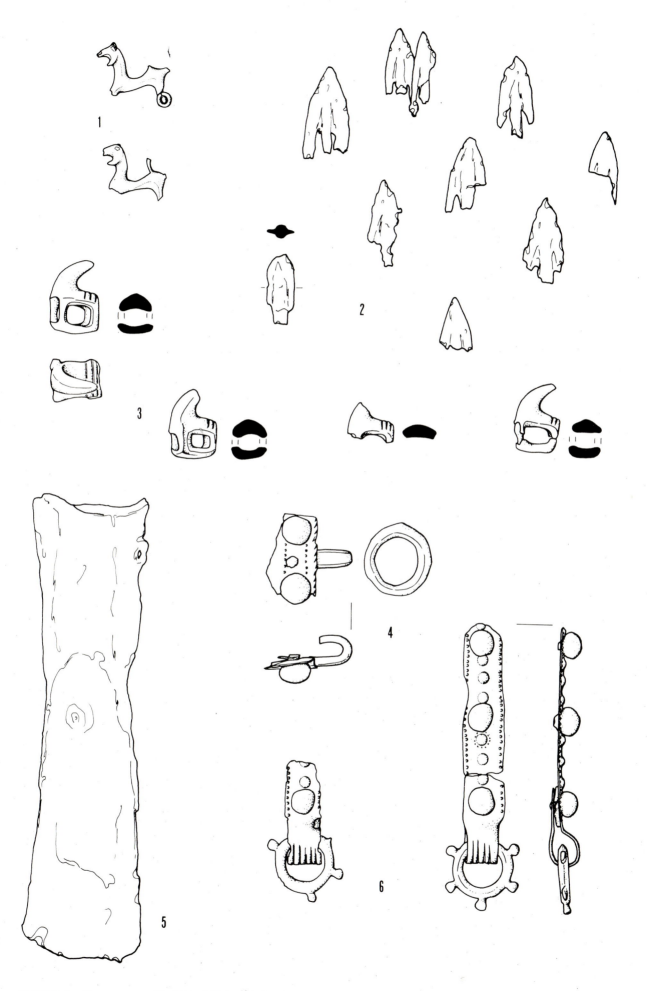

TAFEL 3.   Novo mesto - Grabhügel Malenšek, Grab 2. 1, 3 6-7 Bronze, 2, 4-5 Eisen.

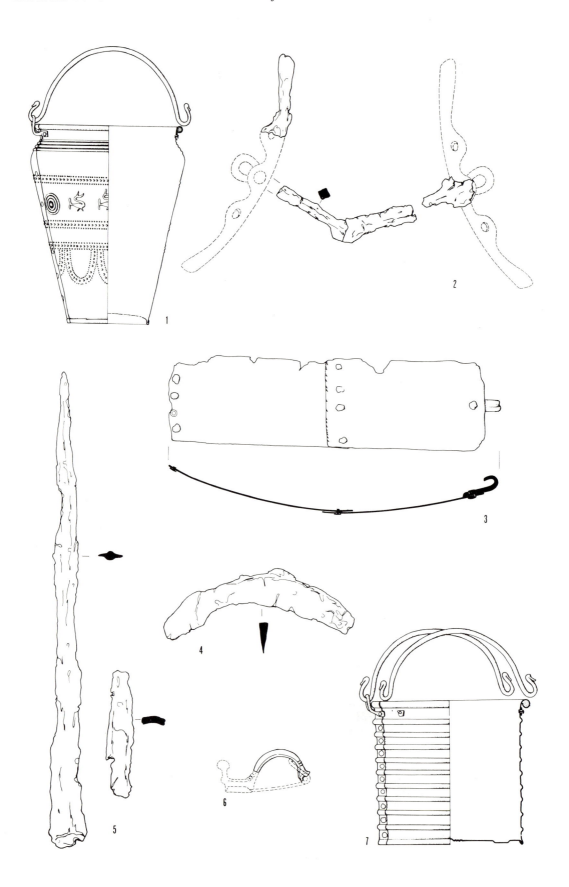

TAFEL 4. Novo mesto - Grabhügel Malenšek, Grab 3. 1, 3, 6-7 Bronze, 2, 4-5 Eisen.

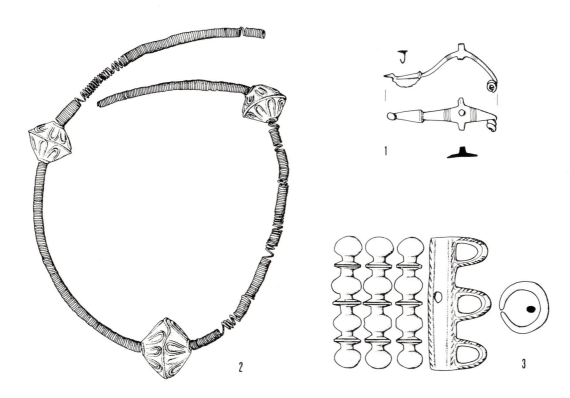

Abb. 2   *Grab aus Sremska Mitrovica. 1, 3 Bronze, 2 Gold.*

Anmerkungen:

1. Garašanin M. 1973, 496 ff; Benac und Čović 1957; Marić 1964.
2. Gabrovec 1966 a = idem 1964-65.
3. Die zweite Hälfte des 6. Jh. wurde bisher in der Fachliteratur als Horizont der Doppelkammhelme bezeichnet (Frey und Gabrovec 1971). Es hat sich jedoch erwiesen, dass die Doppelkammhelme vorwiegend in den Gräbern des Certosahorizonts vertreten sind, deshalb verwenden wir für diese Periode die Bezeichnung Horizont der Schlangenfibeln, denn diese repräsentieren mit ihren jüngeren Varianten die führenden Formen.
4. Parducz 1973, 27 ff mit Literaturverzeichnis.
5. Parducz 1965 a; cfr. auch Bökönyi 1968. Für Boštanj cfr. Guštin 1974, 88, sl. 2.
6. Grabungen des Gradski muzej in Sombor im Jahr 1974.
7. Kossack 1954; Gabrovec 1960; 46 ff; Guštin 1973, 87 ff.
8. Knez und Škaler 1968, T.8:1.
9. Guštin 1974, 90, T.14: 5.
10. Schmid 1908. Durch abermalige Revision des Berichts und des Fundmaterials gelang es uns, im Grabhügel drei Gräber zu unterscheiden, die unterschiedlichen Zeithorizonten angehören.
11. Guštin 1974, 93 ff.
12. Knez und Škaler 1968, T. 6- 8. Die zwei Kopfschmücke stellen im Vergleich mit älteren Pferdegechirr im Bereich Sloweniens eine Novität des 6. Jh. dar, wenn wir sie auch nicht völlig gleichsetzen können, da sie sich typologisch voneinander unterscheiden. Cfr. auch De Marinis 1975 T.7: 1, 2.
13. Parducz 19 65b, 149 ff. Cfr. auch Parducz 1973, 36, Karte 3 mit Literaturverzeichnis auf S. 60 f.
14. Die Verbreitungskarte von Parducz haben wir durch die Fundorte der Variante 4 ergänzt: Garibovac in Badovinci (Arheološki pregled 14, 1972, 165 f, T. 54: 1), Stična, Gr. 99 (Gabrovec 1974, Abb. 4: 3), und für die Variante 6 : Novo mesto, Gr. IV/3 (Knez 1975, T. 32:3) sowie Šmarjeta (Stare 1973, T. 11: 7). Nach abermaliger Uberprüfung der Skythentrensen im nordwestlichen Balkan und in Slowenien haben wir sie aufs neue in die einzelnen Varianten eingeordnet (Karte 1).
15. Zur Verbreitung der Certosafibeln auf Karte 3 cfr. Teržan 1976. Für die Datierung dieses Grabes ist jedoch auch seine Lage im Gefüge des Grabhügels bedeutsam - cfr. Gabrovec 1962, 116 f; idem 1974, Plan 1.
16. Kromer und Gabrovec 1962, Y 43.
17. Frey 1969, 57.
18. Gabrovec 1962 -63, 305 ff.

19. Gabrovec 1966 b, 28 ff, T. 6 - 8.
20. Guštin 1974, 95 ff mit Verbreitungskarte.
21. Teržan 1976. Das Fragment der Armbrustfibel wird in W. Schmids erster Veröffentlichung fälschlicherweise als Griff eines Bronzegefässes rekonstruiert.
22. Kromer 1959 a, T. 17: 1 - lo; Vače : Naturhistorisches Museum Wien - unveröffentlicht.
23. Treasures of Carniola 1934, 74, 77, T.2: 4; 8: 19; Gabrovec 1966 a, 31, Abb. 17: 5.
24. Das Grab ist noch nicht in Gänze veröffentlicht. Für die Einzelgegenstände cfr. Knez 1971, Abb. 63 - 71 und idem 1972, Abb. auf S. 62, 64 und 66, Auch Knez 1975.
25. Gabrovec 1966a, 29, Abb. 16: 1; idem 1962, 114 ff; idem 1966 b, 30 ff. Die Situla aus Novo mesto gehört in die Gruppe von Magdalenska gora, Valična vas, Kuffarn und der Situla Arnoaldi aus Bologna (Gabrovec 1966 a, 29, 36).
26. Kromer 1960; cfr. auch Hencken 1974, 124 ff.
27. Parducz 1973, 34, 60, Karte 2. Seine Verbreitungskarte haben wir mit dem Fundort Rob (Gemeinde Ljubljana, Narodni muzej Ljubljana - unveröffentlicht) und Čavarine auf Glasinac (Benac und Čović 1957, T. 41: 21) ergänzt.
28. Parducz 1973, 32, 59 f, Karte 1. Seiner Karte fügen wir im Bereich Sloweniens hinzu : Boštanj (Guštin 1974, 88, T.3 : 3), Libna (Stare 1962-63, 397, T. 9: 8 - 56; lo: 1 - 62), Lukovica (Gabrovec 1965, lol, T. 11: 8), Velike Malence (Stare 1960 - 61, 60, T. 12: 1), Tržišče bei Cerknica (Guštin, Katalog Notranjske - in Vorbereitung); und im übrigen Jugoslawien : Veliki Kalnik bei Križevci (Arheološki muzej Zagreb - unveröffentlicht), Dalj (Arheološki muzej Zagreb - unveröffentlicht), Glasinac (Fiala 1894, 17, Fig. 44), Atenica (Djuknić und Jovanović 1965, lo f, T. 20: 19 - 20; 24: 1 - 5), obala Zemuna (Todorović 1971, T.39: 5- 17, 19, 21), Vinča (Garašanin 1954, 61), Vršac - At (Narodni muzej Vršac - unveröffentlicht), Banatska Palanka (Narodni muzej Vršac - unveröffentlicht).
29. Kimmig 1971, 49 ff, Abb. 12.
30. Teržan 1976.
31. Jerem 1973, Abb. 6 - 7.
32. Djuknić und Jovanović 1965, T. 15 : 13; Mano Zisi und Popović 1969, T. 27, 29, 37.
33. Parducz 1966, T. 62: 3.
34. Jerem 1973, 82 f.
35. Gabrovec 1966 a, 27, Abb. 14: 2; idem 1962-63, T. 13: 4; Frey 1971, 355 ff, Abb. 11: 5.
36. Schmid 1933, 234 Abb. 13; Kromer 1959 b, T. 50: 15; 94: 5, 13.
37. Jerem 1973, Abb. 7: 8. Djuknić und Jovanović 1965, T. 21: 3, 8. Aber cfr. auch Goldschätze der Thraker. Thrakische Kultur und Kunst auf bulgarischem Boden, Wien 1975, Abb. 89, 145.
38. Vejvoda und Mirnik 1971, T. 13: 6; Mano Zisi und Popović 1969, T. 22, 36.
39. Jerem 1973, idem 1968.
40. Brunšmid 1902; Vinski und Vinski Gasparini 1962; Majnarić Pandžić 1973, 39 f, T. 20.
41. Jerem 1968.
42. Cfr. Anm. 32 und Marić 1959, T. 2: 2, 4.
43. Zu den älteren Fibeln mit viereckiger Fussplatte gehören: Gogoşu (Berciu und Comsa 1956, fig. 141: 2 - 3; 159: 1; 163: 2), Telesti - Dragoesti (ibidem, fig. 192), Grivac (Bogdanović 1971. 149 ff., T. 2: 4), Zemun (Todorović 1971, T. 40: 4, 7, 9), Kupinovo (Garašanin 1954, T. 49: 17), Donja Dolina (Truhelka 1904, T. 58: 4; 59: 7).
     Zu den jüngeren (Karte 3) aber zählen wir : Beremend (Jerem 1973, Abb. 6: 3-4), Sotin (Vinski und Vinski Gasparini 1962, T.8:94), Sremska Mitrovica (Ibidem, T. 9: 106), Kuzmin (Vinski 1960, 59, sl. 3), Vinča (Garašanin 1954, T. 49: 15), Atenica (Djuknić und Jovanović 1965, T. 15: 13), Umčari (Garašanin 1973, T. 11o: 3), Novi Pazar (Mano Zisi und Popović, 1969, T. 27, 29, 37), Rusanovići (Benac und Čović 1957, T. 34: 1), Gosinja planina (Ibidem, T. 47: 21 - 22), Crvena Lokva (Abb. 1: 2), Kačanj (Marić 1959, T.2: 2, 4), Mati und Gajtan (Shqiperia Arkeologjike. Tirane 1971, Ill. 49).
     Hierher gehört auch das Exemplar der Fibel mit viereckiger Fussplate aus Grab 61 aus Vekerzug (M. Parducz, Acta Arch Hung 4, 1954, T. 17: 3), das sich in gewissen Details von den aufgezählten Beispielen unterscheidet. Cfr. auch Jerem 1973, 74 f, Abb. 9.
44. Tetovo, Janjevo, Čavarine : Antička bronza u Jugoslaviji 1969, Abb. 19 a, 22, 23; Prizren: British Museum, London; Atenica : Djuknić und Jovanović 1965, T. 17: 4-5; Novi Pazar : Mano Zisi und Popović 1969, T. 1 - 6 a; Kaptol bei Slavonska Požega : Vejvoda und Mirnik 1971, T. 13: 1; Stična: Gabrovec 1966 a, 27, Abb. 14: 1; Sveta Lucija (= Most na Soči): Frey 1971, T. 2: 1.
45. Parducz 1965 b, 137 ff, T. 1-3.
46. Parducz 1965 b, 217 ff.
47. Parducz 1965 b, Fig. 4, 12, T.9: 3; 14; 21; Djuknić und Jovanović 1965, T. 18: 3 - 4; 25: 5-6; 24: 10.
48. Parducz 1965 b, T. 17 - 19; Djuknić und Jovanović 1965, T. 15: 10, 16; 19 : 10 - 11.
49. Mano Zisi und Popović 1969, T. 15: 1; 27; Brunšmid 1902, 76, sl. 36; Jerem 1973, Abb. 5: 5.

Wir danken Herrn S. Gabrovec, Narodni muzej Ljubljana, B. Čović, Zemaljski muzej Sarajevo, und Frau K. Vinski Gasparini, Arheološki muzej Zagreb, die uns ermöglicht haben die Unterlagen für die Abbildungen zu zeichnen, und Fräulein Darja Grosman, die uns die Zeichnungen gefertigt hat.

Abkurzungen

Acta Ant Hung   Acta Antiqua Academiae Scientiarum Hungaricae
Acta Arch Hung   Acta Archaeologica Academiae Scientiarum Hungaricae
AV   Arheološki vestnik, Ljubljana
Glasnik Sarajevo   Glasnik Zemaljskog muzeja Bosne i Hercegovine, Sarajevo
Vjesnik Zagreb   Vjesnik Arheološkog muzeja u Zagrebu

Bibliographie

Benac, Alojz, und Čović, Borivoj
    1957   Glasinac II.
Berciu, Dumitru, und Comsa, Eugen
    1956   Sapaturile arheologice de la Balta Verde si Gogosu.
            Materiale si cercetari arheologice 2, 251 ff.
Bogdanović, Milenko
    1971   Prilog proučavanju bronzanog i starijeg gvozdenog doba na području centralne Srbije.
            Starinar 22, 145 ff.
Bökönyi, Sandor
    1968   Mecklenburg Collection, Part I. Data on Iron Age Horses of Central and Eastern Europe. American
            School of Prehistoric Research. Bulletin 25.
Brunšmid, Josip
    1902   Prethistorijski predmeti iz srijemske županije. Vjesnik n.s. 6, 68 ff. Zagreb.
Djuknić, Milena, und Jovanović, Borislav
    1965   Illyrian Princely Necropolis at Atenica. Archaeologica Iugoslavica 6, 1-37.
Fiala, Franz
    1894   Die Ergebnisse der Untersuchung prähistorischer Grabhügel auf dem Glasinac im Jahre 1893.
            Wissenschaftliche Mitteilungen aus Bosnien und Herzegovina 3, 1 ff.
Frey, Otto Herman
    1969   Die Entstehung der Situlenkunst. Römisch-Germanische Forschungen 31.
    1971   Fibeln vom westhallstättischen Typus aus dem Gebiet südlich der Alpen. Oblatio. Raccolta di studi di
            Antichità ed Arte in onore del Prof. Aristide Calderini, 355 ff.
Frey, Otto Herman, und Gabrovec, Stane
    1971   Zur Chronologie der Hallstattzeit im Ostalpenraum.
            Actes du VIIIe congres international des sciences prehistoriques et protohistoriques I, 193 ff.
Gabrovec, Stane
    1960   Grob z oklepom iz Novega mesta. Situla 1, 27 ff.
    1962   Chronologie der Negauerhelme. Atti del VI Congresso internazionale delle scienze preistoriche e
            protostoriche III (1966) 114 ff.
    1962-63 Halštatske če lade jugovzhodnoalpskega kroga. AV 13-14, 293-347.
    1964-65 Halštatska kultura v Sloveniji. AV 15-16, 21 ff.
    1965   Kamniško ozemlje v prazgodovini. Kamniški zbornik l0, 89 ff.
    1966 a Zur Hallstattzeit in Slowenien. Germania 44, 1-48.
    1966 b Zagorje v prazgodovini. AV 17, 19-49.
    1974   Die Ausgrabungen in Stična und ihre Bedeutung für die südostalpine Hallstattkultur. Symposim zu
            Problemen der jüngeren Hallstattzeit in Mittelauropa (Smolenice 1970) 163 ff.
Garašanin, Draga
    1954   Katalog metala. Praistorija I.
Garašanin, Milutin.
    1973   Praistorija na tlu SR Srbije.
Goldschätze der Thraker. Thrakische Kultur und Kunst auf bulgarischen Boden.
    1975   Wien.
Guštin, Mitja
    1973   Mahaire. Doprinos k povezavam Picena, Slovenije in srednjega Podonavja v 7. stol. pr. n. št.
            Situla 14—15, 77 ff.
    1974   Gomile starejše železne dobe iz okolice Boštanja. Varia archaeologica 1, 87-119. Posavski muzej.
            Brežice.
Hencken, Hugh
    1974   Bracelets of Lead-Tin Alloy from Magdalenska gora. Situla 14-15, 119 ff.

Jerem, Elisabeth
    1968   The Late Iron Age Cemetery of Szentlörinc. Acta Arch Hung 20, 159 ff.
    1973   Zur Geschichte der späten Eisenzeit in Transdanubien. Späteisenzeitliche Grabfunde von Beremend.
            Acta Arch Hung 25, 65 ff.
Kimmig, Wolfgang und Gersbach, Egon
    1971   Die Grabungen auf der Heuneburg 1966- 1969. Germania 49, 21–91.
Knez, Tone
    1971   Prazgodovina Novega mesta.
    1972   Novo mesto v davnini.
    1973   Figurale Situlen aus Novo mesto. AV 24, 309-326.
    1975   Hallstattzeitliche Funde aus Novo mesto/Jugoslawien. Archäol. Korrespondenzblatt 5, 125 ff.
Knez, Tone, und Škaler, Stanko
    1968   Halštatska gomila na Libni. AV 19, 239-261.
Korkuti, Muzafer
    1971   Shqiperia arkeologjike. Tirane.
Kossack, Georg
    1954   Pferdegeschirr aus Gräbern der älteren Hallstattzeit Bayerns. Jahrbuch des Römisch-Germanisches
            Zentralmuseums Mainz 1, 111 ff.
Kromer, Karl
    1959 a Brezje. Arheološki katalogi Slovenije 2.
    1959 b Das Gräberfeld von Hallstatt.
    1960   Zierstücke östlicher Herkunft aus drei Gräbern in Slowenien. Situla 1, 111 ff.
Kromer, Karl, und Gabrovec, Stane
    1962   L'art des situles dans les sépultures hallstattien en Slovénie. Inventaria Archaeologica Jugoslavija 5.
Majnarić Pandžić, Nives
    1973   Vinkovci. Arheološki pregled 15, 39-40.
Mano Zisi, Đuro, und Popović, Ljubiša
    1969   Novi Pazar. Ilirsko-grčki nalaz.
Marić, Zdravko
    1959   Grobovi ilirskih ratnika iz Kačnja. Glasnik n.s. 14, 87-102, Sarajevo.
    1964   Donja Dolina. Glasnik n.s. 19, 5-128, Sarajevo.
De Marinis, Raffaele
    1975   Le tombe di guerriero di Sesto Calende e le spade e pugnali hallstattiani scoperti nell Italia nord-
            occidentale. Archaeologica. Scritti in onore di Aldo Neppi Modona.
Párducz, Mihail
    1965a   Western Relations of the Scythian Age Culture of the Great Hungarian Plain. Acta Ant Hung 13,
            273 ff.
    1965b   Graves from the Scythian Age at Artánd (County Hajdu Bihar). Acta Arch Hung 17, 137 ff.
    1966   The Scythian Age Cementery at Tapioszele. Acta Arch Hung 18, 35 ff.
    1973   Probleme der Skythenzeit im Karpatenbecken. Acta Arch Hung 25, 27 ff.
Popović, Ljubiša B., und Mano Zisi, Đuro, und Velicković, Milivoje, und Jelicić, Branka
    1969   Antička bronza u Jugoslaviji.
Schmid, Walter
    1908   Tumuliforschungen. Tumulus bei Rudolfswert in Unterkrain. Carniola 1, 202 ff.
    1933   Die Fürstengräber von Klein-Glein in Steiermark. Prähistorische Zeitschrift 24, 219 ff.
Stare, France
    1963-63 Kipec ilirskega bojevnika z Vač. AV 13-14, 383-434.
Stare, Vida
    1960-61 Prazgodovinske Malence. AV 11-12, 50 ff.
    1973   Prazgodovina Šmarjete. Katalogi in monografije 10.
Teržan, Biba
    1976   Certoške fibule. AV 27 (im Druck)
Todorović, Jovan
    1971   Katalog praistorijskih metalnih predmeta.
Treasures of Carniola
    1934   New York
Truhelka, Ćiro
    1904   Der vorgeschichtliche Pfahlbau im Savebette bei Donja Dolina. Wissenscheftliche Mitteilungen aus
            Bosnien und Herzegovina 9, 3 ff.
Vejvoda, Vera, und Mirnik, Ivan
    1971   Istraživanja prethistorijskih tumula u Kaptolu kraj Slavonske Požege. Vjesnik 3.s. 5, 183 ff. Zagreb.

Vinski, Zdenko
    1960   Povodom izložbe "Iliri i Grci". Vijesti muzealaca i konzervatora Hrvatske 9/2, 57 ff.
Vinski, Zdenko, und Vinski Gasparini, Ksenija
    1962   O utjecajima istočno-alpske halštatske kulture i balkanske ilirske kulture na slavonsko-srijemsko
            Podunavlje. Arheološki radovi i rasprave 2, 263-293.

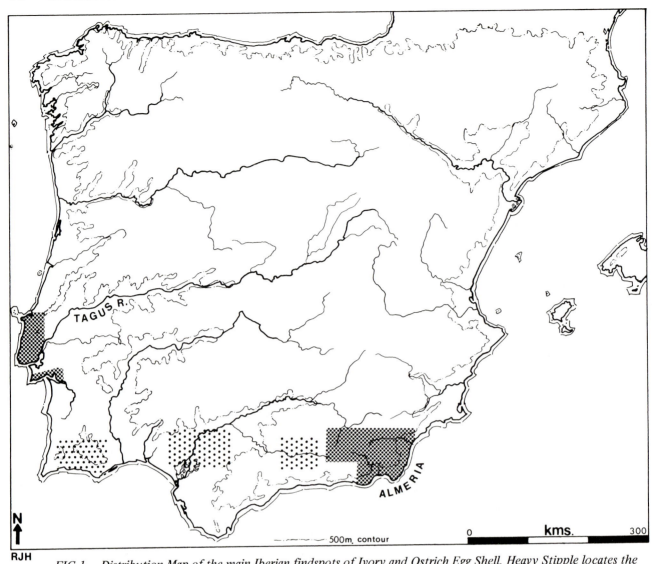

FIG 1.   *Distribution Map of the main Iberian findspots of Ivory and Ostrich Egg Shell. Heavy Stipple locates the VNSP Culture (around the Tagus estuary) and the Millaran Culture (Almeria). Light stipple indicates other areas where ivory imports are known.*

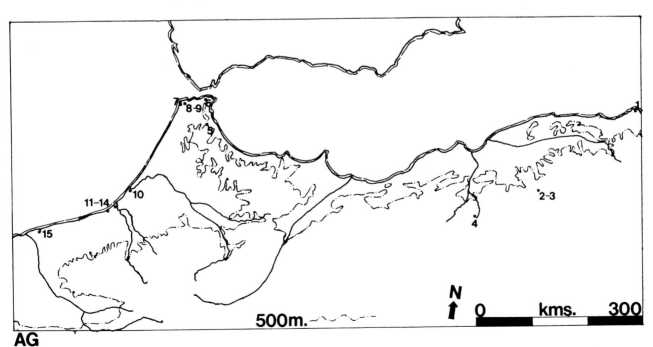

FIG 2.   *Distribution of Iberian materials in the Maghreb*

1. Cap Chenoua, 2. Tiaret, 3. Rhar Oum el Fernan, 4. Oued Saida, 5. Caf Taht el Gar, 6. Gar Cahal, 7. Ashakar, 8. Mers, 9. Ain Dahlia Kebira, 10. Mehdia, 11. Oued Akrech, 12. Grotte des Contrabandiers, Temara, 13. Dar es Soltan, 14. Sidi Messaoud, 15. El Kiffen.

TRADE IN THE SECOND AND THIRD MILLENNIA B.C. BETWEEN THE MAGHREB AND IBERIA
by Richard J. Harrison and Antonio Gilman

One of the intriguing aspects of the sophisticated Millaran and Vila Nova de São Pedro (VNSP) cultures in third millennium Iberia is the range of contacts indicated by a wide variety of imported materials. Two such materials, ivory and ostrich eggshell, were quite unobtainable locally, then as now, and had to be sought across the Straits of Gibraltar in northern Africa. Our purpose is to examine the nature of this long distance resource procurement network and to consider how it operated. This case study will lead us to some general comments on recent archaeological approaches to trade.

Ivory and Ostrich Eggshell as Resources

In prehistoric Iberia ivory and ostrich eggshell were not essential primary raw materials used to make utilitarian items. Rather, they were highly prized socially and buried in quantity with the dead. The magnificence of the burials of select personages in megalithic tombs was apparently directly linked to the number of prestige items in the tombs: metals, semi-precious stones or elaborately carved ritualia. A developing taste in Iberia for increasingly magnificent and varied non-utilitarian items can be traced from the late fourth millennium B.C. onwards.

The nearest source for ivory was the Maghreb, where elephants are known to have survived well into Punic and Roman times. Fossil ivory from Quaternary deposits can be excluded as a primary source because of its composition.[1] Iberian ivory has all the qualities of fresh ivory. Indeed, there is evidence that whole tusks were brought in. In the great Eneolithic passage grave of Matarrubilla pieces of an ivory bracelet, dagger pommel, and sandal were found along with a large piece of tusk (Collantes 1969).

In the western Maghreb the only sites where ivory occurs are Grotte des Idoles, where two pins may be of ivory (Camps-Fabrer 1966: 127), and El Kiffen, where part of an elephant tusk was associated with a Late Neolithic cemetery of the second millennium B.C. (Bailloud and Mieg de Boofzheim 1964).[2] There are also bones of *Elephas* reported from Dar es Soltan (Ruhlmann 1951: 29). There is no sign that ivory was an important resource to the inhabitants of the Maghreb in the third and second millennia B.C. Where ivory does occur, and in considerable quantity, is in southern Spain and around the Tagus estuary in central Portugal (Appendix I). The non-availability of ivory in Iberia, its occurrence in the Maghreb, and its presence in prestigious Copper and Bronze Age contexts in Spain and Portugal suggests its importance in trade.

Ostrich eggshell can only be obtained where there are live ostriches, in the same savannah environment as elephants. In the Maghreb, especially in the eastern interior, whole eggshells were used to hold liquids and pieces were fashioned into beads. In Iberia ostrich eggshell beads are known from Millaran contexts (Appendix 1).

African Imports in Iberia

The evidence for northwest African materials in Iberia is summarized, with full references in Appendix 1.[3] Ostrich eggshell occurs in far more restricted Iberian contexts than ivory. While ivory is known from Portugal as well as Andalusia and southeast Spain, ostrich eggshell occurs only in southeast Spain. Furthermore, while ivory was in continuous use and demand from Millaran to Argaric times, ostrich eggshell occurs exclusively in Millaran contexts. Thus, there is not one instance of ostrich eggshell occurring with Beaker pottery, although ivory was certainly in use in Beaker times and Beaker pottery was taken in quantity to Morocco.

Ivory first appears in Millaran and VNSP contexts (FIG. 1), where it is worked into non-utilitarian wands, rods, 'idols', combs, sandals, and dagger pommels.[4] There are claims for earlier ivory associations in late Almerian contexts (Campos and Los Molinos de Viento) in southeast Spain. There is one possible late Alentejo context in Portugal (Cabeço da Ministra, Alcobaça, north of Lisbon). However, the earliest secure contexts are Millaran and VNSP, in the latter part of the third millennium B.C.

Soundly associated discoveries of ivory (but not ostrich eggshell) in Beaker contexts occur at Palmela I, III, and IV as beads and round V-perforated buttons. At least two other V-perforated buttons of ivory are known from Cerro de La Virgen(one a tortuga button). An old find by Bonsor (1899) at El Acebuchal of a round V-perforated button "of ivory" is also likely to be Beaker in date, especially in view of the enormous amount of Beaker pottery from the site (Harrison *et al.* 1976).

From Argaric contexts[5] we continue to have an abundance of ivory beads, V-bored buttons, and even a comb (Fuente Álamo), although the range of objects appears to be smaller than in Millaran times. The quantity appears to be about the same as in earlier periods. At El Argar alone the Sirets found at least 38 pieces of ivory from 17 graves.

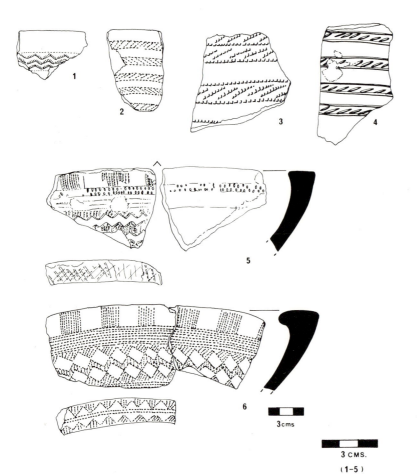

FIG 3.   Beaker Sherds from:
*1. Oued Saida. 2. Rhar Oum el
Fernan. 3. Dar es Soltan.
4. Achakar (after Koehler).
5. Mehdia. 6. Temara (4 probably
not Beaker ceramic)*

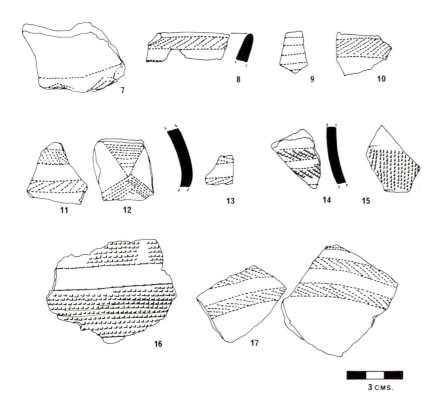

FIG 4.   Beaker Sherds from:
*Caf Taht el Gar (7. Surface.
8-9. Split 1. 10. Split 2
11-14. Split 3. 15, 17 not
located stratigraphically.
16. probably from Split 3)*

In addition to El Argar, ivory is known from Lugarico Viejo, Gatas, Fuente Álamo, Los Eriales 14, Rio de Gor 5, and Fonelas.

Iberian Imports in Africa

In northwest Africa there is far less material of Iberian origin than might be expected from the quantity of ivory in the Peninsula. Indeed, there is nothing specifically Millaran from anywhere in North Africa, despite the abundance of ivory and ostrich eggshell in contemporary Eneolithic contexts in Almeria. Of course, a complicating factor in determining the degree of reciprocity between the two regions is that virtually all the ivory and ostrich eggshell in Iberia is found as grave goods. Thus, their abundance relates to the prescriptions of burial ritual and only indirectly to the quantity imported. The computation of prehistoric "trade statistics" is not as straightforward as Renfrew (1969: 152) asserts.

For the Bell Beaker relations with North Africa we are on far stronger ground. Beaker pottery is readily recognizable as an import in African contexts and, because of its complex and often individual decoration, it can be given a precise source in Iberia. Furthermore, Beaker ceramics do not occur exclusively as grave goods or luxury items, even in Iberia, so their abundance ought to be a more direct reflection of trade intensity than distinctive Millaran or VNSP ritualia.

Jodin (1957) and Camps (1960) have proposed that "Beaker folk" were engaged in the North African ivory trade. The distribution of imports suggests this idea, since most Beakers are found along the coasts and in areas accessible from the Iberian peninsula. All the inland finds (FIG. 3, nos. 1-3) are concentrated on the steppes of western Algeria, which would have been a prime area for the African savannah fauna on which the trade ultimately depended. The modest scatter of imports in this fairly remote area contrasts with the abundance of Beakers at the accessible sites of Caf Taht el Gar and Gar Cahal.

Beakers are reported from at least seven localities in Morocco and Algeria (FIG. 2)[6] and fall into two distinct complexes of Iberian origin: the Maritime and Palmela groups.

The richest and most important sites where Maritime Beakers occur *en masse* are the coastal caves of Caf Taht el Gar near Tétouan (Tarradell 1957/8) and Gar Cahal near Ceuta (Tarradell 1955). At Caf Taht el Gar (FIG. 4) there are at least 12 pieces of comb-decorated Beaker pottery from 10 or 11 separate vessels. A larger assemblage was excavated at the cave of Gar Cahal where a completely typical Portuguese Maritime Beaker complex includes Bell Beakers (FIG. 6: 31-45),[7] Shouldered Bowls (Fig. 5: 18-30), and decorated coarser ware (FIG. 6: 48-49). The great bulk of the Gar Cahal Beakers were stratified in zone IIIa (above a "Bronce I" zone with painted pottery of Serraferlicchio type and below zone II, "Bronce II", with undecorated pottery).[8] It is striking that 33 of the 34 sherds are comb-decorated Maritime Complex sherds, with a Bell Beaker/Shouldered Bowl ratio of at least 7:5. Even more significantly, every single Bell Beaker sherd is of the *Herringbone Variety*, which has the greatest geographic dispersion of any Iberian Beaker type. It is the only Peninsular Beaker type regularly found in Western Europe (FIG. 7). The Caf Taht el Gar and Gar Cahal Beakers are of considerable interest since they are complete *assemblages* of undeniably Peninsular types (probably from central Portugal) on the northernmost coast of Morocco, and not simply a scatter of sherds. The remaining Maritime Beaker finds are single sherds from Oued Saida and Rhar Oum el Fernan on the steppes of the Algerian interior near Tiaret (Camps-Fabrer 1966: Pl. LXV), and one Maritime Bell Beaker fragment from Dar es Soltan, near Rabat (Ruhlmann 1951) (FIG. 3: 1-3). As Figure 7 indicates, there are only three Maritime Beaker centers in southern Iberia, which correspond fairly exactly with the main concentrations of ivory imports (FIG. 1).

Rich and varied Maritime assemblages are commonest in central Portugal around the Tagus estuary, where they are found in most particular association with VNSP sites (Harrison 1974a). Walled settlements such as Penha Verde (Zbyszewski and Veiga Ferreira 1958, 1959), Vila Nova de São Pedro (Jalhay and do Paço 1945; Do Paço and Sangmeister 1956; Savory 1970) and Pedra do Ouro (Leisner and Schubart 1966) all have consistent Maritime Beaker occupations where both Bell Beakers and Shouldered Bowls occur in quantity. Outside the Tagus estuary, Shouldered Bowls occur only in the Lower Guadalquivir estuary near Seville (El Acebuchal; "Sevilla", unprovenanced in Castillo 1954), and from Grave 4 at Cañada Honda de Gandul G (Leisner and Leisner 1943: Taf. 67, 1/19). Figures 8 and 9 carry a selection of Maritime Beakers from the site of El Acebuchal, themselves derived from the Tagus estuary and intrusive in the Seville region. The strong representation of the *Herringbone Variety* Beaker (FIG. 8: a-e, i, k), Shouldered Bowls (FIG. 9: 1-o, s-t) and domestic ware (FIG. 9: u-v) finds very close parallels in the Gar Cahal assemblage (FIG. 5, 19-27; Fig. 6: 31-49) and easily suggest a common Portuguese source for both the El Acebuchal and the Moroccan Maritime assemblages.

Related Maritime concentrations in southeast Spain, Languedoc, and Brittany lack the Shouldered Bowl component so characteristic of Portugal and in general possess far fewer luxury articles in their assemblages. It is not

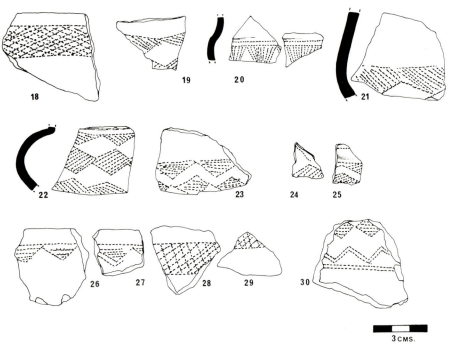

FIG 5.   Beaker Sherds from Gar
Cahal (18. level I; 19-30
level III).

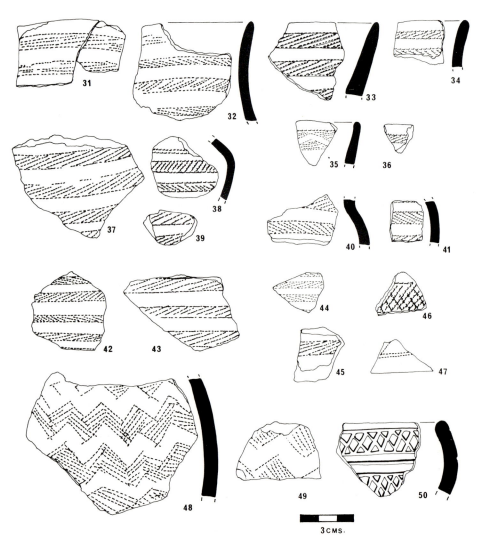

FIG 6.   Beaker Sherds from Gar
Cahal (presumably from
level IIIa).

simply owing to chance that 90% of the Beakers from Los Millares are Maritime types (Leisner and Leisner 1943; Almagro and Arribas 1963) nor that only Bell Beaker shapes are found there. At Los Millares there is not a Maritime Beaker assemblage as at Gar Cahal, El Acebuchal, or the Tagus castros. Beakers at Los Millares are only one of the many luxury commodities gathered into the tomb furniture. If anything, the contacts between the Tagus estuary, El Acebuchal, and northern Morocco were more direct than the Maritime Beaker links between the Tagus estuary, Brittany, Almeria, and Languedoc.

The second intrusive Beaker group in North Africa is the Palmela Complex, represented by single sherds, or pieces of one vessel, from at least three sites. Jodin (1959) published fragments of a Palmela bowl from Grotte des Contrabandiers (not illustrated) near Rabat, as well as a massive, comb-decorated Palmela bowl rim from Temara (FIG. 3: 6). Both pieces have numerous parallels around the Tagus estuary, where the Palmela bowl originated, and both are probably imports from Portugal. The motifs on the Temara rim sherd can be matched individually (although not all on the same sherd) on Palmela bowls around the Tagus.[9]

The comb-stamped Palmela rim sherd from Mehdia (FIG. 3: 5; Jodin 1959: FIG. 2), also near Rabat, is also of Portuguese inspiration, although it cannot be matched very closely around the Tagus. The internal rim decoration that it carries is a trait never found on any Beaker from around the Tagus, although such decoration is highly characteristic of the Ciempozuelos complex on the Spanish Meseta. It is also common at El Acebuchal where Palmela bowl sherds also occur. The Mehdia piece would be more properly placed in the Lower Guadalquivir than around the Tagus and an Andalusian origin is quite acceptable. It is interesting that the only area outside central Portugal where Palmela bowls occur more than once is in the Lower Guadalquivir. Otherwise, the distribution is highly localized around the mouth of the Tagus.

A similar mixture of Peninsular traits is evident on the Dar es Soltan *cazuela* (Ruhlmann 1951: Fig. 61), compared by Castillo (1954) to a vaguely provenanced Beaker from Seville.[10] The shape of the Dar es Soltan vessel is wholly unknown on Beakers around the Tagus estuary, but is common enough in the Ciempozuelos complex. Similarly flaring mouths occur on the Bell Beakers from Écija (Castillo 1928: Lam. XI) and Cañada Rosal (Harrison 1974b) in the Guadalquivir valley. The decorative comb motifs near the rim can be matched exactly on a Palmela rim sherd from El Acebuchal (Harrison *et al.* 1976: Fig. 22. no. 93), but not around the Tagus estuary.

Lastly, the rim from an incised, hemispherical bowl from Gar Cahal (FIG. 6: 50) should also belong to the Palmela Complex and could equally well have come from the Tagus or the lower Guadalquivir. The Beaker sherds reportedly found at El Menzeh near Casablanca (Souville 1965) are of unknown type. In summary, then, it appears that North African materials of the Palmela and related later Beaker complexes have a similar Iberian origin as the earlier Maritime materials: a primary source in the lower Tagus, a secondary source in the lower Guadalquivir.

Other than luxury decorated pottery, only two other artifacts might form part of the normal range of Beaker finds in the Peninsula. There is a two-holed archer's wrist guard of schist from Dar es Soltan (Ruhlmann 1951: Fig. 52) and a bifacially flaked flint point from Caf Taht el Gar (Tarradell 1957/8: Fig. 6). Two Palmela points are also known; one, now lost, from Ain Dahlia el Kebira near Tangier, another from Sidi Messaoud near Rabat (Souville 1965). Two caveats must be entered about the Palmela points and wristguard. They are both predominantly late elements in Beaker complexes; wristguards are much more common in Argaric contexts in southeast Spain than they are in Beaker assemblages (Sangmeister 1964). Wristguards are not common in either the Tagus or Guadalquivir estuaries. Palmela points also had a long life and a restricted distribution (FIG. 10). They occur in non-Beaker and Argaric contexts and could just as well be Argaric as Beaker in date. It is not possible to say from where in the Iberian peninsula the Moroccan pieces originated.

Iberian materials of post-Beaker (Argaric) times are few in North Africa and nearly all are found on or near the coast. They include a flat axe from Oued Akrech near Rabat (Giot and Souville 1964), a tanged copper dagger from Cape Chenoua near Tipasa (Camps and Giot 1960) and a 'halberd' of Argaric type from the Mers 5 dolmen near Tangier (Ponsich 1970: Fig. 14). Another flat bronze axe with a high tin content, like the Oued Akrech specimen, was found inland near Tiaret (Cadenat 1956).

The scarcity and isolation of these finds indicates that they are imports from the Iberian peninsula, but in no case can their origin be as precisely fixed as for the Beaker pottery. Taken as a group, the bronze artifacts of the western Maghreb cannot be referred to specific cultural contexts within Spanish or Portuguese prehistory. It is worth noting, however, that there is nothing particularly Atlantic about any of them and that the identification of the Mers 5 halberd is still an open question. As Schubart (1973) has recently demonstrated, the great majority of Iberian halberds are from the southeast; only two are known from the Algarve in southern Portugal. There are, of course, many *representations* of hafted halberds on rock engravings in the High Atlas (Schubart 1973: Fig. 15, after Malhomme 1959, 1961) and on the engraved slabs from the Alentejo (Schubart 1973: Fig. 14). Their dating is vague, however, and the High Atlas Art cannot be adequately assessed until something more is known of its archaeological context.

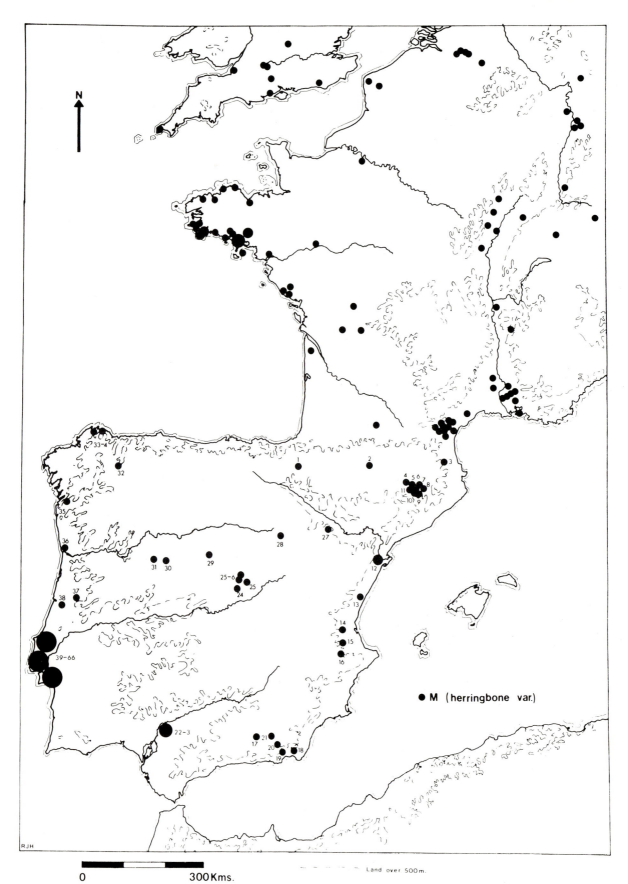

FIG 7. *Maritime Beaker Distribution (Herringbone Variety).* **Spain** *1. Cueva de Echauri; 2. Bauma Margineda (Andorra); 3. Puig Roig; 4. Peu de Roques; 5. Cova d'Aigues Vives; 6. Corderoure; 7. Cista de Coll d'en Bertran; 8. Serrat dels Quadrats; 9. Balma de Solanells; 10. Balma de San Bartolomeu; 11. Collet de les Forques; 12. Calvari d'Amposta I, II; 13. Filomena, Villareal; 14. Cova de les Aranyes; 15. Cami de Alfogas; 16. Cova de Recambra; 17. "Guadix", Almería; 18. Terrera Ventura, Tabernas; 19. Los Millares XI, XII, surface; 20. Loma de Atalaya 6, Purchena; 21. Cerro de La Virgen (Level IIa); 22. El Acebuchal; 23. Cañada Honda de Gandul G; 24. Entretérminos; 25. Arenero de Miguel Ruíz; 26. Casa del Cerro, Madrid; 27. Moncin; 28. Villar de Campo; 29. Cueva de la Tarascona; 30. Aldeavieja de Tormes; 31. Teriñuelo de Salvatierra; 32. San Pedro de Buriz; 33. Veiga dos Mouros, Puentes de García Rodriguez (Tumulus 219); 34. Veiga de Vilavella, tumuli 242, 245; 35. Chan d'Arquiña.*

Portugal *36. Guilhabreu; 37. Seixo; 38. Eira Pedrinha; 39. Vila Nova de São Pedro; 40. Pragança; 41. Ermegeira; 42. Cabeço de Arruda II; 43. Charrino; 44. Zambujal; 45. Gruta de Portucheira I; 46. Castro da Fórnea; 47. Castro da Ota; 48. Castra da Pedra do Ouro; 49. Dolmen de Casal do Penedo; 50. Cova do Biguino, Olelas; 51. Conchadas; 52. Necropole de Trigache; 53. Trigache II; 54. Agualva; 55. São Martinho de Sintra; 56. Monge; 57. Penha Verde; 58. São Pedro do Estoril I; 59. Alapraia II; 60. Alapraia IV; 61. Montes Claros; 62. Rotura; 63. Vale do Nena, Setubal; 64-5. Palmela; 66. Chibannes.*

In summary, we have an abundance of imported elephant ivory in southern Iberia in the third and second millennia B.C. and of ostrich eggshell in south-east Spain in Millaran times. In Morocco and Algeria the clearest evidence of reciprocal contact consists of the scatter of imported Beaker pottery, especially at the cave of Gar Cahal. The older Maritime Beakers can be most closely matched as an assemblage around the Tagus estuary. The slightly later Palmela bowl sherds have counterparts in both the Tagus and Guadalquivir estuary regions. The Dar es Soltan *cazuela* probably is an Andalusian import. The post-Beaker metal finds could all derive from the El Argar culture of south-east Spain.

Discussion

As we have noted, Camps (1960) and Jodin (1957) suggest that Beakers and metal artifacts were imported into the Maghreb in exchange for ivory and ostrich eggshell. This proposition finds mixed support in the evidence we have just reviewed. The abundant ivory in Millaran and VNSP contexts does not conform to the expectations of the ivory trade hypothesis because no characteristic Millaran and VNSP pieces have been found in northern Africa. Other considerations, to be discussed below, suggest, however, that the hypothesis need not be discarded out of hand. For Beaker and Argaric times there is solid evidence of reciprocity and the suggestion that Beaker pottery and metal artifacts were traded into North Africa can be retained. Heuristically, speaking of 'trade' is better than referring to the ivory in Iberia as part of a general North African "contribution" to Iberian Bronze Age cultures (Renfrew 1967: 282) or than arguing that the imported pieces in North Africa are examples of unspecified *"influences ibériques"* (Souville 1965: 421). 'Trade' also covers the facts better than other more concrete explanations, for example that Beakers were taken to North Africa by "pastoralists" of great "speed and mobility" (Savory 1968: 76). Nevertheless, as Kohl (1975) has emphasized, the social context of trade must be specified. Otherwise, 'trade' will only be, at a higher level, a vague and disordered phrase, like the 'contacts' so often mentioned in the literature of the not too distant past.

Recent studies have attempted to erect models of trading mechanisms for the Near East (Lamberg-Karlovsky 1972; Beale 1973), for the Aegean (Renfrew 1972), and in general (Renfrew 1975). Various distributions of presumably traded items in the archaeological record are related to various putative exchange mechanisms ("trickle trade", "down-the-line trade", etc.). These models do not yield straightforward results when considered against the data for North African/Iberian trade in the second and third millennia B.C. Quite different results emerge when the distributions are looked at from different sides of the Straits of Gibraltar. From an African point of view the ivory trade is anomalous, in terms of models such as those referred to, because the traded item is virtually non-existent in archaeological contexts in the source area. From an Iberian point of view, Beakers and metal artifacts are found much more frequently in some homeland regions (the Tagus estuary, the lower Guadalquivir, Almería) than in North Africa. Other parts of Iberia, however, have densities of Beakers quite comparable to those found in parts of the Maghreb (northern Morocco and the Rabat area). Thus, from a North African point of view the models do not fit, while from an Iberian point of view one or another model might indeed fit. [11] This uneven applicability is understandable enough when one realizes that Iberian/North African exchanges were conducted between partners at quite different levels on the social evolutionary scale. The importers of ivory were incipiently stratified (Bronze Age) groups, while the exporters were presumably egalitarian social groups, subsisting largely, if not exclusively, on hunting and gathering (Gilman 1974) . In Iberia the use of ivory was sociotechnic, designed to certify the final status of select and magnificent personages (cf. Binford 1962; Winters 1968), while in the Maghreb ivory was a technomic resource commanding no more value than ordinary bone. Models constructed to account for exchanges between partners who are members of similar social and economic formations do not illuminate the structure of trade between unequal partners.

The asymmetry of the ivory trade suggests that its central motor force lay in the need Iberian elites had for exotic and luxurious materials. A preliminary outline of the case for a local development of the Maritime Beaker complex from a VNSP substratum in central Portugal has been made elsewhere (Harrison 1974a, 1977). It goes some way towards accounting for the strong Portuguese flavor of the Moroccan Beakers and the long-term stability of the exchange network. Ivory was only one of many exotic imports flowing into the walled VNSP castros. An amplification of the repertoire of non-utilitarian items continued into Beaker times. In fact, if the Maritime Beaker complex is interpreted as the latest phase of the VNSP culture, then the continuity of established resource procurement networks into periods when Maritime Beaker pottery was manufactured is understandable. The same hierarchy would have existed (in changing form) throughout the VNSP-Maritime Beaker periods, making use of similar raw materials to enhance its privileged status. A similar continuity of developing elite formations may be posited for the Millaran-Argaric sequence in southeast Spain. These elites had stable means of acquiring luxury materials from areas outside their immediate sphere of control, both within the Iberian peninsula and in the Maghreb. In exchange, they might give prestigious luxury ceramics (Beakers, used in rich graves at home) or valuable metal artifacts. [12]

As we have mentioned, an important characteristic of the ivory and ostrich eggshell trade is its lack of balance or evident reciprocity. For each successive period the amount of Iberian material in the Maghreb bears little relation

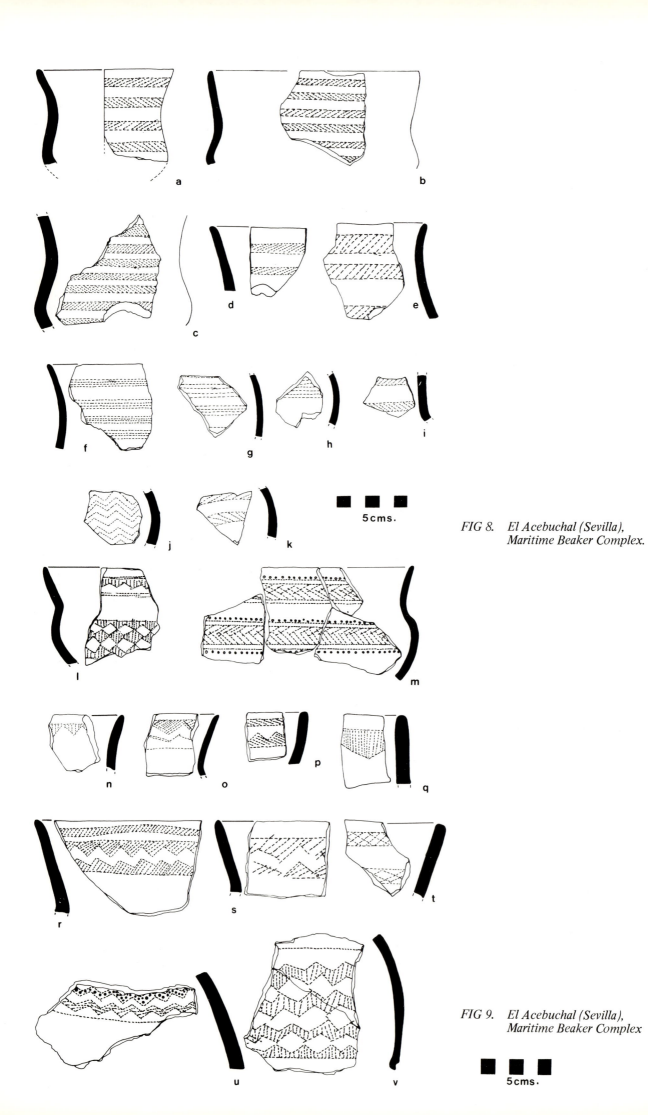

FIG 8. *El Acebuchal (Sevilla),*
Maritime Beaker Complex.

5 cms.

FIG 9. *El Acebuchal (Sevilla),*
Maritime Beaker Complex

5 cms.

to the quantities of ivory found in the Peninsula. Ivory is abundant on the Millaran/VNSP horizon, but no corresponding materials are found in North Africa. There is at the moment no certain hypothesis to account for this imbalance. One possible explanation for the absence of early Iberian imports in North Africa is that the distinctive Millaran/VNSP items are mostly found in ritual assemblages, such as burial lots. Thus, one would not expect to find them outside their proper context. Non-ritual items of the period are to a great extent typologically non-descript and would not be readily recognized as imports in the Maghreb. Nevertheless, characteristic VNSP/Millaran artifacts are not all ritual items. Why were no VNSP channeled, pattern-burnished *copas* (the so-called *Importkeramik*) sent to North Africa like the luxury ware of a later time (Beakers)? It is possible also that in the earlier period some perishable commodity was the only material exchanged for the ivory, leaving no trace in the archaeological record. Both of these suggestions argue that we are dealing with residual distributions which give a distorted picture of the whole system.

Prehistorians can easily argue that their evidence is incomplete and accordingly that the extinct cultural systems in which they are interested cannot (as yet) be reconstructed reliably. Such contentions are often justified, their only defect being that they lead nowhere. It is more interesting to proceed on the speculative assumption that the available evidence is somehow representative of the past totality. On this basis, then, what account can be given of the paucity of imports into the Maghreb in comparison to exports from it? The root, in our opinion, is in the same discrepancy between the trading partners which accounted for the absence of ivory in the archaeological record at its source. Just as the egalitarian natives of the Maghreb found little use for ivory, just so they would relinquish it to Iberians for few goods in exchange. This imbalance tended, however, to disappear over time. At first, no recognizable Iberian goods can be identified in the Maghreb. Then, Beakers appear in some quantity along with copper and bronze implements. Metal artifacts, especially those with a high tin content, like the Tiaret and Oued Akrech axes, would, of course, have commanded a high price even in Iberia. Indeed, Iberian imports appear in elite North African contexts, such as the Argaric halberd in the Mers 5 burial monument. Towards the end of the second millennium B.C. even ivory is included in elite burials: at El Kiffen an ivory tusk is found as gravegoods along with fine pottery with comb-impressed designs apparently of Beaker inspiration (Bailloud and Mieg 1964, cf. Gilman 1975: 110-111). Thus, it seems possible that, in the course of the millennium in which Iberians procured ivory, they may have provided opportunities for some members of Maghreb social groups to obtain superordinate statuses, with consequent effect on the balance of trade and the values placed on the goods exchanged. This view of the dynamics of Iberian-North African trade is, we believe, consistent with the evidence at hand, and will no doubt require substantial modification as more sites in better dated sequences become available, especially from the Maghreb.

Much recent archaeological work on trade has skirted consideration of the class background of social exchange. Trade is viewed as a mutually beneficial interchange between inhabitants of different ecological zones or possessors of complementary skills. The interchanges are tacitly assumed to take place between social equals. This view is further reflected in the inclination to see the 'trader' as a specialist middle-man somehow outside the social system (Kohl 1975: 47). As Robert Adams (1974) has rightly stressed, however, these attitudes tend to ignore the degree to which elites control 'redistribution' and 'exchange' to their own advantage. In order to make sense of the pattern of evidence for North African-Iberian trade in the third and second millennia B.C., we have had to begin by taking into account the basic socio-economic structure of the period. During the Copper and Bronze Ages social evolution took place from more egalitarian to more stratified social and economic formations. The trade was apparently managed by the elite of those formations in its own self-interest, to celebrate and consolidate its power. Since many archaeological studies of trade involve culture-historical situations where analogous social changes were in progress, we assume that, to the extent that those studies do not attempt to take social structural phenomena into account, they will fail to make full sense of their evidence.

Notes

1. After burial ivory loses the oily substance which fills its countless minute pores. Fresh, oil-impregnated tusks are far easier to carve and take on a delicate, transparent polish which is lacking in ancient or desiccated ivory. As Penniman (1964: 13-16) observes, fossil ivory tends either to disintegrate in a cone-within-a-cone fashion or to decay more completely into a dense white powder. In either case the rotted remains are unusable owing to the loss of organic material. With the loss of fat and water ivory frequently absorbs the color of its surroundings, taking on a variety of brown or ochreous hues. The only persistent exploitation of fossil ivory seems to have been in Europe in the 18th and 19th centuries A.D., when it was obtained from Siberian mammoth carcasses in ice deposits. Even here fat loss made carving harder and the polish duller than with fresh tusks (Penniman 1964).
2. The most reliable C-14 determination is NZ-1510: 1142 ± 200 B.C. (cf. Gilman 1974: 279).
3. It should be emphasized that ivory sometimes is hard to distinguish from polished bone. The identifications of the Leisners (1943, 1965) and the Sirets (1887) can be accepted, as can the more recent Spanish discoveries at Matarrubilla and Cerro de La Virgen. Some of the Portuguese claims for ivory in the Lisbon region are more doubtful, however, and are so indicated with a question mark in

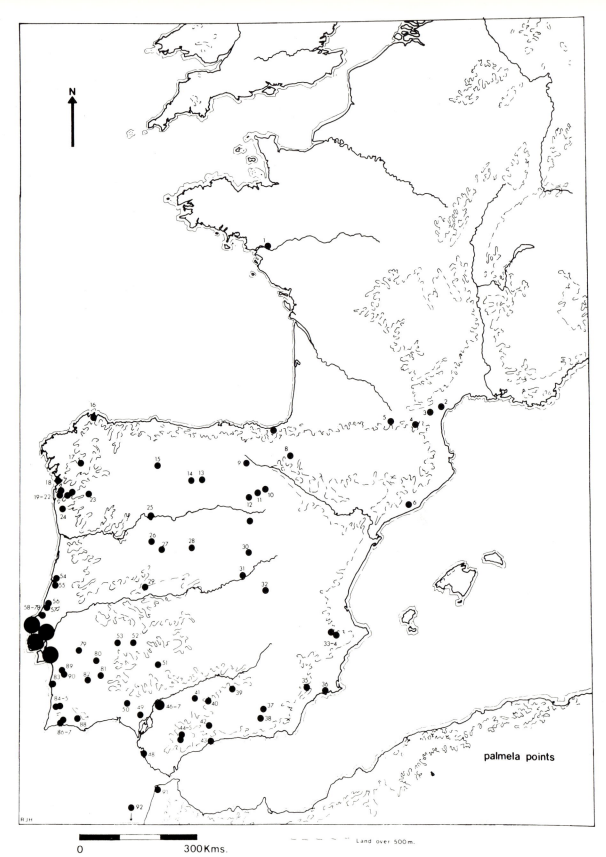

FIG 10. *Distribution of Palmela points.* **France** *1. Loire, Nantes; 2. Fontlaurier, Bizanet, Aude; 3. Massac, Aude; 4. Grotte de Montou a Corbiere; 5. "Haute Ariege"*

Spain & Portugal *6. Cova de "El Pany"; 7. Obionete, San Sebastian; 8. Dolmen de Sakulo; 9. Miranda de Ebro; 10. Arancón, Soria; 11. Alcubilla, Soria; 12. Layna, Soria; 13. Padilla de Abajo; 14. Carrión, Palencia; 15. Grajal de Campos; 16. Vilavella, Puentes de García Rodriguez; 17. Monte das Cabras, Lalín; 18. Limeus, Hío; 19. Gondomar; 20. Cabreiras (Arbo?); 21. Cabeceiras de Basto, Braga; 22. Citania; 23. Castro de São Lourenco, Chaves; 24. São Bento de Balaguês; 25. Los Pasos, Zamora; 26. Salamanca; 27. Aldeavieja de Tormes; 28. Cardeñosa, Avila; 29. Palencia, Cáceres; 30. Mejorada del Campo; 31. "Toledo", Finca de Paloma; 32. Ucles, Cuenca; 33. Cueva de la Pastora, Alcoy; 34. El Cabezo Navarro, Onteniente; 35. Bastetana region; 36. Ifre, Mazarrón, Murcia; 37. Cerro de La Virgen; 38. Cuesta de la Sabina, Gorafe; 39. Villacarrillo, Jaén; 40. Montilla, Cordoba; 41. Cañada Rosal; 42. Alcaide 6, Antequera; 43. Cueva de la Pileta, Malaga; 44. Grazalema, Cadiz; 45. Villaluengo del Rosario, Cadiz; 46. El Acebuchal; 47. Carmona; 48. Coto de Doñana, Cadiz; 49. Villamanrique, Sevilla; 50. Soto, Dolmen 2; 51. Azuaga, Badajoz; 52. Prado de Lacara, Mérida, Badajoz; 53. "Prov. Badajoz"; 54. Crasto, Figueira da Foz; 55. Forno da Cal, Vinha da Rainha, Soure; 56. Gruta IX, Redondas, Alcobaça; 57. Val do Carvalhal, Alcobaça; 58. Casa da Moura, Cesareda; 59. Vila Nova de São Pedro; 60. Pai Mogo I; 61. Serra da Mutelas; 62. Zambujal; 63. "Near Torres Vedras"; 64. Barro; 65. Castro da Fórnea; 66. Cova da Moura, Torres Vedras; 67. Castro do Penedo; 68. Pedra do Ouro; 69. Montelavar; 70. Praia das Maças; 71. Belavista; 72. São Martinho de Sintra; 73. Penha Verde; 74. Ponte de Laje; 75. Palmela; 76. Chibannes; 77. Rotura; 78. Porto Covo; 79. Dolmen EP, Montemor-o-Novo? 80. Anta 2 dos Gorginos; 81. Castro de São Bernado, Moura; 82. Monte Outeiro; 83. Pedra Branca; 84. Vila Nova de Milafontes, Odemira; 85. Odemira; 86. Caldeiroa, Lagos; 87. Paderne, Albufeira; 88. Alcala 4; 89. Lousal; 90. Herdade do Duque, Grandola; 91. Ain Dahlia Kebira, Tangier (Morocco); 92. Sidi Messaoud (Morocco); 93. Dolmen de Kercadoret, Morbihan (France).*

Appendix 1. In at least two cases claimed ivory pieces are in fact hard well-polished bone (Belavista and Charrino). Other bone pieces probably misidentified as ivory occur at Cova da Raposa, the castros of Olelas and Pragança, and possibly also Lapa do Bugio. More certainly identified ivory pieces are known from Grutas do Poço Velho (Cascais), Samarra, Belas, Casainhos, and São Martinho in the Lisbon area, and from Nora and Marcella in the Algarve. The correct identification of ostrich eggshell is less problematic: it is an unmistakeable material.

4.   Millaran-VNSP ivory: Los Millares 2, 5, 7, 8, 12, 20, 40, 63; Los Castillejos; Almizaraque; Matarrubilla; Nora; Marcella; Grutas do Poço Velho; Samarra; Belas; São Martinho de Sintra 2; Casainhos.

5.   El Argar A is now dated to at least 1700 B.C. (Schubart 1973: Fig. 12). It has a substantial chronological overlap with later Beaker complexes (Savory 1968: 260-261). Recent C-14 dates from Cerro de La Virgen would tend to push back the early Argaric groups to around 1850-1800 B.C. (Vogel and Waterbolk 1972: 73).

6.   Henry Koehler's excavations at Grotte des Idoles (Koehler 1931a) produced at least one Beaker-like sherd (FIG. 3, no. 4; Koehler 1931b: Pl. II/1) from layer "B" or "C" (cf. Gilman 1975: 96-98), which Jodin (1957) accepted as a Beaker ceramic. The incised herringbone decoration in thin bands is reminiscent of Maritime Bell Beakers, but cannot be matched precisely to any south Spanish or Portuguese Beaker.

7.   The classic *Seeverkehrbecher* of the Leisners (1943), Sangmeister (1961), and Savory (1968).

8.   For full discussion of the Gar Cahal and Caf Taht el Gar stratigraphies, see Gilman (1975: 100-107).

9.   Particularly rich sites with numerous comb-decorated Palmela bowls include Palmela I-IV (Leisner 1965). Montes Claros (Jalhay and Do Paço 1948; Do Paço and Bartholo 1954), and Ponte de Laje (Zbyszewski *et al*, 1957; Vaultier *et al*, 1958, 1959).

10. Stated only to be "from Seville". It is actually a Shouldered Bowl, not a Bell Beaker, and has exact parallels around the Tagus estuary. Castillo's comparison with the Dar es Soltan Beaker is not apt.

11. It is impossible to assess the goodness of fit of Beaker distribution with respect to any one of Renfrew's (1972, 1975) models as opposed to another because of the unevenness of the available data. Given the low quality of our information it would be hard to discriminate between "freelance commercial" trade (Renfrew 1972: Fig. 20.11) and "directional commercial" trade (ibid.: Fig. 20.12), for example. Thus, the concentration of Beaker finds at Gar Cahal might suggest that it was a temporary base for Iberian traders, but we do not know enough about other contemporary sites to contrast effectively their Beaker frequencies with Gar Cahal's.

12. In most of the literature Beakers tend to be regarded as the material expression of a prehistoric ethnic group, the "Beaker folk". The wide distribution of Beakers is explained by the folk's mobile occupational emphasis. They were nomadic pastoralists (Savory 1968: 166-167) or metal traders (Childe 1957: 222), "*vergleichbar etwa wandernden Schmieden Schwarzafrikas auch den* 'pedlars' *der nordamerikanische Kolonialzeit*" (Sangmeister 1972: 200). This view does not account for two salient features of Maritime Beaker distribution (in south-western Europe, at least): 1) that Beakers are found in great concentration in a few areas, much less frequently elsewhere; 2) that Maritime Beakers are usually found with luxury goods. The position put forward here is that Beakers were a luxury ware made for the emergent elite class of a few nuclear centers and traded by that elite as part of their long-distance procurement activities. This view accounts for the anomalies unexplained by the conventional 'Beaker folk' theory.

APPENDIX I

A.   List of ivory findspots until the Argaric period in Iberia. Questionmark indicates doubtful identification. Asterisk indicates a Beaker item (usually a V-perforated button with Beaker pottery from the same site).

Spain

1.   Los Molinos de Viento, Almería ("lissoire en ivoire") (Siret and Siret 1887: *Texte,* p. 245).

2.   Campos, Almería ("bâtonnet en ivoire creusé de deux trous convergents . . . ") (Siret and Siret 1887: *Texte,* p. 57).

3.   Matarrubilla, Sevilla (section of an elephant tusk; pieces of a sandal, bracelet, and dagger pommel) (Collantes de Terán 1969).

4.   Los Millares, tombs 2, 5, 7, 8, 12, 40, 63 (various: combs, rods, wands, sandals, pots, *etc.*) (Leisner and Leisner 1943).

5.   Almizaraque (Leisner and Leisner 1943).

6.   Los Castillejos, Cuevas de Montefrio, Granada (rod) (Tarradell 1952).

*7.   Dolmen de Sakulo, Roncal, Navarra (V perforated button) (Apellániz and Nolte 1966).

*8.   El Acebuchal, Carmona, Sevilla (V perforated button) (Bonsor 1899).

*9.   Cerro de La Virgen, Orce, Granada (V perforated buttons) (Schüle 1969).

10. Rio de Gor 5 (ivory vessel and wands) (Leisner and Leisner 1943).

11. Fonelas (Leisner and Leisner 1943).

12.   Los Eriales 14 (button) (Leisner and Leisner 1943).
13.   Gatas, Almería (pyramidal button, "identical to those from El Argar") (Siret and Siret 1887: *Texte,* p. 174).
14.   Lugarico Viejo, Almería (two ivory buttons) (Siret and Siret 1887: Pl. 16, Fig. 24-5).
15.   Fuente Álamo, Almería (ivory comb) (Siret and Siret 1887: Pl. 65: no, 62).
16.   El Argar, Almería (all references to Siret and Siret 1887):

      Grave 2 (pl. 41):   1 bead.
      Grave 64 (pl. 36):   1 bead.
      Grave 152 (pl. 51): 2 beads.
      Grave 202 (pl. 41): 6 pyramidal buttons (*Texte,* p.135).
      Grave 289 (pl. 40): 2 beads.
      Grave 301 (pl. 51): arc-shaped pendant.
      Grave 334 (pl. 52): 1 bead.
      Grave 386 (pl. 52): 2 beads.
      Grave 407 (pl. 48): 1 conical V perforated button.
      Grave 429 (pl. 34): 1 bead.
      Grave 439 (pl. 38): 4 beads.
      Grave 454 (pl. 44): 1 bead.
      Grave 494 (pl. 41): 1 bead.
      Grave 501 (pl. 53): 1 bead.
      Grave 579 (pl. 53): 10 beads.
      Grave 584 (pl. 41): 1 bead.
      Grave 623 (pl. 54): 2 beads.
  ? Grave 738 (pl. 39): 7 beads (or teeth).

(N.B.   Buttons from graves 202 and 407 were coated with cinnabar).

Portugal

1.   Nora, Algarve (dagger pommel) (Leisner and Leisner 1943).
2.   Marcella, Algarve (comb) (Leisner and Leisner 1943).
3.   Cabeço da Ministra, Alcobaça ("uma lasca de marfim, apresentando numadas extremidades dois cortes para suspensão. Numa das faces nota-se uma bellissima cor amarella") (Vieira Natividade 1901: p. 56, Fig. 101).
4.   São Pedro do Estoril I (rod?) (Leisner, do Paço, and Ribeiro 1964: 57).
5.   Grutas do Poço Velho, Cascais (comb) (Leisner 1965).
6.   Samarra (comb) (Leisner 1965).
7.   Anta de Belas (beads) (Leisner 1965).
8.   São Martinho de Sintra 2 (box, cylinder idol) (Leisner 1965).
9.   Casainhos (comb) (Leisner 1965).
*10.   Palmela I, IV (V perforated button) (Leisner 1965).
*11.   Palmela III (beads) (Leisner 1965).
?12.   Vila Nova de São Pedro (rods or cylinder idols, some pins) (do Paço 1961: 105).
?13.   Castro de Olelas (rod) (Veiga Ferreira 1966).
?14.   Castro de Pragança (V perforated button) (Veiga Ferreira 1966).
?15.   Cova da Raposa (rod or cylinder idol) (Veiga Ferreira 1966).
?16.   Lapa do Bugio, Sesimbra (rod) (Monteiro, Zbyszewski. and Veiga Ferreira 1971).

Incorrect identifications:

17.   Belavista (V-perforated button) (Leisner and Ribeiro 1964: 56). This button is later described as being made of bone (Leisner 1965).
18.   "Tholos" of Charrino (V-perforated buttons) (Veiga Ferreira 1966). Seen by Harrison in 1973 and identified as being of bone, not ivory.

B.   List of ostrich eggshell findspots in Iberia.

Los Millares 12, 63 (800 and 12 flat beads, respectively): Leisner and Leisner 1943.

References Cited

Adams, Robert McC.
    1974   Anthropological perspectives on ancient trade. *Current Anthropology* 15: 239-258. Chicago.
Almagro Basch, M., and A. Arribas Palau
    1963   El poblado y la necrópolis megalíticos de Los Millares (Santa Fé de Mondújar, Almería).
        Bibliotheca Praehistorica Hispana 3.   Madrid.
Apellániz Castroviejo, J.M., and E. Nolte
    1966   Excavación, estudio y datación por el C-14 de la cueva sepulcral de "Kobeaga" (Ispaster, Vizcaya).
        Munibe 18 (1/4): 37-62. San Sebastián.
Bailloud, G., and P. Mieg de Boofzheim
    1964   La nécropole néolithique d'El Kiffen. *Libyca* 12: 95-171. Algiers.
Beale, T.
    1973   Early trade in highland Iran: a view from a source area. *World Archaeology* 5 (2): 133-148. London.
Binford, L. R.
    1962   Archaeology as anthropology. *American Antiquity* 28 (2): 217-225. Salt Lake City.
Bonsor, G.
    1899   Les colonies agricoles pré-Romaines de la vallée du Bétis. *Révue Archéologique* 35: 125-159, 232-325, 376-391.   Paris.

Cadenat, P.
    1956   Découverte d'une hache de bronze dans la commune-mixte de Tiaret. *Libyca* 4: 283-287.
            Algiers.
Camps, G.
    1960   Les traces d'un Age du Bronze en Afrique du Nord. *Revue Africaine* 104 (1/2): 31-55. Algiers.
Camps, G., and P. R. Giot
    1960   Un poignard chalcolithique au Cap Chenoua. *Libyca* 8: 263-276. Algiers.
Camps-Fabrer, H.
    1966   Matière et art mobilier dans la préhistoire nord-africaine et saharienne. *Mémoires du Centre de
            Recherches Anthropologiques, Préhistoriques, et Ethnographiques* 5. Algiers
Castillo y Yurrita, A. del
    1928   *La Cultura del Vaso Campaniforme: Su Origen y Extensión en Europa.* Barcelona.
    1954   La cazuela de la cueva de Dar-es-Soltan y su procedencia hispánica. *I. Congreso Arqueológico del
            Marruecos Español*: 163-170.   Tetuan.
Childe, V. G.
    1957   *The Dawn of European Civilization.*   London.
Collantes de Terán, F.
    1969   El dolmen de Matarrubilla. *V. Symposium Internacional de Prehistoria Peninsular:* 163-170.
            Barcelona.
Gilman, A.
    1974   Neolithic of Northwest Africa. *Antiquity* 48: 273-282. Cambridge.
    1975   The later prehistory of Tangier, Morocco. *Bulletin of the American School of Prehistoric Research.*
            no. 29. Cambridge, Mass.
Giot, P. R., and G. Souville
    1964·   La hache en bronze de l'Oued Akrech(Maroc). *Libyca* 12: 301-306. *Algiers.*
Harrison, R. J.
    1974a   Origins of the Bell Beaker cultures: some speculations. *Antiquity* 48: 99-109.   Cambridge.
    1974b   A closed find from Cañada Rosal, near Ecija (Sevilla). *Madrider Mitteilungen* 15: 77-94. Heidelberg
    1977   The Bell Beaker Cultures of Spain and Portugal. Cambridge, Mass.
Harrison, R. J; T. Bubner, and V. Hibbs.
    1976   The Beaker Pottery from El Acebuchal, Carmona (Prov. Sevilla). *Madrider Mitteilungen* 17: 79-141.
            Heidelberg.
Jalhay, E., and A. do Paço
    1945   El castro de Vila Nova de San Pedro. *Actas y Memorias de la Sociedad Española de Antropología,
            Ethnografía, y Prehistoria* 20: 5-91. Madrid.
    1948   Lisboa há 4000 anos: a estação pre-histórica de Montes Claros (Monsanto). *Lisboa é Seu Termino* 1:
            51-58. Lisbon.
Jodin, A.
    1957   La céramique campaniforme de Dar-es-Soltan. *Bulletin de la Société Préhistorique Française* 54: 44-48.
            Paris.
    1959   Nouveaux documents sur la civilisation du vase campaniforme au Maroc. *XV. Congrès Préhistorique de
            France (Monaco):* 677-687. Paris.
Koehler, H.
    1931a   La céramique de la grotte d'Achakar (Maroc) et ses rapports avec celles des civilisations de la
            péninsule ibérique. *Revue Anthropologique* 41: 156-157. Paris.
    1931b   La grotte d'Achakar au Cap Spartel. *Collection Marrochitana* 1. Bordeaux.
Kohl, Philip L.
    1975   The archaeology of trade. *Dialectical Anthropology.* 1: 43-50. Amsterdam.
Lamberg-Karlovsky, C. C.
    1972   Trade mechanisms in Indus-Mesopotamian interrelations. *Journal of the American Oriental Society*
            92 (2): 222-229. Baltimore.
Leisner, G, and V. Leisner
    1943   Die Megalithgräber der iberischen Halbinsel: der Süden. *Römisch-Germanische Forschungen* 17. Berlin.
Leisner, V.
    1965   Die Megalithgräber der iberischen Halbinsel: der Westen. *Madrider Forschungen* 1 (3). Berlin.
Leisner, V., A. do Paço, and L. Ribiero
    1964   *Grutas Artificiais de São Pedro de Estoril.* Lisbon.
Leisner, V. and H. Schubart
    1966   Die kupferzeitliche Befestigung von Pedra do Ouro/Portugal. *Madrider Mitteilungen* 7: 9-60. Heidelberg.
Malhomme, J.
    1959   *Corpus des Gravures Rupestres du Grand Atlas* 1. Rabat
    1961   *Corpus des Gravures Rupestres du Grand Atlas* 2. Rabat.
Monteiro, R., G. Zbyszewski, and O. da Veiga Ferreira
    1971   Nota preliminar sobre a lapa pre-histórica do Bugio (Azoia-Sesimbra). *II. Congresso Nacional de
            Arqueologia (Porto):* 107-120.
Paço, A. do, and M.L. Bartholo
    1954   Considerações acerca da estação arqueológica de Montes Claros (Monsanto) e da sua cerâmica
            campaniforme. *Broteria* 59: 200-203.
Paço, A. do, and E. Sangmeister
    1956   Vila Nova de São Pedro: eine befestigte Siedlung der Kupferzeit in Portugal. *Germania* 34 (3/4):
            211-230. Frankfurt.
Penniman, T. K.
    1964   Pictures of ivory and other animal teeth, bone, and antler. *Pitt-Rivers Museum, University of Oxford,
            Occasional Paper on Technology* 5. Oxford.

Ponsich, M.
    1970   *Recherches Archéologiques à Tanger et dans sa Région.* Paris.
Renfrew, C.
    1967   Colonialism and Megalithismus. *Antiquity* 41: 276-288. Cambridge.
    1969   Trade and culture process in European prehistory. *Current Anthropology* 10: 151-169. Chicago.
    1972   *The Emergence of Civilisation: the Cyclades and the Aegean in the Third Millennium B.C.* London.
    1975   Trade as action at a distance: questions of integration and communication. In: Jeremy A. Sabloff
          and C.C. Lamberg-Karlovsky, eds. *Ancient Civilization and Trade:* 3-59. Albuquerque.
Ruhlmann, A.
    1951   La grotte préhistorique de Dar es-Soltan. *Collection Hespéris* 11. Paris.
Sangmeister, E.
    1961   Exposé sur la civilisation du vase campaniforme. *I. Colloque Atlantique* (Brest): 25-55. Rennes.
    1964   Die Schmalen "Armschutzplatten." In: R. von Uslar and K. Narr, eds. *Studien aus Alteuropa* 1:
          93-122. Cologne.
    1972   Sozial-ökonomische Aspekte der Glockenbecherkultur. *Homo* 23: 188-203. Göttingen.
Savory, H. N.
    1968   *Spain and Portugal. The Prehistory of the Iberian Peninsula.* London.
    1970   A section through the innermost rampart at the Chalcolithic castro of Vila Nova de São Pedro,
          Santarém (1959). *I. Journadas Arqueologicas:* 5-18. Lisbon.
Schubart, H.
    1973   Las alabardas tipo Montejícar. In: *Estudios Dedicados al Professor Dr. Luis Pericot:* 247-269.
          Barcelona.
Schüle, G.
    1969   Tartessos y el hinterland (excavaciones de Orce y Galera). *V. Symposium Internacional de
          Prehistoria Peninsular:* 15-32. Barcelona.
Siret, H., and L. Siret
    1887   *Les Premiers Ages du Métal dans le Sud-Est de l'Espagne.* Antwerp.
Souville, G.
    1965   Influences de la péninsule ibérique sur les civilisations post-néolithiques du Maroc. In: E. Ripoll-
          Perelló, ed. *Miscelánea en Homenaje al Abate Breuil:* 409-422. Barcelona.
Tarradell, M.
    1952   La Edad del Bronce en Montefrío (Granada). Resultados de las excavaciones en yacimientos de las
          Peñas de los Gitanos. *Ampurias* 14: 49-80. Barcelona.
    1955   Die Ausgrabung von Gar Cahal (Schwarze Höhle) in Spanish Marokko. *Germania* 33: 13-23. Frankfurt.
    1957/8 Caf Taht el Gar, cueva neolítica en la región de Tetuán (Marruecos). *Ampurias* 19/20: 137-159.
          Barcelona.
Vaultier, M., J. Roche, and O. da Veiga Ferreira
    1958   Novas excavações na gruta da Ponte de Lage (Oeiras). *I. Congresso Nacional de Arqueológia*
          (Lisboa) 111-115.
Veiga Ferreira, O. da
    1966   La culture du vase campaniforme au Portugal. *Serviços Geológicos de Portugal, Memória* 12. Lisbon.
Vieira Natividade, M.
    1901   *As Grutas de Alcobaça.* Porto.
Vogel, J. C., and H. T. Waterbolk
    1972   Groningen radiocarbon dates X. *Radiocarbon* 14: 6-110. New Haven.
Winters, H. D.
    1968   Value systems and trade cycles of the late Archaic in the Midwest. In: S. R. Binford and L. R. Binford,
          eds. *New Perspectives in Archaeology:* 175-222. Chicago.
Zbyszewski, G., and O. da Veiga Ferreira
    1958   Estação pre-histórica da Penha Verde (Sintra) *Communicações dos Serviços Geológicos de Portugal*
          39: 37-57. Lisbon.
    1959   Segunda campanha de escavações na Penha Verde (Sintra). *I. Congresso Nacional de
          Arqueologia (Lisboa):* 401-406.
Zbyszewski, G., A. Viana, and O. da Veiga Ferreira
    1957   A gruta pre-histórica da Ponte de Laje (Oeiras). *Comunicações dos Serviços Geólogicos de Portugal*
          38: 389-400.

THE NEOLITHIC OF WESTERN ASIA: 1945 TO 1975. A RETROSPECT.
by Kathleen Kenyon

Hugh Hencken's wide range of interests spanned the western confines of Europe to the Mediterranean. Though the Neolithic of Asia was not one of his special subjects, it would seem to be sufficiently near to his interests to be a suitable contribution to this volume. Another reason for suitability is that the basis of the article is a lecture given to the Royal Irish Academy, and it was in Ireland that Hugh was working when I first knew him. I am most grateful to have been given the opportunity to join in this tribute to my old friend.

Our understanding of the beginnings of the Neolithic (I am intentionally using the plural) has made enormous strides in the thirty years here discussed. When at the end of the War in 1945 European archaeologists could return to their studies, prehistorians based their comprehension of the metamorphosis of man the gatherer and parasite into man the producer, or in the jargon of the economist today a contributor to the GNP, and then into man the citizen on Professor Gordon Childe's writings, and with Childe they believed that the most important centre from which these innovations spread was western Asia. This was the home of Childe's Neolithic Revolution, though he fully recognized that a similar process probably took place in the New World and in central and eastern Asia. It would still today be accepted that the main centre of progress affecting Europe was western Asia, though some independent progress may have been made in Europe. The great step forward in our knowledge is that today we can no longer talk of a Neolithic Revolution, for it was a process spread over millennia.

This change Childe would have accepted with avidity. Indeed, germs of it were already taking root in his revisions. In the 1929 reprinting of the 1928 edition of *The Most Ancient East*, the third chapter was entitled "The Oldest Farmers." In the re-written 1952 edition of *New Light on the Most Ancient East*, this chapter has become "The Oldest Egyptian Farmers." In 1952, it was no longer dogma that the earliest steps to a settled way of life took place in the Nile valley.

The basis of one's understanding at this period after the War, which was marked by the resumption of archaeological activity in western Asia, was that the Neolithic, at least in this area, was defined as the stage at which man had become sufficiently master of his environment by the development of agriculture and the domestication of animals to become fully sedentary and to establish permanent villages. The diagnostic material artifact was not so much the polished axe of the 19th century classification but pottery.

Nowadays, the picture is so much more complex that some prehistorians prefer not to use the term Neolithic. I continue to do so, making the main criteria a population sufficiently sedentary to build permanent houses and having some form of food production. Even here there are some pluses and minuses and border-line cases.

Though by about 1950 the first puffs of the wind of change had begun to be felt, and the first step forward had been taken, the picture of western Asia still made a nice logical and compact scheme. A map prepared at that date shows the Fertile Crescent between the valleys of the Nile and Tigris-Euphrates marked by the names of villages in which had been found the first Neolithic pottery. On the map there are two exceptions to this characteristic of use of pottery, Jericho and Jarmo.

Jericho was excavated by Professor John Garstang between 1930 and 1936 (Garstang 1948). Most of his excavations were concerned with the Bronze Age levels, but in 1935 and 1936 he cut a great trench near the northeast end of the tell, in which at one point in a very small sounding he claimed to have reached sterile soil (this in fact is doubtful). Beneath Early Bronze Age levels and deposits of Neolithic pottery, he found a long succession of well-built houses and thus clear architectural evidence of permanent settlement, but in which no pottery was used. This idiosyncrasy was regarded with interest by his colleagues, but the general condescending conclusion was that Jericho, and indeed Palestine, was a backwater, lagging behind the achievements of the river valleys and the rest of the Fertile Crescent.

Jarmo, on the Iraq foothills of the Zagros, was first excavated in 1948 by Professor Robert Braidwood (1952), and was the first important excavation in western Asia after the end of the War. The remains were not very impressive, a small village with four superimposed levels of buildings, thus certainly indicating permanent settlement. The importance of the excavations was twofold. The excavations were part of a planned exploration to find the beginnings of settlement and the accompanying agriculture. The site was selected since it seemed to provide the prerequisites of being within the habitat of the wild ancestors of grains subsequently domesticated and an environment - rainfall and soil - favourable for primitive agriculture. The expedition, moreover, included the scientists necessary for the study of such aspects. Secondly, in the excavation of Jarmo dating by radio-active carbon was used for the first time, since Dr. Libby's techniques had just reached the stage that they could be adopted by archaeologists to date their prehistoric levels. Up to this time, fixed dates in western Asia began c. 3000 B.C. when links could be established between local cultures and the culture of Egypt, itself dated with a fair degree of precision by the Egyptian calendar with its astronomical foundation. Professor Garstang could only guess at by how much his Neolithic levels preceded those of the Early Bronze Age, roughly contemporary with the Old Kingdom of Egypt.

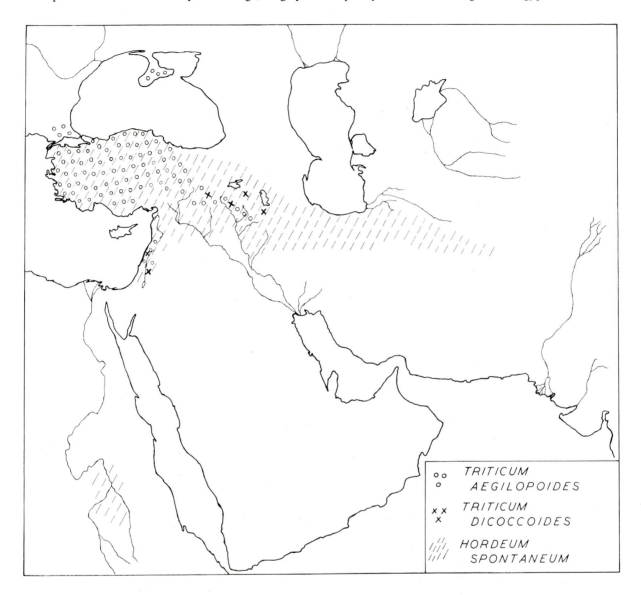

TRITICUM AEGILOPOIDES

TRITICUM DICOCCOIDES

HORDEUM SPONTANEUM

The first Carbon-14 dating for Jarmo was c. 4800 B.C. The 1950 map takes that as a starting point of what appeared to be a reasonable succession and chronology. The framework seemed to be first permanent settlements and primitive agriculture c. 5000-4800 B.C., with preceding less permanent sites, intermediate between full hunting/gathering and full settlement, as the background that could be traced in the foot-hill area of N.E. Iraq and the surrounding countries. It seemed that as this development spread west into the lower and richer area of the Fertile Crescent the manufacture of pottery appeared, and these are the villages shown on the map. For these villages, a date of c. 4500 B.C. seemed to suit. This allowed for the various stages of the later Neolithic and Chalcolithic and beginning of the Early Bronze Age which have to be fitted in before 3000 B.C. Where in this scheme Jericho fitted was still uncertain, for this depended on whether or not the area was a backwater. This then is the picture in the first stage of the period of archaeological investigation under discussion.

One can say that in this first stage the horizon had widened and the outlines had become firmer, but there had been no revolution. The full revolution that has so changed the picture at the end of the period can be ascribed to three main causes - the great increase of excavation concerned with prehistoric sites, with improved and more precise techniques, taking the place of a concentration on great historic cities, a whole new time-scale introduced by the widespread use of Carbon-14 dating, and the new scientific approach in the study of the environmental background, largely initiated by Professor Braidwood.

These environmental studies form the background of the whole story, for the opportunities of primitive man were controlled by his environment. During the decade 1950-1960, the studies initiated by Professor Braidwood and his team provided the framework for future work. A most revealing aspect of this work is the map prepared by Dr. Hans Helbaek of the habitat of wild grains. On the thesis, at that stage of investigation considered to be dogma, though now holes in the dogma are beginning to appear, that permanent, year-round settlement must be dependent on food production - agriculture and the domestication of animals - earliest settlements must lie in this area. Helbaek (1959) claimed that the evidence was that early agriculture was never based on barley only, and therefore the distribution of wheat was the important element. At Jarmo, Helbaek found cultivated wheat and barley, and Braidwood believed that the area in which Jarmo is situated provided all the requisites for the beginning of agriculture and settlement. This it did, but not so exclusively as Braidwood claimed, and the whole picture has become much more complex in the twenty years that have succeeded the investigation of Jarmo.

The investigation of Jericho comes next in the story, with excavations lasting from 1952 to 1958 (Kenyon 1957; 1960). The environment of Jericho is very different from that of Jarmo. The site does however lie within reach of the home of wild wheat, for the map shows the area in which *Triticum dicoccoides,* the ancestor of *T. dicoccum,* as well as barley, is found, stretching right round the Fertile Crescent at least as far as the Galilean Hills.

Starting with the evidence provided by Professor Garstang's excavations, the 1952-58 excavations were able to expose a much greater area of the levels that preceded the Early Bronze Age and by use of more stratigraphical methods to define them in greater detail. Professor Garstang's main Pre-Pottery Neolithic levels started with Level IX. In a sounding that became increasingly smaller he reached Level XVII, c. 4.50 m. lower with 3 m. of microliths below that. These deposits proved to represent a Mesolithic level and two quite separate Pre-Pottery Neolithic cultures, A and B. Professor Garstang further claimed that at the end of Level IX the making of pottery was invented, to be followed by a full Pottery Neolithic in Level VIII. In fact, the Neolithic pottery is found in pits cutting into the pre-pottery levels, and Level VIII as such does not exist, though the lower pits belong to an early stage, Pottery Neolithic A, and the upper pits to Pottery Neolithic B, the finds from which roughly correspond with Level VIII.

The finds at Jericho can indeed be called revolutionary in knowledge of the Neolithic of western Asia, for they pushed the beginnings of the Neolithic back millennia earlier than was believed in 1950, and they traced a continuous evolution from the local Mesolithic. In 1952, the accepted Carbon-14 date for Jarmo was 4800 B.C. Even in 1952, almost the highest surviving Pre-Pottery Neolithic level at Jericho produced a Carbon-14 date of c. 6250 B.C., with evidence that the site had the status of a walled town at that stage. This was at that time considered quite unacceptable by Professor Braidwood and others. It was claimed that Jericho could not have preceded the "area co-tradition" of the Near East, in which the emergence of the era of village-farming communities was assigned to a date of 5000 B.C. ± 500 years. The town was designated as an overgrown village and the defences pejoratively called a "rough stone ring wall." The evidence from Jericho and elsewhere, however, is now overwhelming. There have, moreover, been a number of new Carbon-14 datings from Jarmo, ranging from 10,000 B.C. to 4800 B.C. Of these Professor Braidwood (1953) has accepted a date of c. 6500 B.C. as the most probable.

The earliest structural remains found at Jericho belong to the Mesolithic. They consist not of houses but of an oblong, rectangular platform of natural clay, surrounded by revetting walls, outside which the clay had been stripped to bedrock. In the revetting walls were set side-by-side three stones c. 60 cms. high through which had been bored sockets for posts. The most likely interpretation of these is that they were ceremonial or totem poles, and that the platform was a sanctuary or cult centre, established by Mesolithic hunters beside the magnificent spring of Ain es Sultan. The flint and bone industries, including a lunate and a harpoon head, associate the level with the Mesolithic of the Wadi Mughara on Mount Carmel. The structure was destroyed by fire, and the resultant charcoal provided a Carbon-14 dating of c. 9200 B.C.

This Mesolithic structure at Jericho was the forerunner and ancestor of permanent settlement at that site. To the succeeding stage belongs a deposit 4 m. deep, which accumulated very gradually through the super-imposition of innumerable slight earth floors. These floors were bounded by slight clayey humps, and in debris layers there could be identified rough balls of clay, representing bricks of the most primitive kind. This accumulation must be evidence of a long succession of slight huts, habitations suitable to a nomadic way of life. The inhabitants of the huts, however, were no longer complete nomads. They may not yet have lived at Jericho the year round, but they returned regularly to the same spot. Their flint and bone industry is derived from that of the Natufian Mesolithic of Palestine but not so directly from the Mesolithic hunters who built the sanctuary at Jericho as was believed when the interim report was written. This is the Proto-Neolithic of Jericho.

Eventually the first solid houses appear, circular in plan with a small porch and usually monocellular, being clearly a translation into a permanent structure of the preceding slight huts. To this culture the name Pre-Pottery Neolithic A, PPNA, is given. The flint, stone and bone industries derive directly from the Proto-Neolithic and through it from the Mesolithic. At this stage, the expansion of the settlement seems to have been rapid, and the characteristic PPNA houses are found from end to end of the site, covering an area of c. 10 acres. The interim report on the final season of excavation in 1957-58 is in Kenyon (1960).

The next stage again follows rapidly. After only two or three stages of PPNA houses, the settlement was enclosed by a most impressive defensive system, consisting of a rock-cut ditch 9 m. wide and nearly 3 m. deep, a town wall surviving to a height of c. 6 m., at the rear, in at least one place a massive stone-built tower nearly 10 m. in diameter and surviving to a height of c. 10 m. The Carbon-14 dates for this remarkable development are c. 8000 B.C.

The PPNA town and its defences had a long life, with successive rebuilds of the town wall and the tower, and a long succession of houses in all the areas excavated. It is to be expected that a closely built-up walled settlement of 10 acres, for which the term town seems more appropriate than "overgrown village", must have been dependent, at least in part, on agriculture and the domestication of animals. The evidence on the latter point is not yet clear, since the skeletal criteria for domestication are not yet precise. The evidence for agriculture has been found, though the samples are scanty (Hopf 1969). It must here be noted that the excavations at Jericho preceded the development of techniques, especially flotation, that have so greatly assisted the collection of botanical evidence. Nevertheless, from the PPNA levels comes evidence of domesticated wheat, T. dicoccum as well as of barley and figs. Two important inferences are to be drawn. The ancestor of T. dicoccum, T. dicoccoides, is to be found in the Galilean hills, and a relatively local origin is possible, but it is *not* to be found in the Jordan valley. Somewhere in the Mesolithic or Proto-Neolithic background of settled Jericho lay the agricultural operations that produced the domesticated form of wheat translated by the PPNA inhabitants to their permanent settlement in Jericho. Secondly, the environment of Jericho must have been propitious for agriculture to have supported the population of a town of this size, possibly two or three thousand individuals, even though hunting, on the evidence of the animal bones, still formed an important part of the economy. The liberally-flowing Jericho spring, Ain es Sultan, is the basis for this productivity. But to produce an oasis such as that of modern Jericho requires irrigation. Mid 19th century photographs of the Jericho area during Turkish rule show scrub and sand. An interlocking deduction can be made. An adequate area for agriculture could only be provided by irrigation. Irrigation demands an elaborate communal organisation, and this the defensive system showed existed at Jericho.

Pre-Pottery Neolithic A Jericho comes to an abrupt end. Between it and Pre-Pottery Neolithic B Jericho there are clear traces of erosion, with the higher levels towards the summit partially washed away, and with well-defined stream beds in the lower areas cut, filled and re-cut several times. The cause and period of time of this erosion stage can only be conjectural. Natural causes, such as disease, earthquake or blockage of the stream may have caused desertion of the site. The observed erosion could have been spread over a long period, or two or three winters of strong rain would have been enough to account for the evidence. An enemy destruction of walls could have been responsible for abandonment, the destruction of retaining walls and subsequent erosion. So far, any explanation is conjectural.

What is certain is that following the period of erosion a completely new culture appears. In PPNB are the large multicellular buildings with plastered floors of the type assigned by Professor Garstang to his Level IX and the preceding strata. The flint industry is quite different, the stone utensils such as querns and the bone industry is pedestrian compared with that of PPNA. Burials, though still below the floors of the houses, are recognizably different. There is no doubt that PPNB represents a considerably more sophisticated culture than PPNA, though there is not evidence of the monumental architecture of the latter, and the town wall is not nearly so impressive. Pottery is still not found. The most remarkable achievement is artistic, in the realistically modelled plaster faces on human skulls. Ten of these plastered skulls were found. A central date for PPNB is c. 7000 B.C.

PPNA had been indigenous, with its ancestry in the local Mesolithic clearly traceable. PPNB arrived fully developed and in Palestine it is rootless. The evidence of its relationship to the north Syrian culture, which was postulated when the Jericho sequence was established, was confirmed in the next stage of the exploration of the western Asiatic Neolithic.

PPNB at Jericho ended with another period of erosion, and an abandonment which may have lasted a millennium. In the next stage, Neolithic pottery appears in the pits which confused Professor Garstang's stratification. The earliest Pottery Neolithic A has no obvious ancestry elsewhere, and may have been a local response to the idea of pottery which developed in Syria in the 7th - 6th millennium. Pottery Neolithic B can be linked with sites elsewhere in Palestine and to the north, and can be dated, though not very firmly, to c. 5000 B.C. and a date lasting into the 4th millennium is not impossible. What was happening in Palestine during this long period in which steady progress was being made to the north is a subject which still needs investigation.

When excavations at Jericho finished in 1958, Jericho stood in splendid isolation, thousands of years ahead of its "area co-tradition." In the third stage of this thirty years of investigations of the Neolithic, highly satisfactory steps have been taken to fill in this improbable void.

That PPNA and PPNB were not isolated in chronological space was fully indicated by Professor Renfrew's study of the sources and spread of obsidian (Renfrew *et al* 1966). The obsidian used in the 9th millennium PPNA Jericho came from Anatolia within the area of Çiftlik in Cappadocia. It did not fly to Jericho on the wings of migrating storks, as conceivably seeds might have done. PPNA tool makers are most unlikely to have sent expeditions for hundreds of miles to fetch an exotic tool material. It must have reached Jericho through a long chain of contemporary settlements. We are still a long way from filling in on the map all these 9th - 8th millennium settlements, but the progress in doing so in the last fifteen years has been quite remarkable.

Jericho, in the first place, no longer stands isolated in Palestine. Miss Diana Kirkbride (Mrs. Hans Helbaek) has shown how a systematic search can provide Jericho with neighbours (Kirkbride 1966). Her most concentrated area of search was in the area of Petra, on the east side of the Arabah, some 100 miles to the south of Jericho. Here she located a number of sites, and excavated one, the village of Beidha. The cultural connections with Jericho were clear. A period of circular houses, built by people not very confident in their stone-building techniques, with much use of timber, was followed by a period in which there were rectangular houses with plastered floors. There is thus an architectural sequence comparable with that of PPNA and PPNB at Jericho. In artifacts, however, the distinction is not so clear-cut. It might be tentatively suggested that the first occupants of Beidha were PPNA people pushed out of the Jericho area by the arrival of the PPNB people, acquiring in the process some of the culture and equipment of the newcomers. With them they certainly brought agriculture, and there is evidence of *T. dicoccum* as well as much use of wild barley. The Carbon-14 dates of Beidha, c. 6990-6600 B.C., would fit such an hypothesis. A survey similar to that carried out by Mrs. Helbaek of the area between Jericho and Beidha will certainly fill in the gap and elucidate the general process of development and expansion.

Still more important is the filling in of information in Syria and the adjacent north of Palestine, for here there is likely to be a development of agriculture and settlement parallel to that in Palestine. The full sequence from the hunting-gathering stage has not yet been established, but it is already clear that the origins of Jericho PPNB were in this area, and the map is gradually being filled with related sites.

The basic affiliation is of course established by parallels in architecture and equipment. The most striking link, however, is the discovery of such a very remarkable product as the plastered skulls at Beisamun (Ferembach and Lechevallier 1973), near Lake Huleh and at Ramad (De Conlenson 1971), near Damascus some 120 miles north of Jericho, where there were Carbon-14 dates for the early stages of c. 7500 to 6000 B.C.

At the famous coastal site of Ras Shamra, levels of a similar Pre-Pottery Neolithic culture are now being reached, and are dated to the early 7th millennium. Again, the origins and lowest levels have not yet been reached. One can nevertheless affirm that in north Syria there must have been a centre in which agriculture and settlement developed, parallel with that of PPNA in Palestine.

In Anatolia there is certainly another centre of early Neolithic development. The most famous site is Çatal Hüyük, southeast of Konya, covering an area of thirty acres, excavated between 1961 and 1963 by James Mellaart. It is thus a much larger site than Jericho, and provides evidence of a much more sophisticated culture. The architecture is strange, in that the houses, which contain a number of rectangular rooms have no outside doors, and are entered by ladders to the roof. A triangular segment very roughly of 100 by 100 metres in its maximum dimensions (but of course much less at the apex of the triangle), has been excavated to an average depth of some 7 m. below the surface, in which ten strata have been identified. Another strange feature in the buildings exposed is the large number of rooms apparently to be identified as shrines. The walls, like the floors, are covered with excellent plaster, upon which are painted some amazing scenes, some in the flat, some in rounded relief. There are naturalistic scenes of leopards fighting, a hunting scene reminiscent of the Late Palaeolithic, patterns resembling those of kelim rugs and so on. Applied to the walls are skulls of bulls with wide sweeping horns, and if these rooms are indeed shrines, the bull must have been an important cult object.

The occupants of Çatal Hüyük grew cultivated wheat, both emmer and einkorn, and they had domesticated cattle. Even in the lowest levels there was a little pottery. The Carbon-14 dates for the excavated levels are c. 6250-5400 B.C. These overlap only with the latter part of PPNB Jericho, but it is probable the origins of Çatal Hüyük, as yet unexplored, may reach back very much earlier.

Çatal Hüyük was preceded in Anatolia by Hacilar, dated to c. 7200-6850 B.C. It is technologically more primitive in that no pottery is found. It has, however, its own developed art, mainly consisting of figurines in the round, especially of women. It is the predecessor of Çatal, but not necessarily the ancestor, for the art is very different. The occupants practiced dry farming, growing mainly barley, but some emmer.

It can at this stage be said that there are four different areas in western Asia in which can be traced the development of full settlement with firmly established architecture, based on an agriculture in which cultivated forms of wheat and barley had emerged, and on the domestication of cattle; these were Palestine, N. Syria, Anatolia and N.E.

Iraq. There can be no doubt that these were separate developments, for the products, equipment and architecture are very different, though there may of course have been a spread of ideas. The general period is 10,000 to 5,000 B.C., and so far Jericho is the earliest, and the only place where the complete sequence from hunting-gathering to a developed town has been traced by excavation on the same site. This may no longer be the case when excavation has been carried to the base of sites such as Ras Shamra and Çatal Hüyük.

The next stage in Neolithic investigations is almost certainly going to show that behind the stages described, which can perhaps be described as the full Neolithic, were experimental stages in one direction or another, some of which may have led to dead ends.

Already in the last few years indications have been given of some such experiments. In Palestine, for instance, Jean Perrot (1960) excavated at 'Ein Mallaha ('Eynan) in the Jordan Valley, a small village settlement in which the equipment was pure Mesolithic, but there were houses with foundations of solid stone, which, on the evidence of alterations and adaptations, were occupied over an appreciable period of time. The economy was purely gathering based on the fish in the adjacent Lake Huleh.

At Umm el Dabaghriyeh in Mesopotamia, Mrs. Helbaek has excavated a settlement, Neolithic in equipment, which appeared to be supported on a system of large-scale trapping of onager, which she believes had the objective of a trade in skins. The idea of such a large-scale and organized trade in the Neolithic is certainly a new conception.

At Mureybet (Cauvin 1973) on the Euphrates in Syria there was a settled village of which the earliest Carbon-14 date is c. 8500 B.C. The equipment included flat sickle blades and obsidian brought from Anatolia, but the grain harvested consisted of wild types only. There was therefore here a permanent village based on food collecting. A further difficulty is that the area is far from the natural habitat of wild grain. It has still to be established whether a climatic change is the answer or whether, far from being self-sufficient, these Neolithic villagers travelled hundreds of miles to collect their grain, which seems most unlikely.

These permutations and combinations and the study of such possibilities as the herding rather than domestication of wild animals, cattle, gazelle, sheep and goats, are indications of the lines of investigation that are likely to be followed in the period of thirty years succeeding that which has been discussed in this article.

References Cited

Braidwood, Robert J.
    1952   The Near East and the Foundations for Civilisation. Eugene, Oregon.
    1958   Near Eastern Prehistory. Science 127: 1419-1429.
Cauvin, M. Jacques.
    1973   Découverte sur l'Euphrates d'un village natoufien du IXe millénaire av. J. C. à Mureybet (Syrie). Centre de Recherches d'Ecologie Humaine et de Prehistoire.
de Contenson, Henri.
    1971   Tell Ramad, a village in Syria of the 7th and 6th millennia B.C. Archaeology 24: 278-285.
Ferembach, Denise, and Lechevallier, Monique.
    1973   Découverte de deux crânes surmodelés dans une habitation du VIIeme millenaire à Beisamun, Israel. Paleorient 1.
Garstang, J. and J. B. E.
    1948   The Story of Jericho.   London.
Helbaek, Hans.
    1959   Domestication of Food Plants in the Old World. Science 130: 365-372.
Hopf, Maria.
    1969   Plant remains and early farming in Jericho. In The Domestication and Exploitation of Plants and Animals. P. T. Ucko and G. W. Dimbleby, Eds.   London.   355-359.
Kenyon, Kathleen M.
    1957   Digging up Jericho.
    1960   Excavations at Jericho 1957-58. Palestine Exploration Quarterly 92: 88-113.
Kirkbride, Diana.
    1966   Five Seasons at the Pre-pottery Neolithic of Beidha in Jordan. Palestine Exploration Quarterly 98: 8-72.
Perrot, J.
    1960   Excavations at 'Eynan ('Ein Mallaha). Israel Exploration Journal 10: 14-22.
Renfrew, Colin et al.
    1966   Obsidian and Early Cultural Contact in the Near East. Proceedings of the Prehistoric Society XXXII: 30-72.

A ROMAN INTAGLIO FROM EAST WRETHAM HEATH, NORFOLK
by Eleanor Megaw with a Report by Dr Martin Henig

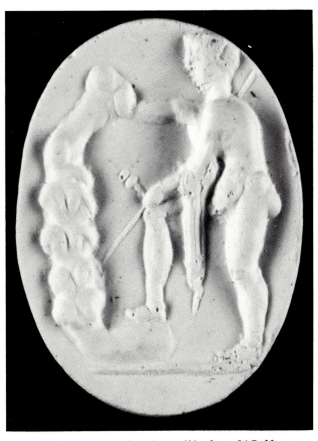

Fig 1.   Intaglio (cast) c. x 6½, photo W.S. Megaw

On 16 March 1930, when visiting the Norfolk Breckland to look for flints, my brother and I noticed a small reddish-brown stone with a flat polished face that lay in one of the then innumerable rabbit scoops. After some weeks in the pocket of my school blazer the hard crust hiding the other face had partly rubbed off, and I saw that it was engraved. Examining it under a microscope, my father Sir William Hardy F.R.S. found the covering contained carbonate of copper holding very fine sand grains. A wax impression which incorporated the rest of this material was sent to the author of *The Archaeology of the Cambridge Region*, Sir Cyril Fox, then at the National Museum of Wales. Professor A. B. Cook, who saw the original, considered the intaglio was Greek work of the first quarter century A.D., and that the engraving represented Theseus having taken his father's sword from the rock. Subsequently it was mounted as a ring and remains in my possession, but has not hitherto been published.[1] I am much indebted to Dr Martin Henig of the Institute of Archaeology at Oxford for contributing the essential descriptive part of this note.

My father had carefully noted the site of the find with reference to a 6" Ordnance Survey map (National Grid Reference TL 911883). The area (fig. 2) is now a Nature Reserve and lies in East Wretham parish, north-east of Thetford, Norfolk. The intaglio was found some 10 metres north of the old Drove Road that runs from the Peddars Way westwards towards Fowlmere and the Devil's Punchbowl. It was some 300 yards south-east of Langmere, and less than a quarter of a mile north of Ringmere. That part of Breckland characterised by its meres was well described by Clarke (1937) in its earlier largely unforested state. Its appearance has greatly changed since, not only through afforestation, but also by the reduction of the large rabbit population which kept the vegetation in check and everywhere burrowed in the surface soil. Now there tends to be a continuous deep cover of grass and herbs so that the soil is scarcely visible anywhere and lies entirely undisturbed. We could not have found the gem in present conditions, and on a recent visit saw no worked flints at all.

Nothing else of the Roman period was noticed where the intaglio was found. Apart from flints, rough hand-made sherds of dark ware containing quartz grains used to be picked up at the site: Rainbird Clarke (1939: 103) thought they were Iron Age, though Miss Barbara Green[2] thinks they might be Neolithic or Bronze Age. The nearest Roman finds come from the little plateau on the far side of Langmere, where "on the sand at the mouth of almost every rabbit's burrow, there are Roman potsherds of various pastes and patterns" (Clarke 1937: 42). Miss Green informs me that in 1932 G. Kingaby made "some slight digging" there, and found several pots, all the material appearing to be late first to early second century A.D. but the exact nature of the site is not known. The only other Roman find Miss Green knows of from Wretham parish was a pot containing about 600 coins found in 1760 in a ditch near Corkmere, at the Glebe, Thorpe Hall Farm (Clarke 1952: 155). The exact site of that find is not known, but it would be a couple of miles north-west of Langmere. This hoard is undated, but the pot and some of the coins apparently went to King's College, Cambridge.

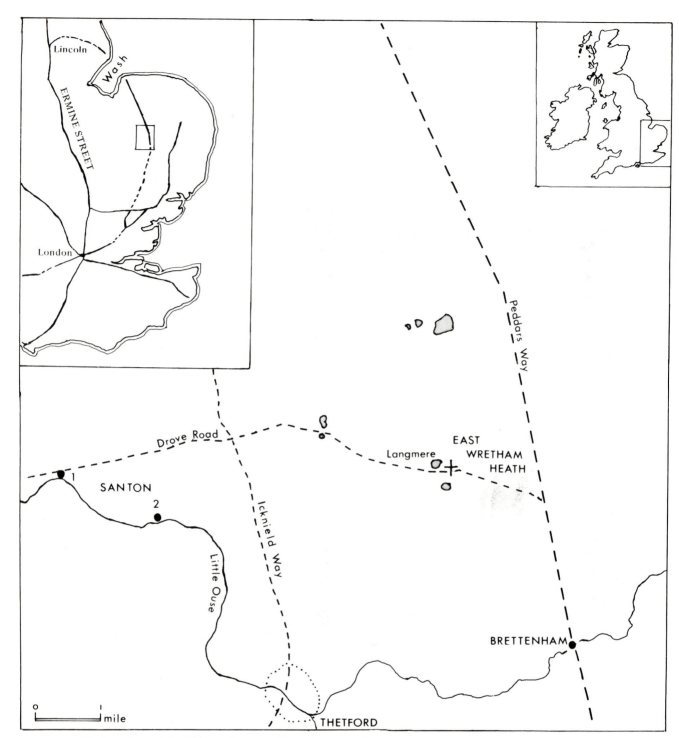

Fig 2.   *Part of the East Anglian Breckland showing + find-site of Intaglio 1. Roman settlement; 2. Hoard. Inset left; Roman routes between London & Lincoln.*

Both the Peddars Way and the Drove Road were used in Romano-British times. The Peddars Way is thought to have led to a ferry-crossing at the Wash, and ultimately to Lincoln (Phillips 1932); Rainbird Clarke (1938: 158) believed it was a Roman highway constructed during the last third of the first century A.D., as an alternative route to Ermine Street, for carrying troops and official traffic from the Romanised area of north Essex through Icenian territory to the north of England. The Drove Road, beside which the intaglio was found, links the Peddars Way and the Icknield Way, and continues in the general direction of Grimes Graves and the Fens: Clarke thought it was probably in use from prehistoric times. Some six miles west of Langmere it passes close to the Roman settlement beside the Little Ouse at Santon, with finds dating from late first to fourth century; and at its western end, on the edge of the Fens, is another Roman site at Hockwold-cum-Wilton. The well-known "Santon Downham" hoard, actually from Santon, but a mile and a half upstream of the Santon settlement, is dated soon after 50-55 A.D. by two brooches of Claudian type, and is thought to have been hidden during the Boudiccan rebellion or its aftermath (Clarke 1935: 203; Fox 1923: 104-8).

In the other direction from Langmere, under 3 miles south-east of our site, was the Roman village at Brettenham, beside the Peddars Way some two miles south of its junction with the Drove Road. Pottery there ranged from late first to fourth century, and among the finds were two seal-boxes of late first or early second century, one of which has affinities with work from the south of England (Clarke 1938: 136).

It is clear therefore that there was considerable Roman activity, both in the immediate locality where the intaglio was found and in the general vicinity, during the latter part of the first century A.D., though the area was not developed much until the second century (Clarke 1938: 144; 1960: 119). Being a stray find the intaglio cannot positively be associated with the Roman site at Langmere, though the dates appear to agree quite well. It certainly seems possible, and in line with Dr Henig's attribution, that this handsome gem could have been brought to this country by a Roman soldier settled in the district at the time of the Icenian uprising of 61 A.D., or posted to it immediately thereafter. Indeed it might well have been seized from a soldier by one of the local inhabitants during the struggle or the repression that followed, for evidence of the Icenian coin hoards suggests that the 'palace' of Prasutagus and Boudicca was somewhere in the Breckland area (Allen 1970 : 15).

Notes

1.   Since writing this Dr. Henig has included the intaglio in his monograph *A Corpus of Roman Engraved Gemstones from British Sites.* British Archaeological Reports 8 (1974), Part ii, 116 No. App. 75.
2.   I am much obliged to Miss Barbara Green F.S.A., of the Castle Museum, Norwich, and also to Mr. C. Green, of the Norfolk Archaeological Unit, for their kind assistance with regard to other finds from the area.

References Cited

Allen, D. F.
    1970   The Coins of the Iceni. Britannia I: 1-33.
Clarke, R. R.
    1935   A Roman Site at Santon. Norfolk Archaeology XXV: 202-206.
    1938   The Roman Villages at Brettenham and Needham and the Contemporary Road System. Norfolk Archaeology XXVI: 123-163.
    1939   The Iron Age in Norfolk and Suffolk. Archaeological Journal XCVI: 1-113.
    1952   Roman Norfolk since Haverfield a Survey of Discovery from 1901. Norfolk Archaeology XXX: 140-155.
    1960   East Anglia. Ancient Peoples and Places series. London.
Clarke, W. G.
    1937   In Breckland Wilds. Second Edition, revised and re-written by R. Rainbird Clarke. First Edition 1925.
Fox, C. F.
    1923   The Archaeology of the Cambridge Region. Cambridge.
Phillips, C. W.
    1932   The Roman Ferry across the Wash. Antiquity VI: 342-348.

A Roman Intaglio from East Wretham Heath, Norfolk
Description by Martin Henig

The stone is a sard or cornelian, reddish-brown in colour and oval in shape with a slightly convex upper surface (dimensions 17 x 12 mm). It is boldly cut in intaglio and yields an impression of a youth standing towards the left with his right leg flexed and his right foot resting on a boulder. Over his left arm is draped a *chlamys* and he holds a sword by its scabbard so that the hilt is showing in his left hand. Another weapon, a spear, is indicated behind him. With his right hand the youth supports a rock standing on a cliff which is rendered in a very schematised manner.[1]

The type is evidently based on a statue by Lysippos which approximated to the Poseidon in the Lateran or the Lansdowne Hermes.[2] We may note that on gems the type was used for Mars, Neptune, Mercury and Achilles amongst other personifications.[3] In the present instance, however, as Professor A. B. Cook realised when the gem was shown to him, the subject is Theseus after he had recovered the sword of his father Aegeus from under a great rock (Plutarch, *Theseus* iii, 4. vi, 3). Theseus is frequently depicted on gems both in the act of finding the sword and in contemplating it after recovery; this is, nevertheless, the only rendering of a 'Lysippan' Theseus to have come my way.[4] I have suggested that heroic gems would have had an especial appeal to members of the Imperial army,[5] and although the gem under discussion appears to be a stray find, its fine, highly classical workmanship is suggestive of an early date - probably in the first century A.D. when the army was still in evidence in Eastern Britain. It appears to have been cut in a good Mediterranean workshop.[6]

Notes

1. For a similar cliff employed for a representation of Oedipus and the Sphinx, G. M. A. Richter, *Engraved Gems of the Romans.* London 1971, 68 No. 317. A much smaller rocky eminence is depicted in front of Theseus in *Ibid.*: 69, No. 323.

2. F. P. Johnson, *Lysippos,* Duke University North Carolina 1927: 143ff. *cf* M. Bieber, *The Sculpture of the Hellenistic Age,* revised edition New York 1961: 50f, Fig. 149 for the type as used for a statue of Demetrius Poliorcetes of Macedon.

3. E. Zwierlein-Diehl, *Die Antiken Gemmen des Kunsthistorischen Museums in Wien.* Munich 1973, No. 416 (Mars).
    G. Sena Chiesa, *Gemme del Museo Nazionale di Aquileia.* Aquileia 1966 No. 46 (Neptune).
    Hesperia supp VIII, 1949, 317 and Pl. XLII No. 21a = G. Horster, *Statuen auf Gemmen,* Bonn 1970, 29f, Pl. VII, 1 (Mercury).
    Sena Chiesa, *op cit.* No. 915 (?Achilles), and J. P. Bushe-Fox, *Richborough* IV, Society of Antiquaries, 1949, 125 and Pl. XXXV, 88 (misdrawn - not Mercury as stated but ? Achilles).

4. Richter, *op cit.* 69 Nos. 322-324 (contemplating sword) No 325 (recovering sword).

5. *Cf.* Martin Henig, 'The Veneration of Heroes in the Roman Army', *Britannia* I (1970): 249-265 and especially 250-252 (Theseus).

6. C. Sourvinou-Inwood, 'Theseus lifting the rock and a cup near the Pithos Painter', *Journal of Hellenic Studies* XCI (1971): 94-109, provides a full discussion of the origin of the theme. She concludes "that the years around 475 are the most likely date for the creation of a sculptural group representing Theseus lifting the rock which influenced later representations of the subject."

LA TENE AND TYPES OF SOCIETY IN SCANDINAVIA
AN OUTLINE
by Carl-Axel Moberg

When an archaeologist and prehistorian on the Scandinavian peninsula would like to construct a map of Europe, *ca* 400 B.C. - O, with an emphasis on societies, he would encounter several difficulties.[1]

First of all, one has to be aware of the fact that La Tène Europe was transected by non-agricultural and agricultural areas; areas with combined economies, or with predominant agriculture.

Another type of difficulty is caused by incompatibilities between literary and archaeological sources. To the Scandinavian prehistorian this situation recalls another one "at home," but a millennium later: the limitations in agreement - mildly expressed - between verbal and archaeological data from the so called Viking Period (cf. Blindheim et al. 1974). The interrelation of historical and archaeological data is critical. A merely "illustrative" archaeology could only add some flesh to a skeleton of historical information but it would be deprived of any real capacity to contribute anything substantially new.

Europe at the time in question is covered by historical sources to a certain extent only; but there are archaeological finds throughout the area. If we want to map this area with pre- and proto- historical sites simultaneously, we have to study compatible traits, common on both sides of the frontier; and these can be archaeological traits only. If we want to study change in an area which was prehistoric at one moment and protohistoric in the next, we have to find common and compatible traits, early and late; and this can be archaeologically based, only. The resulting loss of information - of all incompatible information - is deplorable, but inevitable.

Ethnic concepts, and mainly the concept of "Celts", dominate textbook summaries of the La Tène periods. Almost automatically, the use of an ethnic model involves use of "migrations" in interpretation. Many years ago, the present writer attempted to formulate an outline of some traits in North European prehistory of this period, purposely without even mentioning terms such as "Cimbri", "Teutons", "Vandals" or "Goths", etc. (Moberg 1941); he is still convinced that it is useful to avoid ethnic labels, particularly those such as "Celtic", "Germanic", or "Slav". Recent critical studies by Hachmann, Kossack and Kuhn (1962) and Lönnroth (1972) ought to have made us even more aware of the dangers of using ethnic names drawn from Classical authors in prehistoric archaeology - not at least in the period under discussion.

Furthermore, there is also incompatibility of models. Certainly, there is, in interpretations of La Tène, as of other periods, much use of such terms as "civilization" or "barbarism". One is entitled to wonder whether the writers using them are aware of their inherent load of evolutionism - a load often conveyed by V. G. Childe; and earlier, by L. H. Morgan, whose impact is immense, even if modern users of these terms hardly know his name.

Readers and writers today are more aware of another set of concepts, where evolutionism is largely present, also. As a consequence of the present political structure of Europe, we have to face an archaeology in the East which has to keep inside the conceptual frames of an evolutionism expressed in Marxist economic terms, and nationalism (as often in the West, the Kossinna tradition is now deeply rooted in the East too). One must be aware of such ideological ties in East and West, to be able to use publications with necessary criticism or, at least, to be able to cope with special sets of terms, even where the real difference in underlying ideas is not too deep. A rather clear instance of the Eastern trend is Karl-Heinz Otto's *Deutschland in der Epoche der Urgesellschaft*, 1961, with "dissolving primitive society," "Gentilaristokratie" and "military democracy" etc. Mongait expressed less orthodox views recently; "the synthesis of archaeological data and the writing on the basis of these facts, of the history of Ancient Europe is a task for the future;" the "transition to generalization was limited, on purpose" (Mongait 1974: 379).

There are, indeed, good reasons to emphasize the obstacles to generalization. They exist, and they are created by incomparabilities and incompatibilities, such as those reviewed. One has to be aware of them and make them visible. If, on the contrary, one chooses to harmonize the contrasts and differences, the resulting picture will be one of rather limited usefulness. This is true also of attempts to harmonize chronologically and geographically widely divergent written sources - as e.g. Caesar and mediaeval Irish texts. The result is a static picture of a "generalized Celtic" society. As such, it is similar to what we in Northern Europe are used to: the picture of a "generalized 'Viking'" society towards A.D. 1000, drawn from sparse contemporary texts and late Icelandic sagas. An analysis on the basis of finds will indicate divergent, changing societies for the area and period under discussion. It is tempting to widen Cunliffe's formulation: "behind the popular myth of the 'Celtic nation' there was great variety and sometimes rapid social change" (Cunliffe 1974: 313); and this may be true for several areas as, for example, the Marne (Pollnac and Rowlett 1971).

Possibilities and impossibilities of "social archaeology"

Can the archaeologist actually distinguish "types of societies"? Recently, Edmond Leach seriously questioned the archaeologists' capability of studying 'people'. For archaeologists, he states "social organization as the social anthropologist understands the term, must for ever remain a mystery" (Leach 1973; cf. Moberg, 1975). It may be that a map of Europe with emphasis on types of societies "as the social anthropologist understands" could not be made. However, in these pages, it will be argued that some important indications of types of societies, and some of their constitutive elements might be distinguished, and that these might not be entirely unrelated to concepts of social organization "as the social anthropologist understands the term" (Moberg 1974).

Forms shaped by man are social. Among its kinds are indicators of disjunction, or conjunction between groups of people; such as fortifications and other signs of warfare; material symbols with social loadings - such as differentiating costume, or forms and arrangements of buildings; iconic and aniconic signs, of many kinds and structures - some of these bring us relatively closer to language; sequences of ceremonial signs in the form of gestures and actions, as far as such sequences can be reconstructed from pictures and/or from material traces they left, e.g. in depositions of funerary or votive character.

Certainly, there are situations when such, or comparable, social markers do not exist in the available archaeological record. In these situations, but only in these, the archaeologist has to resign.

The social map of an area like Europe, and the social change trajectory over time, for instance 400 B.C.-O, must remain fragmentary, of course. But it will include some information on subareas and sub-periods where a protohistorically based study is impossible.

If one wishes to relate Northern European and Central-West-European societies to each other, then, obviously, one has to use selected traits such as are present in both areas. The testimonies of three categories of such criteria will be briefly discussed here: fortified settlements, high-rank graves, and "exotic symbols." The isolation of such traits must be a preliminary step to possibly subsequent interpretations in systemic terms.

"Demilitarization - remilitarization?"

All of us know how fortified settlements are conspicuous features, existing in compatible forms within both the zones of Central Europe, England, and in Northern Europe. However, their chronological distributions are quite different. In the southern zone, where they were well developed before La Tène, they continue, with growing importance, toward the Christian era, at least. On the contrary, there seems to be no known well-dated fortified settlements on the Scandinavian peninsula during the Bronze and Early Iron Ages. In Denmark, Borremose is the only unclear case (Brøndsted 1960: 47-54, 390-1).For an occurrence at Havor on the Swedish island of Gotland in the Baltic, see Nylén (1962: 94-6). The appearance of fortified settlements in large numbers in Scandinavia is later, by four or more centuries.

Scandinavia adjoins the westernmost fringes of an impressive Eastern area (including e.g. Ananjino and Djakovo cultures) with traditionally fortified settlements; even areas beyond the Urals are comprised within it. During the Late Bronze Age and Earliest Iron Age, this neighboring area extended westwards, comprising "Lusatian" South Baltic regions, as far southwest as the island of Rügen. But in the northern Continental area, covered by this southwest extension of a settlement pattern common in East Europe, fortified settlements seem to be absent over a long period. The situation is similar even farther west, up to the Ardennes-Meuse regions of Belgium (De Laet 1958: 166-7). Significant contributions to the special problems of this important intermediate zone have been given by Hachmann (1956:19), Hachmann, Kossack and Kuhn (1962) and recently especially by Capelle (1971). For a single, late fortified settlement on the North Sea coast, see Hachmann, Kossack and Kuhn (1962, map 2).

In northern Poland and Germany, the absence of fortified settlements is of long duration, in Poland well into the eighth century A.D. (Hensel 1974: 213; Kukharenko 1969: 115, 120, 125).

Then again, these are dates which seem to coincide roughly with an increase in construction of fortifications, sometimes with settlement in northern Europe.

Does this reflect changes within and among societies? Is it a sign of "demilitarization and remilitarization"? Of course, one very usual answer for the re-appearance in northern Poland - north Germany of fortified settlement is that it reflects a profound change in population, an "invasion of the Slavs". But this is an interpretation in historical and migrationist terms, which is not accepted everywhere. There are alternative interpretations in socio-political or economical frame works also (cf. Bradley 1971, for England).

"Dehierarchization - rehierarchization"?

Does a "change in hierarchization" occur within some societies in Europe? The occurrence of high-ranked graves with rich equipment deposited with elaborate ritual may provide the answer to this question.

There are different ways to study these problems. One would be to "measure" grave furnishings (cf. Moberg 1972: 240), their mutual relations and their geographical distributions. This is what Randsborg recently attempted for the Early Danish Bronze Age, arriving at a conclusion rather similar to a traditional interpretation of Danish society of the period - a "chiefdom" (Randsborg 1973, 1974).

Another way leads to case studies of so-called "princely graves" or *Fürstengräber*. However, these case studies should be carried out with application of identical questionnaires in order to arrive at really comparable "profiles" of the burials. For Scandinavia and the north of the continent, a very promising beginning has been made for post-La Tène periods, by Gebühr's (1974) re-evaluation of the *Fürstengräber* concept, used earlier by Eggers (1953) and Hachmann (1956:17-18). A different type of interpretation - not "prince" but "priest" has been suggested by A. Kietlińska. To a Scandinavian it recalls an analogous attempt at reinterpretation of the Oseberg Viking Period burial by Gjessing (1943). There exists no really comparable study of pre-La Tène graves. On a more intuitive basis, it has been hinted that exceptional high-ranked graves from Middle and Late Bronze Age in north Europe and north Germany should occur mainly in the geographical periphery of areas and not in their centre (Moberg 1965). The pre- and post-La Tène graves should be described in fully comparable terms; and also graves within the La Tène *Fürstengräber* complex of Continental Europe (Schaaff 1969), and their analogies in England. It might be well worth while to try to include attempts at reconstructing ritual programs. Procedures for such reconstructions have been suggested by Brown (1971: 92-112).

Then, we might compare the sequences of occurrences in different regions. Was there a "dehierarchization" going on in the Hunsrück-Eifel areas, a "hierarchization" in England and a "dehierarchization" followed by a later, substantial "rehierarchization" within some Scandinavian societies? And - in the last-mentioned area - how do isolated occurrences of elaborate graves like Kraghede A (Klindt-Jensen 1950: 102-3, 203-5) and Langaa 1 (Albrectsen 1954:29-30; Becker 1961: 272-3) fit into the pattern? How far is, for instance, Kraghede A similar to graves within the Arras group of Yorkshire such as the "King's Barrow" at Arras (Cunliffe 1974: 289; Stead 1965: 89 ff)?

If such graves; prior to, contemporary with, or later than the 400-0 period, are seen in their context against the background of the respective majority of graves (Albrectsen 1954; Becker 1961; Capelle 1971; Stjernquist 1955: 67-8), one might find more accurate answers to the question of whether the more elaborate funerals from these different periods in southern Scandinavia and the north of the continent have such important traits in common that there is a continuity among them; and that they should be regarded as representing one and the same hierarchical level. And then, if so, how this level should be best characterized in terms of social organization.

In Scandinavia, there are only limited possibilities for social analysis of the kind Filip (1965: 59) carried out for central Europe or such as might be indicated at cemeteries like Münsingen-Rain (Hodson 1968, compared with Martin-Kilcher 1973: 37). This is due to mortuary customs. For possible mathematical analysis, see Moberg 1972.

"Displaced signs - displaced meanings"?

When a specialized symbolic or "projective" system (Renfrew 1972: 404) is built up within a human entity, and when isolated items out of their set of symbols are found in a distant environment, the question arises as to what function they have been filling there. Were they just exotic items, imported out of curiosity, or because of appreciation of the objects bearing them - or was the original meaning of the signs themselves accepted? Such questions can be asked about products of Roman craftmanship in non-Roman areas. What did Achilles and Priam mean to the last possessors of the Hoby silver goblets in Denmark (Klindt-Jensen 1957: 103 and Pl. 59)? What did scrolls and animals on Irish Christian paraphernalia mean to those who buried them in fragments in Norway?

Similar questions apply very well to some finds in Jutland and Funen from La Tène periods. The local background is "non-La Tène", indeed. Fortified settlements are absent (?) with one exception. Real continental La Tène types are practically non-existent in grave inventories - something which might reflect a difference in mortuary practices. In pottery, and in other wares there are no signs of contact with nuclear La Tène areas. We are still outside the La Tène world proper, in a zone which can be characterized as "epi-Jastorf", (Rowlett 1968). The abundant settlements, studied from a late stage do not seem to link Jutland to the nuclear La Tène zone either. But - within this area in the far north, the Brå (Klindt-Jensen 1953) and Rynkeby and Gundestrup cauldrons, and the Dejbjerg wagons were deposited (for all three see Klindt-Jensen 1950; for Gundestrup, also Nylén 1967-8; Powell 1971). A number of smaller artifacts with La Tène patterns can also be added (Becker 1961: 273) as well as representatives in the rest of Denmark and on the Scandinavian peninsula (Moberg 1954).

The question as to whether or not this set of symbolic data on objects found in northern Europe kept anything of their original meaning is linked to the question of how far local craftmanship was involved in their making (Nylén 1967-8).

The situation is paradoxical. Judging only from selected archaeological items one might be tempted to characterize the possible impact of symbols from continental Europe between the Black Sea and France as being no less important in Jutland-Funen than in pre-Christian Ireland.

And, undoubtedly, a correct answer to our questions would be of great importance for our understanding of social realities in north Europe and in Ireland.

- - - - - - - - - - - -

These examples were chosen as illustrations of a concept:

"Interregional and interperiodical compatibility"

Within some parts of the central European nuclear La Tène areas, the broad trend seems to be that singular high-rank graves disappear, while *oppida* increase and develop. In England hillforts increase and become more important and so do high-rank graves, whereas large cemeteries do not occur on the same scale as on the continent (Cunliffe 1974).

The north of continental Europe seems to display a reverse trend; high rank graves and fortifications have existed, then disappear early, only to return very much later.

Among the north European regions, there is one with a peculiar situation. Against an average background which is very far from what is usual in the nuclear La Tène area, but which has much in common with north continental areas, there appear outstanding signs of contact with foreign, "exotic" areas. This region, Jutland-Funen, has a unique position in this respect. With not too much imagination, one might draw a sketch of an elite group there, in a very special social and political situation, and with considerable economic resources and exceptional contacts.

But here, and not for the first time in this paper, it is advisable to remember some lines from the final chapters of a magnificent analysis of rich and important grave finds - an analysis of a kind which is lacking within research on La Tène, still:

> "In asking such questions one is indeed in the realm of speculation where no real answers are possible. The clues and hints are very meager, and firm evidence is lacking. Yet I have thought it worth-while to explore this peculiarly difficult area as a stimulus to the enquiries of others." (Hencken 1968: 603.)

Note

1. This paper was also written for the program "Forms of Society in Northern Europe 1500 B.C. - A.D. 500", in the Department of Archaeology especially Northern European, University of Gothenburg.

   The interesting and important work by Carole L. Crumley, *Celtic Social Structure: The Generation of Archaeologically Testable Hypotheses from Literary Evidence.* Anthropological Papers, Museum of Anthropology, University of Michigan, No. 56, Ann Arbor: University of Michigan 1974 was received only after the completion of the manuscript and thus could not be commented on here.

References Cited

Albrectsen, E.
    1954   Fynske jernaldergrave. l. Førromersk jernalder. Zusammenfassung. København: Munksgaard.
Becker, C. J.
    1961   Førromersk jernalder i Syd- og Midtjylland. Mit deutscher Zusammenfassung. Nationalmuseets skrifter, Større beretninger 6. København: Nationalmuseet.
Blindheim, C., G. Gjessing, H. Gjøstein-Resi, C. A. Moberg, M. Stefansson and B. Stjernquist.
    1974   Comments on K Odner, Økonomiske strukturer på Vestlandet i eldre Jernalder. Norwegian Archaeological Review.

Bradley, R. J.
  1971   Economic change in the growth of early hill forts. *In* The Iron Age and its hill forts. D. Hill and M. Jesson eds. Pp. 71-83. Papers presented to Sir Mortimer Wheeler, University of Southampton. Monograph series 1. Southampton.

Brown, J. A. ed.
  1971   Approaches to the social dimensions of mortuary practices. Memoirs of the Society for American Antiquity 25.

Brøndsted, J.
  1960   Danmarks oldtid, 3, Jernalderen. København: Gyldendal.

Cappelle, T.
  1971   Studien über elbgermanische Gräberfelder in der ausgehenden Latènezeit und der älteren römischen Kaiserzeit. Münstersche Beiträge zur Vor- und Frühgeschichte 6. Hildesheim: Lax.

Cunliffe, B.
  1974   Iron Age Communities in Britain. London and Boston: Routledge and Kegan Paul.

De Laët, S. J.
  1958   The Low Countries. London: Thames and Hudson.

Eggers, H. J.
  1953   Lübsow, ein germanischer Fürstensitz der älteren Kaiserzeit. Praehistorische Zeitschrift 34/35:58-111, 1949/50.

Filip, J.
  1956   Keltove v Středni Evrope. Zusammenfassung: Die Kelten in Mitteleuropa. Rezjume: Kel'ty v srednej Evrope. Monumenta archaeologica 5. Praha: C SAV.
  1966   Fürstengräber. J. Filip ed. Enzyklopädisches Handbuch zur Ur-und Frühgeschichte Europas 1:381. Praha: Akademie der Wissenschaften.

Gebühr, M.
  1974   Zur Definition älterkaiserzeitlicher Fürstengräber vom Lübsow-Typ. Praehistorische Zeitschrift 49: 1:82-127.

Gjessing, G.
  1943   Hesten i førhistorisk kunst og kultur. Viking 7: 105-
Gjessing, see also Blindheim

Hachmann, R.
  1956   Zur Gesellschaftsordung der Germanen in der Zeit um Christi Geburt. Archaeologia geographica 5:7-34.

Hachmann, R., G. Kossack and H. Huhn.
  1962   Völker zwischen Germanen und Kelten. Neumünster: Wachholtz.

Hencken, H.
  1968   Tarquinia, Villanovans and early Etruscans. Americans School of Prehistoric Research. Peabody Museum. Harvard University. Bulletin 23:1-2.

Hensel, W.
  1974   Ur und Frühgeschichte Polens. Veröffentlichungen des Zentralinstituts für Alte Geschichte und Archäologie der Akademie der Wissenschaften der DDR.

Hodson, F. R.
  1968   The La Tène cemetery at Münsingen-Rain. Catalogue and relative chronology. Acta Bernensia 5. Bern: Stämpfli.

Kietlińska, A.
  1959-60 Problem tzw. grobow ksiazecych we wczesnym okresie rzymskim. Wiadomosci Archaeologiczne 26.

Klindt-Jensen, O.
  1950   Foreign influences in Denmark's Early Iron Age. Acta archaeologica 20, 1949:1-248.
  1953   Bronzekedelen fra Brå. Tidlige keltiske indflydelser i Danmark. The Bronze cauldron from Brå. Early Celtic influences in Denmark. Jutland Archaeological Society publications 3. Århus : University Press.
  1957   Denmark before the Vikings. London: Thames and Hudson.

Kukharenko, Ju. V.
  1969   Arkheologija Pol'shi. Moskva: Nauka.

Leach, E.
  1973   Concluding address. C. Renfrew ed., The explanation of culture change. London: Duckworth.

Lönnroth, E.
  1972   Die Goten in der modernen kritischen Geschichtsauffassung. U. E. Hagberg, ed. Studia Gotica. Die eisenzeitlichen Verbindungen zwischen Schweden und Südosteuropa. Pp.57-62.Kungl. Vitterhets Historie och Antikvitets Akademiens Handligar. Antikvariska serien 25. Stockholm: Almqvist & Wiksell.

Martin-Kilcher, S.
  1973   Zur Tracht und Beigabensitte im keltischen Gräberfeld on Münsingen-Rain (Kt. Bern). Zeitschrift für schweizerische Archäologie und Kunstgeschichte 30: 26-39.

Moberg, C. A.
   1941   Zonengliederungen der vorchristlichen Eisenzeit in Nordeuropa. Lund: Gleerup.
   1954   Between Horn and Ornavasso. Studies of chronology and style in the La Tène period. Acta
           archaeologica 25:1-48.
   1956   Till frågan om samhällsstrukturen i Norden under bronsåldern. Fornvännen.
   1972   Questions sur l'outillage mathémathique d'une archéologie sociologique. Les méthodes mathématiques
           de l'archéologie, 229-248. Marseille; Centre d'analyse documentaire pour l'archéologie.
   1974   Arkeologi om samhälle. Summary, pp. 13-14.
           Forskningsprofiler vid Göteborgs universitet 4. Göteborg: Göteborgs universitet.
   1975   Anthropologists on archaeology. K. E. Knutsson et. al. ed., (Festschrift for K. G. Izikowitz). Ethnos,
           No. 1-4: 360-4.
           See also Blindheim.
Mongajt, A. L.
   1974   Arkheologija zapadnoj Evropy. Bronzovyj i zheleznyj veka. Moskva: Nauka.
Nylén, E.
   1962   Skatten från Havors fornborg. Proxima Thule. Sverige och Europa under forntid och medeltid.
           Hyllningsskrift till Konungen, 94-112. Stockholm: Norstedt.
   1967-8 Gundestrupkitteln och den keltiska konsten. Summary. Tor. 133-172.
Odner, K.
   1973a   Ethnohistoric and ecological settings for economic and social models of an Iron Age society:
           Valldalen, Norway. D. L. Clarke, ed., Models in archaeology, 623-670.
   1973b   Økonomiske strukturer pa Vestlandet i eldre jernalder. Summary: Economic structures in Western
           Norway in the Early Iron Age. Bergen: Historisk museum.
           See also Blindheim.
Otto, K. H.
   1961   Deutschland in der Epoche der Urgesellschaft. A. Meusel and R. F. Schmiedt, eds., Lehrbuch der
           deutschen Geschichte (Beiträge). Berlin: VEB Deutscher Verlag der Wissenschaften.
Pollnac, R. B. and R. M. Rowlett
   1971   Multivariate analysis of Marnian La Tène cultural groups. F. R. Hodson, D. G. Kendall and
           P. Tăutu, eds., Mathematics in the archaeological and historical sciences 46-58. Edinburgh:
           University Press.
Powell, T. G. E.
   1971   From Urartu to Gundestrup: the agency of Thracian metal-work. Eds. J. Boarman, M. A. Brown and
           T. G. E. Powell, The European community in later prehistory, Studies in honor of C. F. C. Hawkes,
           181-209 + plates with Figs. 26-32. London: Routledge and Kegan Paul.
Randsborg, K.
   1973   Wealth and social structure as reflected in bronze age burials - a quantitative approach. C. Renfrew,
           ed., The explanation of culture change 565-570. London: Duckworth.
   1974   Social stratification in Early Bronze Age Denmark: a study in the regulation of cultural systems.
           Praehistorische Zeitschrift 49, No. 1: 38-61.
Renfrew, C.
   1972   The emergence of civilization. The Cyclades and the Aegean in the third millennium B.C.   London:
           Methuen.
   1973   Social archaeology. Southampton: The University of Southampton.
Rowlett, R. M.
   1968   The Iron Age north of the Alps. Science 161: 123-34.   See also Pollnac.
Schaaff, U.
   1969   Versuch einer regionalen Gliederung frühlatènezeitlicher Fürstengräber. O. H. Frey, ed.,
           Marburger Beiträge zur Archäologie der Kelten. Festschrift für W. Dehn. Fundberichte aus Hessen
           Beiheft 1: 181-202. Bonn: Habelt.
Stead, I. M.
   1965   The La Tène Cultures of Eastern Yorkshire. The Yorkshire Archaeological Society.
Stjernquist, B.
   1955   Simris. On cultural connections of Scania in the Roman Iron Age. Acta archaeologica Lundensia
           Series in 4°, 2.   See also Blindheim.

SWISS ARMS OF THE LA TENE PERIOD AT PRINCETON, N.J.
by J. M. de Navarro

If Hugh Hencken's academic career were stratified, Late Hencken would be Harvard, Middle Hencken Cambridge (England), Early Hencken Princeton. A note on the Iron Age arms from Switzerland housed in the Department of Geology, Princeton University, seems therefore to be a not inappropriate tribute to him from a friend of fifty years.

I am primarily indebted to Professor H. J. Müller-Beck of Tübingen for notifying me of the existence of these objects, most of them unpublished. Small in number though they are, they form the most important collection of La Tène period scabbards known to me on the American continent. My thanks are also due to Dr. Donald Baird, of the Department of Geological and Geophysical Sciences, Princeton, for his unstinted help and for his permission to publish, to Mr. Willard Starks for photographs whence most of my illustrations are taken, and to Mrs. M. Houghton for her drawings for the text figures.

The relevant pieces are listed as follows under the heading Swiss Lake-Dwellers[1] Artifacts.

1162	Shield-boss. Dr. Gross collection. La Tène, Lake Neuchâtel.
1171	Iron scabbard, hilt end,[2] front and back pieces; incised decoration. La Tène, Lake Neuchâtel.
1172	Sword-point in tip of scabbard; scabbard with stamped shagreen decoration and long disc-ended chape bands: Site?
1174	Iron scabbard, hilt end front and back pieces; incised decoration. Site?
1175	Iron scabbard, front piece lacking point; stamped decoration. Site?
1176	Iron scabbard, hilt end, back piece only. Site?
1190	Sword lacking point; hilt restored. Arnold Guyot collection. Site?

Before dealing with this group of objects, I must touch upon the method I have adopted for classifying the scabbards of Middle La Tène type that come from La Tène in FLT I for the benefit of those who have not read that book. I divide the scabbards of this type into two main groups: Groups A (36 or 35 examples, see below, notes 3 and 7) and B (60 pieces). Each of these is characterized by a family of key-factors, the two families being mutually exclusive, as far as the relevant groups are concerned. In addition to these main groups there is also a small one, Group C (10 or 11 pieces),[3] in which the key-factors that distinguish Groups A and B from each other occur on the same piece. Most of the factors that characterize Group A are closely allied to features found on sheaths in Early La Tène form. The contrary is true for Group B. The evidence definitely points to Group A scabbards being made earlier in the Middle La Tène period than those of Group B. For detailed lists of the key-factors and other features found on sheaths of these two groups and a discussion of their chronological significance the reader is referred to FLT I: 302-305). In the following pages I shall restrict myself to dealing with the different factors involved as I come to them.

I am inclined to regard the small Group C as transitional between the two main ones, with some of its scabbards standing closer to Group A, others to Group B (Ibid.: 305-307). There are also eight or nine sheaths of Early La Tène type known to me from the site - nine, if one apocryphal piece is included.[3a] Finally there is a sort of limbo (Group D) into which I consigned scabbards, mainly fragmentary or otherwise ill-preserved, which are less easy to classify or date. It does not concern us here.

I conclude these remarks by emphasizing that the foregoing classification is primarily designed for the scabbards found at La Tène and is not intended to cover the whole La Tène area. If used with all due caution it can, however, enable one to identify certain scabbards found elsewhere over a far-flung area (FLT 1: Fig. 36) as having been made in north Switzerland and some of them as products of a school of armourers that catered for the people who assembled at La Tène, or in some instances sword-sheaths made by smiths outside Switzerland who copied or were inspired by such Swiss models (Ibid.: 136 ff, 180 ff and 310 ff). Again, used with caution, it may sometimes be of help towards classifying sheaths from other north Swiss sites and from regions in close touch with north Switzerland: Württemberg, Upper Bavaria and the middle Rhine.

Nos. PU 1162 and 1171 were found at La Tène, and, as we shall see, so was no. 1175.

Nos. 1171 and 1175 were first published in FLT I under the serial numbers 13 and 111β (Ibid.: 367.201f and 426).

PU 1171 (FIG. 2, 1a-1d) is the upper part of a scabbard 21.8 cm long; its maximum breadth is 5.78 cm. It is the broadest extant sheath known to me from La Tène. Its mouth is what I call Type A2, (see note 3) viz. campanulate, not narrowly pointed and normally low; its height is 1.09 cm. A plano-convex strip of metal, a mouth-guard is

FIG 1. Dragon-pairs a. Type I   b. Type III

FIG 2. PU1171 1a. An early water colour of the piece with its reinforce (Now in MCA Neuchatel). 1b-c.
Front and back of PU1171 still lacking its reinforce. 1d PU1171 with its reinforce restored to it.
(1a-1d approx 1:2). 2. MCA Neuchatel, 422, reinforce for PU1171 (approx 1:1).

rivetted on to the top of the sheath and was originally clipped to its sides (one clip is now missing); this protected the scabbard's mouth against the sword being slammed home. The reinforce is a frontal one and the suspension-loop is what I call Type II (i.e. rectangular and with its top 3 to 7 mm longer than it is wide). Its measurement on this piece are 1.61 x 1.28 cm. The whole of the chape is missing.

I will take first the key-factors on this piece which distinguish it from Group B scabbards. The Type A2 mouth on Group A sheaths is derived from mouths of that shape found on scabbards of Early La Tène form. Though known on Group C sheaths, it is quite foreign to those of Group B. In Group A, including No. 9, it occurs on 31 out of the 32 pieces with classifiable mouths preserved; excluding No. 9, it is the only form of mouth met with in that group. [4]

At La Tène midribs occur in 4 out of the 8 Early La Tène sheaths on which the presence, or absence of this feature is detectable (FLT I: 45 and below note 3a); on 11 out of 32 or 33 (33 1/2 - 34.4%) relevant Group A pieces (FLT I: 129)[5] and on 2 out of 10 or 11 (18.2-20%) of the Group C scabbards (*Ibid.*: 204f). At La Tène midribs are foreign to Group B scabbards, although they occur on 3 swords belonging to sheaths of that group.

The third key-factor that distinguishes Group A from Group B on the present piece is the bird-pair design. This motif is derived from the closely allied dragon-pair (FIG. 1), the birds being usually developed from the hooked upper jaws of the dragons. Indeed it is not always easy to distinguish dragons from birds with this motif.[6] Although scabbards adorned with dragon-or bird- pairs are far better represented at La Tène[7] than on any other site, the dragon-pair motif did not originate there. It is an inter-Celtic feature found on scabbards over a wide area stretching from West Hungary to the Saône and from northern Czechoslovakia (if not from Poland[8]), to Yugoslavia (FLT I, Fig. 15).[9] Jacobsthal and I derive the dragon-pair motif from fourth century B.C. Scythian sources.[10] In its classic form it appears to have originated in Hungary in the fourth century whence it spread rapidly westward. In the westerly area of its distribution the best dated examples come from late Early and early Middle La Tène contexts (FLT I: 71-80). As already noted, it is not always easy to differentiate between dragons and birds in this type of ornament, but from the present state of the evidence, it seems not unlikely that the transformation into birds took place in north Switzerland, where we find an example on a definitely Early La Tène type of sheath discovered at the eponymous site (Vouga 1923, Pl. I, 1: Jacobsthal 1944, Pl. 65, 107; FLT I, Pls. II, 2a-2b and LXXII, la). The rare examples of bird-pairs known to me from the East Celtic zone all occur on scabbards of Middle La Tène form (*Ibid.*: 237).

I have elsewhere pointed out that there are three types of this ornament (de Navarro 1959: 98-100; FLT I: 217-219). Types I and III are very closely allied and concern us here; the lyre-shaped Type II does not. Briefly, the main characteristic that distinguishes Type I is that the scroll-shaped ribbon-like bodies end in free-standing fore-feet: the fore-feet do not touch the dragons' lower jaws(FIG. 1a). From the lower part of the body hangs a very abstract motif which I call the 'tail-pendant' (*Schweifanhängsel*) for want of a better term. In Type III (FIG. 1b) the forefeet touch the dragons' lower jaws, the point of contact being indicated by a nick or an arc. This feature, then, has an organic significance. The scroll-shaped bodies of Type I have developed into a pair of concentric circles; the outer one of these is sometimes not completed at its top (see Fig. 1b), but each of the outer circles is marked by the aforesaid nick or arc. The tail-pendant is still present in Type III. Most of the bird-pairs are of Type III. The birds, perched on the concentric circles, face one another. With bird-pairs the concentric circles, the above-mentioned nicks or arcs and the tail-pendants are retained but have lost their organic significance and have become purely ornamental abstractions. On our piece even the nicks have disappeared and each of the birds is perched on a pair of unbroken concentric circles. The suppression of the nicks suggests that the bird-pair design on No. 1171 is devolved and that the ornament may come late in the bird-pair series.

There are three features on this scabbard still to be discussed and although they are not key-factors that distinguish Group A from Group B scabbards, they are all proportionately better represented on the former.

The mouth-guard is a rare feature that occurs on the front sides of the scabbards. It is unknown to me on any sheath of Early La Tène type. From La Tène there are or were 7 examples on 27 Group Ab sheaths with the fronts of their mouths well enough preserved to tell the presence or absence of this feature (25.9%) (FLT I: 145f). But out of 47 such Group B scabbards I only know of one example (2.1%) that definitely formed an original part of a given sheath (*Ibid.*: 156). Mouth-guards are unknown on any of the few Group C scabbards from the site.

At La Tène the Type II suspension-loop (see above), present on No. 1171 (FIG. 2, 1c) is the dominant form in Group A; it occurs on 13 out of 24 sheaths with loops preserved (54.2%) (*Ibid.*: 133) and in Group C twice out of 6 sheaths (33 1/3%) with loops still classifiable[11] (*Ibid.*: 207); but it is only represented on 3 out of the 40 Group B scabbards with loops still present (7 1/2%) (*Ibid.*: 171).

The frontal reinforce (FIG. 2, 1a, 1d and 2) on No. 1171 is the only class of this feature found at La Tène on Group A scabbards and occurs or has left its mark on 16 of them (FLT I: 131);[12] in Group B there are only 4

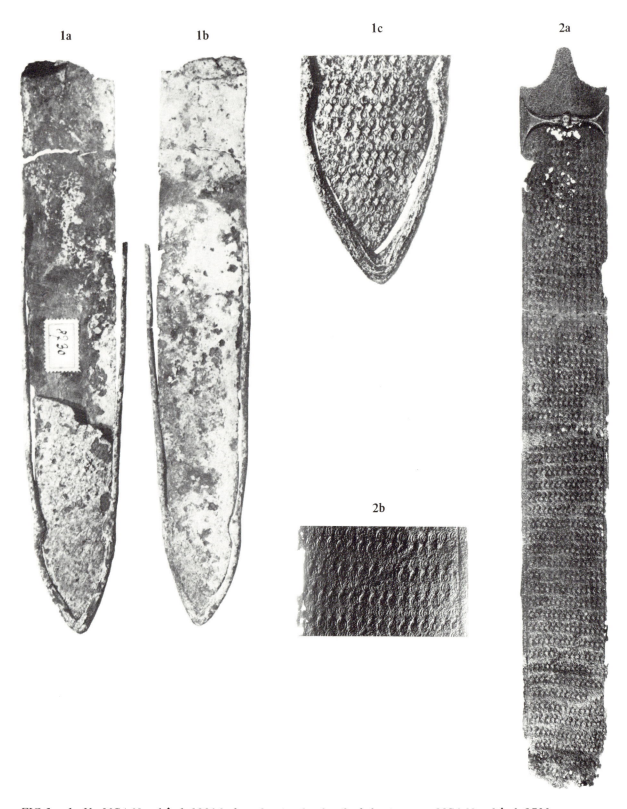

*FIG 3.   1a-1b. MCA Neuchâtel, 1830 before cleaning 1c. detail of chapinage on MCA Neuchâtel, 8730
after cleaning. (1a-1b approx 1:2, 1c approx 1:1).
2a. PU 1175 2b. detail of chapinage on PU1175 (2a approx 2:1, 2b approx 1:1).*

definite examples on the 36 pieces with reinforces preserved (11.1%) (*Ibid.*: 158). In Group C it is only represented for certain once among the 6 relevant pieces of that group (16 2/3%) (*Ibid.*: 205f).

Strangely enough I knew the reinforce of this piece before I was aware of No. 1171's existence. It was No. 422 of the Musée Cantonal d'Archéologie (MCA), Neuchâtel (FIG. 2, 2), a frontal reinforce of an uncommon type; in shape it is not unlike a man's bow tie. After I had visited Princeton and examined No. 1171 - then lacking its reinforce - I returned to Neuchâtel where I found an old water colour of this sheath giving its afore-mentioned reinforce still on it (FIG. 2 1a). Through the co-operation of the then Director of the Neuchâtel museum it has now been restored to its scabbard in Princeton (FIG. 2 1d). The finding of the old water-colour and the reinforce for No. 1171 in MCA, Neuchâtel indicates that Princeton acquired this sheath from Neuchâtel.

The above evidence shows the piece under discussion to be part of a Group A scabbard.

PU 1175 (FIG. 3, 2a), serially numbered as 111β in FLT I is the upper and probably greater part of the front side of a scabbard; the reverse is missing. Its present total length is 39.2 cm, its original maximum breadth was approximately 5.16 cm (one of the overlaps is missing at the upper end of the scabbard). The Type B (viz. narrowly pointed) mouth is 2.02 cm high. It has a reinforce with closed clamps below the mouth; whether it was frontal or bilateral in type one cannot say, owing to the absence of the reverse side of this part of the sheath. The clamps are of the closed type; neither clamp is intact; a composite measurement gives their length as *circa* 3.57 cm. There is no design on the piece. Its most striking feature is its chagrinage done with a patterned stamp and disposed in contiguous horizontal rows, starting below the reinforce and continuing to the end of the fragment. The marks it made consist of an upright figure-of-eight with pointed ends; within each loop of the eight is an oval, eye-shaped motif, the centre of which is sunk (FIG. 3 2b). The marks vary from 6.7 to 6.9 mm in length according to the sharpness of the blow and also the angle at which the tool was held (vertically or slightly obliquely) when struck.[13]

Before I knew of the existence of this piece I came across the lower end of a scabbard from La Tène in MCA, Neuchâtel (FIG. 3 1a-1b), bearing the number 8730 (serially numbered as 111a in FLT I). Its present maximum length is 29 cm and present breadth 4.56 cm at the top of the fragment. The chape-end is Type A1, i.e. long (here 5.76 cm), flattish and with well-defined finials. Only the lower end of the scabbard's front side is preserved; it was coated with white silt through which faint traces of a rare type of chagrinage were to be seen. In view of this the fragment was sent to Schweizerisches Landesmuseum (SLM), Zurich to be cleaned. On the reverse side the dark shadow left by a bird-bridge showed up against the white silty surface above and below it. But in process of cleaning the mark of the bird-bridge unfortunately has disappeared; it is still visible on a photo taken of the piece before it was sent to Zurich to be cleaned (FIG. 3 1b). Measured from the mark of this bridge, the chape was 21.8 cm long. The cleaning brought out the chagrinage very well indeed and showed its marks to be of the same type as those on No. 1175 (FIG. 3 1c). No. 8730 was returned to MCA, Neuchâtel after it was treated, where it was mislaid. Owing to this in FLT I (201f) I could only measure the length of the punch-marks from the approximately 1:1 scale of the photograph taken at Zurich after this fragment was cleaned; these varied between 6.5 and 6.8 millimetres. Even so Dr. Donald Baird of Princeton held this piece to be the lower end of No. 1175 and that both fragments were shagreened with the same tool. Since FLT I was published, the Neuchâtel fragment has come to light again and I have been able to measure the punch-marks. The best struck of these were 6.8 mm long. This has dispelled the very slight doubts I had and I now believe that the two fragments were definitely parts of the same scabbard. I assign it to Group C, the small group on which key-factors that distinguish Groups A and B from each other appear on the same scabbard.

The Group A key-factor on No. 8730 is the Type Ai chape-end (FIG. 3 1c). Including sheath No. 9 (see note 3) 9 out of 10 of the Group A scabbards from La Tène on which this feature is preserved have chape-ends of this type (90%); but if No. 9 is transferred to Group C, Type Ai is the only form of chape-end represented in Group A.[14] It is foreign to Group B,[15] and the only example met with on the 7 or 8 Group C sheaths with chape-end preserved is the one on the present piece (12.5-14.3%).[16]

The Group B key-factors on the present scabbard are the narrowly pointed Type B mouth and the now vanished mark of the chape's bird-bridge. Type B mouths occur or occurred on 53 out of 57 Group B sheaths with mouths or with hilt-ends preserved,[17] 93% of them (FLT I: 154f). This type of mouth (in one case its mark) appears on 3 out of the 9 or 10 relevant Group C pieces (30-33 1/3%), see *Ibid.*: 205. It is unknown on sheaths of Early La Tène type or in Group A.

There are two main forms of chape-bridge: the straight and the bird-head type (FIG. 4b). At La Tène the former is the only type found on Early La Tène type sheaths and in Group A. In Group B it occurs 13, perhaps 14 times (FLT.: 176f), while there are 17, perhaps 19 examples of the bird-bridge or marks left by it (Ibid.: 177f). Taking the lower of the two sets of figures, the percentages in Group B for the straight and the bird type work out at 43 1/3 and 56 2/3 respectively. Including the mark on No. 8730, the bird-bridge occurs twice out of the 7 or 8 Group C sheaths with chape-bridges preserved (25-28.6%)[18] (*Ibid.*: 208).

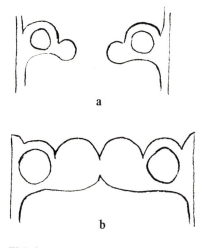

FIG 4.

Tops of chapes a. chape-clamps, bird-head type. b. bird-bridge.

Chagrinage of the type seen on the present scabbard is very seldom met with; the only comparable examples occur on two Group B scabbards from La Tène (FLT I: Pls. LXVII and LXVIII). The chagrinage on the latter stands very close indeed to that on the present piece. It consists of similarly diposed figure-of-eights, but the marks differ from those on the piece under discussion in being less pointed at their ends and were thus done with a different tool.

If, as I am convinced they are, Nos. 8730 and 1175 are parts of the same scabbard, the latter must come from the site of La Tène, since No. 8730 clearly does. The last-named piece originally formed part of the large collection of antiquities amassed from La Tène for Colonel Schwab (see below). About forty years after Schwab's death the then director of the Schwab Museum in Biel sold a number of these objects from La Tène to the Museum für Völkerkunde in Basel. About 1937 the last-named Museum handed this collection over to the Historisches Museum in the same city. The greater part of these pieces including 8730 were subsequently sent to MCA Neuchâtel, where they still bear their old inventory numbers in the five, six and eight thousands.

Part of this 1175-8730 scabbard is missing, as well as the reverse of the former, for the breaks on the two fragments do not fit. But the lower end of 1175 and the top of 8730 show clear signs of having been bent and then broken, perhaps at the time of deposition, for the breaks are old ones. The possibility of the two fragments having been recovered from the site on separate occasions should be borne in mind, for I know of no evidence that PU 1175 had ever belonged to SM Biel. In dealing with PU 1171 we saw that there was good reason for assuming that Princeton obtained it from the Neuchâtel museum. Could the same be true for 1175?

The third piece from La Tène at Princeton is PU 1162, an iron band-shaped shield-boss (FIG. 5 1). Its maximum width is 29.7 cm. One wing is slightly wider than the other, viz. 10.1 as against 9.5 cm. The outer ends of the wings are slightly higher (10.2 and 10.4 cm) than the inner ones (9.15 and 9.41 cm); the wings are therefore slightly expanded but not, as with some of these shield-bosses, noticeably flared. Approximately at the centre of each wing there is a single rivet-hole punched from the front side. The rivets are both missing. The arched centre which spanned a wooden spindle-shaped boss has a shallow horizontal groove along its upper and lower ends. Its sides are slightly convex, giving it a truncated faintly ovoid appearance. On the back of this piece there are many marks made by a narrow rectangular-ended hammer.

A sticker label on this shield-boss indicates its provenance and that it came from the collection of V. Gross. Gross did not excavate at La Tène. He was a collector and the author of *La Tène; un oppidum helvète* (1886), a work full of inaccuracies but the first in which plates illustrating the objects from La Tène were made from photographs. The bulk of his collection of objects found at La Tène is now housed in the SLM Zurich. How Gross acquired his collection is uncertain. Perhaps some of the objects were obtained from F. Borel (see FLT I 13, note 3) who explored the site most unsystematically in 1882-1883. What he found there he sold to pay for further excavations. Most of his finds went to BHM Bern and MAH Geneva.

The earliest La Tène shield-bosses are of wood and spindle-shaped. The earliest iron ones, dating from the Early to Middle La Tène transition, were little more than covers for the wooden spindle-boss; they were usually of the twinned (*zweischalig*) type. Before these went out of fashion, the band-shaped boss with its broad wings and arched centre came in (see W. Krämer 1949-50: 358). If the latter type appears before the end of the Early La Tène period, it had only got its foot in the door of that phase. It is the best represented form in the Middle La Tène times, and still sometimes appears in Late La Tène contexts. It is the only type of iron shield-boss known to me at the eponymous site. In FLT I: 315f, I pointed out that the band-shaped type was already in use early in the second century B.C. among two Celtic peoples: the Boii then in the Bologna area (before they were conquered by the Romans in 191 B.C.) and the Galatians of Asia Minor (190-189 B.C.). The occurrence of the type at this early date in two such widely separated areas of the Celtic world in itself indicates that its origin must go back well into the third century B.C.

Two pieces of wood were found at MCA Neuchâtel in a carton labelled (probably in Paul Vouga's hand) "boucliers 1 et 2 de La Tène". They were sent to Herr A. E. Hollstein of Trier for dendrochronological examination. One piece, with part of its bark preserved, he showed to have come from an oak felled in 256 B.C. The inventory numbers of these pieces are uncertain. From 1909 onward, starting with No. 750, the objects excavated at La Tène are numbered in the MCA Neuchâtel inventory in the order of their finding. In the section on shields in P. Vouga (1923: 59-62) only three examples from the site are mentioned. What is there given as the "first" is MCA

FIG 5.   1. PU1162, band-shaped shield-boss (approx 1:2). 2. PU1190 upper part of sword (approx 1:4)

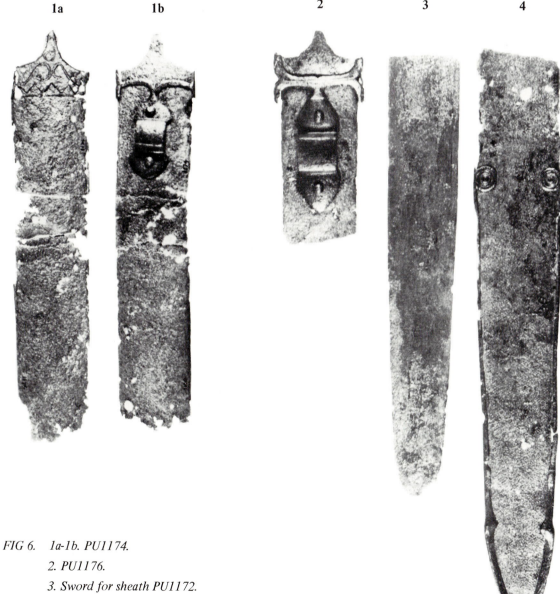

FIG 6.   1a-1b. PU1174.

2. PU1176.

3. Sword for sheath PU1172.

4. PU1172 sheath

(approx 1:2)

Neuchatel No. 1188 (*Ibid.*: Pl. 16, 10a-c). The middle part of it was found in 1911, its sides in 1913. [19] The "second" of these shields is No. 1231 (*Ibid.*: Pl. 17) from the 1913 excavations; the "third" is No. 1315 (*Ibid.*: Pl. 18), found in 1915. All three had iron band-shaped bosses and if one is right in identifying "boucliers 1 et 2" with Nos. 1188 and 1231, this type of shield-boss was already in use at La Tène by 256 B.C. or at all events soon afterwards.

It is an interesting fact that at La Tène offensive weapons far out-number defensive arms.

There are still four pieces which, beyond being inventorized as coming from Switzerland, are not precisely provenanced: PU 1172, 1174 and 1190. Perhaps the likeliest sites they may have come from are La Tène, Port (Kt. Bern) and the river Broye which links the Lake of Morat (Murten) with the Lake of Neuchâtel; all three of them are water-finds. The mouth of the Broye is but little more than five kilometres as the crow flies south-east of La Tène; Port about 20 km northeast of it. During the first correction of the Jura waters (mainly between 1874-1878) a good deal of smuggling went on, the objects being sold *sub rosa*. The four pieces that here concern us are all of Middle La Tène type, the period to which most of the objects found at La Tène belong. At Port objects of that period are relatively rare, though not unknown; there is also some Early La Tène material; but the bulk of the Port finds date from Late La Tène times. As to the Broye, most of the objects found there have disappeared largely owing to a school-master from Morat, one Süsstrunk by name, who used to arrive every Saturday by boat when the dredging was going on and depart with sacks full of antiquities which went to unknown destinations and whose exact provenances are now unknown. [20] We do know, however, that objects of the La Tène period were found at that time in that vicinity. The most famous of them is the big Middle La Tène spearhead from Jorissant with rich engraved ornament on both sides of its blade (Jacobsthal 1944, No. 129 on plates 72 and 73). Now in BHM Bern, it was originally acquired by H. Zintgraff from the dredger, Vanneau. [21]

It should be remembered that the objects that here concern us reached Princeton before 1876, the date of the earliest Princeton accession book in which there is no mention of them. How long before 1876 is uncertain. Arnold Guyot, the geologist, who haled from Neuchâtel, moved to Harvard in 1848 and was called to Princeton in 1854 to set up the Geological Department for the then College of New Jersey. He travelled to Europe in 1861 to collect extensive geological material and artifacts for this purpose. [22] E. Desor, a fellow geologist, was already settled in Neuchâtel by then, where he had been harvesting material from La Tène soon after its discovery in November 1857 by Hans Kopp who fished for antiquities in Swiss waters on behalf of Colonel Friedrich Schwab, founder of the Museum Schwab in Biel (Bienne) with its rich collection of finds from La Tène. We have seen there are strong grounds for assuming that PU 1171 was acquired from the Neuchâtel museum and, though we lack documentary evidence to prove it, it is not unlikely that Guyot obtained the piece through Desor and that the old water-colour of this scabbard (FIG. 2, 1a) was made for the record when the Neuchâtel museum parted with it. We have no written evidence when or from whom the less-precisely provenanced pieces were acquired. But if they were bought by Guyot on his 1861 trip which, despite the lack of documentary confirmation, is by no means impossible, this trip antedated the first correction of the Jura waters that brought so many antiquities to light.[23] By 1861, however, the exploration of La Tène had been in progress for four years. So some sort of case could be made for these unprovenanced pieces coming from La Tène. But if they were acquired by Princeton after 1861, they could equally well have come from Port, where the deepening of the Nidau-Büren canal began in 1867, or possibly from the Broye, though the first correction of the Jura waters did not start there till 1874, only two years before 1876, the Princeton dead-line.

PU 1172 (FIG. 6, 3 and 4) are the lower ends of a sword and its sheath. The present length of the scabbard is 29.4 cm, and its maximum breadth 4.67 cm. The total length of the chape is 23 cm and the lengths of its asymmetric chape-end are 6.6 and 5.9 cm. The chape-end appears to be of piled structure. In front, now only clearly visible at one side, there is an astragaloid finish to the chape-end on the chape's binding; its upper edge is 8.1 cm from the point of the scabbard. There are traces of a fellow to this on the opposite side; the binding there is now abraded. The chape's clamps on the front side of the sheath are round and each is adorned with stamped concentric circles. On the reverse side the bridge at the top of the chape is a straight one. It is now in very poor shape.

No. 1172 is an example of how my classification of scabbards from La Tène must be used with caution in attempting to classify sword-sheaths from possibly, as with this piece, other sites, even for those found in Switzerland.

It is the type of the chape-clamps on this piece that one must treat with circumspection when endeavoring to classify it. Were one sure that this scabbard came from La Tène, round and rounded (i.e. D-shaped) chape-clamps only occur at that site on sheaths of Early La Tène type and those of early Middle La Tène form (Group A). The general shape of 1172 and the form of its chape-end (see below) show clearly that the present piece is not an Early La Tène type scabbard. Already, before Group A scabbards went out of fashion, another type of chape-clamp began to appear at La Tène; I call it the bird-head form (FIG. 4a), though in some instances these clamps look more like the heads of animals. At La Tène on Groups B and C scabbards, the bird-head type completely ousted the round and rounded chape-clamps. I hold the bird-head type to be of importance, for it is one of the hall-marks of a school of armourers that made scabbards for the people who assembled at La Tène. The bird-head type, so richly represented there, rarely occurs elsewhere, even in Switzerland, and when it is found on other sites, it shows that the scabbards on which it is present were either made by that school of armourers or were copied from or inspired by their work (FLT 1, 136).

But although the life of the round and rounded chape-clamps was cut short at La Tène, it continued long in use elsewhere. While at La Tène it is a key-factor distinguishing Group A from Groups B and C scabbards, it is of little importance in attempting a finer classification for scabbards found on their sites, unless other early diagnostic factors are present, as they are on No. 1172. I refer to the type of its chape-end and to long chape.

The chape-end on No. 1172 is Type Ai: long (5.5 cm or more), flattish, and with well-defined (here in-pointed) finials. This feature is definitely a Group A key-factor (see above). As already noted, it is unknown on sheaths of Early La Tène type and on those of Group B and only occurs once on the 7 or 8 Group C scabbards from La Tène with chape-ends preserved: on MCA Neuchâtel 8730 which formed the lower part of PU 1175 (see above). The chape-end on No. 1172 is asymmetric, 6.6 and 5.9 cm long.

The long chape (23 cm on the present piece) is another factor which distinguishes Group A sheaths from those of Early La Tène and Group B character. Viewed statistically the chapes on Group A are significantly longer than those on Early La Tène and Group B scabbards, but they are not significantly longer than the chapes of Group C sheaths (FLT I: 353). In view, however, of its Type Ai chape-end, this scabbard would be more at home in Group A than in Group C.

One other feature on sheath No. 1172 remains to be discussed: its front side is shagreened. The word chagrinage was first employed for the practice of covering scabbards with punch-marks by the famous Swiss antiquary Ferdinand Keller (1858, 152); the term implies that this was done in imitation of leather. Beyond the fact that it is unknown to me on any sheath of Early La Tène form and is essentially characteristic of Middle La Tene type scabbards it is not very helpful for finer chronological shadings. We have already noted a rare type of chagrinage on PU 1175. At La Tène this practice first appears on Group A scabbards (6 examples, all shagreened with different varieties of punches); it occurs definitely on two sheaths of Group C and on over half of the Group B scabbards (32 examples).[24] I refrain from giving percentages since they may prove misleading, as a number of scabbards need cleaning to see if they were shagreened or not. But even on the present evidence this practice clearly reached its zenith at La Tène during the period when Group B scabbards (i.e. those of more advanced Middle La Tène type) were being made. On PU 1172 the chagrinage is very abraded and only here and there faintly visible in a low cross light. But I think it was done by a compound, diamond-shaped punch, probably giving 5x5 squarish marks. The closest parallels known to me come from La Tène and occur on one Group A sheath (my No. 42; SLM Zurich, No. 19775, see FLT I: 145) with 4x3 square marks and on two Group B scabbards, Nos. 55 (SM Biel T2767) with 5x5 marks and 62 (MAH Geneva, M549) with either 4x4 or 5x5 marks (FLT I: Pl. CL, Figs. 1 and 2).

Only the lower end of the sword which goes with sheath No. 1172 is preserved (Fig. 6, 3). Its present length and breadth are 22.5 and 3.92 cm respectively. In section the blade is of flattened lenticular form. It is not of the noticeably tapered Early La Tène type and its broad point is blunt. Both these factors, taken in conjunction with the scabbard to which it belongs, show it to be of Middle La Tène character. Though blunt, the point is what Dr. Donald Baird describes as feather-edged. This sword had evidently been broken in its sheath. Instances of this occur at La Tène (FLT I: 101, note 4, where they are cited as examples of ritual damage before deposition).

PU 1174 (FIG. 6, 1a-1b) was illustrated in FLT I, Pl. CLVI, 3a-3b. It is the upper end of a scabbard. Its present length is 22 cm, its present breadth 4.02 cm; owing to its condition the original breadth is uncertain; Dr. Baird estimates it as 4.25 to 4.3 cm. The narrowly pointed Type B mouth is 1.94 cm high. The reinforce is on the reverse of the scabbard and is clipped to each side of the sheath by short reinforce-clamps. They are of the closed type (i.e. without central openings) and are 1.59 cm long. Taken in conjunction with the suspension-loop to which it is linked by a short vertical element, the reinforce is of the T/V type, a T with curved arms. The suspension-loop is broader than the length of its top, i.e. Type IIIB. The plates above and below the actual loop, through which it is riveted to the scabbard, are shield-shaped. A ternary Swiss Sword Style design is incised below the mouth on the sheath's front side. It consists of two semi-recumbent S-motifs; above and between them hangs a spiral hook, its top ending in a paddle-shaped motif. The design is demarcated above by a plain line that contours the scabbard's mouth, and below by a horizontal line of zig-zags with a plain one running parallel to it and beneath it.

At La Tène the narrowly pointed Type B mouth, foreign to scabbards of Early La Tène character and to those of Group A, is numerically the most important key-factor for Group B and in which it is proportionately far better represented than in Group C (see above). Reinforces on the reverse sides of scabbards only, unknown either on Early La Tène or on Group A sheaths, occur at La Tène on 26[25] out of 36 Group B scabbards and three out of six Group

C sheaths with this feature preserved. The respective percentages are 72.2 and 50.0%. The T/V reinforce is only known at La Tène on Group B scabbards. One should bear in mind, however, that it only occurs on three sheaths from that site and that on one of these it forms the back of a bilateral reinforce (FLT I: 160); for some examples from other sites see *ibid*.: 168f. The Type IIIB loop is the dominant form in Groups B and C; half the scabbards with classifiable loops preserved in each of these groups are of that type (*Ibid*.: 170f and 207). On Group A sheaths from La Tène there are only 5 examples of this type on the 24 sheaths with classifiable loops (20.8%) (FLT I: 133). The form does not occur on any of the sheaths of Early La Tène type found there and is very rarely found on such scabbards from other sites (*Ibid*.: 55f). At La Tène Swiss Sword Style ternary designs (other than triskeles) appear both on Group A and B scabbards - twice on the former, six times on the latter. In Group C they are unknown.

Taking the available evidence into account, No. 1174 would be more at home in Group B than Group C, especially in view of its high, pointed Type B mouth. This factor precludes its being classified as an Early La Tène or Group A sheath.

PU 1176 (FIG. 6, 2) is the top of a scabbard's back plate. Its length is 10.8 cm; its present breadth, taken below the reinforce-clamps is 4.01 cm. In shape the mouth is narrowly pointed (Type B). But it is very low for a mouth of that form, its present height being only 1.42 cm; originally it was fractionally higher as the peak is now abraded. The loop is Type IIIB (broader than the length of its top). Taken in conjunction with the suspension-loop, the reinforce is of the T-type. A horizontal rill is incised along its arms. Each of the reinforce-clamps has a central opening; the better-preserved one is 2.66 cm in length.

As to parallels from La Tène, none of the classifiable key-factors on this piece occur either on scabbards of Early La Tène character or on those of Group A type. The mouth is uncharacteristically low but in shape it is quite unlike the mouths found on the two last-mentioned types of scabbards. In shape, if not in height, it can only be described as a low, narrowly pointed Type B mouth. The significance of that type of mouth I have already stressed (see above). It is a feature which indicates that pieces with this factor are definitely more likely to belong to Group B than to Group C. Owing to the front of this fragment being missing, one cannot say for certain whether the reinforce was confined to the reverse side only or whether it was a bilateral one. But it would be most unusual for a bilateral reinforce to have clamps with open centres.[26] The T-type reinforce confined to scabbards' reverse sides occurs at La Tène on 9[27] out of the 36 Group B sheaths with classifiable reinforces (25%) and once out of 6 such Group C pieces (16 2/3%); for the examples of the T-type forming the backs of bilateral reinforces, the relevant percentages are 8 1/3% for Group B (3 out of 36 pieces with classifiable reinforces) and 16 2/3% (1 out of 6 such pieces)[28] for Group C. As already noted (see above), the Type IIIB loop is proportionately equally well represented at La Tène in Groups B and C, but definitely rarer in Group A (see above). At La Tène the true open reinforce-clamps are only found in Group B (i.e. those with single central openings where the two halves of the clamps diverge from each other).[29] At La Tène in Group B both the closed and the open forms occur. Out of 34 clamps identifiable in this respect 16 are of the open type (47.1%). These open clamps are only represented at La Tène in Group B which strongly indicates that the present fragment was part of a scabbard of that group. I list some instances of sheaths from other sites with open reinforce-clamps, mentioning other diagnostic factors found on them:

Stettlen-Deisswil, Kt. Bern (BHM Bern, 33830a). Type B mouth, mark of a T/V reinforce; surviving chape-clamp of the bird-head type.
Mandach, Kt. Zurich (FLT 1: Pl. CLI, 1). Frame reinforce; shagreened.
Geislingen, Kr. Göppingen, Württemberg (*Ibid*.: 329); F. Fischer 1967:71, Fig. 6, 1). Type B mouth; chape with bird-head clamps and bird-bridge; shagreened.
Schrobenhausen, Upper Bavaria (de Navarro 1955: Pl. XXX, 1; FLT I: Pl. CXLIV, 3). Type B mouth; shagreened; design an ornithomorphic triskele.
München-Obermenzing, Upper Bavaria. From a doctor's grave with his surgical instruments. (de Navarro 1955, Pl. XXX, 2-3 and figure 1). Type B mouth; bird-head chape-clamps and bird-bridge; frame reinforce; shagreened; design, an ornithomorphic triskele.
"Himmelreich", Wattens, Tyrol (FLT I, Fig. 28) Bird-bridge to the chape; two circular stamp-marks on the sword of this scabbard; otherwise lacking in north Swiss characteristics.[30]

The bird-bridge like the bird-head chape clamps, was an invention of the school of armourers that worked for the people who assembled at La Tène (FLT I: 135ff and 180ff). As already noted these two forms rarely occur elsewhere, even in Switzerland, and when they do they show the relevant scabbards to be products of that school (like the one from the above-mentioned doctor's grave) or to be copied from or partly inspired by their work (like the sheath from "Himmelreich", Wattens). Devices like open reinforce-clamps, frame reinforces and chagrinage were certainly employed by these armourers, though it may be premature to regard them as hall-marks of their work. I nevertheless regard it as highly probable that the three last-named features originated in north Switzerland and the same of course holds good for the Swiss Sword Style.

PU 1190 (FIG. 5, 2) is the upper part of a sword, a very poor piece. The total length of the fragment is 55.5 cm; the present length of its blade 40 cm; its maximum breadth is 4.26 cm and the length of its hilt is 15.5 cm. The hilt-end is a thin one made of flattened wire or sheet iron; it is designed to fit a scabbard with a low Type A2 mouth; its internal height is 1.08 cm and at its centre it is only 0.13 cm thick. The tang is rectangular in section and burred for a disc-button; it tapers but little; the hilt's shoulders are stepped. The blade is of flattened lenticular section. It is slightly whippy. The sword has obviously been fought with, as there are four bent-up notches along one of its edges and one on the other. The piece formed part of the Arnold Guyot collection, presumably his private collection and not part of the material possibly collected by him for Princeton (see above).

With swords there are fewer factors that are of help for classification than there are with scabbards. The general shape of a sword can be of use in this respect; those of Early La Tène type begin to taper higher up the blade or taper gradually throughout. But the lower part of No. 1190 is missing and all one can say is that even in its present state the breadth of the blade at its top and its bottom shows that it did not taper throughout. The type of the hilt-end is of primary importance for classifying swords. In its shape, height and thinness the hilt-end on the present piece is characteristic of swords belonging to Early La Tène[31] and Group A scabbards. The midrib, often present on swords of Early La Tène character, is lacking on this piece. Early La Tène swords normally tapered to a sharp point and were used primarily as thrusting weapons. The bent up notches show No. 1190 to have been used in a slashing fray and were either caused by warding off cutting blows or by slashing against a parrying weapon. This damage to the edges shows the poor quality of the iron.

The evidence for classifying this piece is not very helpful. The shape, height and thickness of the hilt-end point, as already noted, to an Early or Middle La Tène date: it was clearly not shaped to fit the narrowly pointed, high mouth proper to later Middle La Tène (Group B) scabbards. The length of the hilt is less characteristic of Early than of early Middle La Tène swords and were I sure it came from the eponymous site, I would be inclined to assign it to the earlier part of Middle La Tene.

Notes

1. The term "lake-dwellers" is in this connotation both obsolete and unfortunate. Though some of the chief Swiss Iron Age assemblages of antiquities are waterfinds, they do not come from "lake dwellings" but from rivers which flowed or flow out of or into lakes: La Tène where the main find came from an old arm of the river Thielle (Zihl), from the river Broye and again from the Thielle at Cornaux below La Tene and from the old bed of that river below Port.

2. In this list the term "hilt end" denotes the upper end of a scabbard and is used in a different sense to mine. I use the term "hilt-end" (with a hyphen) in a more specific sense to describe the ogival 'cross-bar' at the lower end of the sword's hilt which was made to fit the curves of the scabbard's mouth.

3. The above figures for Group C depend on whether the scabbard BMH Bern, 13526 (No. 9 in FLT I: 125), a difficult piece to classify, is retained in Group A or transferred to Group C. This also affects my percentages where a feature found on that scabbard is involved. In such instances I give two percentages for the trait in question. For Group A one of these includes No. 9, the other excludes it; for Group C one percentage excludes No. 9, the other includes it. E.g. in Group A there are 31 or 32 sheaths with mouths preserved to classify (*Ibid*.: 130f); 31 of them have Type A2 mouths (i.e. not narrowly pointed and normally low in height, see FIG. 2, 1a-1d). On sheath No. 9 the mouth is high and subtriangular, and if No. 9 is included in Group A, it is the only certain example in that group whose mouth is not Type A2. The respective percentages are therefore 100 and 97. In Group C 5 out of the 8 or 9 scabbards with mouths preserved have Type A2 mouths (55 1/2 - 62 1/2%). It should be noted that three of these are abnormally high (see *Ibid*.: 205 and 306). My percentages only cover features well enough preserved to classify.

3a. Since FLT I was published the lost volume IV (IV K) of the former MfV Berlin has come to light. In it is inventorized all the material from La Tène once housed there, together with small sketches of some of these pieces. One of the latter is IV K 98, lost in World War II, a partly exposed sword in its scabbard. The sheath is noticeably tapered in form and it has a long band-shaped suspension loop (cf. FLT I: Fig. 8. 1), both of which factors show it to be of Early La Tène type. This brings the total of such scabbards found at La Tène to nine, including one fragmentary apocryphal piece. Neither IV K 98's sword nor the sheath has a midrib.

4. For the relevant Group A and Group C percentages for this feature see above note 3. The mouth of No. 9 is subtriangular in shape and high.

5. With and without No. 9 (see note 3), and including No. 114 (see below note 7). The latter was not included in FLT I: 129.

6. In interpreting these very abstract creatures as griffons, Mossler (1962) obviates this difficulty.

7. In FLT I: 65 eleven examples were cited as coming from La Tène. A sketch of a twelfth is given in the recently recovered volume IV of the former MfV Berlin: it is the top of IV K 100, now lost. The lower part of it is still extant and was serially numbered in FLT I as 114 and illustrated on Pl. L11, 1a-1b of that book, where I classified it in Sub-group D i, (viz. among sheaths which could be of either Early or Middle La Tène form) for I had only its midrib to go on. In view of the dragon- or bird-pair, taken in conjunction with its evidently not very tapered form, it should be transferred to Group A bringing the total of Group A sheaths to thirty-six and Group A sheaths with midribs from ten to eleven. The scale of the sketch is too small to tell if this sheath bore

a dragon- or a bird-pair. Whichever it was, it was not Type II (viz. lyre-shaped); and judging from the sketch it was Type III, not Type I. The scabbard's mouth in the sketch looks rather pointed for Type A2, and could possibly have been of the rare sub-triangular form. It is hardly concave-sided enough to be Type B, which would be quite out of character for any sheath with dragon- or bird-pair design from La Tène or indeed elsewhere. But it is asking a lot of a small sketch to be reliably accurate in such nuances as the type of curve taken by a scabbard's mouth. I have therefore deemed it safer not to include it in footnote 3 among the mouths of Group A scabbards. From the sketch, this sheath appears to have a mouth-guard. Were this certain, it would also point to No. 114 being a Group A sheath and not one of Early La Tène type (see FLT I: 145f). The suspension-loop, though only given in profile, resembles more closely the less long Middle than the longer Early La Tène forms.

8. The ornament on the example from Żerań, Poland is ill-preserved but is, I think more likely to have been a dragon-pair than ornament allied to that motif (FLT I, Fig. 16a).

9. In FLT I: 65-69, I was able to cite 41, with Żerań 42 instances. Since then I have learnt of 4 further examples: the one from La Tène mentioned above in note 7, and 3 from Hungary: 1 from Rezi-Cser and an unprovenanced sheath, both in the Balatoni Museum at Keszthely, and 1 from Muhi in the O. Herman Museum, Miskolc (M. Szabó 1971: 765 with note 2). These bring the total of scabbards with dragon- and bird-pairs known to me to 45 or 46.

10. Jacobsthal (1944) Text: 45 and FLT I: 229f. Szabó (1973: 762), however, would derive the motif from confronted felines found in a very early phase of the Scythian beast-style, the Kelermes-Melgunov horizon. Recent Russian authorities would date the latter as early as the end of the seventh and start of the sixth century B.C., largely because of Urartean contacts (Piotrovsky, 1973-74: 17). But even on Schefold's rather later dating, second quarter of the sixth century, (Schefold 1938: 9), there is an unconscionable time gap between the confronted felines of the Kelermes-Melgunov horizon and our fourth century B.C. dragon-pairs.

11. The loop on No. 9 is too damaged to classify with assurance.

12. No. 9 has no reinforce.

13. For further remarks on chagrinage, see below.

14. The chape-end on No. 9 is Type Aii, a rare form, a short version of Type Ai (see FLT I: 140b).

15. Devolved descendants of the Type Ai chape-end (described in FLT I as Aiii) occur on 5 Group B scabbards from La Tène (Ibid.: 184). They are devolved because their finials are ill-defined.

16. FLT I: 208f.

17. On nine of these 53 scabbards the mouths are ill-defined or missing, but the swords of all these nine pieces have hilt-ends clearly shaped to fit Type B mouths.

18. I have not included a rather doubtful mark of one on my No. 109 (FLT I: 202f), a Group C scabbard.

19. It should be noted that No. 1188 was not the first shield to be found at La Tène but only the first of the three best preserved ones. The MCA Neuchâtel inventory gives three other examples. No. 887 ("morceaux de bois d'umbo") I found in a tray along with pieces of an uninventorized band-shaped iron shield-boss; the association may be fortuitous, as there is no reference to iron in the entry for No. 887 from the 1909 or, 1910 excavations. No. 1022, inventorized as "bouclier et fragment d'umbo; bois", was found in 1911 and No. 1051 ("fragment d'umbo et de bouclier; fer et bois" in 1912. As wood only, not iron, is mentioned in the above entries for Nos. 887 and 1022, it is possible that wooden spindle-shaped bosses, unprotected by band-shaped ones of iron, may also have been in use at La Tène.

20. A letter from an eyewitness, Mme Derron, to F. Louis Ritter.

21. Information in a letter marked 1926/7 from H. Zintgraff to F. Louis Ritter.

22. I am indebted to Dr. Donald Baird for the above information about Guyot.

23. W. Bourquin, Die archäologische Forschung und die 2 Juragewässer-Korrektion, 8, whence the dates given for the start of the work on the Büren canal and the Broye are taken.

24. Cf. FLT I, 145; 189ff; 209f. For instances on scabbards found elsewhere, see ibid., 195f.

25. See below, note 26.

26. In FLT I, 164 I cited scabbard No. 45 from La Tène (BHM Bern, 13575) as being the only instance known to me from that site of a sheath with a bilateral reinforce that had a central opening in each of its clamps. The back of this piece has disappeared and is only known from an old drawing reproduced in FLT I, pl. XX, 3c. Granted that in this respect the drawing is accurate, I erred in taking the mark of a shaped bar on the front side of this sheath for the front part of a bilateral reinforce: it is located too high to have formed part of the T-shaped reinforce on the back of the scabbard (cf. ibid., pl. XX, 3a with XX,3c). The mark of the shaped bar on the front of this piece I now believe to have been left by a non-functional purely ornamental mount welded on to it. Nor in the old drawing of the front of this sheath with the shaped bar still preserved on it (ibid., pl. XX, 3b) does this feature appear to be attached to the scabbard's sides: it stops short of them. The total of Group B sheaths with bilateral reinforces given in FLT I, 161, 199 and 303 should therefore be reduced from seven to six and the total number of sheaths in that Group with reinforces confined to their reverse sides correspondingly increased from twenty-five to twenty-six (ibid., 158, 199 and 303).

27. Including sheath No. 45 (see the foregoing footnote).

28. No. 9 has no reinforce.

29. The surviving reinforce-clamp on a dragon- or bird-pair sheath (No. 16) from La Tène is pierced in two places (*FLT* I, pl. IX, 1b); it is an ornamental afterthought and not, like the type under discussion, something that grew out of the reinforce's structure.

30. To judge from a sheathed sword found with Late La Tène pottery at Niederingelheim (Behrens, *Bodenurkunde aus Rheinhessen,* fig. 228), the open form of reinforce-clamps appears to have outlasted the Middle La Tène period - unless this sword was an heirloom.

31. In its thinness and low height the hilt-end on the present piece resembles the ill-preserved hilt-end on a sword from La Tène rusted in an early La Tène type scabbard (No. 3, *FLT* I, pl. II, 1a). Hilt-ends are uncommon but not unknown on swords of Early La Tène form.

Abbreviations

BHM Bern	Bernisches Historisches Museum, Bern.
FLT I	See s.v. de Navarro 1972 *In* References Cited.
MAH Geneva	Musée d'Art et d'Histoire, Geneva.
MCA Neuchâtel	Musée Cantonal d'Archéologie, Neuchâtel.
MfV Berlin	The former Museum für Völkerkunde, Berlin.
PU Princeton	Princeton University, Dept. of Geology, Princeton, N.J.
SLM Zurich	Schweizerisches Landesmuseum, Zurich.
SM Biel	Museum Schwab, Biel.

References Cited

Behrens, G.
  1927   Bodenurkunden aus Rheinhessen I. Vorrömischezeit.
Bourquin, W.
  n.d.   Die archäologische Forschung aus der 2ten Juragewässerkorrektion.
de Navarro, J. M.
  1955   'A doctor's grave of the Middle La Tène period from Bavaria'. Proceedings of the Prehistoric Society XXI: 231-248.
  1959   'Zu einigen Schwertscheiden aus La Tène. 40 Bericht der Römisch-Germanischen Kommission 1959: 79-119.
  1972   The Finds from the Site of La Tène, Vol. I. Scabbards and the Swords found in them. Part I, Text; Part II, Catalogue and Plates. See abbreviations.
Fischer, F.
  1967   'Alte und neue Funde der La Tène - Periode aus Württemberg'. Fundberichte aus Schwaben, Neue Folge 18: 61-106.
Gross, V.
  1886   La Tène; un oppidum helvète.
Jacobsthal, P.
  1944   Early Celtic Art.
Keller, F.
  1858   'Pfahlbauten 2 Bericht'. Mitteilungen der Antiquarischen Gesellschaft in Zurich XII: 245-320.
Krämer, W.
  1949/50 'Zur Zeitstellung der holzernen Schilde des Hirschsprungfundes'. Praehistorische Zeitschrift 34/35: 354-360.
Mossler, G.
  1962   'Schwert und Scheide der frühen La Tène - Kultur aus Wieselburg, Niederösterreich'. Mitteilungen der Anthropologischen Gesellschaft in Wien XCII: 221-226.
Piotrovsky, B.
  1973/74 'Early Cultures of the Lands of the Scythians'. From The Lands of the Scythians. Metropolitan Museum of Art, New York, Bulletin XXXII, No. 5: 12-31. Special Issue.
Schefold, K.
  1938   'Der Skythischer Tierstil in Südrussland,' Eurasia Septentrionalis Antiqua XII: 1-78.
Szabó, M.
  1973   'Eléments régionaux dans l'Art des Celtes orientaux'. Etudes Celtiques XIII, 2:750-774.
Vouga, P.
  1923   La Tène. Monographie de la station.

THE TIME OF THE HILL-FORTS
by Jiří Neustupný

We are generally inclined to take it for granted that fortified settlements (hill-forts) were built in periods of war-like clashes between different and alien groups of prehistoric, primitive society. Such a matter-of-fact assumption is based upon a simplified understanding of the relations between fortifications and military actions. A deeper analysis of the possible functions of prehistoric fortified settlements, however, shows that such simplified linking of the construction of fortified settlements with simultaneous military actions is much influenced by our knowledge of long-term historic and mainly recent wars, which were of course waged by developed societies and involved advanced military technique. In those periods of history there were constructed and are still constructed in the course of military actions various fortifications, either light and simple, or more sophisticated, all closely linked up with the existing needs of the warriors, as well as with the organization and technique that were necessary to build them. It is not certain, however, if such facts and observations from more advanced and recent stages of the development of human society can be directly transferred into the milieu of prehistoric, primitive society. The character and extent of military clashes in prehistoric times were undoubtedly different from those typical of more highly organised historic society. This difference is shown, among other things, in the wide distinctions between archaeological evidence of prehistoric weapons, armour and fortifications on the one hand and similar archaeological evidence from the milieu of ancient and feudal society, on the other hand. For this reason it is necessary to compare collected archaeological data and study it from all possible aspects.

As far as the present author is informed, the most remarkable theory of the period of the origins as well as the functions of prehistoric fortified settlements was supplied by the Czech prehistorian and protohistorian Emanuel Simek. His opinion, expressed as early as 1948, did not attract the interest of wider circles of prehistorians and protohistorians only because it was published in a journal that had limited circulation and went out of publication shortly afterwards. The article by E. Simek is entitled "When fortified settlements came into being" (Simek, 1948), and in the short concluding part of this article we can read that "primitive nations of prehistoric and early historic epochs started to build fortified settlements only when passing over from the first period of stormy expansion and of occupying new domiciles to a quiet life in territories, which they considered to be their full and legitimate property, inherited from ancestors, and as soon as it became necessary to defend this heritage against attacks of other foreign 'invaders'.

Quite clearly and unambiguously, E. Šimek does not place the construction of fortified settlements into periods of wars and military clashes, but rather into periods of calm and settled life, which had been preceded by stormy expansions and occupation of new domiciles.

As for the period of the construction of fortified settlements, the present author is inclined to agree almost apodictically with the interpretation given by E. Simek, because it is very difficult to imagine that two opposing parts or strata of human society - prehistoric (primitive) society - had the time and energy to build fortified settlements during warlike clashes. It is not possible to exclude the possibility of construction of light and temporary camp fortifications in the course of military actions. Such temporary fortifications were used by the Roman military technique, as evidenced by accounts of Caesar and Tacitus (Simek: 130). Also at the beginning of the Middle Ages the construction of such fortifications was probable during military campaigns (Turek: 134). In earlier pre-historic and protohistoric periods, however, we cannot prove such cases by means of archaeological finds. In the following text the present author will try to prove that fortified settlements in prehistory were linked up with periods of settled life conditions.

Before proceeding to these problems, however, let us give some attention to other opinions and theories of E. Šimek, in connection with his interpretation of the period of origin of fortified settlements. E. Simek was of the opinion that fortified settlements were constructed as defence against foreign invaders. Such an interpretation, of course, cannot be disregarded, particularly for territories in which there would be in contact two different and consequently alien, social, power or ethnic units. But how can we explain the existence of so many fortified settlements within the territory of a certain entity, of an archaeological culture? Does it mean that warriors of one inimical group dared to penetrate deep into the territory of the adversary, and consequently the adversary protected himself by a whole system of fortified settlements? Such extensive and broadbased military campaigns are hardly probable in primitive society, because they are not in keeping with the political disintegration of such society, which can be presumed on the basic of historic ethnographic models. Also, we must pose the question whether the archaeological cultures within whose framework fortified settlements appear could form political units; this is improbable, or almost out of the question, because the territory of an archaeological culture is usually too extensive to form a political unit within the framework of a primitive society of pre-state character. Thus, we cannot assume that archaeological cultures, as units, waged wars on one another and constructed fortified settlements (hill-forts) to protect themselves. In view of the above mentioned analysis it is much more probable to presume that the origin and existence of fortified settlements were rooted in the internal relations of the society that was the bearer of a certain archaeological culture. In the following text the present author will try to substantiate the interpretation that the appearance of fortified settlements (hill-forts) was directly related to the internal tensions in certain primitive societies, i.e. that it was a reflection of socio-economic relations.

Turning our attention to the present research, which is sufficiently advanced for the study of our problem, in the territory of Czechoslovakia and the neighbouring Central European countries (Neustupný, Jiří 1950.-Neustupný, Evžen and Jiří 1961.-Neustupný, Jiří 1970), we take note of a very interesting phenomenon, namely that hill-forts do not exist in all archaeological cultures and in all archaeological periods. Thus, in the territory of Czechoslovakia and Central Europe it is not possible to trace uninterrupted development of prehistoric fortified settlements, including the development of construction techniques. We can only find separate groups of fortified settlements that are not related either in time or culture. These isolated groups of fortified settlements are separated by periods in which settlements were not fortified at all. (Neustupný, Jiří 1969.)

What could be the reasons for the existence of hill-forts in certain periods and for their absence in others?

Let us have a detailed look at some archaeological periods and cultures that display more clearly the phenomena whose explanation and interpretation may be sought with relative certainty in the present state of archaeological research. For example, the Corded Ware culture and the Bell Beaker culture of the Late Eneolithic do not show fortified settlements at all. At present, we know only very little about the settlement of the Bell Beaker people, and settlements of the people with Corded Ware have so far escaped discovery by present archaeological methods. (Neustupný, Evžen 1969.) On the other hand, both these archaeological cultures have already yielded so many burial grounds and burials, that we can describe the Late Eneolithic as a period in which for the first time in prehistory a large part of the population, if not all the population, were ritually buried. (Neustupný, Evžen and Jiří 1961: 79-81, 84.) At the same time attention must be drawn to the fact that in this period we can observe clearly for the first time a distinction between a battle-axe and working tools. Thus, burials of males belonging to the Corded Ware culture seem to be those of warriors. Similarly, in the burials of males belonging to the Bell Beaker culture there appear a bow with arrows furnished with stone arrow-heads, or wrist-guards protecting the wrist against the slash of the bow-string. As a novelty in prehistoric arms there appear copper daggers. The characteristic weapons of both of these cultures of the Late Eneolithic point to a military character of the society, within which there took place various clashes and modifications of relations in the patriarchal system. (Neustupný, Evžen 1967). The society at that time was not settled and did not have either time or energy to build in peace fortified settlements, which certainly require very good organization and considerably high numbers of workers.

The conditions typical of the Late Eneolithic survived into the following Early Bronze Age, which was related to the Late Eneolithic genetically, as far as the population and material culture are concerned. At extensive burial grounds of that period we find in male burials evidence of a warlike character to life - small bronze daggers and in hoards from the same time there come to light even large daggers. Settlements corresponding to the burial grounds of that period are open - no fortified settlements are known. Only after a consolidation of the social relations at the end of the Early Bronze Age (in the so-called Věteřov type) can we observe a start of the construction of hill-forts, which apparently served to stabilize the conditions resulting from armed clashes between and among the units of the patriarchal society of the preceding phase of the Early Bronze Age.

Hill-forts in Czechoslovak territory and in neighbouring countries are particularly characteristic for the Late and Latest Bronze Age, Early Iron Age, and the Early La Tène period. In those prehistoric periods the stratification of patriarchal society reached a considerable degree of development, and we can observe the separation of a leading social stratum - chiefs of patriarchal great families. In Central Europe the situation was very similar to that described by Homer for Greece. The leading social stratum formed a warrior aristocracy, whose members closed themselves up in hill-forts to protect both the economic and social power they had acquired. A warrior aristocracy protected its power from the subjugated population, who worked for them. On the other hand the population was protected by the warrior aristocracy against other warrior groups. By their military might the warriors ensured their population peace for work - in the interest of the warrior aristocracy ("military democracy"). This was the last undoubtedly prehistoric milieu, the milieu of prehistoric Celts, whose original cradle-land was made up of, among other Central Europeans regions, South and Central Bohemia, South Moravia and South-West Slovakia, all substantial parts of the modern Czechoslovak territory. (Neustupný, Jiří 1966 and 1970.) Starting with the 4th century B.C. we may call the population of these regions "protohistoric Celts", because we have written accounts of them, though not quite clear and subject to several interpretations. In the milieu of these protohistoric Celts we encounter in the Czechoslovak territory two very interesting problems. From the 4th, 3rd and 2nd centuries B.C. we know only of burial grounds and very few settlements - all of them are open. There are no hill-forts from this period. At the burial grounds the male graves contain weapons and armour, and the buried individuals seem to have been warriors. (Schránil, Josef 1928:224-49. - Neustupný, Evžen and Jiří 1961: 148, 154.) The overall character of this period points to an unsettled and uneasy life, in which the leading stratum of the patriarchal society fought with weapons for social and economic consolidation, which came about in the 1st century B.C. From the 1st century B.C. we have evidence of both open settlements and *oppida*. The latter represent fortified settlements of almost city-like character, which were at the same time centres of manufacture and social power. These *oppida* were seats of rulers, warrior aristocracy and artisans, who were brought here from villages. The *oppida* protected the leading social stratum, which organized manufacture and trade and controlled the neighbouring territory. It is interesting, however, that so far no burial grounds belonging to such extensive settlements as Celtic *oppida* have been found. (Neustupný, Evžen and Jiří 1961:157.)

The period of Germanic settlement of the present Czechoslovak territory, particularly of Bohemia and Moravia, in the 1st to 6th centuries A.D. has yielded so far, from the archaeological viewpoint, only burial grounds and open settlements. The latter are more frequent in the 1st to 4th centuries A.D. and rather scarce in the 5th and 6th centuries A.D. Hill-forts are not known. Because burial grounds from the 1st to the 4th centuries A.D. are for the most part cremation burial grounds, we have no detailed information about the furnishing of graves, though we have evidence of weapons and armour in male graves. Graves dating from the 5th and 6th centuries A.D. are, on the other hand, inhumation graves, and the males are provided with weapons and armour, though we have only partial information about such finds, because graves from that period were very often looted by contemporaries. (Schránil 1928: 252-281; Svoboda 1965:195, 348; Sakař 1970:68; Sakař 1973:232.) For this reason we can say that the Germanic milieu of the 1st to 6th centuries A.D. was unsettled and disturbed, that clashes took place between tribes or even tribal unions (as evidenced by contemporary written accounts from the ancient world), and that internal tensions within the tribes were adjusted. Apparently, no such internal victory took place, which would assure the leading social stratum both social and economic supremacy resulting in the construction of hill-forts.

From the beginnings of the settlement of present-day Czechoslovak territory by the ancestors of modern Czechs and Slovaks, from the 6th to 8th centuries A.D., hill-forts are very rare or we do not know of them at all. Only in the 9th century A.D. did the construction of hill-forts begin to greater extent, particularly in Moravia, and their prime began in Bohemia and Moravia in the 10th century A.D., at a period of more advanced formation of the Bohemian state. (Turek, Rudolf 1974:134,139.) The society of Slavonic tribes was in the initial stages of the settlement of new territory in Bohemia, Moravia and Slovakia, apparently for a long time unconsolidated not only in relations between individual tribes, but also within the tribes themselves. Only after the adjustment of internal tensions can we observe the development of a firmer social formation, protected by the construction of hill-forts, whose function was to protect the social and economic power acquired by the victorious social stratum. This time, however, is already the beginning of feudalism.

Conclusion

The present article does not represent a full and complete archaeological picture of the distribution of hill-forts (Neustupný, Jiří 1969.) with respect to individual archaeological cultures, but the facts mentioned do show that fortified settlements are not typical of all prehistoric archaeological cultures, and that in the territory of Czechoslovakia and neighbouring countries there was no direct and uninterrupted development from the earlier to later fortified settlements. In certain periods and cultures fortified settlements do not appear at all, only to come into existence in the subsequent cultures and periods. We are now faced with the problem as to whether every new appearance of hill-forts is the result of local invention, or whether this phenomenon had been transplanted from other territories. Taking into account the primitive character of the construction of prehistoric fortified settlements we may consider the first possibility as more probable. On the other hand it is very difficult to prove a transfer of fortification architectures from neighbouring or even more distant territories. In this latter case we must base our conclusions upon certain distinctive differentiating features of architecture, and often we must be content by saying that such features had been intruded into the domestic (local) primitive fortification architecture. A transfer of fortification architecture may come into account in the case of a new population, and for the existence of fortified settlements at the very beginning of such new settlement.

But why were fortified settlements built in certain periods and absent in others?

First of all we will pay attention to the warlike character of the prehistoric periods without fortified settlements, as evidenced in male graves of respective burial grounds. The warlike character of the furniture of such graves points to the fact that these periods were unconsolidated, and there existed tensions within the society which were settled or adjusted in armed clashes. New contradictory social conditions were formed in these periods which at the same time gave rise to a new economic power. Apparently, attempts were made within the society to establish economic and power supremacy of a certain social stratum over the rest of the population. The character of the relations of such a leading social stratum was naturally subject to developmental changes. Its character in the Neolithic was different from that in the Early Iron Age, in the time of Homer, and in the period of military democracies, from which we have conclusive evidence that it was fully developed and established. In these periods of unrest and armed clashes there was, naturally, no time and energy to perform such complicated and demanding work as the construction of hill-forts. Only the liquidation of tensions within the society and gaining of economic and social supremacy by one stratum of the population over the rest of the people brought about the victory of that leading social group. This social group protected its power by the construction of fortified settlements, hill-forts. But fortified settlements at the same time offered protection to this leading social stratum against the subjugated population who, in turn, were under the protection of the leading military power. By building fortified settlements one social group also protected itself against neighbouring groups, which desired aggrandizement of their power and wealth.

The fortified settlements were not built against foreign invaders in general: thus the Celtic tribes did not construct their *oppida* against the invading Teutonic tribes but as the result of internal needs of Celtic society. And the Teutons never built hill-forts - although pressed by invading Slavs.

Hill-forts became economic and social centres, and their development resulted in the appearance of the *oppidum,* of a pre-historic town of the 1st century B.C., whose society was already on the threshold of social stratification and pre-state life.

Thus, there were alternating periods of internal conflicts in the society with periods characterized by established and consolidated political and economic power. The former had a warlike character and were without fortified settlements, the latter are characterized by fortified settlements as centres of economic and political power.

This is then the conclusion of our socio-economic interpretation of the original idea of E. Šimek concerning the period of the appearance of hill-forts. However, it remains an open question whether such interpretation, based upon the archaeological situation in the Czechoslovak territory, may be applied also to other more extensive territories in Europe, or even whether it may be a generally valid interpretation. The relatively uniform development of mankind and human civilization may not exclude the possibility of such application to other primitive societies.

References Cited

Břeň, Jiří
    1966   Třísov, A Celtic Oppidum in South Bohemia. Guides to Prehistory No. 2. Prague.
Neustupný, Evžen
    1967   The Beginnings of Patriarchy in Central Europe. Rozpravy Československé akademie věd, řada
            společenských věd, Transactions of the Czechoslovak Academy of Sciences, Social Sciences
            Series Vol. 77, No. 2. Prague.
Neustupný, Evžen
    1969   Economy of the Corded Ware Cultures. Archaeologické rozhledy. Vol. XXI : 43-67. Prague.
Neustupný, Jiří
    1950   Fortifications appartenant à la civilisation danubienne néolithique Premières bourgades en Europe
            Centrale. Archiv orientální. Journal of the Czechoslovak Oriental Institute Vol. XVIII, No. 4:
            131-158. Prague.
Neustupný, Jiří
    1966   From Indo-Europeans to Prehistoric Celts in Central Europe. Revista da Faculdade de Letras de
            Lisboa, III series, No. 10 : 3-32. Lisbon.
Neustupný, Jiří
    1969   Urgeschichtliche Vorformen des Städtewesens. Siedlung, Burg und Stadt. Deutsche Akademie der
            Wissenschaften zu Berlin. Schriften der Sektion für Vor-und Frühgeschichte, Band 25, pp. 26-41.
            Berlin.
Neustupný, Jiří
    1970   Essai d'explication de la fonction des stations préhistoriques fortifiées en Europe Centrale. Atti del
            Convegno di Studi sulla Città etrusca e italica preromana, pp. 339-43. Imola.
Neustupný, Jiří
    1970   Ethno-Prehistory of Central Europe. Proceedings, VIIIth International Congress of Anthropological
            and Ethnological Sciences 1968, Tokyo and Kyoto, Vol. III, Ethnology and Archaeology,
            pp. 191 - 3. Tokyo.
Neustupný, Evžen and Jiří
    1961   Czechoslovakia before the Slavs. Ancient Peoples and Places. London, New York.
Sakař, Vladimír
    1970   Roman imports in Bohemia. Fontes archaeologici pragenses 14. Prague.
Sakař, Vladimír
    1973   in Archaeologia Polona XIV : 232. Warsaw.
Schránil, Josef
    1928   Die Vorgeschichte Böhmens und Mährens. Berlin-Leipzig.

Svoboda, Bedřich
    1965   Čechy v době stěhovániź národů - Böhmen in der Völkerwanderungszeit. Monumenta archaeologica
           XII. Prague.
Šimek, Emanuel
    1948   When fortified settlements came into being. Z dávných věků /From ancient times/ Vol. I, pp. 127-31.
           Brno.
Turek, Rudolf
    1974   Böhmen im Morgengrauen der Geschichte. Wiesbaden.

A GLANCE AT CORNISH TIN
by Stuart Piggott

The first account of the prehistoric tin trade of Cornwall to be set out in modern terms was that embodied in Chapter V of Hugh Hencken's *Archaeology of Cornwall* in 1932, and to it we can still turn with profit. In the intervening forty years Cornish tin has continued to be the subject of discussion by archaeologists and ancient historians, and it seems appropriate to offer a brief review of some of the problems which have emerged, as a tribute to the original author. The main studies referred to are three: Francois Villard's section on the tin trade in his examination of the economic history of Massalia (Villard 1960); Lloyd Laing's re-examination of the English evidence (1968), and James Muhly's massive review of the copper and tin resources of the Bronze Age in Europe and Western Asia (Muhly 1973). In the chronology of tin exploitation Muhly, an ancient historian, is concerned with the question of bronze working from the earliest times, but as we shall see makes considerable use of the classical literary sources for Europe, just as he does of the Assyrian texts for Mesopotamia. Villard is specifically dealing with the Cassiterides-Massalia trade across Gaul from Hallstatt D times in the sixth century B.C. to the Roman Conquest; Laing is concerned with seeing whether the archaeological and numismatic evidence from Cornwall and southern England 'substantiates the suggestion that there was a flourishing trade conducted by Greeks with Britain in the period from 300 B.C. to 50 B.C.'. We may therefore conveniently begin with the question of Cornish tin in the European Bronze Age from early in the second millennium B.C.

Here, since the early 1960's thanks to the work of the Stuttgart school of archaeological metallurgical analysis, and in Britain the work of Coghlan, Case, Britton and others, we have become accustomed to the model of a technological sequence in which in several geographical localities the use of pure copper is followed by not only increased complexities in the methods of ore extraction and smelting, but the apparently experimental use of additives such as arsenic, and culminating in the use of tin as an alloy to form a true tin-bronze with a composition centred on a copper-tin ratio of 10:1. The documentation for this will be found in Muhly 1973; a correlative problem which need not concern us here, that of the independent invention of the basic copper metallurgy in more than one centre in prehistoric Europe and Western Asia, is summarized by Renfrew (1973). We are here concerned with the developed phase of non-ferrous metallurgy when the demand for tin as a constituent in a bronze alloy was a reality arising from a knowledge (however acquired and of polycentric or monocentric origin) that such an alloy had advantages outweighing all others known at the time. We may pause parenthetically here to pose the question of how, in practical terms, ancient metal-workers obtained the knowledge of the locality of their raw material once they had empirically arrived at its need, in landscapes which in Europe at least would be almost wholly covered with vegetation of varying densities and inhabited by stone-using communities to whom copper or tin were irrelevant stones which were not a part of their world-picture. Some form of initial prospecting, with a growing body of sound field geology of however pragmatic a type, must have taken place, and the recognition of characteristic plant communities on appropriate subsoils may well have played a part, anticipating modern sophisticated techniques (cf. Cannon 1960).

In all considerations of the question of the origins of European Bronze Age tin in recent discussions several sources have been assumed apart from Cornwall, the Ore Mountains of the Erzegebirge and Fichtelgebirge on the northern march of Bohemia being the most important even if, as Childe was careful to point out 45 years ago, the latter deposits were 'neither plentiful nor easily worked' (1929, 6). Presumptive evidence was afforded, as he stressed, by bronzes with very high tin percentages in the earlier bronze-using cultures of Bohemia and Saxo-Thuringia. Minor sources include those of Tuscany but there is no evidence of its pre-Etruscan use (the Monte Bradoni V-bored buttons are not tin, but local antimony), and the Iberian and Breton tin come into the general vague picture presented from the time of Herodotus onwards of far northwestern 'Tin Islands' somehow reached by Atlantic routes. In the Minoan-Mycenean world, though tin-bronze was extensively used from the earlier third millennium B.C., there are no known local sources of tin in East Europe, Asia Minor or West Asia, and while there is documentary evidence of tin (of unknown origin) being traded by Assyrian merchants as far west as Kültepe near Kayseri, this is still ten degrees of longitude from the Aegean. By the fifteenth century Egypt is obtaining tin from Syria and Crete, but Mycenae's huge demands were being met from unknown sources which might plausibly have included Europe, where contemporaneously a comparably massive tin-bronze industry was being developed in East Europe, especially in Hungary and the copper-producing mountains of Transylvania. The central European tin deposits of the Erzegebirge have usually until now been seen as playing a complementary part in this metallurgy, parallel to that developing locally in the Únětice and Otomani bronze industries, but Muhly, in his detailed study already quoted, regards this as an inadmissible assumption. The extensive modern studies on this mining area, he states, 'make it perfectly clear that the Erzegebirge deposits are hydrothermal deposits in veins of granite rock and would have been completely inaccessible to the metal-workers of the Bronze Age. This would seem to rule out the Erzegebirge as a possible source of tin in the Bronze Age' (Muhly 1973: 256). Having thus removed this potential region without further discussion he is left with the north-western Cornish-Breton-Iberian group of deposits as suppliers of all ancient European tin. Taking the classical sources, notably Diodorus Siculus, with their specific description of a trade in tin from Cornwall to Massalia in the second or early first century B.C., and therefore one in which Greeks were involved, he argues that this provides an acceptable model for the second millennium B.C. and the Mycenean world. 'At the time of the shaft graves of Mycenae, a trade developed by means of which the manufactured products of the Greek bronze industry were exchanged for the raw materials of the west, namely Baltic amber, Cornish tin, and Irish gold . . . This is the trade described by Herodotus, the trade recorded in the Greek literary tradition' (Muhly 1973: 349).

Such a statement of bold confidence strikes terror into the heart of the timorous writer of this essay, very conscious that his own more tentative suggestions of contacts between Britain and Mycenae made some years ago have not stood up to the test of time in most respects, and though a small element does seem difficult to dismiss entirely, it is certainly insufficient to use as a basis for establishing such a tin trade. It is not his purpose here to rehearse this debate in detail; in passing though we may remember that the elimination of all European tin sources save Cornwall would affect not only the Aegean tin-bronze technology, but that of Hungarian Bronze III and its East European counterparts already touched on, cumulatively using very large quantities of metal, with the later Bronze Age huge hoards of bronzes such as that of Uiora de Sus in Transylvania, weighing some 1100 kg., as evidence. But in any review of the evidence for a prehistoric Cornish tin trade with whatever customers, there is one striking object that deserves reconsideration, the great ingot of tin dredged from Falmouth Harbour between St. Mawes and Pendinas about 1810 (Way 1859; James 1871; Evans 1881: 426).

This well-known object is H-shaped, plano-convex in cross section, and weighs 72.5 kg. of high purity tin (Tylecote 1962: 67). Its overall dimensions are 0.89 m by 0.28 m and it is not quite symmetrical; furthermore the tip of one arm had been cut off before it was found. This same arm carries a stamp 7.5 cm long and 0.7 cm deep representing an ingot of similar type but with a less pronouncedly waisted outline. The earlier writers were unanimous in equating this with the description of ingots 'shaped like *astragaloi*' and made in Cornwall, contained in the account of the tin trade, given by Diodorus Siculus writing c. 60–30 B.C., and by implication dated it to this period. We will return to Diodorus, but must now follow changing views on the ingot itself. Haverfield (1900) showed wise caution: 'the astragaloid block dredged up in Falmouth Harbour . . . is really undatable. Until some definite criterion of its age be discovered we must content ourselves with the confession that it may be of any age'. Haverfield at least allowed the ingot to be thought of as 'astragaloid' in shape, but Hencken (1932, 166) pointed to no less than six lexical meanings for *astragalos* and (surely unfairly!) goes on 'since none of these things have the least resemblance to the ingot' and it has no parallels, it is undatable. Later commentators were more dogmatic. Forbes wrote 'In Roman times special double-T formed slabs called *astragali* were used in Cornwall' (1950: 247) and Muhly has recently re-affirmed a Roman date (1973: 246); Lady Fox however in 1964 wrote 'This ingot is tangible evidence for the export of Cornish tin in the Iron Age, and corroborates the classical writers' account' (1964: 240).

Sir John Evans had percipiently looked away from Cornwall for light on the St. Mawes ingot, and drew attention to ingots of copper found in Sardinia which 'in their form present a close analogy with this ingot of tin, though they are of much smaller dimensions' (Evans 1881: 426). These Sardinian finds are now recognisable as in fact the westernmost of a type of metal ingot, the so-called 'ox-hide' type, concentrated in the Aegean, represented in Egyptian tomb-paintings and dramatically occurring in the trading vessel ship-wrecked c. 1200 B.C. off Cape Gelidonya on the south-east coast of Turkey (Bass 1967). In the first modern study of these ingots Hans-Günther Buchholz considered that the St. Mawes ingot could be regarded as a possible variant of his Type 2: 'seine Zugehörigkeit zu den Keftiubarren im Bereich des Möglichen ziegt', and it should date from the end of the second millennium B.C. (Buchholz 1959: 25). He is here using the phrase which associates the metal trade in which copper or tin ingots of this type circulated with Cretans, the *Keftiu* of the Egyptian texts, but George Bass, reviewing the evidence afresh in the light of the 34 copper ingots of this type in the Cape Gelidonya wreck, would rather see a sharing of trade between Minoans and Syrians until 1400, with a subsequent Syrian monopoly (1967: 77). For the Cornish problem this is immaterial: the St. Mawes find has been considered to have typological affinities with an East Mediterranean type of metal ingot of the second millennium B.C. and might therefore be used to support the argument of a connection between the Aegean Bronze Age and Cornish tin resources. It is very much larger than the Mediterranean copper ingots, which at Gelidonya have a range of weights below about 25 kg., and the tomb-paintings and other representations show ingots that are conveniently carried by a man on his shoulder. But another point may be noted: the piece removed from one arm of the St. Mawes ingot resembles the similar treatment at Gelidonya, where 12 corners of ingots were found each cut off by two blows with a cold chisel. The mark or stamp on it takes us no further as it has no resemblance to any of the Mediterranean series, but Roman ingots, if stamped, had inscriptions. Even if we accept a typological relationship with the second millennium Aegean ingots, we cannot necessarily assign it to that date. If we take *astragalos* in its normal sense of 'knuckle-bone', a part of the skeleton of the hind foot in mammals affording articulation with the tibia and fibula, it presents, especially in cattle, a characteristically double-notched outline within which the whole 'ox-hide' range (particularly those in ancient representations) could easily be accomodated in a rather loosely defined metaphor. The Cornish ingot could be, as Buchholz thought, of the Bronze Age, but it could equally well be one of those seen by the informant of Diodorus in the Iron Age.

We are back to the Greek literary tradition, behind which Muhly would see a prehistory stretching back to Mycenae. When Hencken discussed this he of course made reference to the textual sources, and Villard has since set them out conveniently in the original and in translation (1960: 143-148). They raise many problems, and only one need be taken up here. The nature of the traffic in tin across Gaul from the north-west to Massalia, was seen by Hencken as a sea-route from St. Michael's Mount to the ancient trading-settlement of Corbilo at the mouth of the Loire, and then again by a coasting voyage to the mouth of the Garonne, and thence overland through the Carcassonne Gap between the Pyrenees and the Massif Central to Narbonne and Marseilles. It is Diodorus (V.38) who mentions the two latter towns as recipients of tin from the Cassiterides; Strabo mentions Corbilo in connection with traders in all three centres (Hencken 1932: 173, map Fig. 46). It is a natural trans-peninsula route of a kind well-known to geographers, joining the Mediterranean to the Atlantic coasts. Diodorus says the land journey across Gaul took thirty days and that pack-horses carried the tin, a point to be returned to.

On the other hand, another trade route had been described in one of the Posidonian sections of Strabo (IV.1.14; cf. Tierney 1960), up the Rhône, Saône and Doubs valleys, then by a land portage to the Seine, 'down to the Ocean and to the Lexobii and Caleti; and from these to Britain is less than a day's sailing'. This was taken up by more than one writer in connection with the tin trade, and the influence of Déchelette was of course great: he saw the Aeduan *oppidum* of Cabillonum (Chalons-sur-Saône) as a decisive factor, dominating the trade routes along the Seine, Rhône and even the Loire (1913: 72). The discovery of the Vix burial and the recognition of the importance of the adjacent Mont Lassois *oppidum* gave this route new importance, for an assumed tin trade could be used to explain Greek interest in this region in late Hallstatt D, and Joffroy suggested that Mont Lassois was an entrepôt and trading centre mainly concerned with tin, with the Heuneburg controlling a Danubian gold trade (Joffroy 1954: 55). From this point the tin trade and Vix have become associated as a fact and accepted as a faith by many, although Joffroy's wistful hope - 'Il est à souhaiter que la découverte de quelque lingot d'étain dans les fouilles du Mont Lassois vienne confirmer cette hypothèse' - remains unfulfilled. Since so much has been based on this assumption, as opposed to the route favoured by Hencken, it is worth while making one or two points not considered by Villard in his judicious examination of the question. The first is that the Seine-Saône-Rhône route almost necessarily demands the acceptance of the philological equation of the *Ictis* named as the tidal island entrepôt whence tin was shipped with the *ouektis* of Ptolemy, the *uectis* of Latin sources, the Roman name for the Isle of Wight (cf. Richmond & Crawford 1949, 50), and not St. Michael's Mount in Cornwall, the alternative candidate. Laing for instance feels (1968: 19) that one must accept the statement from Timaeus in Pliny that Ictis was six days' sailing from Britain 'inwards' - *a britannia introrsum* - and that this would mean up-channel from the Cassiterides, or Belerion (Land's End); the geomorphological evidence for a tidal land-bridge with the Isle of Wight in antiquity leaves however much to be desired. A journey from Mounts Bay to the mouth of the Seine seems far less probable than one from the Solent.

It is not surprising that the classical texts dealing with the Tin Islands of the north-west - Cassiterides, Oestrymnides, Ictis - are vague and confused. The region was at the limits of the known world in the Ocean for one thing, and we may also have a situation in which deliberate mystification may have been practiced. The story in Polybius about the failure of Scipio Aemilianus around 135 B.C. to obtain information on Britain from Corbilo and Narbonne merchants may well have been due to deliberate concealment of trade secrets, as Hencken saw. A good parallel might well be found in the Roman spice trade, when certain commodities, notably cinnamon and cassia, were confidently believed to originate in East Africa, and not in East Asia, their true habitat, because of the Arabian entrepôts which handled the trade and held the monopoly by concealing its sources (Miller 1969). Such entrepôts were often on offshore islands or promontories, and Rhys Carpenter pointed out that the Tin Islands precisely fitted this rôle, and may have 'contained only the tin that was brought to them to be bartered on their neutral territory' (Carpenter 1973: 206-207). It is amusing too in this connection to notice how with both trades fragments of information on strange shipping came through with accuracy, as with Pliny's circumstantial account of the double outrigger Indonesian canoes coming with spices to East Africa on the one hand, and his and others' repeated references to skin-boats of the curragh type engaged in the tin trade on the other (Miller 1969: 156; Hornell 1938).

We may finally look at the alternative tin routes across Gaul from the practical point of view of the transport difficulties involved. Diodorus gives us the invaluable information that 'the merchants buy the tin from the natives and carry it over to Gaul, and after travelling overland for about thirty days, they finally bring their loads on horses to the mouth of the Rhône'. The stress is on pack-horse transport, for which we have archaeological evidence in the form of the wooden frames of split-saddle type from La Tène (Vouga 1923, Fig. 10, Pl. XXXV; Clark 1941, Fig. 9; cf. Fenton 1973) and confirmation from classical sources (Vigneron 1968: 130 ff.). Vigneron gives a maximum figure of up to 150 kg. for a mule-load in antiquity, suggesting that horses could take a comparable load on the flat and 100 kg. in mountainous country, and also gives an estimate of an average speed of 25 km. per day for pack animals. The Diodorus reference was of course taken up in the early publications of the St. Mawes ingot, and in one is an appealing illustration of a pony loaded with a pair of such (James 1871: 199): the double weight of 145 kg. would come near to Vigneron's limit for easy going, and we know from the Assyrian texts that the 'black donkeys' engaged in the tin trade with Anatolia only carried 68 kg. (2½ talents) apiece (Lewy 1965: 21). We may therefore wonder whether the St. Mawes ingot was intended for pack-horses or for other means of transport. But reverting to the figures for the speed of pack animals, it might be mentioned that the land route from the mouth of the Gironde to Carcassonne, Narbonne and Marseilles is very approximately 700-800 km., precisely what would theoretically be attained by a pack-train moving for a month at 25 km. per day. On all counts then this route, if worked by pack-horses, would be a practical proposition.

River transport has many advantages for heavy bulk cargoes but has its attendant problems. 'The Rhône being swift, and hard to sail up,' wrote Strabo, 'part of the goods from here rather go by land on wagons . . . the road being level and not long, about 800 stadia, induces people not to use the river because the journey by land is easier' (IV.1.14). Recent comment on river traffic has been made in the context of the classical world and the early middle ages. The towed boat was the only answer to traffic against the current in a major river: it 'still exists today in places where labor is cheaper than power. Indeed, until the invention of steam it was practically the only way to get a vessel upstream' (Casson 1971: 332). 'A great variety of goods can move downstream efficiently and relatively quickly, but the journey upstream is difficult and slow' (Leighton 1972: 125). Towing is not only labour-intensive, but presupposes if not tow-paths, at least clear dry river margins, a clear channel, and a more elaborate mechanism of hire with arrangements for portages than a caravan demanded: European explorers in the seventeenth century took a month to make a canoe journey of some 1450 km. up the River Ottawa, and this involved 35 land portages and 50 occasions on which the canoe had to be partially unloaded to lighten it over shallows (Scott 1951: 21). In ancient Mesopotamia all up-stream traffic was maintained by organised towing teams of from 2 to 18 men, and whereas downstream times were 30-35 km. a day, a medium team worked an average boat of 6 tons upstream at only 9-10 km. a day (Casson 1971: 29). Again, an early medieval journey upstream from Avignon to Lyons took nearly a month with both horses and oxen for towing (Leighton 1972, 126). The Seine-Mont Lassois-Saône-Rhône route would involve, if the rivers were followed, some 450 km. upstream to Mont Lassois from the channel coast; a minimum land portage of 100 km. over the Plateau de Langres to the River Saône, and then a downstream run on that river and the Rhône for about 500 km. to Massalia, a total of about 1050 km.

The question of the route or routes taken by Cornish tin across Gaul in late Hallstatt, La Tène, and earlier classical times must then remain unsolved and perhaps incapable of solution. Apart from the land routes, the Atlantic sea-route known to the sixth century source behind Avienus and to Pytheas, and available when political circumstances allowed shipping to pass through the Straits of Gibraltar was again to be used when Iberian tin supplies replaced those of Cornwall in Roman times. The early medieval traffic on these routes between the east Mediterranean and west Britain is now well documented archaeologically, and when in the late fourteenth century Datini, the Merchant of Prato, needed tin for his armour business, he imported it to Avignon from Cornwall together with Cotswold wool, both being shipped by the long sea route from the Channel to the Mediterranean, touching ports in Spain and Majorca on the way to the Rhône mouth (Origo 1963: 37, 73).

References Cited

Bass, G. F.
    1967   Cape Gelidonya: a Bronze Age shipwreck. Transactions of the American Philosophical Society NS LVII: 3-177.
Buchholz, H. G.
    1959   Keftiubarren und Erzhandel im zweiten vorchristlichen Jahrstausend. Prähistorische Zeitschrift XXXVII: 1-40.
Cannon, H. L.
    1960   Botanical prospecting for ore deposits. Science CXXXII: 591-98.
Carpenter, R.
    1973   Beyond the Pillars of Hercules. London.
Casson, L.
    1971   Ships and Seamanship in the Ancient World. Princeton.
Childe, V. G.
    1929   The Danube in Prehistory. Oxford.
Clark, J.G.D.
    1941   Horses and Battle-Axes. Antiquity XV: 50-70.
Déchelette, J.
    1913   Manuel d'Archéologie . . . Vol. III. Paris.
Evans, J.
    1881   Ancient Bronze Implements . . . . London.
Fenton, A.
    1973   Transport with Pack-Horse and Slide-car in Scotland. In Fenton, A. & Podolatz, J., Land Transport in Europe. Copenhagen.

Forbes, R. J.
    1950   Metallurgy in Antiquity.   Leiden.
Fox, A.
    1964   South West England.   London.
Haverfield, F.
    1900   [Roman ingot of Cornish tin . . .] Proceedings of the Society of Antiquaries 2nd. S. XVIII: 1
            (1899-1900), 117-122.
Hencken, H. O' N.
    1932   The Archaeology of Cornwall and Scilly.   London.
Hornwell, J.
    1938   British Coracles and Irish Curraghs.   London.
James, H.
    1871   The block of tin dredged up in Falmouth Harbour and now in the Truro Museum. Archaeological
            Journal XXVIII   196-202.
Joffroy, R.
    1954   Le Trésor de Vix: Monuments et Mémoires. Fondation Eugène Piot. Paris.
Laing, L. R.
    1968   A Greek tin trade with Cornwall? Cornish Archaeology VII: 15-23.
Leighton, A.C.
    1972   Transport and Communication in Early Medieval Europe. (1971). Newton Abbot.
Lewy, H.
    1965   Anatolia in the Old Assyrian Period. Cambridge Ancient History (rev. ed.) I, chap. xxiv, sec. VII-X.
Miller, J. I.
    1969   The Spice Trade of the Roman Empire.   Oxford.
Muhly, J. D.
    1973   Copper and tin: the distribution of mineral resources and the nature of the metals trade in the
            Bronze Age. Transactions of the Connecticut Academy of Arts & Sciences XLIII: 155-535.
Origo, I.
    1963   The Merchant of Prato.   London.
Renfrew, C.
    1973   Before Civilization, Chap. 9. London.
Richmond, I. A. & Crawford, O.G.S.
    1949   The British Section of the Ravenna Cosmography. Archaeologia XCIII: 1-50.
Scott, W. L.
    1951   The Colonization of Scotland in the Second Millennium B.C. Proceedings of the Prehistoric Society
            XVII: 16-82.
Tierney, J. J.
    1960   The Celtic Ethnography of Posidonius: Proceedings of the Royal Irish Academy LX (C): 189-275.
Tylecote, R. F.
    1962   Metallurgy in Archaeology.   London.
Vigneron, P.
    1968   Le Cheval dans l'antiquité Gréco-Romaine.   Nancy.
Villard, F.
    1960   La céramique Grecque de Marseille: Essai d'histoire économique.   Paris.
Vouga, P.
    1923   La Tène. Leipzig.
Way, A.
    1859   Enumeration of blocks or pigs of lead and tin . . . discovered in Great Britain. Archaeological
            Journal XVI: 22-40.

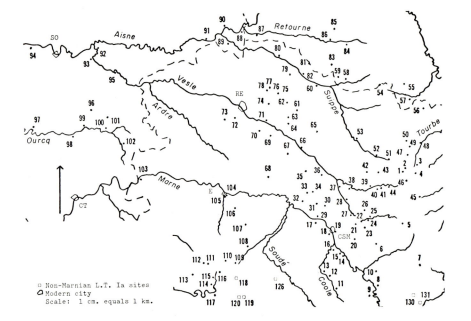

FIG 1. *Map of Marnian sites. See Table A for key to site numbers.*

Table A
La Tène Ia Marnian Sites

1. La Gorge Meillent, Marne
2. Somme-Tourbe "La Bouvandeau", Marne
3. Somme-Tourbe "l'Orgemont", Marne
4. Somme-Bionne, Marne
5. Poix, Marne
6. Marson, Marne
7. Venault-le-Châtel, Marne
8. La Chaussée, Marne
9. Songy, Marne
10. Pogny, Marne
11. Fontaine-sur-Coole, Marne
12. Cernon, Marne
13. Breuvery, Marne
14. Mairy, Marne
15. Sogny, Marne
16. Ecury-sur-Coole, Marne
17. Saint-Gibrien, Marne
18. Châlons-sur-Marne "Côte de Troyes", Marne
19. Châlons-sur-Marne "Avenue Strasbourg", Marne
20. Sarry, Marne
21. Saint-Memmie, Marne
22. L'Epine, Marne
23. Courtisols "Charmont", Marne
24. Courtisols "Grand Ayeux", Marne
25. Courtisols "Côte 141", Marne
26. Courtisols "L'Homme Mort", Marne
27. Melette, Marne
28. Saint-Etienne-au-Temple, Marne
29. Recy "Graviers", Marne
30. Recy "Voie Chanteraine", Marne
31. Juvigny, Marne
32. Vraux "Mont Vraux", Marne
33. Vraux "Le Buisson", Marne
34. Grandes Loges, Marne
35. Livrey, Marne
36. Bouy "Varilles", Marne
37. Saint-Hilaire-au-Temple, Marne
38. Cuperly, Marne
39. La Cheppe, Marne

40. Bussy-le-Château "La Croix-Meuniere", Marne
41. Bussy-le-Château "Les Govats", Marne
42. Bussy-le-Château "Piemont", Marne
43. Bussy-le-Château "Mont Dinet", Marne
44. Saint-Remy-sur-Bussy, Marne
45. Auve, Marne
46. La Croix-en-Champagne, Marne
47. Saint-Jean-sur-Tourbe, Marne
48. Wargemoulin, Marne
49. Mèsnil-les-Hurlus, Marne
50. Hurlus, Marne
51. Somme-Suippe, Marne
52. Suippes, Marne
53. Saint-Hilarie-le-Grand, Marne
54. Saint-Etienne-sur-Arne, Ardennes
55. Liry, Ardennes
56. Fontaine-en-Dormois, Marne
57. Manre, Ardennes
58. Saint-Clement "La Motelle de Germiny", Ardennes
59. Hauvine, Ardennes
60. Pontfaverger, Marne
61. Beine "L'Argentelle", Marne
62. Beine "Petit Cri", Marne
63. Les Commelles, Marne
64. Prunay, Marne
65. Prosne, Marne
66. Sept-Saulx, Marne
67. Villers-Marmery, Marne
68. Bouzy, Marne
69. Sillery, Marne
70. Puisieulx, Marne
71. La Pompelle, Marne
72. Murigny, Marne
73. Les Mesneux, Marne
74. Cernay, Marne
75. Berru "Flogères", Marne
76. Berru "le Terrage", Marne
77. Vitry-les-Reims "La Neufosse", Marne
78. Vitry-les-Reims "Voie de la Haute-Chemin", Marne

79. Lavannes, Marne
80. Bazancourt, Marne
81. Warmeriville, Marne
82. Heurtegeville "Mont Sapinois", Marne
83. Neuville-en-Tourne-à-Fuy, Ardennes
84. Ville-sur-Retourne, Ardennes
85. Annelles, Ardennes
86. Juniville, Ardennes
87. Poilcourt, Ardennes
88. Pignicourt, Ardennes
89. Aguilcourt, Ardennes
90. Guignicourt, Ardennes
91. Berry-au-Bac, Aisne
92. Chassemy, Aisne
93. Ciry-Salsogne, Aisne
94. Pernant, Aisne
95. Limé, Aisne
96. Arcy-Saint-Restitute, Aisne
97. Chouy, Aisne
98. Armentières, Aisne
99. Trugny, Aisne
100. Sablonnières, Aisne
101. Château de Fere-en-Tardenois, Aisne
102. Caranda, Aisne
103. Dormans, Marne
104. Epernay "Malakoff", Marne
105. Epernay "Mont Bernon", Marne
106. "Les Jogasses", Marne
107. Avize, Marne
108. Mont Gravet, Marne
109. Bergères-les-Vertus, Marne
110. Etrechy, Marne
111. Loisy-en-Brie, Marne
112. Etoges, Marne
113. Congy, Marne
114. Vert-la-Gravelle "Gros Pierres", Marne
115. Vert-la-Gravelle "Le Moulin", Marne
116. Vert-la-Gravelle, "Charmont", Marne
117. Bannes, Marne

REPRESENTATIVE ASSEMBLAGE AND TYPE SELECTION:
A LA TENE MARNIAN EXAMPLE
by Ralph M. Rowlett.

One of the most recently developed approaches to archaeological investigation, comparative archaeology, attempts to reach nomothetic conclusions by ignoring variation along the dimensions of space and time. Instead, generally applicable variables are formulated, predicting the relationship among these variables, and testing the predictions by means of case studies. This research strategy both asks questions of data and calls upon techniques which demand that the information be as representative as possible. As late as 1974, when this paper had been in preparation for over a year for this Festschrift, Rouse (1974: 29) bemoaned that this sampling problem thus raised by comparative archaeology had not yet been met, although noting that social anthropologists had already made progress in selecting and finding cases which illustrated typical form.

The theoretical and practical requirements of representativeness in diverse, highly variegated, normally polythetic data sets in archaeology effectively brings some newer concerns of archaeologists back to an old unsolved one. A recurrent problem in archaeology has been to determine the most representative or typical unit, site or artifact in a given body of data either for analysis or communication. Which site should be the type site? Bad choices for such purposes are proverbial. Just as Rouse has raised the problem of representativeness of sample with regard to the more novel problems of archaeology, more classically-oriented French (1971) issued a call for methods enabling an accurate characterization of the material one wishes to study or portray. This problem becomes increasingly acute as there has grown not only an ever greater body of data, much of it in recent years recovered by relatively sophisticated techniques and under well-controlled conditions, but also there has been a greater demand for precision in analysis and synthesis as well as a much wider availability of the tools to achieve this kind of precision.

With the increased tempo of archaeological activity all over the world and with more and more sites and artifacts from various cultural groups available for study, even as a practical matter one cannot study them all. While certain relatively simple sampling procedures are sometimes in order (Cowgill 1964, Rootenberg 1964, Mueller 1974, including R. Benfer) for certain situations their use only introduces further possibility of another error--sampling error.

Awareness of the necessity of finding the central tendency in a data set and at the same time coping with and including in one's consideration the range of variability of archaeological evidence was among the numerous insights conveyed by Dr. Hugh O. Hencken to his students. His precocious awareness of this desiderata of archaeological research preceded the development of computers, which best can handle the often numerous variety that a number of similar archaeological sites can present. It was this perception which enabled Dr. Hencken to formulate his synthetic theory of Etruscan origins (1968), effectively combining lines of evidence and disparate processes, such as migration, acculturation, and local adaptation which in the past had been used to buttress three or more seemingly contradictory hypotheses about the origins of the Etruscans.

As a consequence of the stimulus given by Dr. Hencken and others, I present here one method by which such a representative selection could be made. This problem of representativeness of data set is akin to that of ethnographers to determine the representativeness of particular informants, families, or communities for the societies of which they are part (Robbins 1969).

The particular data used in this study will be from the Marnian Variant in northeastern France, i.e. Champagne, of the wider-spread La Tène culture. This particular data set was chosen because for Iron Age and early Classical studies there is often an implicit or explicit comparison with the Marnian Variant, and at the same time this material is largely inaccessibly situated in museums and the publications on it are extremely diverse, scattered, and often incomplete. Therefore, we hope to find a way of presenting this material to facilitate the comparisons which others may wish to make.

The distinctiveness of the Marnian Variant of the La Tène Iron Age Culture is such that not even the most hardened sceptic of archaeological basic unit groupings can doubt the existence of the Marnian Variant. The loosely aggregated cemeteries with predominant inhumations oriented uniformly to the west, with small clusters of flat graves refilled with black earth, lie near or among village sites. In the graves are practically always pottery, mostly handmade with a high frequency of rectilinear vases, although virtually all the rare wheelmade urns are either elongate or squat piriforms. Burials of children seldom have more than pots or food offerings, but the adults exhibit additionally personal gear laid out in functional arrangement. Men have swords at hand and carving knives lying on the food offering, sometimes with fibulae, belt hooks, and bracelets or rings, while spears may also be present. Almost every woman was originally buried with a torc and bracelets, but grave-robbing has often bereft them of such accouterments. About 15% of the women have fibulae, finger-rings, earrings and other finery as well. In eastern Marne Departement, chariot burials may run as high as 15% of the total during the La Tène Ia.

Among these artifacts twisted torcs with hooked catches, twisted and multi-noded bracelets, openwork belt hooks, basket earrings, and openwork sword chapes are ubiquitous.

To all directions, even in southern Champagne, there is soon a rapid break up of these consistent patterns. Mounds and distinctive wares start in the northeast and east. To the north are mounds as well as different pottery shapes and the black grave fill is absent. The west witnesses both the disappearance of pottery and black fill in stone-lined graves, while house site pottery shows a different ware. To the south the black fill continues, but pottery is not included with burials and special types such as tri-lobate motifs on jewelry and other devices like trumpet ended torcs and bracelets appear in the west. In the southeast there are multiple burials under mounds, with practically no weapons being buried. In all these non-Marnian neighboring areas villages are hard to find and seem remote from the cemeteries.

Despite these regularities permitting the easy distinguishing of a Marian Variant of La Tène from its neighbors, it has long been noted also that there was much cultural heterogeneity subsumed under the term Marnian. Rademacher (1927: 47), in one of the first attempts at a Marnian synthesis, struggled with "a partly branching off of local forms" (translated from German). Before him, Fleury (1877: 158) contrasted the relative poverty of arms in the graves of the Aisne (north-western Champagne), as opposed to the central Champenoise burials in the Marne. Lapierre (1924: 558) actually stated that there were four regional groups in the early La Tène of Champagne. He did not have the opportunity on this occasion to describe either the content of these regional groups or his reasons for recognizing them, and apparently was never able to extend his work further.

Other prehistorians seem to have recognized these same variations, but usually in isolation and with regard only to a certain class of artifacts. The Abbé Favret and Prieur (1950: 17-19) explained the intense concentration of the ternary torc (Fig. 2, 1) (for an example of the type)in south-central Champagne as being due to its association with the prehistoric antecedents of the Tricassi tribe. Bretz-Mahler (1957: 3-5) noted the polarization of large, close-packed cemeteries in the northern Marne as opposed to small, dispersed cemeteries of La Tène I date in the southern Marne, and that "there are certainly rather important local differences (in ceramics) from one region of Champagne to another." (Bretz-Mahler 1961: 10). Chevallier and Ertlé (1965) contended that the pottery found at Berry-au-Bac (Aisne) is different from that found in the central Aisne.

Bretz-Mahler and Brisson (1958: 194-196) have mentioned the sharp increase in central European La Tène I bronzes on the right bank of the Marne and the Vesle Rivers. Brisson (1960: 26-30) alone broached the problem more openly than anyone since Lapierre, mapping the differential distribution of three La Tene I torc types within Champagne and explaining the coincidence of this distribution with historically known tribal areas of Gaul by attributing each of the torc-types to the appropriate tribe which inhabited each region four centuries later.

Such is the prospect for the worker who would clarify and analyze the Marne Culture, which presumably is such a significant complex in European prehistory; the closer one tries to examine the Marne Culture, the more elusive it becomes, until the serious researcher becomes ensnared in a net of interwoven clines, crisscrossing one another in several different directions (Bretz-Mahler 1971). Therefore, these differences cannot be explained away as the expectable linear variation which is simply the function of distance from any given starting point. The multi-directional aspect of these clines make it unlikely that this may be simple North-South or East-West or cultural center-hinterland differentiation. Some means must be devised to handle such regional variation, a problem becoming increasingly pressing as the amount of archaeological data from any given area becomes ever greater.

A detailed multi-variate study utilizing cemeteries from the La Tène Ia horizon (Hodson 1968; Rowlett 1968b) showed that during La Tene Ia these polythetic distributions result in the clustering of some distinctive artifacts into three or four distinct regional groups (Rowlett 1968a; Rowlett and Pollnac 1972). Since this grouping results in geographical contiguous areas including both cemetery and settlement sites, they must represent some sort of socio-cultural grouping.

However that may be, for someone working in another area, there may be little interest in making comparison to each of the special regional groups, as the Marnian Variant itself is so distinct. Since it has taken me twelve years of work on just one of these groups, the eastern one, and it is still not 100% ready for the press, obviously, a comparative archaeologist concentrating on some other area has not the time either to go over every site of every group of Champagne either. Much of the data is unpublished and even the published data is in very obscure locations. With the method presented here, a researcher can help ensure the validity of his results by choosing the most representative Marnian assemblage for comparison with his own research sample.

What is needed to present such polythetic materials for valid comparisons are techniques that can enable the researcher to identify reliable and representative cases. To accomplish this, the underlying structural components of the group being studied must first be determined to decide how many important independent dimensions exist. These dimensions should best be developed objectively rather than *a priori*. What is needed is information on the structure

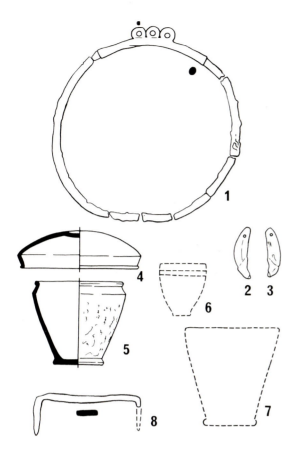

FIG 2.   *La Chaussée grave 3 (child), 1: bronze and iron, 2-3: teeth, 4-7: pottery. La Chaussée 17 (disturbed by second burial). 8: iron. Scale: 1/2 except for pottery, which is 1/4. Objects in the Musée de Châlons-sur-Marne.*

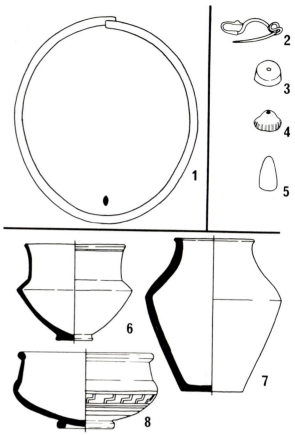

FIG 3.   *La Chaussée 6 (intact), 1: bronze. La Chaussée 75, 2: bronze, 3-4: pottery, 5: polished stone axe (3-5 after Baffet Notes). La Chaussée 27, 6-8: pottery. Scale: 1/2 except pottery, which is 1/4. All objects except 3-5 in the Musée de Châlons-sur-Marne.*

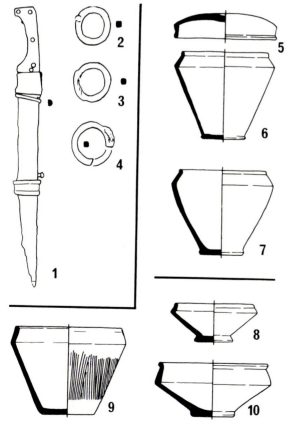

FIG 4.   *La Chaussée 39, 1-4: iron. La Chaussée 47, 5-7: pottery. La Chaussée 48. 8-10: Pottery Scale: All 1/4 except 2-3, which are 1/2. All objects in the Musée de Châlons-sur-Marne.*

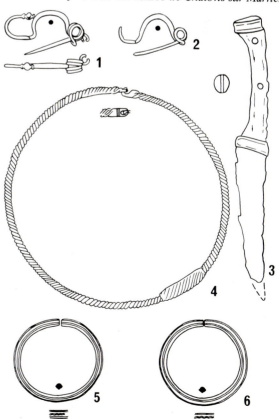

FIG 5.   *La Chaussée 63, 1-2 and 4-6: bronze, 3: iron and bronze. Scale: 1/2 Objects in the Musée de Châlons-sur-Marne.*

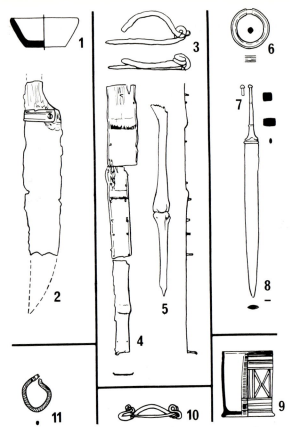

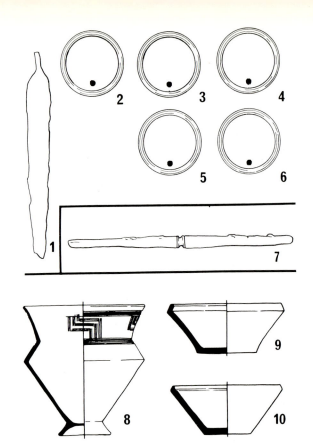

FIG 6.   *La Chaussée 49, 1: pottery, 2: iron and bronze. La Chausée 73 3-4a: iron, 5 adult male femur on which 4 lay. La Chaussée 80, 6-7: bronze, 8: iron with bronze clamp. La Chaussée 163, 9: pottery. La Chausée 103, 10: bronze (after Baffet Notes). La Chausée 232, 11: bronze. Scale: 1/2 except for 1 and 9 (1/4), and 4, 7, 8 (1/6). All objects except 10 in the Musée de Châlons-sur-Marne.*

FIG 7.   *La Chaussée 95, 1: iron, 2-6: bronze, La Chaussée 178 (looted chariot burial), 7: iron. La Chaussée 167, 8-10: pottery. Scale: 1/2 except 1 (1/6) and 8-10 (1/4). Objects in the Musée de Châlons-sur-Marne.*

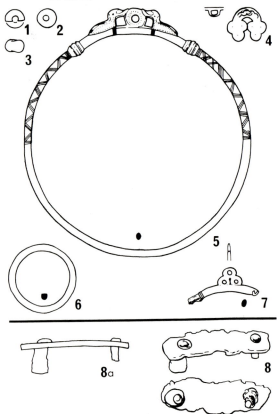

FIG 8.   *La Chaussée 101, sometimes reported as being from Pogny since it was found near the border of that neighboring commune, 1-3 and 6: glass, 4-5: bronze 7: bronze and iron. La Chaussée 235, 8-8a: iron. Scale: 1/2. Objects in the Musée de Châlons-sur-Marne.*

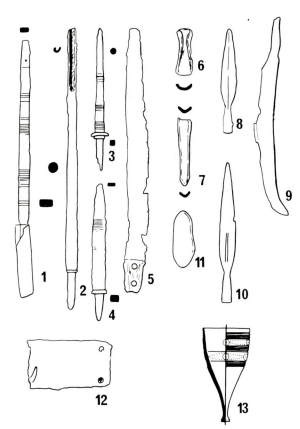

FIG 9.   *La Chaussée 126, 1: iron and antler file, 2-10: iron files, gouges, saw, spearheads and knife, 11: whetstone, 12: iron, 13: pottery. Scale: 12 is 1/2, other objects 1/4. Objects in the Musée de Châlons-sur-Marne.*

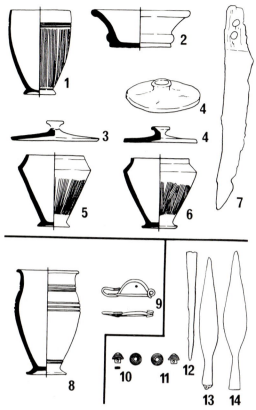

FIG 10. *La Chausée 215, 1-6: pottery, 7: iron.*
La Chaussée 217, 8: pottery, 9: bronze.
La Chaussée 241 (looted chariot burial)
10-11: bronze and coral, 12-14: iron.
Scale: 1/2 except for pottery which is 1/4.
Objects in the Musée de Châlons-sur-Marne.

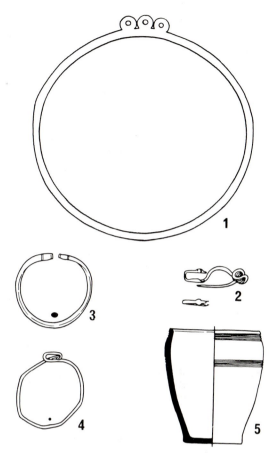

FIG 11. *La Chaussée 220, 1-4: bronze, 5: pottery.*
Scale: 1/2 except for pottery, which is 1/4.
Objects in the Musée de Châlons-sur-Marne.

of the set and we must first make measurements to determine the total structure before figuring out exactly which cases, be they individual sites or assemblages or individual artifacts, are the most representative of the overall structure. From the several techniques available which go under the general heading Numerical Taxonomy, it was decided to use a factor analytical approach. This was done for several reasons, one of which is the ability of the technique to produce in one analysis the several major independent dimensions that characterize a data set from a wider body of data. Since most of the methods applicable for our purpose require the use of computers, programs for factor analysis are readily accessible at most university computational centers. Because of the large quantity of accessible literature on factor analysis, the mathematical technique will not be described in detail here. See Rummel (1970) and Cooley and Lohnes (1971) on this particular technique.

It should be stressed, however, that factor analysis does little more than resolve a set of variables linearly in terms of a small number of categories or factors, thus achieving economy of description. Therefore, nothing comes out of factor analysis that does not go into it, and if the variables have not been carefully selected, the factor analysis will probably produce useless information. When we factor analyze a correlation matrix of variables each variable receives a weight representing its involvement in each of the underlying patterns. In some instances a variable will be weighted only in one pattern, but in many instances the variance of a variable is due to the involvement in more than one pattern. This is often the result of imprecision in the definition of variables, but also results from the fact that they may truly be related to several dimensions. Usually the set of factors extracted from the data and their associated variable weights suffice for the researchers' purpose when this is to classify, or reduce data, or define domain, or define relationships.

For our purposes, where we wish to define the position of each case on the several dimensions, we take these individual factor results and construct scores for each case on each factor. Assuming the reliability and validity of the basic analysis of attributes (for objects or features) or types (for sites), relative positions of the cases scored on each of the factors offer a reliable and objective representation of the variables underlying each dimension on the data set. It is possible to identify not only the case most typical of each factor but also the most atypical as well as intermediate cases. We can determine the modal score for our sample on each of these factors, then try to find a single case whose score approximates this mode in the most important factors. This will probably be the representative case of the group since it has a modal score on several important dimensions.

Another method for finding this average case is to factor by cases and then attempt to find one which loads approximately the same on a number of important factors. Thus we begin to study the entire range of positions of the sample on any of the basic components of the culture that may emerge. A case which had a relatively high loading on all factors would be then arch-typical and while it would contain a great deal of information, it would not necessarily be one which was most exemplary. Likewise the ones which tend to score the minimum on each factor would be equally atypical but in divergent directions, and thus would be of a certain interest too. Thus this particular technique will find the epitome as well as the most and least representative examples.

The data analyzed consist of 104 assemblage items which are distributed in varying degrees among 77 archaeological sites of the Marne Culture in northern Champagne (see Fig. 1, Table A). All of these are from graves dating from La Tène Ia, that is from about 480 to 400 B.C. These sites are distributed in an area approximately 100 by 75 kilometers. The assemblage items categories reflect mainly stylistic traits such as location of vessels in the grave, vessel shape, color, motif, jewelry, knife, and scabbard styles, and chariot pit shapes. These 104 assemblage items were the ones found to be those least uniformly distributed among the Marnian sites and thus chiefly responsible for the regional variation noted among the three main groups (Rowlett 1968a; Rowlett and Pollnac 1972). The data are set up by listing vertically the assemblage items and then horizontally indicating the presence or absence in each particular case, within the individual sites from which these types originate. This is the "Q" technique and it will provide a measure of the degree of association between the sites based on the patterns of assemblage items.

Because we get a factor loading for the sites we can tell which sites participate fully in the factors (see Table B). Which artifacts are the most significantly involved in the particular factors are indicated by a quantity called the factor score (see Table C). In the analysis presented here, the technique of factor analysis with factor scores is used to provide a value for each site that indicated its degree of association with a pattern or factor underlying each grouping of sites and to provide a score for each assemblage item which makes it possible to determine the assemblage items responsible for these factors. The first step in the factor analysis is to correlate sites on the basis of assemblage items as discussed above. A principle components factor analysis of the resultant correlation matrix was then performed by BMDO8M (formerly BMDX72) to determine regularities that underlie its complex relationships. Squared multiple correlations were used as the initial communality estimates and iterations were performed on the estimates so that the mean absolute deviation of the communalities was reduced to less than .0001. Since the goal here was to define the distinct cluster relationships that were present in the data, the factors were rotated to orthogonal simple structure utilized in the Varimax criterion. The first three factors rotated arranged the sites into

Table B
Factor Loadings

Site No.	Fac. I	Fac. II	Fac. III	Site No.	Fac. I	Fac. II	Fac. III
1	.01	-.12	.07	60	.07	-.06	-.54
3	-.39	-.28	.13	61	.04	-.14	-.46
4	-.12	-.22	.9	63	.05	-.20	-.47
5	-.51	-.09	.17	64	-.30	-.06	-.44
6	-.50	-.05	.2	65	.16	.05	-.45
7	-.25	-.10	.8	66	.14	.10	-.05
8	.03	.03	.2	68	.07	.30	-.46
9	-.44	-.03	.13	70	.10	-.08	-.43
11	-.01	-.10	.15	71	.08	-.03	-.66
12	-.58	.05	-.14	72	.04	-.06	-.62
13	-.45	.03	.05	74	.09	.22	-.36
14	-.53	-.22	.20	76	.16	-.22	-.48
15	-.49	-.12	.13	78	.05	-.03	-.46
16	-.38	-.04	0	79	.11	-.13	-.32
18	-.39	.01	.18	80	.02	-.14	-.40
20	-.59	-.01	.10	82	.05	.08	.07
21	-.51	-.04	.07	85	-.01	.20	-.54
24	-.64	.10	.03	88	.12	-.12	-.57
28	-.11	.22	-.04	91	.14	-.17	-.02
29	-.47	-.01	.16	92	.13	.59	.07
31	-.56	-.16	.08	93	.07	.56	.01
32	-.49	.02	.05	95	.14	.30	.16
34	-.52	-.02	.04	96	.00	.46	-.03
35	-.21	-.06	.18	98	.04	.17	.07
37	-.04	.07	.11	99	.19	.59	.17
38	-.56	-.01	.09	100	.19	.45	.06
40	-.70	.02	0	102	.28	.45	-.06
41	-.18	-.12	.11	103	.11	.46	-.03
44	-.01	-.13	.10	104	-.02	.28	.08
45	-.31	.11	.07	106	-.14	.53	.08
46	.01	-.15	.14	107	.03	.24	.12
48	-.60	-.04	.07	108	.00	.60	.11
49	-.43	-.09	.04	109	-.09	.63	-.02
51	-.36	-.13	.11	110	.09	.53	.03
53	-.42	-.09	.02	111	-.22	.20	.16
54	-.29	.10	.01	112	-.22	.24	.07
55	-.08	-.02	.03	114	-.18	.39	.05
58	.13	-.01	.05	117	.02	.19	-.14
59	.10	.14	-.27				

Table C
Assemblage Items and Factor Scores

	FACTORS		
	I	**II**	**III**
1. Vases chiefly to right at foot	-1.22	0.28	0.39
2. Lances chiefly to the left	-0.50	-0.34	0.26
3. a -la bowls	-0.37	-0.07	-1.76
4. A -la jar	-1.12	3.48	-1.30
5. A jar with neck cordon	0.04	-0.53	0.65
6. B vase with flat, everted rim	-0.82	-0.06	-0.40
7. B vase with vertical rim	-0.11	-0.18	0.20
8. Rimless B and b vases	-0.41	-0.13	0.44
9. Bi-conic plates with foot	-0.29	-0.70	0.66
10. Footless carinated cup	-0.19	-0.71	0.63
11. Footless ovoid cup c -2b	0.06	-0.72	0.68
12. Rectilinear conical cist predominant form	-0.89	-0.87	0.74
13. Orange-yellow pottery at least 10% of ceramic colors	-4.32	-0.25	0.07
14. Thin red paint	-4.21	0.22	-0.10
15. Wide-band painting technique	-4.56	0.21	-0.00
16. Triple chevron ceramic motif	-0.88	0.52	0.12
17. Inverted chevron ceramic motif	-1.29	0.12	0.14
18. Zig-zag line ceramic motif	-0.58	-0.45	0.09
19. Recticular ceramic motif	-1.17	0.16	0.05
20. Circular ceramic motif	0.33	0.20	0.54
21. Vertical wavy combmarks on ceramics	-0.35	0.75	0.57
22. Less than 50% twisted torcs	-1.50	-0.31	0.21
23. Majority of twisted torc hooks in the plane of the torc	-1.54	-0.50	-0.48
24. Bird torcs and bird vases, and other bird images (except on fibulae)	-0.19	-0.57	0.36
25. Torcs with exterior annelets	-0.38	-0.21	0.59
26. Bracelet with continuous series of incised lines	-0.61	-0.09	0.62
27. Bracelet with serpentine decoration around the exterior	0.33	-0.67	0.17
28. Pin-and-socket bracelet with flattened wire section	-0.56	0.05	0.48
29. Multiple-node bracelet	0.03	-0.99	0.43
30. Fibula terminal semi-hemispherical (as at La Gorge Meillet)	0.48	-0.70	0.48
31. Fibula with false spring on foot	0.24	-0.98	0.81
32. Disc fibula	-0.23	-0.69	0.69
33. Bronze sword scabbards	0.62	-0.86	0.56
34. Predominantly high arc on scabbard mouth	0.00	-1.16	0.09
35. Knife with complete handle and rectangular pommel	-0.35	-0.48	-0.08
36. Knives with convex dorsal lines and short rivetted handles (D-1 and D3e)	-1.15	-0.20	0.48
37. Narrow felloe clamp	-0.00	-1.16	0.71
38. Trapezoidal chariot burial pit	0.81	-1.06	0.82
39. Vases chiefly to the left side, not at foot	0.29	-0.75	-1.92
40. Black piriform wheelmade urns	0.20	-0.62	-1.57
41. A-3c urn with short, flat upper shoulder	0.48	-1.06	-0.66
42. Spheroid jars A -3	-0.17	0.52	-3.82
43. b -3 spherical pots	0.72	-0.18	-1.09
44. Ta chalice with flaring rim	0.80	-0.25	-1.02
45. Tc -3 conical chalice	0.25	-0.17	-1.43
46. Black pottery predominant (50% or more)	0.21	-0.41	-5.09
47. Relief decorative technique	0.45	-1.01	-1.59
48. Nested serial lozenge ceramic motif	0.78	-0.27	-0.60
49. A vases with rounded bellies	0.64	-0.35	-1.05
50. Concentric semi-circle decorative motif	0.60	-0.81	0.06
51. Vertical comb marks with top section curved	0.46	0.09	-0.39
52. Punctate decoration with relief margins	0.30	-0.57	-0.96
53. Pyramidal ceramic motif	0.35	-0.74	-0.99

	FACTORS		
	I	**II**	**III**
54. La Tene curvilinear designs on wheelmade pottery	0.41	-0.76	-0.73
55. Bracelet of flattened wire with square-chipped ends (B2a)	0.03	0.22	0.09
56. Knife with complete handle with splayed butt	0.65	-0.80	-0.67
57. Knife with concave dorsal line, short handle	0.71	-0.28	-0.20
58. Wide felloe clamp	0.83	-0.48	-0.03
59. Square or rectangular chariot pit	0.43	-0.34	-0.32
60. Cremations as well as inhumations	0.63	0.82	0.34
61. Pots chiefly at the head	0.99	0.71	0.68
62. A-3b urn with short cylindrical neck, wide flat rim	0.67	0.56	-0.10
63. A-2b vase with drooping upper shoulder	0.57	1.22	0.67
64. b -2	0.65	0.56	0.60
65. Cylindrical cist predominant cist form	0.66	0.99	0.57
66. Many grey pots (over 33%)	0.51	1.81	0.44
67. Triplet parallel lines on ceramic cists	0.72	0.30	0.66
68. Single and stacked lozenges ceramic motif	0.01	1.70	0.95
69. Left-oriented step ceramic motif	-0.41	1.59	0.46
70. Solid dot ceramic motif	0.15	0.65	0.46
71. Over 50% twisted torcs	0.67	3.00	-0.41
72. Plaque catch-plate on torcs	0.59	2.02	0.68
73. Majority of torc hooks perpendicular to the plane of the torc	0.48	3.29	-0.28
74. Bracelet with alternate band decoration with lines at right angles to the bands	0.36	0.55	-0.27
75. Rectangle and triangles bracelet motif	0.04	2.09	1.00
76. Pointed-ended bracelet with flattened section, overlapping ends	0.79	0.94	0.36
77. Predominantly low arc scabbard mouth	0.70	1.94	-1.18
78. Knife with arched back, stepped pommel	0.84	-0.13	0.32
79. Knife with short, stepped handle	0.86	0.55	0.57
80. Red piriform wheelmade urns	0.56	-1.15	0.56
81. Piriform flasks	0.06	-0.75	0.50
82. B -3 jar (high rounded shoulder)	0.20	-0.08	0.48
83. b -1 bowl (high rounded shoulder)	-0.35	-0.72	0.31
84. Rimless chalice Tc -2a	0.23	-0.21	0.95
85. Triangle ceramic motif	-0.38	-0.70	0.26
86. Asymmetrical rectangular meander ceramic motif	-0.04	-0.93	0.50
87. La Tene curvilinear designs on handmade pottery	0.46	-0.80	0.40
88. Bracelet of ribbon twist with pointed ends	0.32	-0.77	0.62
89. Pointed oval design on fibula bow complemented by tick marks	0.56	-0.57	0.83
90. Knife with pointed handle	0.09	-1.01	0.71
91. Spear with long socket	0.18	-0.83	0.34
92. Lances chiefly at the feet	0.82	0.34	0.24
93. B vase with incurvate upper shoulder (B-3)	0.84	-0.20	-1.20
94. B rimless ceramic situla	0.23	-0.79	-0.79
95. Cross-hatched decoration on fibula bows	0.11	-0.33	-0.57
96. Lances chiefly at the right	0.61	0.47	0.48
97. Symmetrical rectangular meander ceramic motif	0.30	0.15	-0.20
98. Pin-and-socket bracelets with round section	0.43	-0.31	-0.14
99. Flat rectangular fibula terminal with X-design incised	0.82	0.53	0.68
100. Vases chiefly at foot, no side preference	0.68	-0.27	0.55
101. Orange-brown pottery over 10%	0.42	0.45	0.77
102. Thick paint predominant technique of ceramic decoration (50% plus)	0.37	0.03	0.57
103. Double chevron design	-0.66	0.87	0.34
104. Series of small circles decorating bronzes	0.18	1.06	0.46

three distinct groups. All the factors beyond these three accounted for very small increments of a total variance explained, and thus were considered inessential to our objective of determining the most representative sites. These first three factors accounted for a total of 20.5% of the variance. Factor one has a 9.3%, two 6.0% and three 5.2%. The low per cent of the variance accounted for is not unexpected in the light of the stylistic heterogeneity in this area and often is the case in the more elaborate archaeological cultures.

Examples from the Marnian data would indicate that site no. 8, La Chausée, is the most representative for comparison (Figs. 2-11). This site contains chariot burials, but were too looted to enter in the analysis, a fact which would probably surprise archaeologists who consider the Marnian culture by more conventional and intuitive methods. If one wished to choose the most representative chariot burial site, however, one could simply find the chariot burial which is nearest the modal point. This one is the famous "La Gorge Meillet" chariot burial from Somme-Tourbe (Marne) (Fourdrignier 1877; Jacobsthal 1944: Pls. 75-76, 157-158, 196-199; Hodson and Rowlett 1974: 185, Pls. 70-71). Note that these are the assemblages which are the most representative, exhibiting the modal participation in the Marnian Variant. They are real entities and not abstractions lacking actual manifestation, as "average cases" can be.

While the above sites are the most representative, for some purposes one might be interested in the assemblages which epitomize the Marnian during La Tène Ia times. The most extreme cases are sites 109 and 108. Bergères-les-Vertus (Marne) (Morel 1898) or Villeneuve-Renneville "Mont Gravet" (Marne). The latter has the advantage, for comparative purposes, of also being the most completely published La Tène Ia Marnian site (Brisson 1957; Mahler and Brisson 1958; Brisson, Roualet and Hatt 1971 and 1972). These sites have the least average deviation, .418 and .429 respectively, from the highest loadings on the three factors. Interestingly, both cemeteries lack chariot burials. The epitomizing assemblage with chariot burials comes from Prunay (Marne), where one (Coulon 1930) of the two (Rowlett 1969; Figs. 5-7) produced a helmet. Its average deviation from the maximum loading is .437.

Although our example dealt with determining the representative or type site, the same approach can be applied to individual artifacts as well. If one wanted to work out the typical artifacts, then one would simply treat as the cases particular artifacts, for instance, and one would list as the variables the attributes of these particular artifacts; such things as indented rims, incised decoration, red color, funicular handles, and the like. This technique has the advantage of not only providing insight as to representativeness of cases, but it also uses the correlation matrix showing the relationship of the variables to each other in terms of their strengths of association. There are also a number of things that can be distinguished as well, such as the archtypical example and the least representative. Note that these examples are also real objects and not some mythical abstraction, such as the "average case" would be.

By finding the representative assemblages or specimens, and at the same time identifying precisely extreme cases, archaeological data can be considerably reduced without losing a sense of its variation. This has the effect of making computerized analyses, such as applied here to find the representative case, usable by those who do not have ready access to computers. Unfortunately in the past few years, heavy reliance upon the computer has tended to exclude those archaeologists without handy computer facilities from methodological developments. Such divisiveness need no longer be perpetuated, for if researchers with convenient access to computers and who do extensive syntheses of data would identify their representative and extreme cases, then those lacking computers could apply their normal hand manipulative techniques even more readily than before. Progress in research can thus be extended across the entire field.[1]

1.   Michael C. Robbins, University of Missouri - Columbia, and Richard B. Pollnac made several helpful suggestions during the preparation of this paper.

References Cited

Bretz-Mahler, Denise
    1957   Observations sur quelques cimetières de La Tène I. Bulletin de la Société Archéologique
            Champenoise 44 année: 3-5. Reims.
    1961   Musée d'Epernay. Catalogue de la céramique des cimetières de l'époque de La Tène I.
            Mémoires de la Société d'Agriculture, Commerce, Sciences et Arts du Département de la Marne 76:
            7-60. Châlons-sur-Marne.
    1971   La Civilisation de La Tène I en Champagne. XXIIIe supplement à Gallia. Paris.
Bretz-Mahler, Denise and André Brisson
    1958   Le Cimetière Gaulois du Mont Gravet à Villeneuve-Renneville (Marne). Revue Archéologique de l'Est
            et Centre-Est IX: 194-223, 289-302. Dijon.

Bretz-Mahler, Denise and René Joffroy
    1959   Les Tombes à char de La Tène dans l'est de la France. Gallia. I: 5-36. Paris.
Brisson, André
    1957   Notes sur la nécropole gauloise de Villeneuve-Renneville (Marne). La Fosse au cerf. Bulletin de la
            Sociéte Archéologique Champenoise 50e année: 9-12. Reims.
    1960   Limites septentrionales des Tricasses. Mémoires de la Société d'Agriculture, Commerce, Sciences et
            Arts du Département de la Marne LXXV: 26-30. Châlons-sur-Marne.
Brisson, Andre, Pierre Roualet, and J. -J. Hatt
    1971   Le cimetière gaulois La Tène Ia du Mont-Gravet, à Villeneuve-Renneville (Marne). Mémoires de la
            Société d'Agriculture, Commerce, Sciences et Art de la Marne. 86: 43, Pls. I-XXXIII.
    1972   Le cimètiere gaulois La Tène Ia du Mont-Gravet, à Villeneuve-Renneville (Marne). Mémoires de la
            Société d'Agriculture, Commerce, Sciences et Art de la Marne 87: 8-48.
Chevallier, Roger and Robert G. Ertlé
    1965   Un fond de cabane gauloise à Berry-au-Bac (Aisne). Revue Archéologique de l'Est et Centre Est
            XVI: 206-214. Dijon.
Cooley, William W. and Paul R. Lohnes
    1971   Multivariate Data Analysis. New York.
Coulon, Pierre
    1930   Note sur un casque gauloise trouvé dans une tombe à char, près Prunay (Marne). Bulletin de la
            Société Préhistorique Française 27: 183-184. Paris.
Cowgill, George
    1964   The Selection of Samples from Large Sherd Collections. American Antiquity. 29: 463-473. Salt Lake
            City, Utah.
Favret, P. M. and Jacques Prieur
    1950   Les torcs ternaires de La Tène I en Champagne. Revue Archéologique de l'Est et Centre Est I:
            11-21. Dijon.
Fleury, Edouard
    1877   Antiquités et monuments du département de la Aisne. Vol. I. Paris.
Fourdrignier, Edouard
    1877   Double sépulture gauloise de la Gorge Meillet. Mémoires de la Société d'Agriculture, Commerce,
            Sciences et Arts du Département de la Marne. 1875-76: 125-133. Châlons-sur-Marne.
French, Elizabeth
    1971   Note on "A Chart of Mycenaean and Late Minoan Pottery." American Journal of Archaeology
            75: 329-330. New York.
Hencken, Hugh, O.
    1968   Tarquina, Villanovans and Early Etruscans. Bulletin No. 23, American School of Prehistoric Research,
            2 Vols. Cambridge, Massachusetts.
Hodson, F. Roy
    1968   The La Tène Cemetery at Munsingen-Rain. Acta Bernensia V. Bern.
Hodson, F. Roy and Ralph M. Rowlett
    1974   The Iron Age. In France Before the Romans. Glyn Daniel, Charles MacBurney and Stuart Piggot.
            Eds. London. 157-191.
Jacobsthal, Paul
    1944   Early Celtic Art. Oxford.
Lapierre, G.
    1924   Les sépultures Gauloises de Courtavant (Aube). Congrès de l'Association Française pour l'Avancement
            des Sciences. 48e session. Liege. 554-558. Paris.
Morel, Leon
    1898   La Champagne souterraine. 2 Vols. Reims.
Mueller, James W., ed.
    1974   Sampling in Archaeology. Tucson.
Rademacher, E.
    1927   Marne Kultur. In Reallexikon der Vorgeschichte, edited by Max Ebert 8: 44-46. Berlin.
Robbins, Michael C., A. V. Williams, P. L. Kilbride, and R. B. Pollnac
    1969   Factor Analysis and Case Selection in Complex Societies: A Buganda Example. Human Organization
            28: 227-234.
Rootenberg, S.
    1964   Archaeological Field Sampling. American Antiquity. 29: 181-188. Salt Lake City, Utah.
Rouse, Irving
    1974   Analytic, Synthetic, and Comparative Archaeology. In Research and Theory in Current Archaeology,
            Charles L. Redman, Ed. 21-31. New York. Pp. 21-31.

Rowlett, Ralph M.
    1968a   The East Group of the Marne Culture at the Debut of the La Tène Iron Age. Ph.D. thesis, Harvard University.
    1968b   The Iron Age of Europe North of the Alps. Science. 161: 123-134. Washington.
    1969   Une Tombe à char de Prunay (Marne). Bulletin de la Société Archéologique Champenoise. 62e année: 12-17. Reims.
Rowlett, Ralph M. and Richard B. Pollnac
    1972   Multivariate Analysis of Marnian La Tène Cultural Groups. *In* Mathematics in the Archaeological and Historical Sciences, D. G. Kendall, F. R. Hodson, and P. Tautu. Eds. Edinbourgh and Chicago. Pp. 45-48.
Rummel, M. J.
    1970   Applied Factor Analysis. Evanston.

STRABO, OCRA AND ARCHAEOLOGY
by Jaroslav Šašel

That reciprocal communications existed between the East-Alpine border settlements of the Balkan and Apennine Peninsulas is attested by the archaeological evidence.[1] Thus, in the Iron Age, the south east Alpine provinces were reached from the North-Italian area by technical influences identifiable in the production of arms and tools and in the technique of combat, and by stylistic impulses appearing distinctly in applied-art creation, for example in the Orientalizing style; other influences have been discovered on working amber imported from the Baltic area. In the same way products arrived such as Apulian ceramics, Corinthian vessels, metal weaponry and other warfare equipment which were exported by the inhabitants of north-east Italy and soon abundantly imitated by local toreutic artisans. Victuals, wine and horses were also exported. In the opposite direction - mostly from Lower Carniola to Italy - stylistic influences were spreading, noticeable particularly on certain South-Alpine and North-Italian situlae. Raw materials and semi-finished articles made from iron, lead, and other metals were exported as well as amber which was resold. Some finished products, like helmets made of several pieces, some types of fibulae, glass, ironware, which had afterwards a long, intensive and glorious tradition, as well as slaves, honey and other foodstuffs, raw hides, and barrels were also exported from the Eastern Alps to Italy.

This mutual trade is still difficult to pinpoint geographically by attempting to construct the communication network. What partly supports us in this regard is the ancient literature. The first topographical data on communications are found in Strabo's Geography, Books IV and VII, written about the year 18 A.D.[2] In the former he deals with Gallia Transalpina, the Alps and Cisalpina, and in the latter with Germany and the Balkans.

It is true, his data are in some parts meagre, and in other parts contrary to what we expect. One would suppose that the roads listed by Strabo led to the important settlement centres of the late Republican or early Augustan period but this is not the case. Furthermore, in his descriptions he discusses the geographical point of contact of the two Peninsulas from two different directions. Also he treats a given area in two ways in geographical references as is seen in the following translation.

4.6.10 And further, the Iapodes (we now come to this mixed tribe of Illyrii and Celti) dwell round about these regions; and (*Mount*) Ocra is near these people. The Iapodes, then, although formerly they were well supplied with strong men and held as their homeland both sides of the mountain (*Albius=Velebit*) and by their business of piracy held sway over these regions, have been vanquished and completely outdone by Augustus Caesar (*35 B.C.*). Their cities are: Metulum (*perhaps somewhere near Ogulin*), Arupini (*hill-fort on Vital at the city of Prozor in Lika*), Monetium (*hill-fort at Brinje in Lika*), and Vendo (*rightly Avendo, hill-fort at Kompolje in Lika?*). After the Iapodes comes Segestica, a city in the plain, past which flows (*the River*) Saus (*Sava*), which empties into the Ister. The situation of the city is naturally well suited for making war against the Daci. The Ocra is the lowest part of the Alps in that region in which the Alps join the country of the Carni, and through which the merchandise from Aquileia is conveyed in wagons to what is called Nauportus (over a road of not much more than four hundred stadia) (*74 km., rightly 100 km.*); from here, however, it is carried down by the rivers as far as the Ister and the districts in that part of the country; for there is, in fact, a river which flows past Nauportus; it runs out of Illyria, is navigable, and empties into the Saus, so that the merchandise is easily carried down to Segestica and the country of the Pannonii and Taurisci. And the Colapis too joins the Saus near the city; both are navigable and flow from the Alps . . . .

7.5.2. . . . The city Segestica, belonging to the Pannonians, is at the confluence of several rivers, all of them navigable, and is naturally fitted to be a base of operations for making war against the Dacians; for it lies beneath that part of the Alps which extends as far as the country of the Iapodes, a tribe which is at the same time Celtic and Illyrian. And thence, too, flow rivers which bring down into Segestica much merchandise both from other countries and from Italy. For if one passes over (*Mount*) Ocra from Aquileia to Nauportus, a settlement of the Taurisci, whither the wagons are brought, the distance is three hundred and fifty stadia (*71,95 km., rightly 100 km.*), though some say five hundred (*88,88 km.*). Now the Ocra is the lowest part of that portion of the Alps which extends from the country of the Rhaeti to that of the Iapodes. Then the mountains rise again, in the country of the Iapodes, and are called 'Albian'. In like manner, also, there is a pass which leads over Ocra from Tergeste, A Carnic village, to a marsh called Lugeum. Near Nauportus there is a river, the Corcoras, which receives the cargoes. Now this river empties into the Saus, and the Saus into the Dravus, and the Dravus into the Noarus near Segestica. Immediately below Nauportus the Noarus is further increased in volume by the Colapis, which flows from the Albian Mountain through the country of the Iapodes and meets the Danuvius near the country of the Scordisci. The voyage on these rivers is, for the most part, towards the north. The road from Tergeste to the Danuvius is about one thousand two hundred stadia (*202,40 km. rightly around 450 km.*). Near Segestica, and on the road to Italy, are situated both Siscia, a fort, and Sirmium.

After Jones (1923:287; 1924:253)

Several discrepancies indicate that Strabo was relying on various sources, but he - as he did not personally know the pertinent regions - failed to unify his various data. According to Book IV, *Aquileia* is 400 *stadia* off *Nauportus,* and according to Book VII 350 or 500 *stadia.* In Book IV Strabo has knowledge of two rivers in this area (*Kolapis* and *Sava*), while in Book VII five rivers (*Korkoras, Kolapis,* Sava, Drava, *Noaros*) are mentioned. According to Book IV the Iapods live around Mt. Ocra, while according to Book VII they are separated from it. Elsewhere there are other discrepancies, e.g. *Tergeste* is firstly an Istrian and later a Carnian agglomeration, or the Iapod-Liburnian relations, etc.

Analyses have shown Strabo's sources to stem from two levels (Kahrstedt 1927: 1–36). The groundwork of his data in Book VII was largely the work of older authors, such as Polybios (about 203-120 B.C.) or Artemidoros (2nd half of the 2nd century B.C.), while those in Book IV are of Poseidonios (135-50 B.C.) and Diodoros (in mid first century B.C.). Of course, all sources contained facts from their own or older periods, which were certainly founded on the prehistoric caravans travelling to Italic, East-Alpine tribal centres; hence Strabo's text is necessarily a reflection of Iron-Age communications.

Strabo's data are shown in the map. The narrower location of Mt. *Ocra* - already the central landmark in prehistory - is connected with Mt. Nanos and the saddle below it.[3] Strabo and the sources separately mention *Tergeste, Nauportus, Siscia, Noreia* and Škocjan. He enumerates the following communications by land and by river; via the *Ocra* Pass, past the *Lugeon* Swamp, by the rivers Ljubljanica, Sava, Krka, Kolpa, the (still unspecified) river *Noaros* in the *Siscia* region,[4] moreover the road to the *Danuvius,* or the Amber Road, or by Sava and Drava rivers. The prehistoric network of communications via the point of contact between the Apennine and the Balkan Peninsulas is relatively well known to us. Furthermore, we are now able to specify this network even more precisely, thanks to the map of Iron-Age Slovenia[5] covering the entire border area between the two Peninsulas. It shows the indubitable relations of the Iron-Age settlements with Strabo's data, and the communications among them. The brisk traffic as has been shown above, has been topographically specified and economically motivated; the map has also laid a true foundation for interpreting the incessant tension in this area. The map has partly pointed out the reasons for the continuous struggle for the wealth of fortified places, the ore deposits, the processing handicrafts, and the desire for the economic-political control of the market potentialities in this so critical area because the geographically simple communications tempted either side into inroads and raids.

By combining Strabo's text which preserves uncommon topographical details of the communication network and the archaeological colonization map which shows the corresponding grouping of settlements, one sees that the routes were directed exactly to the urban Hallstatt centres in Lower Carniola.

These routes led from the nearest Adriatic harbours, chiefly *Aquileia, Timavon, Tergeste,* probably also *Aegida,* to the Karst region, to Škocjan and Mt. *Ocra,* i.e. Razdrto, and past Šmihel. A bifurcation to the Reka valley and the Postojna Gap followed. Soon after it, there was another bifurcation, leading either to *Nauportus* and then by river to *Siscia* perhaps with a branching-off at Vače for *Celeia* or via the *Lugeon* Swamp i.e. periodic Lake Cerknica and from there, via the Krka or the Kolpa sources, further on.

In the Iron Age, the central settlements in this area were the following:[6] Magdalenska gora, accessible by the shortest road directly via *Lugeon,* the Krka source, and Stična - all three indirectly mentioned by Strabo; Vače (accessible via *Nauportus* by the Sava), Novo mesto (*Lugeon* - Krka), Libna (*Nauportus* - Sava), Podzemelj (*Lugeon* - Kolpa), then Škocjan (at the *Ocra* pass), Ulaka (*Lugeon* Swamp), Vinji vrh (via *Korkoras*).

From what has been said, Strabo's sources were in possession of certain data; the Iron-Age traffic between Venetia-Carnia and the hill-forts of Inner and Lower Carniola or at least some reflection of this traffic. Certainly the traffic frequencies of these routes fluctuated considerably. Our presently available data already seem to indicate occasional ebbings on one route and activation of another; the Iapod invasion late in the second century B.C. might have blocked the route of the Taurisci and Carni for some time. This may be true for the Liburnian invasion of the Kvarner region,[7] or the still earlier Celtic thrusts. Similarly, during the development of the La Tène principalities - after the political decline[8] of the old Hallstatt organization - in some way the focal points were transferred from the old hill-forts to easier-to-reach centres and emporia.

When the Romans occupied this country, they took over this network of communications, but the network of new roads shows that the old settled centres - the hill-forts - were completely eliminated, whereas the old route had led to Vače and further to *Celeia,* the new Roman road was traced out via *Atrans*; or: neither Stična nor Novo mesto were considered by the new Roman road, which ran through newly constructed *Praetorium* and *Neviodunum.* The old tribal organization was no longer relevant, and under Roman sway Carniola actually presented no settlements of the Hallstatt population; but rather the Celtic centres such as *Celeia, Iuenna, Neviodunum* and others which had been situated in places exactly suiting the Roman plans, and consequently, almost all of them survived and continued prospering. Almost the entire La-Tène society also survived, and was rapidly assimilated. This is why we possess in Roman monuments a rich documentation of the La-Tène population.

Sketch of the Iron Age settlements (small and large dots) in the South of Slovenia (border line: Italian-Yugoslav boundary) and the prehistoric communication ways (interrupted line: water transports) following Strabo, attested also through archaeological topography. Ancient place- and river-names:

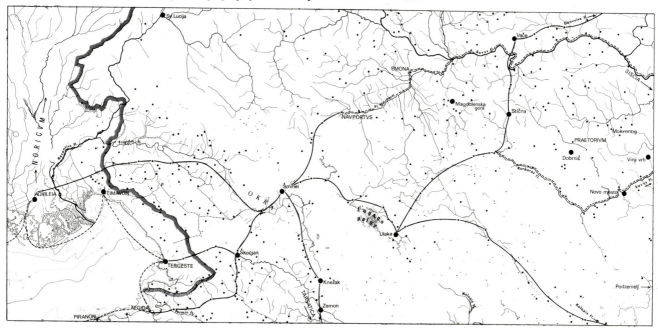

Aegida	Koper	*Nauportus*	Vrhnika
Aesontius fl.	R. Isonzo (in Slovenian : Soca)	*Noricum*	Roman province
Aquileia	Aquileia	*Okra*	Mt. Nanos and Razdrto pass
Danuvius fl.	R. Danube	*Piranon*	Piran
Emona	Ljubljana	*Praetorium*	Trebnje
Formio fl.	Rižana, brook	*Savus fl.*	R. Save
Frigidus fl.	R. Vipava and Hubelj brook	*Siscia*	Sisak
Kolapis fl.	R. Kolpa (in Croatian : Kupa)	*Tarsatica*	Rijeka
Korkoras fl.	R. Krka	*Tergeste*	Trieste
Lugeon palus	Cerkniško jezero (Lake of Cerknica)	*Timavon*	San Giovanni della Tuba

Notes

1. This paragraph has been written after a talk with Professor S. Gabrovec. The analyzed material has been published quite dispersed; let us mention just three instances: S. Gabrovec, 1970:5-65; Hugh Hencken, 1974:119-127; and J. Šašel, 1966:198-204.
2. W. Aly, Strabon von Amaseia, passim. As to the sources, cf. in the first place: E. Honigmann, Pauly-Wissowa, Realencyclopädie der classischen Altertumswissenschaft IV A 1971: 103. seq., and F. Lasserre, Strabon (Budé) II (1960): 101 seq. (for Book IV). For the passages quoted below, cf. also W. Brandenstein (1948:34-37). For the period after the foundation of Aquileia (181 B.C.) we do have knowledge of Roman military expeditions and diplomatic missions to the NE borderland of Italy and beyond, yet without topographical details.
3. B. Saria, Pauly-Wissowa, Realencyclopädie der classischen Altertumswissenschaft XVII 1937:1775. J. Šašel (1974:9-17).
4. The river Noaros is unidentifiable; I personally would think of the river Korana; cf. also Brandenstein's (1948:34-37) attempt. The entire mentioned material represents details relatively uncommon in the literature of that time and in analogous geographical descriptions, and uncommonly located; the question arises why and to which localities the route ran through the mentioned places.
5. Arheološka najdišča Slovenije. Slovene Academy of Science and Arts. Ljubljana 1975.
6. For the documentation of the several centres see the preceding note.
7. S. Kahrestedt (1927:1-36). Yet from Strabo's context, in my opinion, this invasion cannot be securely ascertained.
8. This ruin appears, *mutatis mutandis,* within certain bounds also in this organization's declining standard of life.

References Cited

Aly, W.
    1957   Strabon von Amaseia. Antiquitas I, 5.
Brandenstein, W.
    1948   Frühgeschichte und Sprachwissenschaft I:34-37.
Gabrovec, S.
    1970   Die zweischleifigen Bogenfibeln.Godišnjak. Academy of Science and Arts in Bosnia-Hercegovina, 8:5-65. Sarajevo.
Hencken, Hugh
    1974   Bracelets of Lead-Tin Alloy from Magdalenska gora. Situla 14-15:119-127.
Jones, H. L.
    1923-1924 Strabo. The Loeb Classical Library. Vol. II:287; Vol. III:253.
Kahrstedt, V.
    1927   Studien zur politischen und wirtschaftsgeschichte der Ost- und Zentralalpen vor Augustus. Nachrichten von der Gesellschaft der Wissenschaften zu Göttingen. Philologisch-historische Klasse. Pp. 1-36.
Lasserre, F.
    1960   Strabon (Budé) II:101 ff.
Šašel, J.
    1966   Keltisches portorium in den Ostalpen. *In* Corolla memoriae Erich Swoboda dedicata. Pp. 198-204. Graz-Köln.
Šašel, J.
    1974   Okra. Kronika 22:9-17. Ljubljana.

THE ROLE OF IBERIAN COMMUNAL TOMBS IN MEDITERRANEAN AND ATLANTIC PREHISTORY
by H. N. Savory

Introduction

At an early stage of his career Dr. Hencken made notable contributions to the study of megalithic communal tombs in Cornwall and Scilly (Hencken 1932, Chapter II; 1933). Since then the literature dealing with such tombs in Europe generally has been enriched by a great number of studies - many of them wider in scope but few of them more objective in spirit - and the number of firm facts placed at the disposal of the student by properly conducted excavations and field surveys has greatly increased. Undoubtedly the most important of these contributions has been the publication of the late Georg and Vera Leisner's (Leisner, G. and V., 1943, 1956, 1959; Leisner, V. 1965; Leisner V. and G. 1960) great works on the Iberian monuments which has placed the study of what has long been considered to be the primary concentration of megalithic tombs in Europe on an entirely new basis. But during the last twenty years the study of the Neolithic and earliest metal age in Europe as a whole has been transformed by a flood of radiocarbon dates which has lengthened perspectives and purported to fix more firmly the relative chronology of various cultures in Europe and western Asia. The result, at the moment, certainly seems to some to be rather like an eclipse of the primary role of Iberia in the development of the European tradition of megalithic communal tombs. It may well be that this impression will be dispelled when an adequate number of dates, precisely related to all the phases of the Iberian development, has become available, and that a detailed review of the question ought to await that distant day, but it seems to me that some of the misapprehensions revealed by recent discussions of the Iberian contribution could usefully be pointed out even now in a brief essay which I hope will be a suitable tribute to Dr. Hencken.

The attack on the Iberian role in recent years has been two-fold. On the one hand radiocarbon dates have seemed increasingly to show that communal tombs, both megalithic and drystone, were being constructed in Brittany by the early part of the 4th millennium b.c., while there were until recently no dates for comparable sites in Iberia earlier than the end of the 4th millennium b.c. This encouraged a conception of two relatively independent spheres of megalithic development, which Daniel attributed first to "Northmen" and "Southmen" respectively (Daniel 1967) and then to "Eastern" and "Western" groups (Daniel 1970). This shift of ground reflects a growing realization, first of the antiquity of a tradition of long mound-building on the north European plain, and then of the possibility that this may have originated in the eastern parts of this area, as a result of an adaptation of domestic house types constructed in timber, to ritual and mortuary structures which were initially built of similar materials and imparted their shape to covering mounds. It is easy to see this line of development as a part of the westward trend of cultural groups originating in the Danubian Neolithic, but increasingly fused with local Mesolithic elements, which has lately been coming to light in northern France (Bailloud 1964; 1974). The suspicion then arises that the building of megalithic communal tombs started among a number of different cultural groups along an "Atlantic façade", as Giot put it (Giot 1963: 3), stretching from northwest to southwest Europe, in areas where geological and climatic circumstances would encourage the substitution of stone for timber by marginal communities influenced to varying degrees from central Europe, whose local Mesolithic ancestors had sometimes buried their dead in small family groups in rough cists covered by small cairns as at Téviec (Morbihan) (Péquart, Boule and Vallois 1937). This leads (Daniel 1970) to a rejection of the idea of a "megalithic colonisation" of western Europe from Iberia or anywhere else, and Case adopts a similar position (Case 1969: 19-20).

On the other hand, the old assumption that the distribution of communal tomb types can be explained, at least partially, in terms of cultural diffusion, even of migration, has lately come under attack from the modern school of ecological, anti-diffusionist prehistorians. This school, it seems to me, has sometimes so overworked the ecological "model", where there is no historical evidence to restrain it, that it has risked making itself as ridiculous as the extreme diffusionists were in their day. C. Renfrew (1967) has been an able exponent of this approach and has had no difficulty in demolishing the thesis of B. Blance (1961) that Early Bronze Age colonists from the Aegean played a large part in founding the early metal-using and "tholos" -building communities of southern Iberia. In a more recent treatment of this theme Renfrew has used radiocarbon evidence to emphasize the priority of Breton "tholos" tombs over alleged prototypes in the Aegean area, and advocated the independent development of several megalith-building groups in western and northern Europe from local early Neolithic communities in response to local ecological *stimuli*; in so far as he accepts that neighbouring groups might have influenced each other, he hints at the possibility, on radiocarbon evidence, that Iberia might have derived its megalithic tradition from Brittany (Renfrew 1973, chapters 5 and 7).

It is true, of course, that Brittany, at the moment, can show several communal passage graves with radio-carbon dates which were, at any rate until very recently, much earlier than any in Iberia, or, indeed anywhere else in Europe. But the simplicity of the picture is marred when we consider that the earliest of these dates, Kereado (Morbihan) 3880 b.c. $\pm$ 300 (Sa 95) relates to a megalithic structure set in a circular cairn (Fig. 4.6), while two equally early dates at Barnenez (Finistère) 3800 b.c. $\pm$ 150 (GIF 1309) and l'Ile Gaignog (Finistère) 3850 b.c. (GsY 165) relate to corbelled passage graves ("tholoi") built entirely of drystone walling and set in trapezoidal long cairns (Fig. 5.1). Are we to be guided solely by these "uncorrected" dates and conclude that both the chambered round cairns and chambered long cairns are inventions of Brittany? For to be consistent, we must admit that the Breton sites, on this evidence, are not only earlier than the Iberian passage graves, but also earlier than any of the "unchambered" long mounds of northern Germany or Poland, which Daniel once suggested were the specific contribution of the "Northmen" to the megalithic tradition of Europe. At present, in fact, the radio-carbon evidence for the Kujavish long barrows of Poland would set their beginning two or three centuries later than the earliest Breton long cairns and the same applies to related barrows in other parts of the north European plain (Jazdzewski 1973; Bakker, Vogel and Wislanski 1969: 222-6). Perhaps we should ask whether the few radiocarbon dates so far available from Iberia really cover the whole development of the communal passage grave there; whether the Aegean was the only part of the east Mediterranean area from which that tradition might have been inspired; and what were the origins and functions of the various types of long burial mound in northern Europe? Above all, we need to consider something more fundamental than tomb morphology - the distribution and origin of communal burial itself. For this is the proper point of departure for a study of the dynamism by which the secondary features - burial in natural or artificial caves and in megalithic corbelled or wooden chambers, as conditioned by the local geology - was disseminated.

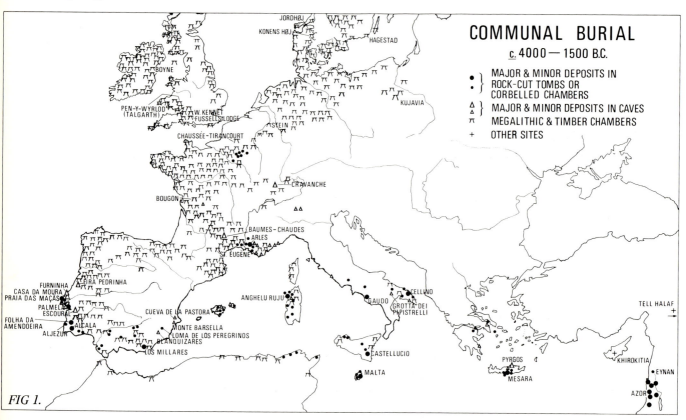

FIG 1.

The Distribution of Communal Burial in Neolithic and Early Metal Age Europe.

As the map shows (FIG. 1) the European distribution of communal burial chambers in the 5th, 4th and 3rd millennia B.C. has a strongly maritime bias. Known communal tombs, whether in natural or artificial caves, drystone structures or true megalithic chambers occur, in the south, close to a line stretching from Palestine through Crete, southern Italy and Sicily to Sardinia, Iberia and Languedoc, and thence in a broader zone stretching through France to the British Isles and northern Europe. Throughout this area the human remains in the chambers, where they have not been destroyed by unfavourable conditions, have proved to represent scores, sometimes even hundreds of individuals; some attempt has been made on the map to indicate the larger deposits. This maritime distribution almost completely excludes the area occupied by the early farming communities of central and south-eastern Europe, which constitute Professor Gimbutas's "Old Europe" (1974). Throughout that area, in Neolithic and

Copper Age times, separate burial in pit graves within or outside the settlements remains the normal practice (Tringham 1971; Müller-Karpe 1968: 361-6). The failure of true communal burial, as opposed to family burial, to establish itself towards the end of this period to any extent in the Aegean area or mainland Greece, or in Italy outside of southern or western coastal areas, is particularly striking; equally impressive are the numbers of individuals - up to several hundreds - even thousands in the case of Hal Saflieni, Malta - involved at certain sites near the central line of the distribution. At the eastern end of this line a form of collective burial was already being practised by the Natufians at Einan c. 8000 B.C. (Anati 1963: 170-171) and the special treatment of skulls is characteristic of the early rock-cut tombs of the proto-urban culture of Palestine as it is of Neolithic cave burials in Portugal (e.g. Eira Pedrinha and Escoural). Throughout the Levant and the Mediterranean, as well as Atlantic Europe, Mesolithic communities were evolving into Neolithic ones and they were certainly not doing it in isolation from each other; when one finds communal burial associated, in southern Iberia, with specialized artifacts and architectural forms which have striking parallels at the opposite end of the Mediterranean, it is hard to believe that the people buried separately in the middens at Muge (Savory 1968: 50-2) or even the people buried in small groups at Téviec had invented then quite independently as has been suggested lately. The relative chronology of the developments in various parts of the Mediterranean and Atlantic Europe will be decisive, when sufficient radiocarbon dates are available for all these areas, but even now it does not seem likely that the earliest Breton passage graves will prove to be earlier than the earliest communal graves of Iberia or the Levant, whatever one may think of recent thermoluminescence dates purporting to place the early development of southern Portuguese megalithic tombs in the 5th and 4th millennia B.C. (Whittle and Arnaud 1975). That they should be earlier than those of the Aegean north of Crete is of no significance, *pace* Renfrew, since it is already clear that this area lay well off the main line of distribution of communal burials and it is in the Levant, rather than the Aegean, that the best parallels to other features of the earliest communal burying groups of Iberia lie (p. 175 below).

Whatever the difficulties with radiocarbon dates may be at present, it is at any rate already clear that communal burial in rock-cut tombs, no doubt ultimately derived from local Mesolithic practices, had already been established in Palestine by the beginning of the 4th millennium B.C. (de Vaux 1970; 527 f., cf. Müller-Karpe 1968: 352 and Anati 1963: 285-300), and the function of the despoiled megalithic chambers of north Palestine and Jordan is not generally doubted, nor their ascription to the same general horizon (Anati 1963: 278-83 and de Vaux 1970: 537 f.). It is also clear that the earliest communal burials in caves in south-east Spain, like those in rock-cut tombs and the earliest drystone or megalithic chambers belong to a horizon much earlier than that of the bulk of the tombs at Los Millares itself, which are at present dated around the middle of the 3rd millennium b.c. (KN 72, 73 and H 284/247). That horizon is linked by various types of artifacts to cultures located near the south-east corner of the Mediterranean in the 4th millennium B.C. or earlier (Savory 1968: 90-93, 118-23). The multiple burial caves of central Portugal also are shown by their associated pottery to have been used already at the time of the local impressed ware (*Ibid.*: 75-8) and Guilaine and Da Veiga Ferreira (1970: 314-6). The apparent absence of equally early communal burial sites in some intermediate Mediterranean areas may reflect the secondary nature of settlement there or the strength of connections with "Old Europe".

The Function of the Northern Long Mounds

We return to the "Northmen" who, according to a theory recently fashionable, were the founders of one of the two great traditions of megalithic communal burial in Neolithic Europe. Daniel, indeed, in his first article (1967) was careful to distinguish between "long graves" and "non-megalithic long barrows", both of them phenomena found to be spreading widely across the north European plain, and both of them sometimes involving the use of timber structures which could be invoked to explain the timber "mortuary houses" associated with some British "unchambered" long barrows, study of which had just been brought into focus by Ashbee's publication of Fussell's Lodge (1966). It is, moreover, hard to believe that the oblong and trapezoidal plans of the long houses built by various Danubian Neolithic and Copper Age groups from the 5th millennium B.C. onwards did not have something to do with the similar outlines of early "unchambered" long barrows built on the north European plain, and even in Britain (Daniel 1970: 267-8). However, as Jazdzewski shows (1973: 63-64) the Kujavian barrows were not built originally to cover collective burials, but a very limited number of separate burials in pits or on pavements; the megalithic communal burial chambers which occur in them are secondary and like those in various parts of northern and central Germany reflect the influence of the northern French SOM group in the 3rd rather than the 4th millennium B.C. (Fischer 1973:60; Schrickel 1957). The sunk "gallery graves" which are characteristic of the communal tombs of this relatively late group in northern France are sometimes constructed of timber instead of stone slabs and have been subject to ritual burnings, which produce the effect of partially cremated bones. These phenomena, too, now appear to have spread from west to east into north central Europe, since the earliest of them so far dated by radiocarbon is the site of Neville-en-Dunois (Eure-et-Loir) 3300 ± 100 b.c. (Gif. 785) (Masset 1968).

In south Scandinavia too, and neighbouring parts of Germany, the onset of true collective burial in megalithic passage graves has recently been fixed on the same late horizon as the SOM gallery graves by a series of radiocarbon dates around the middle of the 3rd millennium b.c.: at Jordhøj, Denmark (K 978), at Vroue, Denmark (K 1567-8),

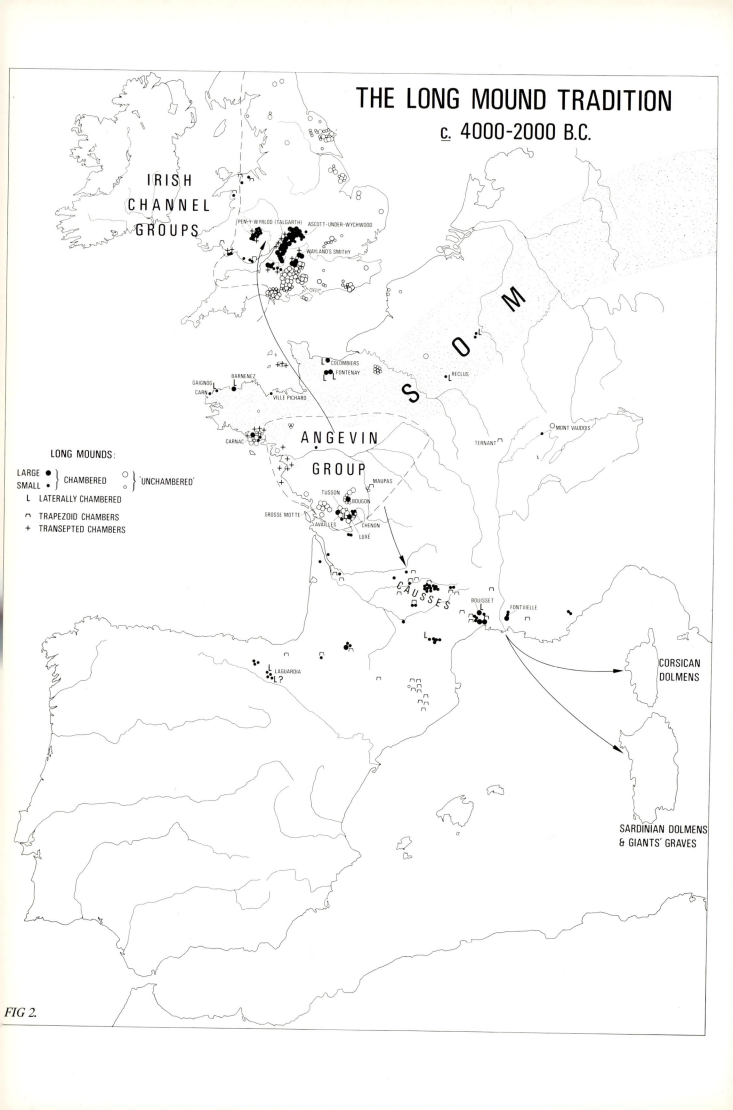

THE LONG MOUND TRADITION
c. 4000-2000 B.C.

IRISH
CHANNEL
GROUPS

PEN-Y-WYRLOD (TALGARTH)   ASCOTT-UNDER-WYCHWOOD

WAYLAND'S SMITHY

S O M

L COLOMBIERS
L FONTENAY

L RECLUS

GAIGNOG   BARNENEZ
CARN
VILLE PICHARD

MONT VAUDOIS

TERNANT

ANGEVIN

CARNAC

GROUP

MAUPAS

TUSSON
BOUGON

GROSSE MOTTE

AVALLES   CHENON
LUXÉ

LONG MOUNDS:

LARGE ● } CHAMBERED   ○ } 'UNCHAMBERED'
SMALL ● }   ○ }
L LATERALLY CHAMBERED
⌐ TRAPEZOID CHAMBERS
+ TRANSEPTED CHAMBERS

C A U S S E S

BOUISSET
FONTVIELLE

LAGUARDIA
L?

CORSICAN
DOLMENS

SARDINIAN DOLMENS
& GIANTS' GRAVES

FIG 2.

at Carlshogen, Hagestad, south Sweden (Ly 277, 255, 254) and at Ramshøg, Hagestad (Ly 276, 257, 278). Before this one has various kinds of oblong or trapezoid mound which may be megalithic only in the sense of having massive stone kerbs, but covering separate burials, or have small megalithic chambers which may be later additions and generally do not contain many individuals. But it is to this earlier horizon that the site at Konens Høj in Jutland to which Daniel referred (1967) belongs and which has a radiocarbon date of 2900 ± 100 b.c. (K 919). This is a type of long grave in which a pavement was covered by a wooden ridge-roof supported by two massive posts, as in some contemporary British long barrow deposits like Wayland's Smithy I (Atkinson 1965) and Fussell's Lodge (Ashbee 1970, Fig. 34) - but with no trace of a covering mound. But here, unlike most of the British sites, there was only one skeleton, so that, in fact, the normal burial practice of the associated Funnel Beaker culture had not been departed from. It seems likely that the practice of communal burial in some kind of chamber was something that spread rather slowly from west to east on this earlier horizon in northern Europe, since we know that long mounds and indeed trapezoidal cairns were being built and even provided with chambers for communal burial in parts of western France, certainly by the early 4th millennium b.c., and earlier than the Kujavish barrows (map, FIG 2). In this case we have to suppose that fusion took place between the Danubian elements building oblong or trapezoidal long houses, which we now know to have been widespread in northern France, and communal-burying groups already established in Atlantic France early in the 4th millennium. At the same time the existence of a primary focus of "unchambered" long barrow-building in northern and western France, with local resort, in response to geological factors, to wooden burial chambers or "mortuary houses" is a possibility which would help to explain the British sites of this type with a radiocarbon time range of 3600-2250 b.c. The spread of the custom of building long mounds, first for separate burials, then for limited numbers of individuals in cists or small megalithic chambers to south Scandinavia, north Germany and Poland, would be a parallel phenomenon anticipating a similar spread of SOM traditions several centuries later.

The Sequence in North-west Europe

We have seen that trapezoid long cairns with multiple lateral passage graves, drystone or megalithic (FIG. 2) were being constructed on the northern coasts of Brittany, and in Lower Normandy, before the middle of the 4th millennium b.c., as a number of dates at Barnenez (Fin.) (Gif 1309-10 and 1556), l'Ile Gaignog (Fin.) (GsY 165), l'Ile Carn (Fin.) (Gif 1362) and La Hoguette, Fontenay-le-Marmon (Calvados) (Ly 131) indicate. We have, therefore, to suppose that by this time the Danubian tradition of the large trapezoid house had already established itself enough in northern France to provide a model there for the House of the Dead. As it happens, the plans of several large trapezoidal houses have recently come to light in the Seine and Yonne valleys (Mordant 1970) (FIG. 5.9) and at Cys-la-Commune on the Aisne (Bailloud 1974: 106) and the associated late Danubian "Cerny" pottery has lately been identified below a Chassey layer at Brèche-au-Diable, Soumont St. Quentin (Calvados) with a radiocarbon date of 3780 ± 150 b.c. (Gif 2139) (Edeine 1972). We have, however, at the same time to recognize that the process which we have postulated for the channel coast of Lower Normandy and Brittany may not have been reproduced in other parts of Armorica or western France south of the Loire. For in other parts of this area, as we have already seen (p. 162), early forms of megalithic or drystone passage graves are associated with circular cairns, sometimes with concentric revetment walls which recall those of some Iberian "tholos" tombs, apparently of much later date (FIG. 4. 3-6) and at the same time relate to the multiple revetment walls at Barnenez and other northern Breton chambered long cairns (FIG. 5.1) which contain similar passage graves. Such comparisons bring home to us the possibility that influences from south-west Europe, as well as central Europe, were combining with local Mesolithic and early Neolithic ones in western France to produce a variety of regional architectural traditions which were, however, united in the pursuit of collective burial as the result of an external stimulus as early as the 4th millennium b.c., which at that time can only have come from south-west Europe. It would, indeed, be unreasonable to reject the early date for the chambered round cairn of Kercado (Morb.) 3880 ± 300 b.c. (Sa 95), based on a deposit under the cairn, while accepting those based on similar deposits under the early chambered long cairns of the Barnenez groups. At the same time, we must notice that the long cairn tradition in southern Brittany and Poitou pursued a somewhat different course from the Barnenez group, and must have run parallel to the round cairn tradition of Brittany, for something like a millennium.

The long mound groups of western France are indeed complex. First the low trapezoid long cairns, with single burials (sometimes cremated) in multiple cists have long been recognized in the Carnac area of the south Morbihan coast (Piggott 1937; Arnal and Burnez 1961: 28-29; the only date is Castellic, Lann-Vras: 3075 ± 300 b.c. (GsY 198B)). Next is a related but rather different group of very large, high and oblong (not trapezoid) mounds in the Carnac area with primary closed cists, one of which, in the great Mont-St. Michel at Carnac has yielded the date of 3770 b.c. (Sa 96). It is possible that this separate, oblong group of *Tumulus Géants,* stretching as it does from Morbihan to Poitou, the Angoumois and Saintonge, had a different origin and represents the primary nucleus of long barrows in western and northern Europe (Burnez and Gabet 1967). The mounds of this group range from 50 to 150 m. in length and from 2 to 4 m. high - one, the Gros Dognon at Tusson (Charente) is said to be 150 m. long and 10 m. high (Arnal and Burnez 1961:35) - and although some in Morbihan and in the regions south of the Loire have had megalithic passage-graves inserted in them long after their erection, they seem normally to have contained closed

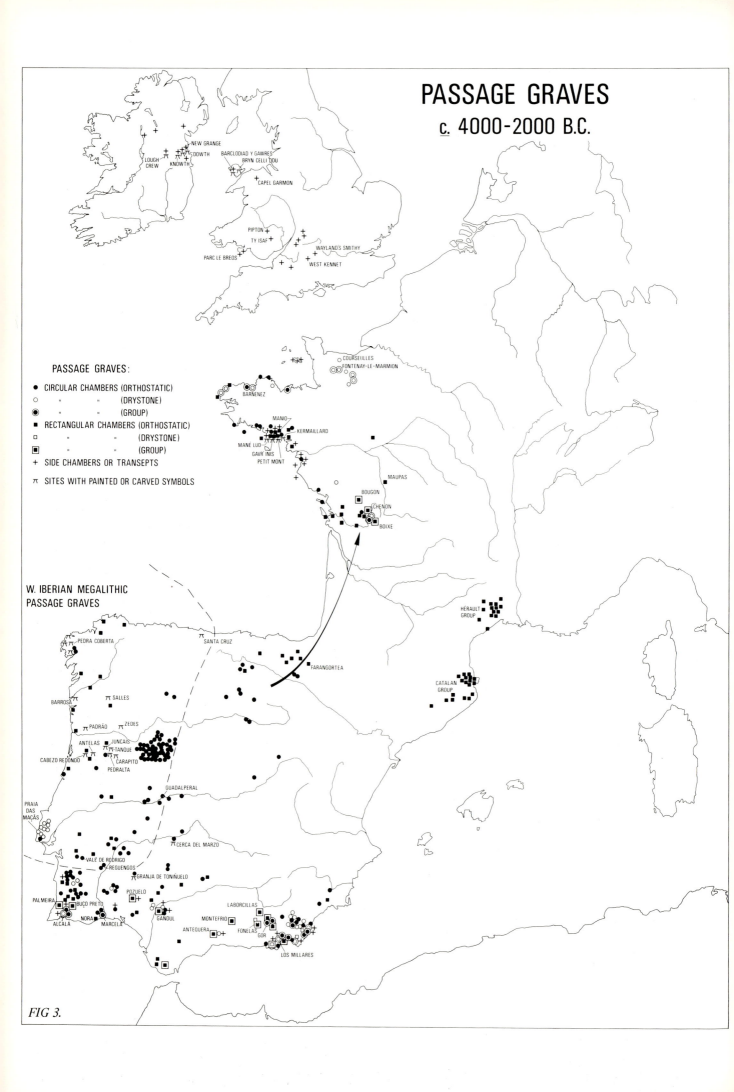

PASSAGE GRAVES
c. 4000-2000 B.C.

PASSAGE GRAVES:

- ● CIRCULAR CHAMBERS (ORTHOSTATIC)
- ○   "   "   (DRYSTONE)
- ◉   "   "   (GROUP)
- ■ RECTANGULAR CHAMBERS (ORTHOSTATIC)
- □   "   "   (DRYSTONE)
- ▣   "   "   (GROUP)
- + SIDE CHAMBERS OR TRANSEPTS
- π SITES WITH PAINTED OR CARVED SYMBOLS

W. IBERIAN MEGALITHIC
PASSAGE GRAVES

LOUGH CREW

NEW GRANGE
DOWTH
KNOWTH
BARCLODIAD Y GAWRES
BRYN CELLI DDU
CAPEL GARMON

PIPTON
TY ISAF
PARC LE BREOS
WAYLAND'S SMITHY
WEST KENNET

COURSEULLES
FONTENAY-LE-MARMION

BARNENEZ

MANIO
KERMAILLARD
MANÉ LUD
GAVR' INIS
PETIT MONT

MAUPAS
BOUGON
CHENON
BOIXE

HÉRAULT GROUP

CATALAN GROUP

PEDRA COBERTA
SANTA CRUZ
FARANGORTEA

BARROSA
SALLES
PADRÃO
ZEDES
ANTELAS
JUNCAIS
TANQUE
CARAPITO
CABEZO REDONDO
PEDRALTA
GUADALPERAL
PRAIA DAS MAÇÃS
CERCA DEL MARZO
VALE DE RODRIGO
REGUENGOS
GRANJA DE TONIÑUELO
PALMEIRA
BUÇO PRETO
POZUELO
GANDUL
LABORCILLAS
MONTEFRIO
ANTEQUERA
FONELAS
GOR
ALCALÁ
NORA
MARCELA
LOS MILLARES

FIG 3.

cists or small rectangular chambers which in some cases were not primary. Thus at the Grosse Motte, Bouhet (Charente-Maritime) there seems at first to have been some kind of mortuary enclosure, lined with wooden posts, on the main axis of the mound, which was afterwards heightened to cover at least one group of lateral cists with single burials or at any rate a limited number of corpses. The pottery is of early Peu-Richard type, hardly earlier than the beginning of the 3rd millennium and the cists may be secondary (Burnez and Gabet 1967). Another great mound at Thou (Charente-Maritime) had a cist on its main axis which also seems to have been secondary (Arnal and Burnez 1961: 33). The Tumulus du Crucheau (Charente-Maritime) was 100 m. long, 30 m. wide and tapering to each end, and had a single flexed inhumation burial, and one of the mounds at Availles-sur-Chizé (Deux-Sèvres) had primary cists and an intrusive megalithic chamber with Peu-Richard Ware. The famous groups of long and round mounds at Luxé and Chenon (Charente) and Bougon (Deux-Sèvres) have been re-excavated in recent years and the results, when fully published should throw much light on the sequence. A small outlier of the group, at Bernet in Gironde (*Ibid.*: 35, Fig. 7) is a clear case of a central, probably primary cist with Chassey pottery and an intrusive megalithic chamber with Copper Age deposits. But it is at St-Martin-La Rivière (Vienne) that one may perhaps see the beginnings of the group (Tartarin 1885; Patte 1971) in that here a large number of cists have been found, apparently without mounds in many cases, and some of them containing several individuals, with inventories which seem to run from the Middle to the late Neolithic, while others are in small circular mounds.

It is unfortunate that there are as yet no radiocarbon dates available which would enable one to fix the chronology of the "giant" long mounds south of the Loire at their inception and determine their relationship to the early long cairns of Brittany and Lower Normandy. It is, however, already probable that their influence lies behind a tradition of long or trapezoid barrows, usually quite small, with simple oblong or trapeze-shaped and apparently primary megalithic chambers placed exactly at the broad end, which spreads through the limestone plateaux ("causses") of the southern edge of the Massif Central, particularly in Aveyron (Daniel 1939; 1950). One of the sites at Salles-la-Source, near Rodez, with its narrow, oblong outline and relatively great length - 50 m. - as well as its terminal dolmen - seems to recall the "giant" barrows of western France, especially tumulus F at Bougon (Arnal and Burnez 1961, Fig. 11), but most of these southern sites are much smaller and their grave-goods suggest a late horizon, overlapping with the local Copper Age (Clottes and Lorblanchet 1968; Costantini and Fages 1971; Rouqayrol 1971; Clottes and Darasse 1972; Lagasquie 1973), the same appears to be the case with the chambered long mounds of coastal Languedoc and Provence (Arnal 1956a and b, and 1963, Arnal and Burnez 1961: 36; Courtin 1974: 59-61 and 165-87). In general one has the impression of a delayed penetration of eastern France by the practice of large-scale communal burial, whether in caves, natural or artificial, or in megalithic chambers, and even in south-western France there seems to have been retardation. None the less, it is important to note that mounds were sometimes oval even in this area (Arnal and Daniel, 1952: 39-48; 1956: 521, Fig. 1, 2 and 6) and that this practice actually crossed the Pyrenees to appear, with a small trapezoid chamber, at Venta de Arrako, Navarre (Maluquer 1964: 15-17), and with passage graves of Iberian types at Alto de la Huesera, Laguardia and Layaza, Alava (De Barandiaran and Medrano 1958: 31-3; De Barandiaran 1962: 95-96) and possibly at S. Martin, Laguardia (De Barandiaran and Medrano 1971b: 147-73). Though many of the recorded grave-goods from these Alava sites are Copper Age or even Early Bronze Age, there is a Neolithic element, most clearly represented by trapezoid flint arrowheads of Iberian types, and at S. Martin these are stratified below Copper Age levels.

So far we have been concerned with the origin and long development, over a vast area of western Europe, of a type of burial mound, the original inspiration of which, in some part of northern France, probably came from a house-form derived from central Europe. But this has told us nothing about the origins of collective burial, or of the associated burial chambers. The "Northmen" or "Eástmen", or whatever they were, had little to do with that. So we must return to the collective burial chambers, in long or round cairns in Brittany, which so far have the earliest radio-carbon dates, and consider the various types of chamber which they incorporate. L'Helgouach has analysed them in a masterly book (1965) and more recently (1973) he has summarized his views on origins and subsequent evolution, in the light of radiocarbon dates. He points out the structural variety which exists even in the earliest phase, referable to the 4th millennium B.C. There are circular chambers and rectangular ones, built either in drystone or with a mix-ture of orthostatic and drystone construction, with fully corbelled roof or massive capstone with passage long or short, entering the chamber centrally or at one corner (FIG. 4). Finally in addition to those set in trapezoidal mounds whose dates we have already considered, are those set in circular cairns which include Kercado (Morbihan) with its square, orthostatic chamber and its date of 3880 b.c. ± 300 (Sa 95) (l'Helgouach 1965, Fig 7) and l'Ile Bono (Côtes du Nord) with its orthostatic circular chamber, short passage in a simple circular cairn (*Ibid.*: Fig. 15.3) and date of 3215 b.c. ± 130 (GsY 64a). It might be said that the specialization already discernible in these early monuments is to some extent regional, in that the multi-chambered long cairns are proportionately commoner on the northern coast of Brittany, and this is matched by the coastal distribution of the similar sites in Lower Brittany which, however, show a more marked preference for drystone-walled chambers. Near the Morbihan coast, on the other hand, is a concentration of circular cairns containing several passage graves (l'Helgouach 1965, Fig. 9).

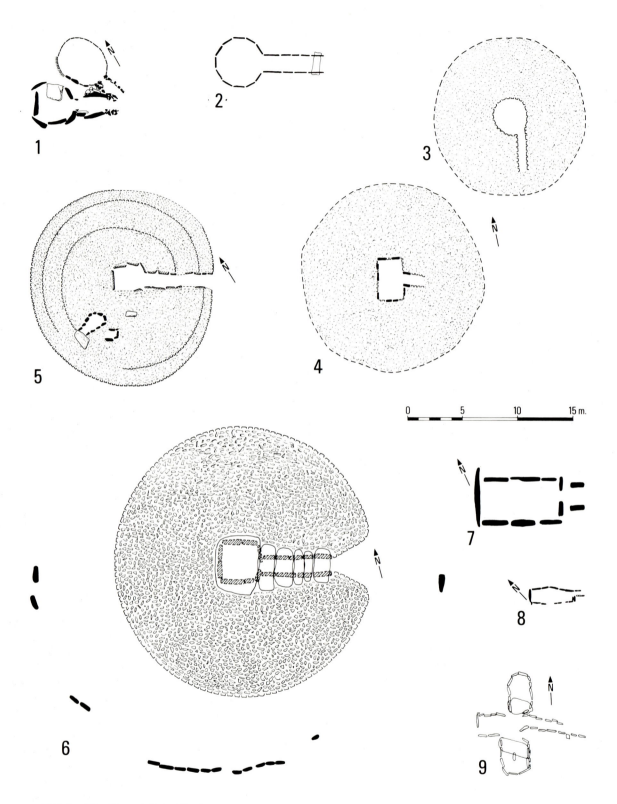

FIG 4.   *The Round Cairn Tradition. 1. Farisoa (Alto Alemtejo) Portugal. 2. Prado de las Navas (Salamanca) Portugal. 3. - 4. La Boixe, (Charente) France. 5. Le Noterio (Morbihan) France. 6. Kercado (Morbihan) France. 7. Le Bernard (Vendée), France. 8. Palmeira (Algarve) Portugal. 9. Pozuelo (Huelva) Spain.*

(1-2, 8-9 after Leisner, 3-4, 7 after Daniel, 5-6 after l'Helgouach).

L'Helgouach, in his analysis, recognizes that passage graves representing most of the Breton variants of the 4th millennium B.C. are thinly scattered throughout a coastal belt stretching south of the Loire, as far as the river Charente, among them being the cemetery of La Boixe (Charente) (Chauvet and Lièvre 1877). The exceptional importance of this site lies in the fact that it contained at least fourteen mounds, all of which were circular, and in those which were explored by Chauvet and Lièvre were found circular chambers, wholly drystone or partially orthostatic, closed or with entrance passage (that of Tumulus E is lopsided, like examples at Barnenez, Ile Carn and Ile Gaignog) as well as rectangular chambers which were partially orthostatic and closed or provided with a passage (FIG. 4). The Charente sites with exclusively circular mounds contrast with those nearby, at Bougon, Luxé, Chenon, etc., which contain long as well as circular mounds. Each of the structural variants just referred to can be matched in the peninsula, and elements in the symbolic carvings on Breton monuments of this early phase can be related to Iberian practice (p.174 below). At the same time, the Chassey culture in its primary form was not addicted to communal burial or megalith-building, so that the pottery of Chassey tradition which forms a distinctive part of the grave-goods of some early passage-graves in Brittany, Lower Normandy and western France south of the Loire cannot indicate the source of the inspiration which led to their construction.

If, in spite of the lack of radiocarbon dates, so far, from the primary phases of sites south of the Loire, we are prepared to believe as l'Helgouach appears to do (1973: 204-205) that the circular and rectangular burial chambers, largely of drystone construction, with central or one-sided entrance passages, in Poitou and Charente, represent a coastal movement spreading from south to north, we can perhaps see here the beginning of several regional lines of evolution which lead, on the one hand, to the various specialized Breton types of passage grave which l'Helgouach recognizes (*Ibid.*: 206-8, map 3) and, on the other, to axially-elongated rectangular chambers, Angevin dolmens with porticos, and finally the *allée couverte* form which spread to Brittany, Languedoc and the Paris Basin on the SOM horizon during the latter part of the 3rd millennium and ultimately had repercussions in Sardinia and southern Italy (FIG. 2) (*Ibid.*: 208-11, map 4). The intermediate forms of rectangular megalithic passage graves, together with l'Helgouach's transepted passage graves of Morbihan and the Loire mouth (1965: 134-9 and 177-88) are of special significance for the origins of the types of chambers found in British long cairns of the Cotswold-Severn group. They may well have been transmitted on the line Poitou-Lower Loire - Lower Normandy and have brought with them a tradition of vestigial drystone circular structures (as at Notgrove, Nympsfield and Ty-isaf), transepted chambers (FIG. 5.7) and simple terminal chambers set in trapezoidal cairns like Chez Vinaigre and Champ Pourri near Angoulême (FIG. 5.6) (Daniel 1960, Fig. 56, 2-3) which resemble the Tinkinswood and St. Lythans chambered long cairns even to the point of apparently possessing funnel-shaped forecourts. Moreover, if one can forget the misleading antithesis between "passage grave" and "long cairn" groups in Britain, we can see how the earliest Breton-Lower Normandy tradition of laterally-chambered trapezoid long cairns could live on in the laterally chambered long cairns of the Cotswold-Severn group (FIG. 5.8), one of which, Pen-y-wyrlod Talgarth (Breckn.) has been now dated 3020 ± 80 b.c. (Har. 674), and how the original circular drystone chambers could be replaced in so many of the British cairns, by axially elongated rectangular passage graves with short entrance passages. We can also see how the transeptal tendency would have been transmitted from the Loire estuary to the lower Severn area, North Wales, and the Boyne Group in Ireland all about the same time, early in the 3rd millennium b.c. as recent radiocarbon dates show.

The Iberian Contribution

We return to the problem of Iberia, which until recently had failed to produce a radiocarbon date for a communal tomb which is earlier than the end of the 4th millennium b.c. One thing that must be pointed out here at once is that the total number of dates involved represents an extremely small proportion of the many thousands of sites which exist in the vast subcontinent which is the Iberian peninsula; what is more, they relate to specialized groups of sites which do not necessarily represent early stages in the development of collective tombs in the peninsula. In fact there are two main groups of relatively early dates which are referred to by Renfrew (1973:9) in his most recent analysis: those from megalithic passage graves in Beira Alta, central Portugal: Carapito I, (Leisner and Ribeiro 1968: 61-62), and Seixas, (Almagro Gorbea 1972: 231) suggesting a primary use about the end of the 4th millennium b.c. and those relating to the settlement and "tholos" cemetery at Los Millares, Almeria which suggest the middle of the 3rd millennium b.c. In neither case is it probable that the sites dated represent the earliest phases in the evolution of the series to which they belong. In the case of the Portuguese megaliths it is necessary to point out that these are classical passage graves of the fully evolved Pavian type with polygonal chambers roofed with massive capstones and with symmetrical centrally aligned passage. It is most unlikely that such tombs, located as they are in the remote inland and mountainous region of northern Beira, were built as early as the earliest monuments of the same type in northern Alemtejo, south of the Tagus, where the type was probably evolved in response to the local geological environment of granite and related rocks which impose a departure from the tradition of "tholos"· building, with circular chambers formed of numerous fine upright slabs below, and drystone corbelling above, which flourished on the schists and other more recent strata of southern Alemtejo, Algarve and Andalusia. The Leisners, moreover, have isolated a primitive group of megalithic passage graves, in the Reguengos and Montemor areas of northern Alemtejo and in Beira Baixa, which have short, lop-sided passages, often consisting only of two large slabs, and are shown by their inventories in the Reguengos area (V. and G. Leisner 1951: 40-3, Pls. I, V-VIII; Leisner,

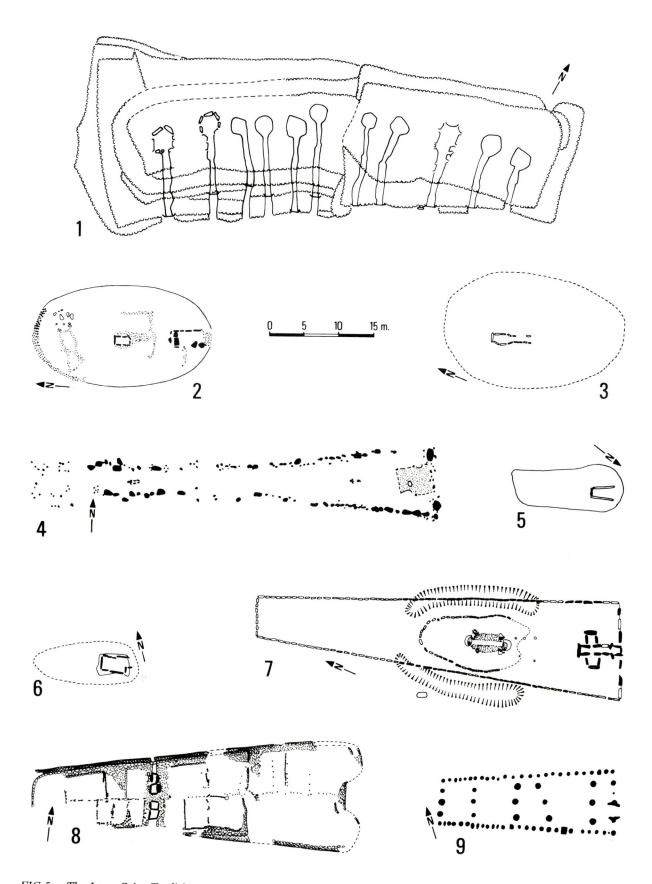

FIG 5. **The Long Cairn Tradition.** *1. Barnenez (Finistère); 2. Bernet (Gironde); 3. Layaza (Alava); 4. Gaj (Poland); 5. Vitarelle (Aveyron); 6. Champ Pourri (Charênte); 7. Wayland's Smithy (Berks.); 8. Ascott-under-Wychwood (Oxon.); 9. Charmoy (Yonne).*
(1 after Giot; 2 after Arnal and Burnez; 3 after De Barandiaran and Medrano; 4 after Ashbee; 5-6 after Daniel; 7 after Atkinson; 8 after Benson; 9 after Mordant).

G. and V. 1956: 43; 1959: 303-40) to be earlier than the Pavian group: in fact two of these, Anta I do Poço da Gateira and Anta 2 dos Gorginos, have been dated around the middle of the 5th millennium b.c. by the thermo-luminescence method (Whittle and Arnaud 1975: 6) and, as it happens, this date is now supported by the radio-carbon date obtained for those layers in the Cueva de los Murciélagos (Cordoba) which contained "cerámica a almagre" like that found in the two early Alemtejan tombs just mentioned (Vicent and Muñoz 1973: 106-10).

Though the chronological gap between the west Iberian and the early Breton tombs may now have been closed by the new thermoluminescence dates, there is still a typological gap. The latter are, after all, nearly all of them drystone, corbelled structures and when they are at least partially megalithic their passages are often much longer or narrower than the early Alemtejan ones, and their chambers have a tendency to be rectangular. We are dealing here with two distinct, locally specialized traditions, which none the less have one particular connecting link, in that some of the early chambers, alike in Brittany and Poitou-Charente, have "lop-sided" entrance passages (FIG. 4) like the early tombs of the Reguengos district. We have, none the less, to notice that tombs of the "tholos" tradition, with circular chambers built with numerous thin slabs carrying corbelled roofs, or built entirely in drystone, with small horizontal slabs, are common in various parts of Iberia; the difficulty is that the only radio-carbon dates from tombs of this type so far available are relatively late, not only at Los Millares but in southern Portugal. In the latter area, indeed, a domed structure, with orthostatic entrance passage and a circular chamber partially corbelled above, apparently primarily sepulchral in purpose, was built as late as the Late Bronze Age at Roça do Casal do Meio near Sesimbra, Estremadura (Ferreira and Spindler 1973). One must accept that the "tholos" tradition had a long life in southern Iberia, whatever the date of its introduction may have been. But it must be pointed out that circular burial chambers, built wholly of drystone walling or with thin vertical slabs below and corbelled above, certainly appear in south-eastern Spain on a horizon which is much earlier than that represented by the Los Millares cemetery and in fact corresponds to Siret's periods I and II of the Almerian culture (Savory 1968: 90-3), characterized by asymmetrical trapezoid arrowheads, with an admixture of bifacial ones of tanged and occasionally of leaf, triangular or concave-based form (G. and V. Leisner 1943, Pls. 1-7, 32). Many of the circular chambers on these early Almerian sites have no entrance passage, others have a short passage and there is clearly an evolution towards large passage graves of the Millaran type. On this same horizon, however, above all further inland in the province of Granada but also near Almeria itself, there is a tendency for megalithic passage graves with square, trapezoid or coffin-shaped chambers to appear (Savory 1968: 93-94) and at Los Millares itself these are probably the earliest tombs in the cemetery, since they are the only ones to contain trapezoid arrowheads (G. and V. Leisner 1943, Pl. 24), and a similar association occurs nearby at Huéchar Alhama (*Ibid.*: Pl. 34). These early megalithic chambers probably derive from the early Almerian closed rectangular chambers, with drystone construction, which are con-temporary with the circular chambers. To this same horizon, too, belong the earliest rock-cut tombs of Andalusia (Savory 1968: 118-23) and here again there are suggestions of a westward spread to the Tagus estuary and the Algarve. We have no radiocarbon dates from any of these pre-Millaran sites in Andalusia, so we have no fully objective way of estimating how many centuries they cover, but the earliest of them are certainly no later than the end of the 4th millennium B.C. The date of 3420 ± 350 b.c. (Harwell, 155) obtained at the copper-using settlement of Terra Venturas, Almeria, by Dr. M. J. Walker, provides a general hint that the Almerian culture which introduced the collective burial chambers may have begun well before the middle of the 4th millennium, and set in train reactions on the western side of the peninsula.

We must, of course, reiterate that the direct origins of the earliest communal tombs of western France are not likely to be found in the Portuguese megalithic passage graves or the related monuments of Galicia, not only because of their specialized structural features and characteristic grave goods, like engraved schist-plaques and "croziers" which do not appear in France: these are, indeed, local Copper Age developments which probably did not appear much before the end of the 4th millennium B.C. Even the early megalithic passage graves already mentioned, which have Neolithic inventories, include in the latter much pottery of specialized forms which, again, do not appear in France. But if we go to the extreme south-west of the peninsula we gain some clues which may help us to an under-standing of the probable line of development towards France. For in the Alemtejo megalithic cists were being built, first for single burials and then for a larger number of individuals well back in the Neolithic, certainly from the beginning of the 4th millennium B.C. (Savory 1968: 96, Figs. 26 and 28, Pl. 13) and at the Buço Preto and Palmeira cemeteries near Monchique in Algarve we can see these small oblong chambers being developed for com-munal burial by enlargement to an oval or coffin shape, while retaining their purely Neolithic inventory of trapezoid arrowheads and small plump axe-heads. At Buço Preto 7, however, (Leisner G. and V. 1959, Pl. 45.4) the provision of a short, lop-sided entrance passage at one narrow end of a coffin-shaped chamber (FIG. 4.8) occurs close to the horizon on which concave-based arrowheads were replacing trapezoid arrowheads and geome-trically decorated schist plaques were appearing, immediately before that of the early "tholos" tombs of Lower Alemtejo - sites like Folha da Amendoeira, Odivelas and Monte Velho, Ourique (Leisner, G. and V. 1959 Pls. 42-3), Malha Ferro and Nora Velha, Ourique (Leisner, V. 1965, Pls. 123.2 and 125-6) and Marcela in the Algarve (Leisner 1943, Pl. 76) We do seem at this stage to have a zone of contact, along the present Spanish-Portuguese border, in which the Almerian culture is blending with the Portuguese megalithic and certain features appear - lop-sided entrance passages, elongated oblong chambers, multiple chambers with or without common

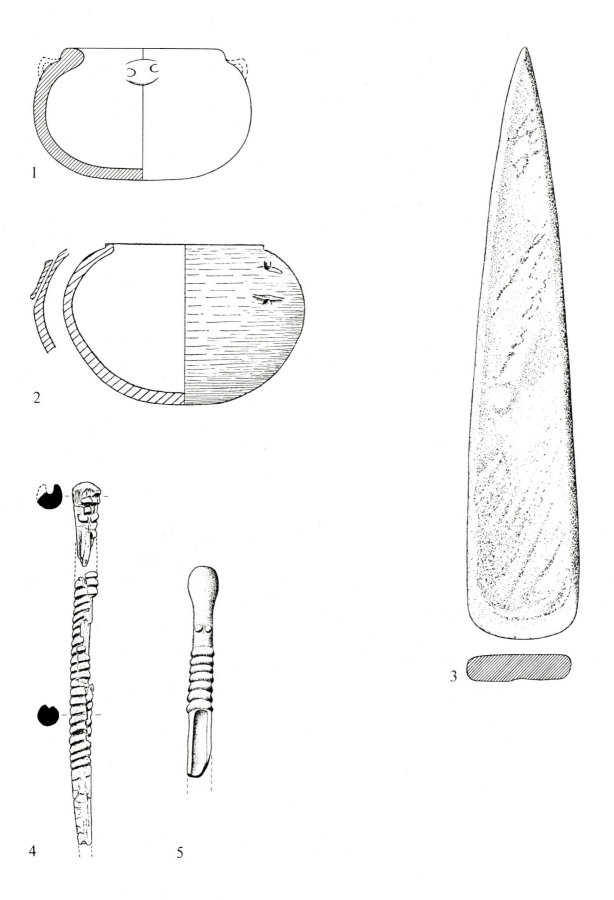

FIG 6. *Pottery bowls, Votive stone axe-head and bone objects.* 1. *Pottery bowl, Gruta dos Alqueves (Coimbra), Portugal.* 2. *Pottery bowl of Souc'h type, Brittany,* after L'Helgouach. 3. *Votive stone axe-head from Carapito (Beira Alta), Portugal,* after Leisner. 4. *Bone object from Knowth, Ireland,* after Eogan. 5. *Bone object from S. Martin, Laguardia (Alava), Spain,* after De Barandiaran and Medrano.

entrances, and transepted chambers (i.e. El Pozuelo 7) (FIG. 4.9) - which do appear in western France.

Is it possible to demonstrate that the Almerian culture at an early stage of development, before the appearance of the anthropomorphic idol, was expanding through Andalusia and the Meseta, to the east of the pure Neolithic rectangular megalithic chambers of Portugal, at the same time as the earliest corbelled passage graves of western France? This would at least account for the development in southern Portugal of the earliest megalithic passage graves, with polygonal chambers, short, lop-sided passages and purely Neolithic inventories - as at Poço da Gateira, Gorginos and Vidigueiras (Leisner, V, and G. 1951, Pls. I-VIII) in place of the local closed rectangular chambers, and the spread of megalithic passage graves with a purely Neolithic inventory north of the Tagus. There is, at any rate, no doubt of the existence in the western Meseta, throughout the provinces of Badajóz Cáceres and Salamanca (Map FIG. 3) of a tradition of large "tholos" type chambers, generally orthostatic, with circular cairns and long entrance passages (Leisner, G. and V. 1956, 28-29, Pls. 2-3, 74). Some of the chambers in Salamanca province are so exceptionally large (e.g. Prado de las Navas (FIG. 4.2) and Torredillas) that the method of roofing is problematic. One of them, El Guadalperal (Cáceres) (Leisner, G. and V. 1959, Pl. 56 and 1960) is of particular interest because of its multiple concentric revetment walls and its primary inventory, which includes many crescents, triangles and trapezes as well as bifacial arrowheads, and several plump axeheads of Neolithic type as well as rectangular section ones. It might be argued that provincial retardation has played a part here as at Carapito, but the size and elaboration of this tomb, as of the Salamanca monuments, does not suggest a poor and backward community. It may be that the considerable destruction of Megalithic monuments which seems to have occurred during periods of agricultural activity in the western Meseta, coupled with the backwardness of fieldwork in the area in recent times has made it appear less important in relation to the Portuguese megalithic passage grave culture than it really is, and that its role during the opening stages of Almerian expansion in influencing the development of the Portuguese megalithic passage graves to the west may have been fundamental. Certainly the grave-goods published long ago by Moran (1930 and 1935) though they suggest much re-use of the chambers on the Beaker horizon, as at El Guadalperal, include a considerable proportion of pure Neolithic types of arrowhead and axehead, as well as nail-impressed pottery which relates to the Neolithic "cave pottery" of central Portugal and the upper levels of the shell mounds of Muge (a radiocarbon date is available here: 4100 $\pm$ 300 b.c. at Cabeço da Amoreira, Sa 194). It is also possible that agricultural destruction may have removed the more vulnerable structures built purely in drystone which might have been present in this western *Meseta* group. There is a great need for further field-work in this vast and rather inaccessible area and until this is done the questions I have raised will have to remain open.

The possibility that collective burials in passage graves of orthostatic or drystone construction may once have been much commoner and more widely distributed in the cereal-growing areas of the northern *Meseta* than available publications have suggested, at least until recently, is emphasized now by the publication by Osaba and his collaborators (1971) of two fine orthostatic passage graves set in circular mounds with circular chambers and long, straight passages like those of Spanish Estremadura and Leon, at Porquera de Butrón (Villarcayo) and Cubillejo de Lara in the province of Burgos, which are shown to have a number of analogues, some of them now destroyed, in the same province and in that of Palencia. A glance at the map (FIG. 3) will show this cluster partly filling the gap round the northern fringe of the *Meseta,* between the Leonese passage graves and another group, recently augmented, near the Upper Ebro in the province of Alava. This latter group, however, in La Rioja, is one which we have already noticed (p.167 above) as showing a tendency to long, rather than circular mounds, and the chambers themselves, though passage graves, are for the most part no longer circular, but polygonal or coffin-shaped and more definitely megalithic in structure, with capstones, instead of the bases of corbelled roofs, surviving in some cases (De Barandiaran and Medrano 1971a; 1971b). The site of S. Martin, Laguardia, is of particular interest because of its apparently lateral siting in what may originally have been a long mound and its primary gravegoods, which include arrowheads all of unifacial type - triangular and trapezoid (some asymmetrical) as well as round sectioned axe-heads and gouges and fragments of several curious bone objects which appear to be large pins, with carved, slightly anthropomorphic heads (FIG. 6.5) which seem to relate on the one hand to the segmented pin heads and pendants of the early Almerian and on the other to the massive bone pins of the Boyne Culture which are sometimes transversely furrowed e.g. Fourknocks and at Knowth (FIG. 6.4) (Hartnett 1957: 241-3; Eogan 1974: 47). A chamber with broad passage leading into it through a large carved "port-hole", at Farangortea, Artajona, Navarre (Maluquer 1964: 22-40) seems to be of later date to judge by its inventory resemblance to monuments in Andalusia like Pantano de los Bermejales (Granada) (Arribas and Del Corral 1969) which are no earlier than the Los Millares cemetery itself. But this convergence of influences from the western *Meseta,* Andalusia and western France (the latter represented by the long mound and the cremations found at some sites) does seem to point to the Rioja and the western end of the Pyrenees as the main channel for early megalithic contacts between south-west and north-west Europe.

Can the suggestion that the earliest passage graves of western France, with their marked tendency to drystone building and corbelled roofs, were inspired by persons and ideas moving mainly by land routes from Andalusia through the *Meseta* and the western ends of the Pyrenees, be confirmed by any common elements in the grave goods? The globular bowls of the Souc'h group associated with early passage graves in Brittany, with their bead rims and perforated or tubular lugs (l'Helgouach 1965: 1973: 204-6, Pl. V) have close analogues in the early Copper Age of central Portugal and Andalusia (FIG. 6. 1-2) (Savory 1968, Fig. 30; Leisner, G. and V. 1959; Leisner V. 1965) as well as Catalonia and at the Balma de Montbolo (Guilaine 1974: 131-204); these like the large triangular and flat sectioned votive axe from the passage-grave of Carapito I, Beira Alta, for which we have the date of 2900 ± 40 b.c. and which has analogues in Galicia (Leisner and Ribeiro 1968: 51-52) and in the "giant" long barrows of Morbihan (l'Helgouach 1965: 109) seem to point to connections between the northern parts of Iberia and Brittany towards the end of the 4th millennium b.c. which excluded south-west Iberia, since the engraved schist plaques characteristic of the latter area must have come into use by then, as the thermoluminescence date for the great Pavian passage grave of Comenda da Igreja (3235 ± 310 b.c.) suggests (Whittle and Arnaud 1975: 7). Moreover the general indication of a common influence from the Italian Middle Neolithic represented by the Portuguese schist plaques and the similarly decorated pottery of the Chassey Culture (Arnal and Gros 1962: Roudil 1973) warns us against accepting certain very low radiocarbon dates from the peninsula itself, for the horizon of schist plaques - e.g. in the west chamber at Praia das Maças (Savory 1968: 73-74 and 122). But the virtual absence of engraved schist plaques from the early passage graves outside the south-west cf the peninsula (Savory 1968. Fig. 32) does focus attention on these areas as the immediate source of Iberian influences in western France on this early horizon. In this connection one must note that vessels of the Souc'h type occur in passage graves and burial caves in Beira, north of the schist plaque line (FIG. 6.1) and that nail-decorated pottery which also probably reflects Italian Early Neolithic influence about the beginning of the 4th millennium B.C. (*Ibid.*: 72) occurs on a number of megalithic sites in the same area and in Leon as well as at El Guadalperal (Leisner, G. and V. 1959, Pl. 56.116; Leisner G. and V. 1960, Fig. 9).

That links may have existed between Iberian passage grave groups established outside of the Alemtejo and the Lower Tagus area and some north-west European groups is suggested not only for the early horizon to which the earlier Breton tombs belong but for the later one to which the Irish Channel passage graves are assigned, not only by the bone objects mentioned above (p.173)but by the stone basins which are a distinctive feature at New Grange, Knowth and Matarrubilla (Seville), and by the common elements in the symbols carved or painted on the interiors of some of the passage graves of the various groups. It is, of course, well known that the total repertoires of symbols in Iberia, Brittany and the Irish Channel area differ from each other considerably. This must be because what we see in each area is an accumulation, reflecting more than one external influence, as well as a long local development in which the primary elements, forming a common denominator, are more or less obscured. If we isolate the "art" of the earliest Breton passage graves (l'Helgouach 1965: 80-4) we see that "yoke" symbols, "croziers", axes, bows, boats, "shields", snakes, undulating lines and concentric semi-circles are the recurrent forms. Some of these are not particularly characteristic either of the Irish Channel or of Iberia, but others certainly are. Croziers form a common element carved out of slate in the Alemtejo, in the form of a bone amulet at the Cova da Moura, Torres Vedras (Belo, Trindade and Ferreira 1961: 410, Fig. 5.25), or engraved on the orthostats of megaliths, not only in Brittany but in Charente (Chauvet and Lièvre 1877:6). Snakes, in explicit form, and the undulating lines which are sometimes associated with them, are a striking feature alike in north-western Iberia, Brittany and the Irish Channel area (FIG. 8). As I have recently dealt with this question in a short paper (Savory 1973) and Shee has also drawn attention to the wealth of material in the area north of the Tagus (1973: 347) I need not recapitulate all the details, but I should mention that though serpentiforms do not seem to occur in the Alemtejan passage grave culture, good examples occur on one of the uprights of an orthostatic "tholos" type passage grave at Cerca del Marzo in Badajoz province (Leisner 1959, Pl. 51.9). An important point to note here is that the use of color for the painting of elaborate symbolic compositions on the inner walls of passage graves, as at Antelas in Beira Alta and the Pedra Coberta near Coruña, is really an attempt to reproduce the frescoes painted on the plaster-rendered inner surfaces of Almerian "tholos" tombs, which are known to have existed but were unfortunately inadequately studied by L. Siret (Leisner, G. 1934: 32, 40-44). That these frescoes originated well before the Millaran phase in southeast Spain is shown by the appearance of the Almerian flat "idol" painted, as on the rocks of the Sierra Morena, among the patterns at Antelas, Pedra Coberta and Pedralta; its appearance at these latter sites, like that of the snake symbol at Carapito, belongs to the beginning of the 3rd millennium B.C. The Almerian idol did not, it is true, go on to Brittany or Ireland, but the resemblance between the curious net-like patterns painted at Antelas (Albuquerque e Castro, Ferreira and Viana 1957, Pls. VI, VII, IX) and those carved in the early Breton passage grave at Kercado (Paquart and Le Rouzic 1927, Pls. 28-9) is very striking. At a later stage the elaborate serpentiform patterns carved on slabs in the Anglesey passage graves of Bryn Celli Ddu and Barclodiad y Gawres invite comparison with certain sites in Galicia and northern Portugal, and the affinity between the lozengic element at Barclodiad and the carving on the terminal slab of the coffin-shaped megalithic chamber at Chão Redondo, Talhadas (Beira Alta) (Albuquerque e Castro 1960) is particularly noteworthy. The use of the carvings at Barclodiad and Chão Redondo, to constitute a form of anthropomorph presiding as it were, over the House of the Dead, like the Copper Age "Statue Menhirs" of eastern Languedoc and the carvings of the Marne rock-cut tombs and SOM Gallery Graves, brings one to the question of the "Mother Goddess."

It is not the purpose of this essay to defend the idea of a universal Mother Goddess as the motive force for the spread of collective burial - an idea which has recently been attacked quite cogently by Fleming (1969). The fact is, of course, that anthropomorphic representation, female or otherwise, is not at all prominent in the early Breton passage graves, nor is it, in fact, in the earlier Iberian tombs. The fully developed "Eye Goddess"

FIG 7.   Engraved schist plaque from Lapa do Bugio (Setubal), Portugal. After Monteiro.

symbolism is Millaran, belonging to the 3rd millennium B.C.,and that is the reason for the contrast revealed by Fleming's map (*Ibid.*: Fig. 34), which is based on the fact that Millaran influences made themselves felt in the late passage grave group of Herault and the Fontbouisse Copper Age culture with its rock-cut tombs, which in turn influenced the SOM culture of the Marne, at an advanced date in the 3rd millennium B.C. In fact, the earliest female figurines so far known from western Europe have been found on settlement sites of marginal Danubian and early Chassey groups in the Paris Basin (Bailloud 1964, 94.9. Fig, 24 and Mordant 1972) quite unrelated to collective burial, and these are in all probability part of the contribution of the Italian Middle Neolithic to the development of the Chassey culture, like obsidian and *vase support* patterns, although it is obvious that their ultimate inspiration comes from the Levant and southeast Europe. Their appearance, however, has a bearing on the chronology of the west Iberian passage grave culture because the recently discovered figurine from Noyen-sur-Seine (Mordant 1972) which is hardly later than the early 4th millennium B.C., is making a gesture with downward-spread hands which reappears on a number of schist and sandstone plaques from passage graves in the neighborhood of the Lower Tagus (Ferreira 1973).

The Contribution of the Near East

We have already seen how improbable it is that the early communal passage graves of Atlantic Europe should have been evolved independently by the local Mesolithic communities. One obvious difficulty is that some of the amulets from the early communal tombs of southeast Spain do show definite links with those of Neolithic or Copper Age groups in areas adjoining the southeast Mediterranean - especially the Levant - I need not repeat the details already accessibly published (Savory 1968: 90 f.) - and it is precisely in the Levant, as we have seen (p. 163 above) that communal burial appears early and can be traced back to local Mesolithic practice. It cannot, therefore, surely be without significance that beehive-shaped structures were being built for domestic and possibly also for religious purposes at Neolithic Khirokitia in Cyprus (FIG. 1), as early as *c.* 6000 B.C. and at a not very

much later date in the urbanized Tell Halaf culture in Syria (Mellaart 1970: 248-313). Some of the structures at Arpachiyah were exceptionally large, may have been cult buildings, and sometimes have had burials near them; while at Khirokitia it was common practice to bury the dead within the "tholos"-like houses, digging holes in the floor for the purpose and raising the floor-level from time to time as convenience might require (Müller-Karpe 1968: 442). It is here that we may very likely find the origin of communal burial in the form in which it was first practised in the Almerian culture of southeast Spain - in circular chambers normally constructed in drystone, with roofs which were either completely corbelled, or covered with clay domes. In Palestine, by the 4th millennium B.C. this practice had been replaced, among some communities, by the cutting of round or oval chambers in the living rock and this tradition, too, was transmitted to south Iberia. It is not surprising, then, that Branigan should be attracted by the idea that the Halafian culture might have played some part in the ultimate origins of the Mesara "tholos" tombs (Branigan 1970: 123). On this view, the House of the Dead in parts of southern Europe would derive its shape and some of its structural features from the house of the living, not, as in northern Europe, from the Danubian long house but from the circular house which had such a wide distribution in Mediterranean lands, from Mesolithic time onwards. There is no reason why this tradition should not have been established with the addition of a rudimentary entrance passage in some Iberian communities not as yet illuminated by radiocarbon dates, before the beginning of the 4th millennium B.C.

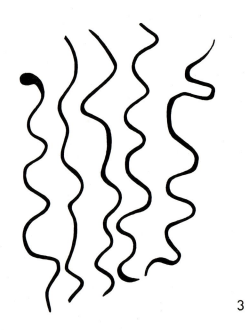

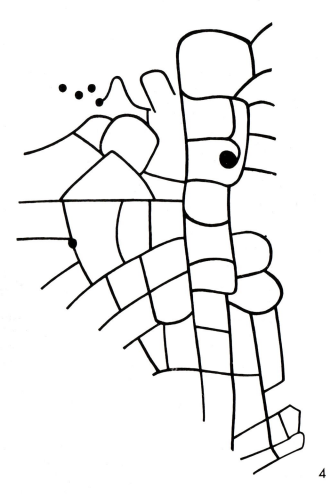

FIG 8.   *Painted and carved serpentiforms and labyrinth.*   *1. Painted serpentiforms in the Anta de Zedes (Tras-os-Montes),*
Portugal, after Santos Junior.   *2. Painted serpentiform and labyrinth, Anta de Antelas, (Beira Alta), Portugal,* after
Albuquerque & Castro.   *3. Carved serpentiforms, Manio, Morbihan,* after Pequart and Le Rouzic.   *4. Carved labyrinth,*
Kercado, Morbihan, after Pequart and Le Rouzic.

Conclusion

What one is dealing with, when studying the distribution of communal burial, in various types of chamber, covered by different kinds of mound, along the Atlantic coasts of Europe, is not an "Atlantic Façade", along which the flotsam and jetsam carried by folk-movements from central and northern Europe finally came to rest. Rather it is an "Atlantic Corridor", which is wide enough to allow the passage of two cultural streams, flowing in opposite directions. The minor, north-south one sometimes affected the form of the covering mound. The major south-north one was responsible for the spread of the practice of communal burial and for most of the architectural forms taken by the chambers required by this practice.

References Cited

Albuquerque e Castro, L de, Ferreira, O. da V. and Viana A.,
    1957   O dolmen pintado de Antelas, Communicações dos Serviços Geológicos de Portugal 38 (ii).
Albuquerque e Castro, L. de,
    1960   Monumentos Megalíticos de Chão Redondo. Estudos, Notas e Trabalhos do Serviço de Fomento Mineiro, Porto XIV (1-2) (1-34 of reprint).
Almagro Gorbea, M.,
    1972   C14, 1972. Nuevas Fechas para la prehistoria y la Arqueología Peninsular. Trabajos de Prehistoria. Madrid XXIX: 228-42.
Anati, E.
    1963   Palestine Before the Hebrews, London.
Arnal, J.
    1956a   Tombes du Serre de Bouisset, Bulletin de la Société Préhistorique Française, Paris LIII: 16–18.
    1956b   Petit Lexique du Megalithisme, Bulletin de la Société Préhistorique Française LIII: 518-31. Paris.
    1963   Les Dolmens du Departement de l'Hérault. Préhistoire XV. Paris.
Arnal, J., and C. Burnez
    1961   Les Longs Tumulus en France. Bericht über den V International Kongress für Vor-und-Fruhgeschichte, Hamburg 1958: 27-37.
Arnal, J. and G. E. Daniel 1952 ,
    1952   Les monuments mégalithiques et la forme des tumuli en France et en Angleterre. Bulletin de la Société Préhistorique Française, XLIX: 39-48.
Arnal, J., and A. C. Gros
    1962   A Propósito das Placas de Xisto Gravadas do Sul da Península Ibérica. Revista da Guimarães LXXII: 301-18.
Arribas, A., and J. M. Sanchez del Corral
    1969   Informe de la Excavación del Sepulcro de Galeria del Pantano de los Bermejales. Noticiario Arqueológico Hispánico X-XII (1966-8): 65-70.
Ashbee, P.
    1966   The Fussell's Lodge Long Barrow Excavations in 1957. Archaeologia, London C: 1–80.
    1970   The Earthen Long Barrow in Britain. London.
Atkinson, R. J. C.
    1965   Wayland's Smithy. Antiquity. Cambridge XXXIX: 126-33.
Bailloud, G.
    1964   Le Néolithique dans le Bassin Parisien (= IIième Suppl. à Gallia Préhistoire), Paris.
    1974   The First Agriculturalists. In France before the Romans. Piggott, Daniel and McBurney, Eds. London.
Bakker, J. A., Vogel, J. C., and Wislanski, T.
    1969   TRB and other C14 Dates from Poland. Helinium, Wetteren IX: 3-27 and 209-38.
Barandiaran, J. M. de
    1962   Excavaciones en Alava, 1957. Noticiario Arqueológico Hispánico Madrid VI: 93-9.
Barandiaran, J. M. de and Medrano, D. Fz.
    1958   Excavaciones en Alava. Zephyrus, Salamanca IX: 5-49.
    1971a   Excavaciones en Alava. Excavaciones Arqueológicas en Alava, Vitoria: 33-86.
    1971b   Excavación del Dolmen de S. Martin. Ibid.: 147-73.
Belo, R., Trindade, L. and O. Da Veiga Ferreira
    1961   Gruta da Cova da Moura. Communicações dos Serviços Geológicos de Portugal, XLV: 391-418.
Blance, B.
    1961   Early Bronze Age Colonists in Iberia. Antiquity, Cambridge XXXV: 191-202.
Branigan, K.
    1970   The Tombs of Mesara, London.

Burnez, C. and C. Gabet
    1967   Destruction du Tumulus Géant de la Grosse Motte à Bouhet (Charente-Maritime) Bulletin de la
                  Société Préhistorique Française   LXIV: 623-38.

Case, H.
    1969   Settlement Patterns in the North Irish Neolithic. Ulster Journal of Archaeology. Belfast, 3s,
                  XXXII: 3-27.

Chauvet, G.
    1881   Deux Sépultures Néolithiques près de Fouqueure. Bulletin de la Société Archéologique et
                  Historique de la Charente. Angoulême 3-10.

Chauvet G. and E. Lièvre
    1877   Les Tumulus de la Boixe. Bulletin de la Société Archéologique de la Charente, Angoulême.

Clottes, J. and P. Darasse
    1972   Les Mobiliers Dolmeniques du Musée de St. Antonin-Noble-Val. Gallia Préhistoire, Paris XV:
                  199-228.

Clottes, J. and M. Lorblanchet
    1968   Le Dolmen du Verdier, Cajarc (Lot). Bulletin de la Societe Préhistorique Française
                  LXV: 559-74.   Paris.

Costantini, G., and G. Fages
    1971   Le Coffre de Vallongue, commune de Prades (Lozère).
                  Bulletin de la Société Préhistorique Française LVIII: 430-9.

Courtin, J.
    1974   Le Néolithique de la Provence. Mémoire II de la Société Préhistorique Française. Paris.

Daniel, G. E.
    1939   On Two Long Barrows near Rodez in the South of France. Antiquaries Journal XIX: 157-65.
    1950   The Long Barrow in Western Europe. In The Early Cultures of Northwest Europe. Fox and
                  Dickens, Eds. Cambridge. Pp. 3-20.
    1960   The Prehistoric Chamber Tombs of France, London.
    1967   Northmen and Southmen, Antiquity. Cambridge XLI: 313-7.
    1970   Megalithic Answers. Antiquity, Cambridge XLIV: 264-9.

Edeine, B.
    1972   Nouvelles Datations par le C14 concernant les sites de la Brèche-au-Diable. Bulletin de la
                  Société Préhistorique Française: 197-9.

Eogan, G.
    1974   Report on the Excavations of some Passage Graves at Knowth, Co. Meath. Proceedings of the Royal
                  Irish Academy, Dublin LXXIV C: 11-112.

Ferreira, O. da Veiga
    1973   Acerca das Placas-Idolos com Mãos Encontradas em Portugal e o Culto da Fecundidade. Estudios
                  Dedicados al Profesor Dr. L. Pericot, Barcelona 233-40.

Ferreira, O. da Veiga and K. Spindler
    1973   Der Spätbronzezeitliche Kuppelbau von der Roça do Casal do Meio. Madrider Mitteilungen XIV:
                  60-108.

Fischer, U.
    1973   Zur Megalithik der Hercynischen Gebirgschwelle. In Megalithic Graves and Ritual. Daniel and
                  Kjaerum, Eds. Copenhagen. pp 51-62.

Fleming, A.
    1969   The Myth of the Mother-goddess. World Archaeology, London I: 247-61.

Gimbutas, M.
    1974   The Gods and Goddesses of Old Europe. London.

Giot, P. R. Ed.
    1963   Les Civilisations Atlantiques du Néolithique à l'Age du Fer. Rennes.
    1969   Circonscription de Bretagne et des Pays de Loire. Gallia Préhistoire XII: 439-63.
    1971   Circonscription de Bretagne. Gallia Préhistoire XIV: 339-61.

Guilaine, J.
    1972   La Nécropole Mégalithique de la Clape (Laroque de Fa. Aude), Carcassonne.
    1974   La Balma de Montbolo et le Néolithique de l'occident méditerranéen. Toulouse.

Guilaine, J. and O. da Veiga Ferreira
    1970   Le Néolithique Ancien au Portugal. Bulletin de la Société Préhistorique Française. LXVII:
                  304-22. Paris.

Hartnett, P. J.
    1957   Excavation of a Passage Grave at Fourknocks County Meath. Dublin.

l'Helgouach, J.
    1965   Les Sépultures Mégalithiques en Armorique. Rennes.

1973   Les Mégalithes de l'Ouest de la France: Evolution et Chronologie. *In* Megalithic Graves and Ritual. Daniel and Kjaerum, Eds. Copenhagen. pp. 203-19.

Hencken, H. O'N.
   1932   The Archaeology of Cornwall and Scilly. London.
   1933   Notes on the Megalithic Monuments of the Isles of Scilly.
          Antiquaries Journal   XIII: 13-29. London.

Jazdzewski, K.
   1973   The Relations Between Kujavian Barrows in Poland and Megalithic Tombs in Northern Germany, Denmark and Western European Countries. *In* Megalithic Graves and Ritual. Daniel and Kjaerum, Eds. Copenhagen. pp. 63-74.

Lagasquie, J. - P.
   1973   Le Dolmen de la Lécune, Flaugnac. Bulletin de la Société Préhistorique Française   LXX: 152-6. Paris.

Leisner, G.
   1934   Die Malereien des Dolmen Pedra Coberta. Jahrbuch für Prähistorische und Ethnographische Kunst. Berlin.

Leisner, G. and V.
   1943   Die Megalithgräber der Iberischen Halbinsel Erster Teil: der Süden. Berlin.
   1956   Die Megalithgräber der Iberischen Halbinsel Erster Teil: der Westen I/I.
   1959   Die Megalithgräber der Iberischen Halbinsel Erster Teil: der Westen I/2.

Leisner, V.
   1965   Die Megalithgräber der Iberischen Halbinsel Erster Teil: der Westen I/3.

Leisner, V. and G.
   1951   Antas do Concelho de Reguengos de Monsarez. Lisbon.
   1960   El Guadalperal. Madrider Mitteilungen I: 20-72.

Leisner, V. and G. and L. Ribeiro,
   1968   Die Dolmen von Carapito. Madrider Mitteilungen IX: 11-62.

Maluquer de Motes, J. M.
   1964   Notas sobre la Cultura Megalítica Navarra. Barcelona.

Masset, C.
   1968   Les Incinerations du Néolithique Ancien de Neuvy-en-Dunois. Gallia Préhistoire. Paris XI: 205-18.

Mellaart, J.
   1970   Cambridge Ancient History, 3 edn. Vol. I, Ch. VII.

Moran, P. C.
   1930 and 1935 Excavaciones en Dólmenes de Salamanca y Zamora. Mem. Junta Sup. de Excavaciones.

Mordant, C. and D.
   1970   Le Site Néolithique des Gours-aux-Lions à Marolles-sur-Seine. Bulletin de la Société Préhistorique Française, Paris LXVII: 345-71.
   1972   L'Enceinte Néolithique de Noyen-sur-Seine (S. et M). Bulletin de la Société Préhistorique Française. Paris LXIX: 554-69.

Muller-Karpe, H.
   1968   Handbuch der Vorgeschichte, Band II: Jungsteinzeit. Munich.

Osaba, B. et al.
   1971   El Dolmen de Porquera de Butrón Burgos . . . y de Cubillejo de Lara de los Infantes. Noticiario Arqueológico Hispánico. Madrid XV: 77-123.

Pequart, M. and St. J. and Z. Le Rouzic
   1927   Corpus des Signes Gravés des Monuments Mégalithiques du Morbihan. Paris.

Pequart, M. and St. J., and H. Vallois
   1937   Téviec. Paris.

Piggott, S.
   1937   The Long Barrow in Brittany. Antiquity   XI: 441-55.

Renfrew, C.
   1967   Colonialism and Megalithismus. Antiquity. Cambridge XLI: 276-88.
   1973   Before Civilization. London.

Roudil, J.-L.
   1973   Le Néolithique de l'Italie du Sud et ses Affinités avec le Chasséen Meridional, Bulletin de la Société Préhistorique Française. Paris LXX: 108-11.

Rouqayrol, J.
   1971   Fouille du Dolmen de Barjac. Bulletin de la Société Préhistorique Française   LXVIII: 109-11. Paris.

Savory, H. N.
   1968   Spain and Portugal. London.

1972   The Cultural Sequence at Vila Nova de S. Pedro. Madrider Mitteilungen XIII: 23-37.
1973   Serpentiforms in Megalithic Art: A Link between Wales and the Iberian North-west. Cuadernos de Estudios Gallegos. Santiago de Compostela XXVIII: 80-89.

Schrickel, W.
1957   Westeuropaische Elemente im Neolithikum und in der Fruhen Bronzezeit Mitteldeutschlands. Leipzig.

Shee, E. A. and Garcia Martinez, M. C.
1973   Tres Tumbas Megalíticas Decoradas en Galicia. Trabajos de Prehistoria. Madrid XXX: 335-48.

Tartarin, E.
1885   L'Age de la Pierre Polie à St. Martin-la-Rivière. Paris.

Tringham, R.
1971   Hunters, Fishers and Farmers of Eastern Europe, 6000-3000 B.C.   London.

Vaux, R. de
1970   Palestine during the Neolithic and Chalcolithic Periods.
        Cambridge Ancient History I. Prolegomena and Prehistory, Chapter IXb: 498-538.

Vicent, A. M. and A. M. Muñoz
1973   Segunda Campaña de Excavaciones en la Cueva de los Murciélagos (Córdoba), 1969, Madrid.

Whittle, E. H. and J. M. Arnaud
1975   Thermoluminescent Dating of Neolithic and Chalcolithic Pottery from sites in central Portugal. Archaeometry 17: 5-24.

THE DISPERSAL OF THE INDO-EUROPEANS AND CONCEPTS OF CULTURAL CONTINUITY AND CHANGE
by Homer L. Thomas

The two successive radiocarbon revolutions, together with the increasingly rapid development of the "new" archaeology, have dramatically altered or changed many of our concepts concerning the prehistoric past. In the Old World, the long gap once thought to separate us from our Palaeolithic ancestors has vanished. Early Neolithic cultures such as the *Bandkeramik* culture of central Europe, previously thought to occupy a few centuries in the third millennium before our era, are now reckoned to have spanned the entire fifth millennium. The long duration of the Neolithic cultures of Europe together with the destruction of their long-established connections with the Aegean, southwestern Asia and Egypt have led to the abandonment of the diffusionist concepts of Montelius (1899), which we know best through the models of V. Gordon Childe (1939). Not only have there been projections of new chronologies, but also a search for new explanations of cultural change and continuity (Renfrew 1973).

After the first radiocarbon revolution, it was clear to many archaeologists that the Corded Ware-Battle Axe cultures, once thought of as short episodes, no longer occupied a narrow horizon limited to the early second millennium, but had beginnings which could be pushed back as early as 2600 B.C. (Thomas 1967). Now, as a result of the second radiocarbon revolution, their initial phases must be placed in the closing centuries of the fourth millennium. This affects our approach to the problems defining the initial dispersal of the Indo-Europeans. Obviously their dispersal can no longer be linked with the Hyksos invasion, the appearance of the Hittites and the first occurrence of Indo-Iranian names. This forces a complete rethinking of the relations of the first Indo-Europeans to the historic civilizations of the Near East, relationships which have underwritten past chronologies as well as explanations of how the first Indo-Europeans reached the Aegean and the highlands of southwestern Asia. With cultures having a life-span of more than a millennium rather than two or three hundred years, it is necessary to project new concepts concerning the character of their development.

These new concepts must cope with the fact that the arrival of the Indo-Europeans marked the end or brought about the transformation of many older cultural traditions, many of which can now be traced back to Mesolithic and even Palaeolithic times. Some of the older traditions were absorbed by the newcomers, but often the archaeological record suggests that they were completely displaced by new traditions. Whatever the case, the Indo-European expansion constitutes a watershed in man's development as significant as the agricultural revolution which set man on his way toward settled life. It marks the beginning of a long transitional period leading through the Bronze Age to proto-historic and historic times. Today, the Indo-European problem must be scrutinized from an entirely different point of view than was possible when Professor Hencken (1955) made his excellent review of theories and concepts concerning the origin and dispersal of the Indo-Europeans.

The second radiocarbon revolution began in 1965 with the publication of the bristlecone pine calibration of the radiocarbon time scale which was based upon the radiocarbon measurements of dendrochronologically-dated wood samples (Suess 1965). By the time of the Twelfth Nobel Symposium (Stockholm, 11-15 August, 1969), bristlecone corrections had been extended back to 5200 B.C. (Suess 1970). There was an almost immediate impact upon archaeological chronology. E. Neustupný's article, "A New Epoch in Radiocarbon Dating", which was published in *Antiquity* in March, 1970 pointed out that measurements made at La Jolla, Tucson and Philadelphia laboratories indicated that while there were only slight variations during the last two thousand years, there was then a steady growth of deviations to the late sixth millennium with the deviation amounting to as much as 800-900 years between 5000 and 4000 B.C. (Neustupný 1970).

The publication by E. K. Ralph, N. N. Michael and M. C. Han of "Radio-carbon Dates and Reality" in the *MASCA Newsletter* in August, 1973 provided tables for the correction of radiocarbon dates at ten-year intervals extending back to 4750 B.C. (Ralph et al 1973). These tables made it relatively easy to check chronologies based upon radiocarbon dates. In Egyptian and Mesopotamian chronologies, the available radiocarbon dates, when corrected for the bristlecone pine calibration, tend to support high historical chronologies such as that of W. C. Hayes (1970) for Egypt, which would place the beginning of the First Dynasty *ca.* 3100 B.C. and for Mesopotamia, which would date the beginning of the Early Dynastic period *ca.* 2900 B.C. (Montelius 1899).[1] The agreement of historical and radiocarbon chronologies, when corrected by the bristlecone pine factor, extends to the Aegean. Here the dating of Early Helladic I still rests upon the Eutresis dates, 2490 ± 64 B.C. (P—307 and 2500 ± 75 B.C. (P—306), which now become 3200-3180 and 3310-3190 B.C. when corrected on the basis of the *MASCA* tables. (Ralph and Stuckenrath 1962: 149). These dates now place the beginnings of Early Helladic I and Troy I less than a century before 3100 B.C., a date assumed on the basis of a high historical chronology in terms of connections between the beginning of the Early Bronze Age in the Aegean and the transition from Jemdet Nasr to Early Dynastic in Mesopotamia and the beginning of the First Dynasty in Egypt (Childe 1939).[2] All this is of considerable importance, because it means that there can be no change in the dating of either historical or archaeological events in Egypt, southwestern Asia or the Aegean that have any significance for the dating or interpretation of the initial dispersal of the Indo-Europeans. On the other hand, Renfrew (1973) is perfectly right in stating that there is a chronological fault-line which marks off the world of Europe beyond the Aegean. Here there is archaeological evidence, which, when redated for the bristlecone pine corrections, suggests that the initial dispersal took place five to six hundred years earlier than could be assumed in 1967 (Thomas 1970). Re-analysis along relatively traditional lines suggests that it is possible to develop a model for the dispersal of the Indo-Europeans which will bring Near Eastern and European evidence into agreement, notwithstanding the recent shifts in chronology brought about by the bristle-cone pine corrections.

Linguistic and historical evidence from the Aegean and southwestern Asia establishes the existence of Greek, Luwian, Hittite and Indo-Iranian speakers by the middle of the second millennium. The existence of these languages indicates that there had already been a relatively long period of linguistic development. Estimates of how far back in time the arrival of these people should be placed in the Aegean and Anatolian and Iranian highlands must be based upon archaeological evidence for definitive breaks in deeply rooted cultural traditions, breaks in cultural tradition indicative of radical cultural change due to the arrival of new peoples.

Evidence for such change is found in both Iran and Anatolia. In Iran, where the deeply-rooted Chalcolithic cultures form parts of a tradition extending back through the Chalcolithic and Neolithic into the Mesolithic, the first of such changes came in the north. Here the Gray Ware culture, which at first appears alongside traditional elements in Hissar IIA and then displaces them in Hissar IIB, ushers in a new culture known not only from Hissar, but also from Tureng Tepe and Shah Tepe. R. Dyson (1965) has dated the beginning of the Hissar II culture to the time of Early Dynastic II, suggesting that it must go back to the early third millennium. Once established, the development of the Hissar II culture can be followed into that of the Hissar III culture, which lasted down until 2000-1900 B.C. After this the cities of northern Iran were deserted, suggesting that the lands were falling into the hands of nomads.

The arrival in Iran of peoples who could have been Indo-Iranians can be placed in the time of either the Hissar II culture or of the nomads who put an end to the Hissar III culture. The magnitude of the intrusion of the peoples who brought the Gray Ware culture may in part be judged by the extent of the so-called Khirbet Kerak movement. Similarities in pottery found in Trans-Caucasia, eastern Anatolia, Syria and Palestine are not sufficiently strong to permit one to determine whether the sudden spread of Khirbet Kerak ware at the time of the Egyptian Old Kingdom and during Early Bronze III in Palestine was due to cultural diffusion or to migration (Todd 1973). Furthermore there are no grounds for connecting it directly with the Indo-Europeans. Yet it may be indicative of disturbances *ca.* 2600-2500 B.C. in the highlands of southwestern Asia resulting from the movements of new peoples into either Iran or Anatolia.

In Anatolia, the old cultural traditions, which extend back through the Chalcolithic to the Neolithic, were gradually destroyed or restricted to the south after three periods of destruction which might be connected with the arrival of the Indo-Europeans. The first period of destruction was marked by the fall of Troy I (usually dated 2600 B.C., but more recently as early as 2800 B.C.). The extent and direction of the movement which destroyed Troy I may be judged by the appearance of Troadic elements at Beycesultan and in Macedonia, where they played a part in the formation of the Early Bronze Age (Lloyd and Mellaart 1962). The second wave of destruction, which is usually placed *ca.* 2300 B.C., affected a broader area and was marked by the destruction of Troy II, Polatli II and Beycesultan (Early Bronze II) (Weinberg 1965). The third movement is more difficult to define because of the lack of a fully detailed view of the archaeological development throughout Anatolia during the entire Early Bronze Age. It was marked by the appearance of a monochrome "Hittite" pottery and the destruction of towns in the Ankara and Halys regions of Anatolia in the late third millennium. Mellaart (1971) has associated the first two movements, which affected mainly northwestern and western Anatolia, with the arrival of the Luwians from southeastern Europe. The third movement would have marked the coming of the Hittites from the east. Crossland (1971) however is probably correct in pointing out that the close linguistic relationships between Luwian and Hittite argue against bringing Luwian from the west and Hittite from the east and above all against a chronological separation of over five to six hundred years in their introduction. In view of the present state of archaeological and linguistic evidence, it is probably best to conclude that these three movements marked by the destruction of towns can only suggest the possible times of the arrival of the Luwians and Hittites. Movements into Anatolia could just as easily have been connected with the Khirbet Kerak movement as the movement of the Gray Ware culture in Iran.

In Greece the discovery of the destruction of Lerna III, the level of the now-famous House of the Tiles, and the subsequent identification of destructions marking the end of Early Helladic II at Tiryns, Asine and Zygouries has led to the widespread acceptance of an invasion of the Aegean *ca.* 2300 B.C. (Caskey 1957: 1971). The discovery of a gray "Minyan" pottery in Lerna IV, which is dated to Early Helladic III, indicates that Minyan pottery, long associated with Middle Helladic I, must be earlier than has been assumed. Since Minyan pottery was associated with a culture that was to evolve into the Mycenaean culture, whose Linear B Tablets guarantee that its creators were speakers of Greek, it is now assumed that the people who destroyed Lerna III were probably Proto-Greeks, surely

Indo-Europeans. Their arrival marks the beginning of a new culture and of the displacement and assimilation of older Helladic elements that was to continue into Middle Helladic times.

Archaeological evidence available from the Aegean and southwestern Asia clearly suggests that the third millennium was marked by the destruction of older traditions and the arrival of new cultures which it is tempting to associate with the Indo-Europeans. If one accepts the presence of Proto-Greeks, possibly Achaean Greeks, on the Greek mainland before the end of the third millennium, it is then possible to place Luwians and Hittites in Anatolia and possibly Indo-Iranians in Iran in the third millennium. This makes it possible to suggest tentatively that the initial dispersal of the Indo-Europeans might be pushed back into the fourth millennium, a dating, which, as we shall see, is required by the European evidence.

European cultures traditionally associated with the dispersal of the Indo-Europeans fall into two groups, one associated with the Corded Ware-Battle Axe cultures, the other with the Baden culture. The Corded Ware-Battle Axe cultures consist of an extraordinarily complex group of cultures found in central, northern, and eastern Europe. In recent years there have been attempts to classify these cultures on both geographical and archaeological grounds. K. Sturve (1955) proposed that they should be subdivided into two groups, one being characterized by the use of both amphorae and beakers, the other group by beakers alone. In the same year, K. Kilian (1955) pointed out that this classification was unsatisfactory because amphorae occur in small numbers in all these cultures, and instead attempted a geographic classification. U. Fischer (1958) advanced a classification similar to that of Sturve, but with a geographical emphasis. He proposed a south central European or Hercynian group characterized by beakers and amphorae, a Balto-Rhine group, which was similar to Sturve's group without amphorae, and an eastern European group.

At the Halle conference (June 1967) on Corded Ware cultures, L. Klejn sought to resolve the problem of classification in terms of a complex set of criteria based on all aspects of culture. He proposed four main groups: the amphorae cultures of southern central Europe (Saxo-Thuringian, south-west German, Bavarian, Austrian and southern Polish), the beaker cultures of northern Europe (Single Grave culture of northern Germany and Scandinavia and the Oder Culture), the Boat Axe cultures (Boat Axe cultures of Sweden, Finland and the Baltic States and the Fatyanovo culture), and the eastern European cultures (Usatovo, Catacomb Grave and Middle Dnieper cultures). He excluded the Pit Grave culture of the Pontic steppe and the North Caucasian Catacomb culture (Klejn 1969).

In these attempts at classification, little was done with the problem of chronological relationships between the various Corded Ware cultures, so important for the determination of the origin of the initial Corded Ware culture. This was probably because they were thought of as occupying a relatively narrow chronological horizon to be dated to the early second millennium or, at the earliest, to the closing centuries of the third millennium. Today radiocarbon dates recalculated for the bristlecone pine correction suggest that the dispersal of the Corded Ware culture must have taken place in the late fourth millennium.

Among the Corded Ware cultures, corrected radiocarbon dates indicate that the earliest in central and northern Europe were those of the North European Plain. It was here that the Corded Ware cultures displaced the Funnel Beaker culture, which had pioneered the Neolithic from the Netherlands to Poland, the Passage Grave culture and its derivatives such as the Kujavian Barrow culture, and the Globular Amphorae culture, which had arisen in the eastern part of the North European Plain just before the intrusion of the Corded Ware culture. Although the Corded Ware culture absorbed elements of these older cultures, it marks the beginning of new cultural traditions that were to serve as the basis for subsequent cultural development in the Bronze Age and because of the continuity of cultural development are to be associated with the Indo-Europeans. The dating of the initial phases of the Corded Ware culture rests upon dates for the Dutch Corded Ware culture known from single burials furnished with beakers with a protruding foot and battle axes (Waals and Glasbergen 1955).[3] Corrected radiocarbon dates from Schaarsbergen (Gro-318: 2485 ± 320 (low half-life), 2618 ± 320 (high half-life) or 3180-3200 B.C. when corrected by the bristlecone pine factor), Ede (Gro-330: 2245 ± 120, 2370 ± 120 or 2920-2940 B.C.) (Vries, Barendsen, Waterbolk, 1958: 135), and Anlo (GrN-1865: 2470 ± 55, 2602 ± 55 or 3180 B.C.) (Vogel and Waterbolk 1963: 180) suggest that the Corded Ware culture had penetrated across the North European Plain before the end of the fourth millennium.

The Single Grave culture of Denmark and southern Sweden probably derived from the North European Plain. Its earliest phase is difficult to define, but the distribution of Type I Battle Axes in western and central Jutland points not only to a derivation from North Germany (Glob 1944: 206-209), but also to the existence of a phase to be dated as early as the Danish Middle Neolithic II (Becker 1961). By Middle Neolithic III, the succession of the Single Graves can be correlated with that of the Middle Neolithic Megalithic Passage Grave culture, whose development can be traced through five distinct phases. Radiocarbon dates for Middle Neolithic I, which come from Tustrup (K-727: 2490 ± 120, 2571 ± 120 or 3160 B.C. and K-718: 2490 ± 120, 2623 ± 120 or 3180-3200 B.C.) (Tauber 1964: 217-218) suggest that the first phase of the Single Grave culture, which dates later than Middle Neolithic I, was later in Denmark than on the North European Plain. Once they were established in southern

Scandinavia, there was a gradual amalgamation of Corded Ware and Middle Neolithic elements that led to the Cist Grave culture of the Late Neolithic and then the cultures of the Bronze and Iron Age of Scandinavia, which are assuredly Indo-European.

The Corded Ware-Battle Axe cultures of the uplands of southern Germany, central Germany, Bohemia, Moravia and southern Poland are characterized by burials often under barrows and furnished with both beakers and amphorae. In Saxo-Thuringia, where Corded Ware was discovered just over one hundred years ago, most of the finds date to the mature Kalbsreith and Mansfeld phases whose development can be traced into the Early Bronze Age (Matthias 1969). The earliest evidence for the presence of the Corded Ware culture consists of sherds found in Salzmünde context. Radiocarbon dates from Salzmünde settlements such as Dölauer Heide (B1n-64: 2830 ± 100, 2973 ± 100 or 3620 B.C. and Bln-53: 2680 ± 100, 2819 ± 100 or 3390 B.C.) (Kohl and Quitta 1963: 290) suggest the Corded Ware culture was penetrating into this region as early as the late fourth millennium.

In Czechoslovakia, there are no radiocarbon dates for the early phases of the Corded Ware culture as defined either in Neustupný's system (E. and J. Neustupný 1961: 75-80) or by Find Group I of the new system proposed by M. Buchvaldek (1966). The only available date is for the destruction of the hilltop settlement of Homolka, which belonged to the Rivnác culture. This date (GrN-4885: 2310 ± 70, 2438 ± 70, or 2970 B.C.) probably marks the end of the first phase of the Corded Ware culture in Bohemia (Vogel and Waterbolk 1967: 133). Again our evidence points to a dispersal in the late fourth millennium.

The evidence for the dating of the Corded Ware cultures of southwestern Germany, Switzerland and Austria suggests that they arrived during the mature phase of the Corded Ware cultures of central Europe (Sangmeister and Gerhardt 1965; Strahm 1969). In Poland, where the Corded Ware culture of the North European Plain extended through western and central Poland to differentiate later as the Oder Culture, the Corded Ware culture of the south-west (Marszowiskiej) and south (Krakowsko-Sandomierskiej) had developments which paralleled those of Bohemia and Saxo-Thuringia (Hensel 1973: 106-126). Again much of our evidence comes from the mature phases of the Corded Ware culture, when one finds obvious instances of the assimilation of surviving Funnel Beaker and Globular Amphora elements (Machnik 1966). The persistence of older cultures as well as of cultural elements is ideally illustrated by the Złota culture which is now regarded as a late Globular Amphora culture (Krzak 1961).

In eastern Europe the Corded Ware cultures are marked off from those of central Europe by their round- or pointed-base pottery. Unfortunately the chronology and particularly the dating of initial phases is difficult to determine for the Strzyzowskiej Gorodsk culture of eastern Poland and Volhynia, the Pre-Carpathian culture of southeastern Poland and the western Ukraine, the Middle Dnieper culture of the central Ukraine, and the Desna-Dnieper culture of the northern Ukraine (Bérézanskaia 1971). With these eastern cultures may be placed the Fatyanovo culture of central Russia and the Boat-Axe cultures of the Baltic region and Sweden (Sturms 1961). The connection between the mature Single Grave culture of Scandinavia and the Swedish Boat-Axe culture dates the eastern Corded Ware cultures to much the same period as the Corded Ware cultures of central and northern Europe. Support for such dating comes from the fact that the beginning of the Middle Dnieper culture should date just after it displaced the Tripolye C I culture from the Middle Dnieper region, an event to be placed in the late fourth millennium (Passek 1962).

The westward expansion of the Middle Dnieper culture, which is marked by the destruction of eastern Tripolye settlements, was accompanied by the formation of the Usatovo and Gorodsk cultures, a hybrid of Steppe and Tripolye elements, and the southwestward movement of those steppe elements which created the Cernavoda I-Ezero culture of the Dobrudja (Brjussow 1957: 280-285). Radiocarbon dates for wood from ochre graves of the Cernavoda I-Ezero culture found at Baia-Hamangia (GrN-1995: 2580 ± 65, 2716 ± 65 or 3350 B.C.) (Vogel and Waterbolk 1963: 184) and Ezero (Bln-61a: 2555 ± 100, 2690 ± 100 or 3230 - 3340 B.C.) (Kohl and Quitta 1963: 297) place the beginning of this culture in the late fourth millennium. This westward thrust of Corded Ware and Steppe elements, presumably derived from the Yamno III culture, led to the displacement of indigenous Balkan elements. In Greece this movement is marked by the appearance in the Late Neolithic of crusted ware of Gumelnitsa Sălcutsa-Krivodol background, where it is characteristic of the Rakhmani culture (Weinberg 1965). To the west the influx of Krivodol and Sălcutsa elements into southern Serbia played a part in the formation of the Bubanj-Hum Ia culture (Srejović 1963).

Archaeological evidence from southeastern Europe suggests that the older traditions persisted into the third millennium notwithstanding these pressures from the steppe. The Tripolye and Cucuteni cultures reached their final phases. This is indicated by finds made at Foltesti I in Transylvania, where Cucuteni B II pottery was found with Usatovo elements (Berciu 1961a) and at Grodek-Nadbuznanski on the Upper Bug, where late Funnel Beaker D/E pottery contemporary with Zlota and Polish Corded Ware was found with Tripolye C II pottery (Driehaus and Behrens 1961: 262). In the Lower Danubian Valley and central Transylvania, the Gumelnitsa, Sălcutsa and Petreshti cultures also continued into final phases contemporary with the Cernavoda I-Ezero culture, which had already displaced the Gumelniţsa from the Dobrudja and much of Muntenia (Berciu 1961b: 479-484).

Further movements from the steppe brought the destruction of the Cucuteni-Tripolye cultures, a destruction marked by ochre graves sunk in settlements. Somewhat later the Coţsofeni culture crystallized in western Rumania. Exact dating is difficult but pottery connections suggest they belong to the time of the Veselinovo group and Karanovo VII (Upper Layers) of eastern and southeastern Bulgaria and thus to the time of Troy II and the Early Bronze Age of Macedonia (Georgiev 1961: 87-89). It is tempting to connect the consolidation of the Coţsofeni culture with the movement which accounted for the destruction of Troy I, ca. 2600 B.C.

In the Middle Danubian Basin, the break with older traditions came with the Baden culture, whose people made use of the horse and wheeled vehicles and kept sheep and cattle, which has led many archaeologists to associate them with the Indo-Europeans (Childe 1957: 124-129). The Baden culture can be traced through two phases, early Baden (without Kostolac elements) and late Baden or Baden with Kostolac elements (Bognár-Kutzián 1963: 540). The early Baden can be traced in western Hungary, where it displaced the Balaton culture, inheritor of Lengyel and ultimate *Bandkeramik* traditions, in southwestern Slovakia, where it replaced the Ludanice culture, and in eastern Austria, Bohemia, Moravia and southern Poland, where it took over from the Funnel Beaker cultures that had displaced still earlier Neolithic traditions going back to the *Bandkeramik* culture. Baden influence penetrated westward and southwestward into Serbia (Garašanin 1958). It is now thought that the Bodrogkeresztur culture, which had inherited the traditions of the Tiszapolgár culture, occupied eastern Hungary until or into earliest Baden times before it was displaced by the Baden culture. The maturity of the Baden culture came with the Baden-Kostolac phase found throughout Hungary and eastern Jugoslavia and the Late Baden of Austria, Bohemia, Moravia and southern Poland. The consolidation of the Baden culture laid the foundations for a cultural development destined to play a part in the formation of the Bronze Age of the Middle Danubian Basin.

The dating of the two phases of the Baden culture is a matter of great importance for the interpretation of movements affecting not only southeastern Europe but also the Aegean and Anatolia. The chronological problem is very much involved with the question of origins, which have been ascribed to Anatolia (Kalicz 1963), the Steppe (Gimbutas 1965: 490-491), and central Europe (E. and J. Neustupný 1961: 67-75). The chronology of the Baden culture is based on Jevišovice in Moravia and Bubanj and other sites in Jugoslavia. At Jevišovice Early Baden occurs in the upper layers of level C1, stratified above a Funnel Beaker occupation datable to the time of the Salzmünde culture of the late fourth millennium, and below the Jevišovice occupation of the late third millennium (J. Neustupný 1961; Zapotocky 1957). In Serbia this dating is supported by Early Baden elements found at Vinča E (2.50-1.50 m), Bubanj III/3 and Hissar I a/b, but the presence of Baden-Kostolac elements at Bubanj II-IIa/Ia and Hissar II a/b, usually dated to the time of Early Helladic III, suggests that the Baden culture continued to the end of the third millennium (E. Neustupný 1973; Morintz and Roman 1973).

Present evidence suggests that the Corded Ware and Baden cultures spread during the late fourth millennium. The Corded Ware culture spread through eastern, central and northern Europe, developing distinct traditions that we associated with the Corded Ware cultures of the Hercynian uplands of southern central Europe, the North European Plain, southern Scandinavia and eastern Europe. Their expansion, together with the movement of steppe elements that account for the formation of the Usatovo and Cernavoda I-Ezero culture, accounts for the southward flight of Balkan elements, then accounts for the formation of the Bubanj-Hum Ia culture and the Rakhmani culture. It is difficult however to fit the Baden culture into this general picture unless it is regarded simply as a derivative from the steppe caught up in this general movement.

It is only with the secondary movement within southeastern Europe, which has been associated with the consolidation of the Coţsofeni culture, here placed at the time of the destruction of Troy I, that any real contact can be established between the possible movements of Indo-Europeans in Europe and southwestern Asia. The second contact between movements in Europe, southwestern Asia and the Aegean, which came at about 2300 B.C., was much more extensive than the first and might be linked with the widespread expansion of the Late Baden culture within the Carpathian Basin. The widespread use of cups with high-loop handles in the Late Baden which has long suggested to archaeologists that it should date to the time of Minyan pottery may well indicate that the Late Baden was involved in movements within the Balkans that are somehow connected with the destructive invasions that beset the Aegean and Anatolia *ca.* 2300 B.C.

The restructuring of European chronology, which has come as the result of the correcting of radiocarbon dates for the bristlecone pine factor, points to more than a "chronological fault-line" between southwestern Asia and the Aegean and Europe. It strongly suggests that the initial dispersal of the Indo-Europeans was essentially a European, probably Eurasian, movement and that the movements in the Aegean and southwestern Asia were secondary affairs involving at most southeastern Europe.

Notes

1. It is interesting to note that when the radiocarbon dates for Early Dynastic I are corrected for the bristlecone pine factor they support the historical chronology. The radiocarbon dates of 2322 ± 65 (P–819) and 2140 ± 62 (P–120) for charcoal from Level IXA of the northwest part of the Inanna Temple become 2970 and 2700 B.C. when corrected, thus bringing them into agreement with the historical dating for Early Dynastic I. Braidwood, (1970, 87-88); Stuckenrath and Ralph, (1965, 189).
2. See various articles in R.W. Ehrich (1965).
3. The work of J.D. van der Waals and W. Glasbergen (1955) is still fundamental.

References Cited

Becker, Carl J.
      1961   Probleme der neolithischen Kulturen in Nordeuropa vom Anfang der Trichterbecherkultur bis zum Auftreten der Schnurkeramiker. *In* L'Europe à la fin de l'âge de la pierre. Jaroslav Böhm and Sigfried J. De Laet, Eds. Praha; Editions de l'Académie tchécoslovaque des Sciences. pp. 585-594.

Berciu, Dumitru
      1961a   Chronologie relative du Néolithique du Bas Danube à la lumière des nouvelles fouilles faites en Roumanie. *In* L'Europe à la fin de l'âge de la pierre, Jaroslav Böhm and Sigfried J. De Laet, Eds. Praha; Editions de l'Académie tchécoslovaque des Sciences. pp. 101-124.
      1961b   Contributii la Problemele Neoliticului in Romînia in Lumina noilor Cercetari. Bucuresti: Editura Academiei Republicii Populare Romîne.

Bérézanskaia, S.S.
      1971   A propos de l'horizon commun européen des cultures de la céramique cordée en Ukraine et en Biélorussie. Sovietskaya Archeologiya No. 4, 36-49.

Bognár-Kutzián, Ida
      1963   The Copper Age Cemetery of Tiszapolgár-Basatanya. Archaeologia Hungarica 42.
      1973   The Relationship between the Bodrogkeresztúr and the Baden Cultures. *In* Symposium über die Entstehung und Chronologie der Badener Kultur. Bohuslav Chropovský, Ed. Bratislava: Verlag der Slowakischen Akademie der Wissenschaften. pp. 31-50.

Braidwood, Robert J.
      1970   Prehistory into history in the Near East. *In* Proceedings of the XII Nobel symposium on radiocarbon variations and absolute chronology. I. Olsson, Ed. Stockholm: Almquist and Wiksell-Gebers forlag AB. . pp. 81-91.

Brjussow, A. Ja.
      1957   Geschichte der neolithischen Stämme im europäischen Teil der UdSSR. Berlin: Akademie Verlag.

Buchvaldek, M.
      1966   Die Schnurkeramik in Mitteleuropa. Památky Archeologické 57: 126-171.

Caskey, J. L.
      1958   Excavations at Lerna, 1957. Hesperia 27: 125-144.
      1971   Greece, Crete and the Aegean Islands in the Early Bronze Age. *In* The Cambridge Ancient History 3rd Ed. Vol. I, Pt. 2. I.E.S. Edwards, C. J. Gadd, N. G. L. Hammond Eds. Cambridge: University Press. pp. 771-807.

Childe, V. Gordon
      1939   The Orient and Europe. American Journal of Archaeology 43:10-26.
      1957   The Dawn of European Civilization. London: Routledge and Kegan Paul.

Crossland, R. A.
      1971   Immigrants from the North. *In* The Cambridge Ancient History, 3rd Ed. Vol. I, Pt. 2. I.E.S. Edwards, C. J. Gadd, N.G.L. Hammond, Eds. Cambridge : University Press. pp. 824-876.

Driehaus, Jürgen, and Hermann Behrens
      1961   Stand und Aufgaben der Erforschung des Jungneolithikums in Mitteleuropa. *In* L'Europe à la fin de l'âge de la pierre. Jaroslav Bohm and Sigfried J. De Laet, Eds. Praha: Editions de l'Académie tchécoslovaque des Sciences. pp. 233-275.

Dyson, Robert H.
      1965   Problems in the Relative Chronology of Iran, 6000-2000 B.C. *In* Chronologies in Old World Archaeology. Robert W. Ehrich, Ed. Chicago. The University of Chicago Press. pp. 215-256.

Ehrich, Robert W.
      1965   Chronologies in Old World Archaeology. Chicago: The University of Chicago Press.

Fischer, U.
      1958   Mitteldeutschland und die Schnurkeramik. Jahrresschrift für Mitteldeutsche Vorgeschichte 41/42: 254-298.

Garašanin, M.
    1958   Kontrollgrabung in Bubanj bei Nis. Praehistorische Zeitschrift 36: 223-244.
Georgiev, Georgi I.
    1961   Kulturgruppen der Jungstein- und der Kupferzeit in der Ebene von Thrazien. *In* L'Europe à la fin de
            l'âge de la pierre. Jaroslav Böhm and Sigfried J. De Laet, Eds. Praha: Editions de l'Académie
            tchécoslovaque des Sciences. pp. 45-100.
Gimbutas, Marija
    1965   The Relative Chronology of Neolithic and Chalcolithic Cultures in Eastern Europe North of the
            Balkan Peninsula and the Black Sea. *In* Chronologies in Old World Archaeology. Robert W. Ehrich,
            Ed. Chicago: The University of Chicago Press, pp. 459-502.
Glob, P. V.
    1944   Studier over den jyske Enkeltgravskultur. Aarbøger for nordisk Oldkyndighed og Historie, pp. 5-282.
Hayes, W. C.
    1970   Chronology I. Egypt - To the end of the Twentieth Dynasty. *In* The Cambridge Ancient History 3rd
            Ed. Vol. I, Pt. 1. I.E.S. Edwards C. J. Gadd, N.G.L. Hammond Eds. Cambridge: University Press.
            pp. 173-193.
Hencken, Hugh
    1955   Indo-European Languages and Archeology. American Anthropological Association Memoir No. 84.
Hensel, Witold
    1973   Polska Starozytna. Wrocław, Warszawa, Kraków, Gdańsk: Zakład Narodowy Imienia Ossolińskich
            Wydawnictwo Polskiej Akademii Nauk.
Kalicz, N.
    1963   Die Péceler (Badener) Kultur und Anatolien. Studia Archaeologica 2: Academiae Scientiarum
            Hungaricae. Budapest.
Kilian, K.
    1955   Haffküstenkultur und Ursprung der Balten. Bonn: Rudolf Habelt.
Klejn, L. S.
    1969   Zum Problem der Aussonderung und Gliederung des Streitaxtkulturkreises. *In* Die neolitischen
            Becherkulturen im Gebiet der DDR und ihre europäischen Beziehungen. H. Behrens and
            F. Schlette Eds. Halle: Veröffentlichungen des Landesmuseums für Vorgeschichte 24. pp. 209-214.
Kohl, Günther and Hans Quitta
    1963   Berlin - Radiokarbondaten archäologischer Proben I. Ausgrabungen und Funde, Nachrichtenblatt
            für Vor- und Frühgeschichte 8:281-301.
Krzak, Zygmunt.
    1961   Materiały do Znajomości Kultury Złockiej. Wrocław, Warszawa, Krakow: Zakład Narodowy Imienia
            Ossolińskich Wydawnictwo Polskiej Akademii Nauk.
Lloyd, Seton and James Mellaart
    1962   Beycesultan I. London: British Institute of Archaeology at Ankara.
Machnik, J.
    1966   Studia nad Kultura ceramiki sznurowej w Małopolsce. Wrocław, Warszawa, Kraków: Zakład
            Narodowy Imienia Ossolińskich Wydawnictwo Polskiej Akademii Nauk.
Matthias, W.
    1969   Die Schnurkeramik im westliche Mitteldeutschland. *In* Die neolithischen Becherkulturen im Gebiet
            der DDR und ihre europäischen Beziehungen. H. Behrens and F. Schlette Eds. Halle: Veröffentlichung-
            en des Landesmuseums für Vorgeschichte 24. pp. 9-28.
Mellaart, J.
    1971   Anatolia c. 2300-1750 B.C. *In* The Cambridge Ancient History 3rd Ed. Vol. I, Pt. 2. I.E.S. Edwards,
            C. J. Gadd, N.G.L. Hammond Eds. Cambridge: University Press. pp. 681-706.
Montelius, O.
    1899   Der Orient und Europa. Stockholm.
Morintz, S. and P. Roman
    1973   Über die Übergangsperiode vom Äneolithikum zur Bronzezeit in Rumanien, *In* Symposium über die
            Entstehung und Chronologie der Badener Kultur. Bohuslav Chropovsky, Ed. Bratislava: Verlag der
            Slowakischen Akademie der Wissenschaft, pp. 259-295.
Neustupný, Evžen
    1970   A New Epoch in Radiocarbon Dating. Antiquity 44:38-45.
    1973   Die Badener Kultur. *In* Symposium über die Entstehung und Chronologie der Badener Kultur.
            Bohuslav Chropovsky, Ed. Bratislava: Verlag der Slowakischen Akademie der Wissenschaft.
            pp. 317-352.

Neustupný, Evžen and Jiří Neustupný
1961   Czechoslovakia before the Slavs. Ancient Peoples and Places 22. London: Thames and Hudson.
Neustupný, Jiří
1961   En marge de certains problèmes de l'Enéolithique en Tchécoslovaquie. In L'Europe à la fin de l'âge de la pierre. Jaroslav Böhm and Sigfried J. De Laet, Eds. Praha: Editions de l'Académie tchécoslovaque des Sciences. pp. 289-302.
Passek, T.
1962   Relations entre l'Europe Occidentale et l'Europe Orientale à l'époque néolithique. In Relazioni Generali I, Atti del VI Congresso internazionale delle Scienze preistoriche e protostoriche, Roma, 29 Agosto - 3 Settembre, 1962. Florence: G. C. Sansoni Editore. pp.127-144.
Ralph, E. K., H. N. Michael, and M. C. Han
1973   Radiocarbon Dates and Reality. MASCA Newsletter, Applied Science Center for Archaeology, The University Museum Vol. 9, No. 1. Philadelphia: University of Pennsylvania.
Ralph, E. K. and R. J. Stuckenrath, Jr.
1962   University of Pennsylvania Radiocarbon Dates V. Radiocarbon 4: 144-159.
Renfrew, Colin.
1973   Before Civilization. New York: Alfred A. Knopf.
Sangmeister, E. and K. Gerhardt
1965   Schnurkeramik und Schnurkeramiker in Südwestdeutschland. Badische Fundberichte, Sonderheft 8.
Srejović, D.
1963   Versuch einer historischen Wertung der Vinča-Gruppe. Archaeologia Jugoslavica 4:5-17.
Strahm, Christian
1969   Die späten Kulturen. In Die Jüngere Steinzeit II, Ur- und Frühgeschichtliche Archäologie der Schweiz. Walter Drack Ed. Basel: Verlag schweizerische Gesellschaft für Ur- und Frühgeschichte. pp. 97-116.
Stuckenrath, Robert Jr. and Elizabeth K. Ralph
1965   University of Pennsylvania Radiocarbon Dates VIII. Radiocarbon 7: 187-199.
Sturms, E.
1961   Die Herkunft der Becher-Bootaxt-Kultur. In Bericht über den V. Internationalen Kongress für Vor- und Frühgeschichte,Hamburg,vom 24. bis 30. August 1958. Berlin: Verlag Gebr. Mann. pp. 779-786.
Struve, K.
1955   Die Einzelgrabkultur in Schleswig-Holstein und ihre kontinentalen Beziehungen. Offa-Bücher N.F. 11.
Suess, H. E.
1965   Secular variations of cosmic-ray-produced carbon-14 in the atmosphere and their interpretations. Journal of Geophysical Research 70: 5937-5950.
1970   Bristlecone-pine calibration of the radiocarbon time-scale 5200 B.C. to the present. In Proceedings of the XII Nobel symposium on radiocarbon variations and absolute chronology. I. Olsson, Ed. Stockholm: Almquist and Wiksell-Gebers forlag AB. pp. 303-311.
Tauber, Henrik
1964   Copenhagen Radiocarbon Dates VI. Radiocarbon 6: 215-225.
Thomas, Homer L.
1967   Near Eastern, Mediterranean and European Chronology. Lund: Studies in Mediterranean Archaeology 17, 1.
1970   New Evidence for Dating the Indo-European Dispersal in Europe. In Indo-European and Indo-Europeans. George Cardona, Henry M. Hoenigswald and Alfred Senn, Eds. Philadelphia: University of Pennsylvania Press. pp. 199-215.
Todd, I. A.
1973   Anatolia and the Khirbet Kerak Problem. In Orient and Occident, Essays presented to Cyrus H. Gordon on his Sixty-Fifth Birthday. Alter Orient und Altes Testament. Veröffentlichungen zur Kultur und Geschichte des Alten Testaments. pp. 181-206.
Vogel J. C. and H. T. Waterbolk
1963   Groningen Radiocarbon Dates IV. Radiocarbon 5: 163-202.
1967   Groningen Radiocarbon Dates VII. Radiocarbon 9: 107-155.
de Vries, Hl., G. W. Barendsen and H. T. Waterbolk.
1958   Groningen Radiocarbon Dates II. Science 127: 129-137.
van der Waals, J. D., and W. Glasbergen
1955   Beaker Types and their Distribution in the Netherlands. Palaeohistoria 4: 5-46.
Weinberg, Saul S.
1965   The Relative Chronology of the Aegean in the Stone and Early Bronze Ages. In Chronologies in Old World Archaeology. Robert W. Ehrich, Ed. Chicago: The University of Chicago Press. pp. 285-320.
Zápotocky, M.
1957   Problemu počatku kultury nálevstých poháru. Archeologické rozhledy 9: 206-235.

LATE HALLSTATT INTERACTIONS WITH THE MEDITERRANEAN: ONE SUGGESTION
by Peter S. Wells

Introduction

A number of Greek and Etruscan objects have been found in burial and settlement contexts belonging to that phase of the Iron Age designated 'Hallstatt D' in west-central Europe (see MAP 1), dating roughly 600-500/480 B.C. (on the chronology see Reinecke 1911: 146-150; Zürn 1942, 1952; Dehn and Frey 1962). Recent archaeological research has added much to this body of material, particularly excavations at the settlements on the Heuneburg (Kimmig and Gersbach 1971) and on Mont Lassois (Joffroy 1960a), and at several important burial locations (Joffroy 1954; Zürn 1970). Most of the 'southern imports' consist of Attic fine pottery and other Greek ceramics, Greek and Etruscan bronze veseels, and coral; other materials occur in isolated instances, some of which will be mentioned below.

Attic pottery has been found at Mont Lassois (Joffroy 1960a: 120-21), Château-sur-Salins (Dayet 1967: 98-99), the Heuneburg (Kimmig 1971: 40-41), and the Britzgyberg (Schweitzer 1971), with small amounts from Würzburg (Mildenberger 1963) and the Ipf (Schultze-Naumburg 1969) - see MAP 2. Two Attic *kylikes* were recovered in the Vix grave. The great majority of datable Attic pottery in central European Hallstatt contexts falls within the period 535-500 (see literature cited). Greek ceramic amphorae are well represented at Mont Lassois (Joffroy 1960a: 123), Château-sur-Salins (Benoit 1965: 183), and the Heuneburg (Kimmig 1971: 41-43), and occur at other settlements and in several graves in eastern France (list in Benoit 1965: 186).

The Greek and Etruscan bronze vessels are found in graves (MAP 2). Dates for individual bronzes in late Hallstatt contexts range from the end of the seventh or beginning of the sixth century B.C. for the Kappel and Vilsingen jugs (Dehn and Frey 1962: 201) to the end of the sixth or beginning of the fifth for the Conliège amphora (*Ibid.* : 202). Most recent attributions for the individual pieces suggest Greek manufacture for the Vix *krater* (Joffroy 1962: 83-86; Jucker 1966), the Grächwil *hydria* (Jucker 1966, 1973), the tripod and cauldron from Sainte-Colombe (Joffroy 1960b), and the tripod from Grafenbühl (Herrmann 1970: 31-34). Thought to be of Etruscan origin are the beaked jugs (*Schnabelkannen*) from Vix, Mercey-sur-Saône, and Hatten (Bouloumié 1973:1), the Kappel and Vilsingen trefoil-mouth jugs (Frey 1963), the pair of basins and the large bowl from Vix (Joffroy 1954:34-36), the Conliège amphora (Lerat 1958), the Hatten trefoil-mouth jug (Frey 1957: 237), and the boss-rimmed bowls (Hencken 1958: 265-267; Frey 1963:22; Dehn 1965: 133).

Among other kinds of Mediterranean products found in late Hallstatt central Europe, the silver *phiale mesomphalos* from Vix is Greek (Strong 1966: 55-56), as are the carved sphinxes, the ivory lion's foot, and the bone, ivory, and amber fragments from Grafenbühl (Herrmann 1970: 25-30). The Vix diadem may be Greek, but its origins are unclear (Megaw 1966: 41).

Several of the graves richest in Greek and Etruscan 'imports' are closely associated topographically with Mont Lassois, the Heuneburg, and the Hohenasperg[1] (see MAP 2). Kimmig (1969) has provided a study of this association of rich graves with major settlement sites; the evidence suggests that 'contact' between Hallstatt Europe and the Mediterranean world was centered at these sites. The two richest graves, Vix and Grafenbühl, are associated with Mont Lassois and the Hohenasperg respectively; both graves date to the end of the sixth or very beginning of the fifth century B.C. (Dehn and Frey 1962: 201-2; Zürn 1970:51).

Reasons for the Interaction.

What explanation can we offer to account for Greek and Etruscan objects on settlements and in graves in late Hallstatt Europe? The word 'trade' provides no answer, because it does not suggest specific mechanisms which might have been involved. Recently several scholars have proposed a number of mechanisms by which the objects in question may have reached central Europe (see Reinecke 1958; Zürn 1970: 119; Dehn 1972; Fischer 1973). These studies have made clear the need to differentiate between various kinds of southern materials in Hallstatt contexts, rather than assuming that a single type of 'contact' would account for the presence of all of them. If we hope to come closer to understanding the processes behind the arrival of Greek and Etruscan goods in Hallstatt Europe, we need to ask both (a) why central Europeans might have wanted to acquire Mediterranean products, and (b) what interest Greeks and Etruscans might have had in developing contacts with central Europe. In this paper we shall consider the second question, and suggest one possible explanation for the presence of 'southern imports' in late Hallstatt Europe.

Greek materials predominate among the 'imports' during late Hallstatt times: pottery from the Mediterranean world is mostly Greek; the Vix silver *phiale* and the Grafenbühl carvings are Greek (except the ivory disc -

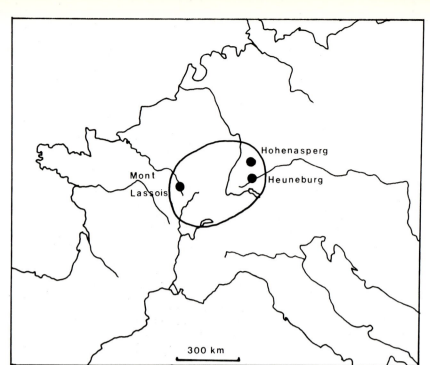

MAP 1   *The west-central European Hallstatt culture-area.*

MAP 2a   *Sites in west-central Europe at which Attic pottery or Greek/Etruscan bronze vessels have been found in late Hallstatt contexts.* (adapted from Kimmig 1968:85)
1. Mont Lassois
2. Vix. 3. Sainte-Colombe.
4. Conliège. 5. Château-sur-Salins. 6. Mercey-sur-Saône.
7. Britzgyberg. 8. Portalban
9. Grächwil. 10. Kappel.
11. Hatten. 12. Vilsingen.
13. Giessübel-Talhau.
14. Heuneburg. 15. Römerhügel. 16. Grafenbühl.
17. Würzburg. 18. Ipf.
19. Pürgen.

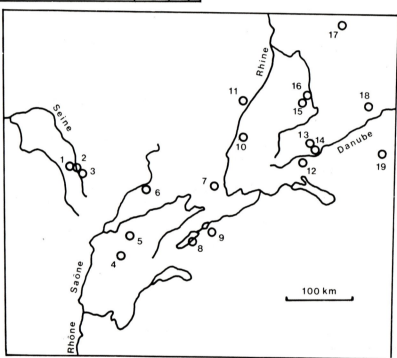

MAP 2b ● *Attic pottery*
○ *Greek or Etruscan bronze vessel.*
(adapted from Kimmig 1968:85).

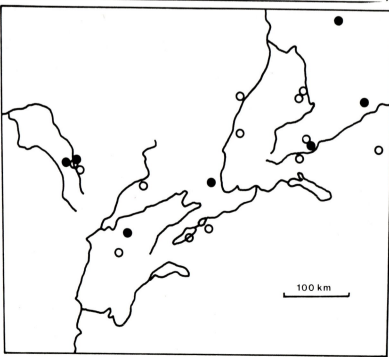

Herrmann 1970: 30-31); and among the bronzes, all of the extraordinary pieces are Greek (Vix *krater,* Grächwil *hydria,* tripod and cauldron from Sainte-Colombe, and Grafenbühl tripod - see p. 189 above). The jugs and basins, types manufactured in quantity and found in many areas of Europe and the Mediterranean (some 250 *Schnabelkannen* are known - Bouloumié 1973:1), are all thought to be Etruscan in origin. This qualitative difference between Greek and Etruscan objects in Hallstatt contexts suggests that relations between Greeks and central Europeans may have been very different from those between Etruscans and central Europeans at that time. The Greek materials arrived for the most part by way of the Greek city of Massalia and the Rhône valley, rather than across the Alps (Carcopino 1957; Blanc 1958; Gallet de Santerre 1962: 392-399). Finds in the Rhône valley area of Etruscan bronzes of the same types as those in Hallstatt graves make it possible that Greeks were also bringing Etruscan vessels to central Europe (Benoit 1956: 19-20, Hatt 1959: 23-26; Megaw 1966:40); quantities of Etruscan *bucchero* found in the area of modern Marseilles indicate active commerce between that region and Etruria during the sixth century B.C. (Benoit 1965: 51-56).[2]

Although major differences exist between the kinds of Greek objects and those of Etruscan origin found in late Hallstatt Europe, all of these materials are luxury items: fine pottery, bronze vessels, gold jewelry, and ivory, bone, and amber carvings; coral from the Mediterranean belongs in the same category (on coral see Kimmig 1971: 57-59). Wine was certainly brought to late Hallstatt Europe as well: Massalia produced wine (Strabo IV 1, 5), and probably exported it during the sixth century (Py 1968:71; Lepore 1970:23). The bronzes and Attic pottery in central Europe are mainly types used in the Mediterranean world for mixing, serving, and drinking wine, and the amphorae were primarily wine transport vessels. In early La Tène contexts in Germany actual remains in Etruscan bronze vessels attest to the presence of wine (Jacobsthal 1944:142). Olive oil also may have been imported, but probably not to the same extent as wine was (see Benoit 1965:202-3; Kimmig 1971:43).

We do not possess much archaeological evidence in Greek contexts (e.g. at Marseilles) indicating the presence of central European materials, but from documented instances elsewhere on the borders of the Greek world and from eastern Gaul during later times, we may infer that some goods were being transported from central Europe to the Mediterranean. Tin has been much discussed in relation to the Greek finds in eastern France (see Villard 1960: 137-161 for a summary of the issues). Massalia participated in the metal trade in the western Mediterranean, dealing in tin as well as other metals (Roebuck 1959: 94-101; Langlotz 1966: 16-17). Some tin may have been arriving at Massalia from across Gaul at this time (Carcopino 1957; Joffroy 1962: 129-139) as well as from tin sources in Spain (Jannoray 1955:297; Benoit 1965: 192), presumably to be shipped to the eastern Mediterranean where tin was in short supply (Roebuck 1959: 94-101). Since commerce in metals generally leaves no archaeological evidence, the sixth century tin traffic across Gaul must remain hypothetical. Some scholars have suggested that exportation of iron from west-central Europe at this time may account for the wealth in Greek and Etruscan finds (Powell 1958:94; Pittioni 1966). But as Villard points out (1960:158 note 5), iron ore is quite plentiful in Mediterranean lands and probably would not have been difficult for Greeks to obtain there.

Massalia lacked good agricultural land and hence needed to import grain (Strabo IV 1, 5); it is likely that other organic products were also lacking around the city (see Strabo IV 1, 4-5). The degree of commercial and building activity at Massalia during the sixth century (Villard 1960: 82-106: Benoit 1965) suggests a substantial population requiring food and other products. Proximity of the Rhône waterway meant relatively easy transport from inland areas of bulky materials such as grain (Finley 1973:128), and Benoit indicates that lands in the Rhône delta and in the lower Durance valley served as sources for Massalia's grain supply (1965:92). A recently excavated grain storage structure at Le Pègue on the eastern edge of the Rhône valley north of the Durance-Rhône confluence (see MAP 2) may relate to local stockpiling for export southward to Massalia (Lagrand and Thalmann 1973:108). Le Pègue has yielded amphorae from Massalia, recovered in levels dating to the end of the sixth century, indicating that contact between the two sites existed (Lagrand and Thalmann, p. 108). Such foodstuffs may also have been coming to Massalia from farther north - grain from rich agricultural lands of eastern France could have been shipped down the Saône-Rhône system with little difficulty; regular shipments of grain from Egypt and south Russia to Greece show that such distances over water were no hindrance.

During the last century before Christ quantities of salted pork and wool were coming from eastern France to supply Rome and other parts of Italy (Strabo IV 3, 2; 4, 3). We might well suspect, with Déchelette (1913:149-150), that such goods were being carried along the same routes during earlier periods of the Iron Age as well.

None of these products - unworked metals, grain, meats, wool - usually survives for the archaeologist to recover. These and other materials such as timber, honey, wax, pitch, hides, and leather may have been in short supply at Greek Massalia and at other settlements on the Mediterranean coast, but available from rich agricultural areas and forests of central Europe. If means for collecting and stockpiling such goods existed at major settlements, as evidence from Le Pègue might suggest, then Greeks from Massalia may have arranged to secure these resources and bring them to the coast.

Rather than looking for a single product such as tin to account for Greek interest in central Europe, we need to consider a variety of such goods. Strabo's remarks concerning the importance of meat and wool from the area are instructive. Literary sources from a period after late Hallstatt describing Greek activity in south Russia (an environment comparable in some respects to southern and eastern France - see Wasowicz 1966) indicate a wide range of products utilized by Greeks there, including grain, timber, fish, salt, hides, slaves, gold, wax, honey, amber, and drugs (Polybius IV 38, 4-5; Minns 1913: 438-441). Archaeological evidence for sixth century Greek activity in that same region suggests that similar materials may have been sought after at that time. Benoit (1965: 191-213) shows the wide variety of natural products from coastal and inland areas of southern France exploited by Massalia; we might expect a similarly broadly-based pattern of resource utilization for Massalia's interactions with central Europe.

Forms of Interaction.

Several kinds of archaeological evidence indicate that some central Europeans and Greeks were in personal contact, as opposed to simply exchanging goods through middlemen. Among the fortifications at the Heuneburg is a wall built of sun-dried clay bricks, a feature unique in central Europe and surely modeled after Greek walls (Dehn 1957; Kimmig 1968: 47-57 with figs. 18-25). The wall must have been built by a Greek architect, or by a central European who had learned the technique in the Mediterranean world; in any case, the wall provides evidence of face-to-face contact between individuals, and of interchange of ideas between members of the two societies. The structure belongs to Heuneburg period IV, which Dehn (1957: 90) has shown to be contemporary with Hallstatt D1, the earlier phase of late Hallstatt (see references on chronology, p. 189). Some kind of personal contact between members of the two societies is also suggested by the stone sculpture from Hirschlanden; the figure combines Archaic Greek and non-Greek Iron Age features, and is made of local north Württemberg sandstone (Zürn 1970: 67-68). Finally, if the Vix *krater* was assembled in eastern France, as several scholars suggest (Megaw 1966:41 with note 37), this would necessitate the presence of a Greek craftsman, or of a central European who had learned how to assemble the vessel. Such evidence for direct contact between individuals is important: it suggests that information about late Hallstatt society must have been passing to the Greek world of southern France, and vice versa.

In a recent study Fischer (1973) has considered a number of possible explanations for the presence of Greek materials in central Europe (p. 438). Reviewing literary evidence from Homer and ancient historians, Fischer suggests that certain of the Mediterranean 'imports' may have been 'political gifts' from powerful persons in Greek society to potentates in central Europe (pp. 455-6). Several objects stand out from the rest in being unique pieces, and clearly were manufactured for some special purpose. These include the Vix *krater,* the Grächwil *hydria,* and probably the Vix diadem; the Sainte-Colombe tripod and cauldron and the Grafenbühl tripod belong to a class of objects frequently used in Greek society as gifts or dedications (Fischer 1973: 455 with note 69). Such objects would probably have been made on special order, as was the huge *krater* commissioned by the Lacedaemonians for Croesus (Herodotus I, 70), and would not have circulated in regular commercial channels (Piggott 1965: 195; Fischer 1973: 455). This distinction between highly ornamental and often exceptionally large objects on the one hand, and the more common types on the other (the various Etruscan jugs and basins) must be re-emphasized, because different kinds of 'imports' probably served different functions in passing from the Mediterranean societies into the hands of central Europeans (Fischer pp. 455-6; see pp. 189-191 above). Scholars have suggested that the Vix *krater* and the Grächwil *hydria* were produced specifically for non-Greek, 'barbarian' taste (Kimmig 1958:85; 1964: 472 note 15; Jucker 1966:121-3). In fact the Vix *krater* is the largest Archaic Greek bronze vessel known, and finds its parallels in non-Greek contexts: e.g. the enormous *krater* made for the Lydian king Croesus (Herodotus I, 70), and the large volute *krater* painted on the wall of the Tomb of the Lionesses at Tarquinia.

'Political' gift-giving is well documented in classical literature (see Fischer 1973), and a few examples here will help to make our point. In the case already cited, the Lacedaemonians had made for Croesus 'a bronze bowl . . . large enough to hold two thousand five hundred gallons and covered with small figures round the outside of the rim' (Herodotus I, 70); the purpose of the gift was to make a 'pact of friendship and alliance', and to express gratitude for past favors. When Cambyses dispatched an embassy to meet with the king of Ethiopia, the messengers brought as gifts 'a scarlet robe, a gold chain-necklace and bracelets, an alabaster casket of myrrh, and a jar of palm-wine' (Herodotus III, 20). And in the *Iliad* we read of a silver mixing-bowl presented by Phoenician traders to a king into whose port they sailed, apparently as a gift to win his favor (XXIII 745). Upon receiving a gift, a person incurs with it an obligation to the donor (Fischer 1973:447; see also Sahlins 1972:208); in each case cited above, one party gives a gift - something of exquisite workmanship or special value - to a powerful individual from whom the party wishes some concession or privilege.

If the Vix *krater* and perhaps the diadem, the tripod and carvings from Grafenbühl, the Grächwil *hydria,* and the Sainte-Colombe tripod and cauldron were 'gifts' made by Greeks to central European potentates, what was the purpose of the gesture? We will probably never know with certainty, but can suggest some reasonable possibilities. Fischer (1973:458) has proposed that political and military alliances may have been one important aim of relationships established through the gifts. In our discussion we wish to emphasize another likely reason for the gift-giving -

to establish treaty relationships by means of which natural products from central Europe (pp. 191-2 above) could become available to Greeks and brought to the Mediterranean.

In a paper dealing with trade between Greeks and non-Greeks Finley (1962) demonstrates the priority of political and administrative arrangements over what we would call 'economic' matters (such as supply and demand). He discusses textual evidence concerning Greek interest in grain from the Bosporus and timber and other natural products from Macedonia (*Ibid.*: 26-27). The critical factor from the Greek point of view was not the 'value' of the materials, but rather the establishment of favorable relations with the king who controlled them. If he so wished, the king might give materials away (Finley: 26; see Herodotus I, 162 for an example of such royal gifts), or he might fix the 'prices' of them (Finley p: 26). In the Bosporus and in Macedonia, natural products were thus obtained by making treaties with the king - not by arriving with trade goods. The same principle is illustrated for medieval Europe: Duby (1973:56) cites instances of shipments of lead metal in ninth century western Europe for which no payment of material goods was made; the metal was sent as 'royal gifts'.

We suggest that one reason for the gift-giving outlined by Fischer may have been to establish treaty relationships with individual kings (or whatever we wish to call them) controlling resources in central Europe (see Lepore 1970:21-22). Once such relationships had been established, the Greeks concerned might have acquired materials they desired, perhaps sometimes by direct gift from the king (as a return gesture of goodwill), or through an arrangement such as the 'administered trade' defined by Polanyi (1957:262) and documented for historical Africa by Arnold (1957: 168-175). In such a system, exchange of goods might have taken place at certain designated locations, and at 'prices' set by the king. Some special arrangement of this kind existed between Greeks at Naucratis and the Egyptian king (Herodotus II, 178), though that situation was different from ours in that Naucratis became a Greek colony. It is possible that through a system of administered trade similar to that outlined by Arnold (1957), products such as metals, foodstuffs, and forest resources were exchanged for Attic pottery, wine, Mediterranean coral, and perhaps Etruscan bronzes.

Thus the success of Greek efforts to obtain natural products in central Europe probably would have depended primarily upon the power of the late Hallstatt potentates over the resources, and upon Greek ability to win their favor. Special gifts may have been presented by Greeks to European kings for the purpose of creating friendly relations, thereby opening the possibility of trade arrangements. It may be the reflection of such gifts which we find in the graves at Vix and Grafenbühl, and perhaps at Sainte-Colombe and Grächwil.

We reiterate that the Greek interest in central European products suggested in this paper was surely only one of several reasons for the establishment of congenial relations between Greeks and late Hallstatt kings. The interpretation offered here needs further investigation; we present it now in the hope of stimulating research in this direction.

Notes

1. For discussion of the Hohenasperg, see Zürn (1970:118). Later building activity on the site has prevented modern excavation, and has probably destroyed the Iron Age settlement remains.
2. In this paper our discussion centers on Greek interests in central Europe; the role of the Etruscans will be dealt with elsewhere.

References Cited

Arnold, R.
1957 A Port of Trade: Whydah on the Guinea Coast. *In* Trade and Market in the Early Empires. K. Polanyi, C. M. Arensberg, H. W. Pearson, Eds. New York: Free Press, pp. 154-176.
Benoit, F.
1956 Relations de Marseille grecque avec le monde occidental. Rivista di Studi Liguri 32: 5-32.
1965 Recherches sur l'hellénisation du midi de la Gaule. Publications de la Faculté des Lettres, Aix-en-Provence, n.s. 43.
Blanc, A.
1958 Le commerce de Marseille dans le bassin du Rhône d'après les trouvailles de céramique. Revue archéologique de l'Est et du Centre-Est 9: 113-121.
Bouloumié, B.
1973 Les oenochoés en bronze du type Schnabelkanne en France et en Belgique. Gallia 31: 1-35.
Carcopino, J.
1957 Promenades historiques aux pays de la Dame de Vix. Paris: L'artisan du livre.
Dayet, M.
1967 Recherches archéologiques au 'Camp du Château' (Salins), 1955-1959. Revue archéologique de l'Est et du Centre-Est 18: 52-106.

Déchelette, J.
    1913   La collection Millon. Antiquités préhistoriques et gallo-romaines. Paris: Paul Geuthner.

Dehn, W.
    1957   Die Heuneburg beim Talhof unweit Riedlingen (Kr. Saulgau): Periode IV nach den Ergebnissen der Grabungen 1950 bis 1955. Fundberichte aus Schwaben, n.s. 14: 78-99.
    1965   Die Bronzeschüssel aus dem Hohmichele, Grab VI, und ihr Verwandtkreis. Fundberichte aus Schwaben, n.s. 17: 126-134.
    1972   'Transhumance' in der westlichen Späthallstattkultur? Archäologisches Korrespondenzblatt 2, No. 2: 125-127.

Dehn, W. and O. -H. Frey
    1962   Die absolute Chronologie der Hallstatt - und Frühlatènezeit Mitteleuropas auf Grund des Südimports. Atti del VI Congresso Internazionale delle Scienze Preistoriche e Protostoriche, Rome: 197-208.

Duby, G.
    1973   The Early Growth of the European Economy: Warriors and Peasants from the Seventh to the Twelfth Century. Trans. by Howard B. Clarke, Ithaca: Cornell University Press 1974.

Finley, M. I.
    1962   Classical Greece. Trade and Politics in the Ancient World. Vol. I of Deuxième Conférence Internationale d'Histoire Economique, Aix-en-Provence. Paris, The Hague: Mouton 1965, pp. 11-35.
    1973   The Ancient Economy. London: Chatto and Windus.

Fischer, F.
    1973   KEIMHΛIA: Bemerkungen zur kulturgeschichtlichen Interpretation des sogenannten Südimports in der späten Hallstatt- und frühen Latène-Kultur des westlichen Mitteleuropa. Germania 51: 436-459.

Frey, O. -H.
    1957   Die Zeitstellung des Fürstengrabes von Hatten im Elsass. Germania 35: 229-249.
    1963   Zu den 'rhodischen' Bronzekannen aus Hallstattgräbern. Marburger Winckelmann-Programm, pp. 18-26.

Gallet de Santerre, H.
    1962   A propos de la céramique grecque de Marseille. Revue des études anciennes 64: 378-403.

Hatt, J. -J.
    1959   Histoire de la Gaule romaine. Paris: Payot.

Hencken, H.
    1958   Syracuse, Etruria, and the North: Some Comparisons. American Journal of Archaeology 62: 259-272.

Herodotus
    1972   The Histories. Trans. by Aubrey de Sélincourt. Harmondsworth: Penguin, revised ed.

Herrmann, H. -V.
    1970   Die südländischen Importstücke des Fürstengrabes von Asperg. In: Hallstattforschungen in Nordwürttemberg. H. Zürn, Ed. pp. 25-34.

Homer
    1950   The Iliad. Trans. by E. V. Rieu. Harmondsworth: Penguin.

Jacobsthal, P.
    1944   Early Celtic Art. Oxford: Clarendon.

Jannoray, J.
    1955   Ensérune. Contribution à l'étude des civilisations préromaines de la Gaule méridionale. Paris: de Boccard.

Joffroy, R.
    1954   Le trésor de Vix (Côte-d'Or). Paris: Fondation Eugène Piot: Monuments et Mémoires 48.
    1960a   L'oppidum de Vix et la civilisation hallstattienne finale dans l'est de la France. Dijon: Bernigaud et Privat.
    1960b   Le bassin et le trépied de Sainte-Colombe (Côte-d'Or). Paris: Fondation Eugène Piot: Monuments et Mémoires 51: 1-23.
    1962   Le trésor de Vix. Histoire et portée d'une grande découverte. Paris: Fayard.

Jucker, H.
    1966   Bronzehenkel und Bronzehydria in Pesaro. Studia Oliveriana 13-14: 1-128.
    1973   Altes und Neues zur Grächwiler Hydria. Zur griechischen Kunst: Festschrift Hansjörg Bloesch, 9. Beiheft zur Antike Kunst, Bern: Francke. pp. 42-62.

Kimmig, W.
    1958   Kulturbeziehungen zwischen der nordwestalpinen Hallstattkultur und der mediterranen Welt. Actes du colloque sur les influences helléniques en Gaule. Publications de l'Universite de Dijon 16: 75-87.
    1964   Ein attisch schwarzfiguriges Fragment mit szenischer Darstellung von der Heuneburg a.d. Donau. Archäologischer Anzeiger 3: 467-475.
    1968   Die Heuneburg an der oberen Donau. Führer zu vor- und frühgeschichtlichen Denkmälern in Württemberg und Hohenzollern, I, Stuttgart.

1969   Zum Problem späthallstättischer Adelssitze. Siedlung, Burg, und Stadt: Studien zu ihren Anfängen. Deutsche Akademie der Wissenschaften zu Berlin. Sektion für Vor- und Frühgeschichte 25: 96-113.

1971   Grabungsverlauf und Funde. *In* Kimmig and Gersbach, Die Grabungen auf der Heuneburg. Germania 49: 21-60.

Kimmig, W. and E. Gersbach.

1971   Die Grabungen auf der Heuneburg 1966-1969. Germania 49: 21-91.

Lagrand, C. and J. -P. Thalmann.

1973   Les habitats protohistoriques du Pègue (Drôme). Grenoble: Centre de Documentation de la Préhistoire Alpine 2.

Langlotz, E.

1966   Die kulturelle und künstlerische Hellenisierung der Küsten des Mittelmeers durch die Stadt Phokaia. Arbeitsgemeinschaft für Forschung des Landes Nordrhein-Westfalen. Geisteswissenschaften 130. Köln and Opladen: Westdeutscher Verlag.

Lepore, E.

1970   Strutture della colonizzazione focea in Occidente. La Parola del Passato 25: 19-54.

Lerat, L.

1958   L'amphore de bronze de Conliège (Jura). Actes du colloque sur les influences helléniques en Gaule. Publications de l'Université de Dijon 16: 89-98.

Megaw, J.V.S.

1966   The Vix Burial. Antiquity 40: 38-44.

Mildenberger, G.

1963   Griechische Scherben vom Marienberg in Würzburg. Germania 41: 103-104.

Minns, E. H.

1913   Scythians and Greeks: A Survey of Ancient History and Archaeology of the North Coast of the Euxine from the Danube to the Caucasus. Cambridge: University Press.

Piggott, S.

1965   Ancient Europe from the Beginnings of Agriculture to Classical Antiquity. Chicago: Aldine.

Pittioni, R.

1966   Grächwil und Vix handelsgeschichtlich gesehen. Helvetia Antiqua: Festschrift Emil Vogt. Zurich Corzett and Huber. pp. 123-128.

Polanyi, K.

1957   The Economy as Instituted Process. *In* Trade and Market in the Early Empires. K. Polanyi, C. M. Arensberg, H. W. Pearson, Eds. New York: Free Press. pp. 243-270.

Polybius

1922   The Histories. London and New York: Loeb Classical Library.

Powell, T. G. E.

1958   The Celts. London: Thames and Hudson.

Py, M.

1968   Les fouilles de Vaunage et les influences grecques en Gaule méridionale (commerces et urbanisation). Rivista di Studi Liguri 34: 57-106.

Reinecke, P.

1911   Funde der Späthallstattstufe aus Süddeutschland. Altertümer unserer heidnischen Vorzeit 5: 144-150 and Plate 27.

1958   Einfuhr - oder Beutegut? Bonner Jahrbücher 158: 246-252.

Roebuck, C.

1959   Ionian Trade and Colonization. New York: Archaeological Institute of America.

Sahlins, M.

1972   On the Sociology of Primitive Exchange. Stone Age Economics. London: Tavistock 1974. pp. 185-275.

Schultze-Naumburg, F.

1969   Eine griechische Scherbe vom Ipf bei Bopfingen/Württemberg. Fundberichte aus Hessen, Beiheft I: Festschrift für Wolfgang Dehn. pp. 210-212.

Schweitzer, R.

1971   Découverte de tessons attiques à figures noires au Britzgyberg près d'Illfurth. Bulletin du Musée Historique de Mulhouse 79: 39-44.

Strong, D. E.

1966   Greek and Roman Gold and Silver Plate. London: Methuen.

Villard, F.

1960   La céramique grecque de Marseille (VIe - IVe siècle): Essai d'histoire économique. Bibliothèque des Écoles Françaises d'Athènes et de Rome. 195.

Wasowicz, A.

1966   A l'époque grecque: le peuplement des côtes de la mer Noire et de la Gaule méridionale. Annales, Economies, Sociétiés, Civilisations. pp. 553-572.

Zürn, H.
    1942   Zur Chronologie der späten Hallstattzeit. Germania 26: 116-124.
    1952   Zum Übergang von Späthallstatt zu Latène im südwestdeutschen Raum. Germania 30: 38-45.
    1970   Hallstattforschungen in Nordwürttemberg: Die Grabhügel von Asperg (Kr. Ludwigsburg),
            Hirschlanden (Kr. Leonsberg) und Mühlacker (Kr. Vaihingen). Stuttgart: Staatliches Amt für
            Denkmalpflege, ser. A. vol. 16.

INDEX OF PRINCIPAL CULTURAL, GEOGRAPHICAL, AND PERSONAL NAMES